MW01493551

Irenaeus

Irenaeus

Life, Scripture, Legacy

Edited by
Sara Parvis and Paul Foster

Fortress Press
Minneapolis

IRENAEUS
Life, Scripture, Legacy

Copyright © 2012 Fortress Press. All rights reserved. Except for brief quotations in critical articles or reviews, no part of this book may be reproduced in any manner without prior written permission the publisher. Visit http://www.augsburgfortress.org/copyrights/contact.asp or write to Permissions, Augsburg Fortress, Box 1209, Minneapolis, MN 55440.

Cover image: Icon of Saint Irenaeus. © Joshua Coolman, 2011
Cover design: Tory Herman

Library of Congress Cataloging-in-Publication Data
Irenaeus : life, scripture, legacy / Sara Parvis and Paul Foster, editors.
        p. cm.
Based on a conference held in 2009 at the University of Edinburgh.
Includes bibliographical references (p.   ) and index.
ISBN 978-0-8006-9796-9 (hardcover : alk. paper) — ISBN 978-1-4514-2444-7 (ebook)
1. Irenaeus, Saint, Bishop of Lyon—Congresses. I. Parvis, Sara. II. Foster, Paul, 1966–
BR65.I64I73 2012
270.1092—dc23   2012007892

The paper used in this publication meets the minimum requirements of American National Standard for Information Sciences—Permanence of Paper for Printed Library Materials, ANSI Z329.48-1984.
Manufactured in the U.S.A.

16 15 14 13 12 1 2 3 4 5 6 7 8 9 10

Contents

Acknowledgments

The editors would like to thank all those who helped to make the Irenaeus conference—at the School of Divinity at the University of Edinburgh in August 2009—on which this volume was based such an enjoyable and stimulating occasion. This includes all those who attended, as well as our colleagues at the Centre for the Study of Christian Origins, and particularly Professor Larry Hurtado. Heartfelt thanks are also due to Kirsty Murray, Mrs. Murray, Alex Peden, and Karl Shuve, and also to Scott Manor and the other students who looked after the bar, as well as to all the relevant University of Edinburgh staff.

Regarding the volume itself, we would like to thank all those at Fortress Press who have worked on this volume, particularly Neil Elliott and Josh Messner. We would also like to thank the Atelier Saint André for their permission to use the icon on the cover. As usual, our debts to Paul Parvis are legion.

Contributors

D. Jeffrey Bingham is Chair and Professor of Theological Studies at Dallas Theological Seminary. He is the author of *Irenaeus' Use Of Matthew's Gospel in* Adversus haereses (Peeters, 1998) and the editor of the *Routledge Companion to Early Christian Thought*, Routledge Religion Companions (Routledge, 2010).

Allen Brent is Senior Research Fellow at King's College, London, and a member of the Faculty of Divinity at the University of Cambridge. He is the author of a number of books on pre-Constantinian Christianity, including *Hippolytus and the Roman Church in the Third Century: Communities in Tension before the Emergence of a Monarch-Bishop*, Supplements to Vigiliae Christianae 31 (Brill, 1995) and *A Political History of Early Christianity* (Clarke-Continuum, 2009).

Sophie Cartwright is currently completing her doctoral dissertation, at the University of Edinburgh, on the theological anthropology of Eustathius of Antioch.

Paul Foster is Senior Lecturer in New Testament Language, Literature, and Theology at the University of Edinburgh. He is the editor of a number of collections of essays on pre-Constantinian Christianity and also the author of *The Apocryphal Gospels: A Very Short Introduction* (Oxford University Press, 2009) and of *The Gospel of Peter: Introduction, Critical Edition, and Commentary*, Texts and Editions for New Testament Study 4 (Brill, 2010).

Charles E. Hill is Professor of New Testament at Reformed Theological Seminary in Orlando. He is the author of *The Johannine Corpus in the Early Church* (Oxford University Press, 2004) and *From the Lost Teaching of Polycarp: Identifying Irenaeus' Apostolic Presbyter and the Author of* ad Diognetum, Wissenschaftliche Untersuchungen zum Neuen Testament 186 (Mohr Siebeck, 2006).

Denis Minns is a Dominican friar resident in Sydney, Australia. He is the author of *Irenaeus: An Introduction* (Continuum, 2010) and, with Paul Parvis, *Justin, Philosopher and Martyr: Apologies*, Oxford Early Christian Texts (Oxford University Press, 2009).

Sebastian Moll is Wissenschaftlicher Mitarbeiter at the Theological Faculty of the University of Mainz. He is the author of *The Arch-Heretic Marcion*, Wissenschafliche Untersuchungen zum Neuen Testament 250 (Mohr Siebeck, 2010).

Paul Parvis teaches early Christianity at the University of Edinburgh. He is the author, with Denis Minns, of *Justin, Philosopher and Martyr: Apologies*, Oxford Early Christian Texts (Oxford University Press, 2009).

Sara Parvis is Senior Lecturer in Patristics at the University of Edinburgh. She is the author of *Marcellus of Ancyra and the Lost Years of the Arian Controversy, 325–345*, Oxford Early Christian Studies (Oxford University Press, 2006) and coeditor, with Paul Foster, of *Justin Martyr and His Worlds* (Fortress Press, 2007).

Stephen O. Presley is Assistant Professor of Biblical Interpretation at Southwestern Baptist Theological Seminary. He recently completed a doctoral thesis at the University of Saint Andrews entitled "The Intertextual Reception of Genesis 1–3 in Irenaeus of Lyon."

Jared Secord is a doctoral candidate in the Interdepartmental Program in Greek and Roman History at the University of Michigan. His dissertation is a study of the interactions and debates that took place in the city of Rome between Greek, Roman, Christian, and Jewish scholars during the late republic and early empire.

Karl Shuve is Assistant Professor of Religious Studies at the University of Virginia. He is preparing a monograph on the interpretation of the Song of Songs in early Latin Christianity.

Michael Slusser is a Catholic priest and was chair of the Department of Theology and Professor at Duquesne University in Pittsburgh until his retirement in 2006. He is the author of a number of influential articles on early Christianity and the translator of *Saint Gregory Thaumaturgus: Life and Works*, Fathers of the Church 98 (Catholic University of America Press, 1998).

Irenaeus M. C. Steenberg is Professorial Research Fellow in Theology at Leeds Trinity University College, England, where he was chair of Theology and Religious Studies until 2010. His recent work includes *Of God and Man: Theology as Anthropology from Irenaeus to Athanasius* (T&T Clark, 2009), *Irenaeus on Creation: The Cosmic Christ and the Saga of Redemption* (Brill, 2008), and *Irenaeus of Lyons: Adversus haereses, Book III—Critical Translation and Commentary* (Paulist, 2012).

ALISTAIR STEWART is an Anglican priest. He is the author of a number of works on early Christian liturgy, including *The Lamb's High Feast: Melito, Peri Pascha, and the Quartodeciman Paschal Liturgy at Sardis*, Supplements to Vigilianae Christianae 42 (Brill, 1998) and *From Prophecy to Preaching: A Search for the Origins of the Christian Homily*, Supplements to Vigilianae Christianae 59 (Brill, 2001).

PETER WIDDICOMBE is Associate Professor of Patristics and Historical Theology in the Department of Religious Studies at McMaster University. He is the author of *The Fatherhood of God from Origen to Athanasius* (Oxford University Press, 2000) and is currently working on a monograph entitled *Drunkenness, Nakedness, and the Redemption and Fall of an Image: Noah and Christ.*

The Writings of Irenaeus

Two genuine works of Irenaeus survive: *Against the Heresies* and the *Demonstration*.

1. *Refutation and Overthrow of the Knowledge Falsely So Called, or Against the Heresies*

The main witnesses for the text of *Against the Heresies* are:

(a) extensive fragments of the original Greek, including the evidence of two damaged and fragmentary papyri:

(i) P. Oxy 405, dated palaeographically to the beginning of the third century and containing portions of III.9.2-3;[1]

(ii) a Jena papyrus, probably of the early fourth century, containing portions of V.3.2–13.1;[2]

(b) a Latin version of all five books; and

(c) an Armenian version of the whole of books IV and V, together with fragments of the other books.

The best edition is published in ten volumes in the Sources chrétiennes series:

Adelin Rousseau and Louis Doutreleau, eds., *Irénée de Lyon, Contra les hérésies, Livre I*, 2 vols, SCh 263 and 264 (Paris: du Cerf, 1979);

———, *Irénée de Lyon, Contra les hérésies, Livre II*, 2 vols., SCh 293 and 294 (Paris: du Cerf, 1982);

———, *Irénée de Lyon, Contra les hérésies, Livre III*, 2 vols., SCh 210 and 211 (Paris: du Cerf, 1974);

Adelin Rousseau, with Bertrand Hemmerdinger, Louis Doutreleau, and Charles Mercier, eds., *Irénée de Lyon, Contra les hérésies, Livre IV*, 2 vols., SCh 100 (Paris: de Cerf, 1965);

Adelin Rousseau, Louis Doutreleau, and Charles Mercier, eds., *Irénée de Lyon, Contra les hérésies, Livre V*, 2 vols., SCh 152 and 153 (Paris: de Cerf, 1969).

The Armenian of books IV and V was published, from a manuscript then as now in Yerevan, by Karapet Ter-Mekerttschian and Erwand Ter-Minassianz, *Irenaeus, Gegen die Häretiker, ΕΛΕΓΧΟΣ ΚΑΙ ΑΝΑΤΡΟΠΗ ΤΗΣ ΨΕΥΔΩΝΥΜΟΥ ΓΝΩΣΕΩΣ, Buch IV u.*

V in armenischer Version, TU 35.2 (Leipzig: Heinrichs, 1910); its evidence is factored in to the edition by Rousseau.

There is a full English translation by Archibald Roberts and W. H. Rambaut in *The Ante-Nicene Fathers*, vol. 1, reprinted from *The Ante-Nicene Christian Library*, vols 5 and 9 (Edinburgh: T&T Clark, 1868–1869) and available online. It is basically accurate and reliable, if rather woodenly Victorian, though it does not, of course, reflect the very significant improvements that have been made to the text of Irenaeus in the past century and a half.

F. R. Montgomery Hitchcock published an abridged translation, *The Treatise of Irenaeus of Lugdunum, Against the Heresies*, 2 vols (London: SPCK, 1916), and excerpts are translated in Robert M. Grant, *Irenaeus of Lyons*, Fathers of the Church (New York: Routledge, 1977). Saint Irenaeus of Lyons, *Against the Heresies, Book I*, trans. D. J. Unger, rev. J. J. Dillon, Ancient Christian Writers 55 (Westminster: Newman, 1992), contains the first book with extensive notes. *Book III*, by Ungar and Irenaeus M. C. Steenberg, appeared in the same series at the beginning of 2012, and further volumes are promised. A complete one-volume translation is being prepared by Paul and Sara Parvis and Denis Minns.

2. Demonstration (*Epideixis*) of the Apostolic Preaching.

The *Demonstration* is mentioned by Eusebius (*HE* V.26) but was only published from the same Armenian manuscript that contains Haer. IV and V, in 1907: Karapet Ter-Mekerttschian and Erwand Ter-Minassianz, *Des heiligen Irenäus, Schrift zum Erweise der apostolischen Verkündigung*, ΕΙΣ ΕΠΙΔΕΙΞΙΝ ΤΟΥ ΑΠΟΣΤΟΛΙΚΟΥ ΚΗΡΥΓΜΑΤΟΣ, *in armenischer Version*, with notes by Adolf Harnack, TU 31.1 (Leipzig: Heinrichs, 1907). Reliable English translations include:

The Demonstration of the Apostolic Preaching, trans. J. A. Robinson (London: SPCK, 1920);

Proof of the Apostolic Preaching, trans. J. P. Smith, Ancient Christian Writers 16 (Westminster: Newman, 1952);

Saint Irenaeus of Lyons On the Apostolic Preaching, trans. John Behr (Crestwood: Saint Vladimir's Seminary Press, 1997).

Eusebius of Caesarea, writing shortly before 300, gives the titles of six other works, quoting fragments from three of them:

3. A letter *Against Blastus, On Schism* (*HE* V.20.1);

4. A letter *Against Florinus, On the Monarchy, or On the Fact That God Is Not the Maker of Evil* (*HE* V.20.1, with a fragment at V.20.4-8);

5. A treatise *On the Ogdoad*, written "because of Florinus" (*HE* V.20.1, with a fragment at V.20.2);

6. A letter to Victor of Rome, written "on behalf of the brethren throughout Gaul over whom he was presiding" on the controversy with the churches of Asia

Minor over the date of Easter (*HE* V.24.11, with a fragment quoted at 24.12-13 and another at 24.14-17);

(7) *On Knowledge* (ἐπιστήμη), against the pagans (*HE* V.26);

(8) A book of various discourses (*HE* V.26).

Eusebius also claims in passing that Irenaeus wrote a book against Marcion (*HE* IV.25) but that, as *HE* V.8.9 shows, is simply an inference from Irenaeus' own expressed intention (*Haer.* I.25.2 and III.12.16) to produce such a work.

There are in addition (9) a number of fragments—many of dubious authenticity—in Greek, Syriac, and Armenian. There is a list in *CPG* 1 (1983), numbers 1311–17 (= 112–17).

Among spurious works should be noted (10) the so-called "Pfaffian fragments"—four fragments in Greek, primarily relating to the eucharist, which Ch. M. Pfaff "discovered" in a manuscript in Turin—a manuscript, oddly enough, never seen again —and published in 1715. Their authenticity was vigorously debated from the moment of their publication. They are still included, as genuine, by Harvey in his 1859 edition of Irenaeus (fragments xxxv–xxxviii = vol. 2, 498–506), but Harnack proved conclusively in 1900 that they were forgeries: Adolf Harnack, *Die Pfaff'schen Irenäus-Fragmente als Fälschungen Pfaffs nachgewiesen*, TU 20.3 (Leipzig: Hinrichs, 1900).

Timeline

Names of Roman emperors are in SMALL CAPS *under year of accession.*

138	ANTONINUS PIUS
140 (?)	Valentinus the Gnostic comes to Rome from Egypt
Mid-140s (?)	Birth of Irenaeus—at Smyrna?
157 (23 Feb.)	Martyrdom of Polycarp in Smyrna
161	MARCUS AURELIUS (with LUCIUS VERUS until 169)
Early 160s (?)	Irenaeus moves to Lyon
175–189	Eleutherus bishop of Rome
177/180	Persecution in Lyon and Vienne; Irenaeus becomes bishop of Lyon
180–185 (?)	Writing of *Against the Heresies*
181	COMMODUS
185–190 (?)	Writing of *Demonstration of the Apostolic Preaching*
189–199	Victor bishop of Rome
193	Civil war and accession of SEPTIMIUS SEVERUS
???	Death of Irenaeus

Introduction

Irenaeus and His Traditions

SARA PARVIS AND PAUL FOSTER

renaeus is the star witness of the post-sub-apostolic period of early Christianity, the period of the late second century. By then, not only were the eyewitnesses, the generation that had known Jesus, dead, but so also were the generation that had known the apostles. Irenaeus himself, who became bishop of Lyons in Gaul in the late 170s or early 180s, was one of the last Christian writers who could plausibly claim to have learned directly from someone who had known the apostles, that someone being Polycarp of Smyrna.

Christianity was thriving but diverse. It continued to wrestle with its relationship to Judaism past and present, as it had done since the beginning. But increasingly it was also attracting converts who situated their knowledge within the Greek and Roman cultural worlds of rhetoric and philosophy. In place of the apostles who had founded the oldest churches were the writings they had left, the long-term memories of the individual communities they had left, and a succession of more recent teachers, preachers, and charismatic individuals. These latter had preached or taught or prophesied in different places, made a mark, and in some cases left writings, new communities, or strong memories of an exemplary death for the faith. Among these was to be found some considerable theological divergence. Irenaeus, the most comprehensive writer that Christianity had yet produced (at least in terms of surviving work), who on the one hand celebrated diversity of tradition, education, geography, and charismatic gifts, but on the other fiercely opposed divergence of doctrine, allows us to take stock of all this, and much else.

This book, based on a conference that took place at the University of Edinburgh in 2009 under the auspices of the Centre for the Study of Christian Origins, seeks to bring together a number of aspects of Irenaeus's witness and a number of current strands in Irenaeus scholarship. To bring together all would be impossible in a book of this size. In planning the conference, we had intended to give equal room to both lovers and critics of Irenaeus, but it was mainly Irenaeus's lovers who accepted our invitation. These included, as well as some of the foremost writers in English on Irenaeus today, scholars expert in other areas of biblical studies and patristic thought who were conscious of

1

Irenaeus's strong influence on their own areas of work. One of the features of current Irenaeus scholarship is a shift away from studying him for what he says about Gnosticism (which was itself a shift away from studying what he says about church order) toward studying him for what he says about scripture and about early Christian theology. These last are the two areas on which we have concentrated in this volume, though we include also three essays on Irenaeus's historical context. Amidst the lovers, who for the most part and in varying degrees accept Irenaeus as a credible witness to the make-up of the church of his day and its handling of its own traditions, Allen Brent and Paul Foster do duty for the sceptics and read Irenaeus to some extent as a witness against himself.

New trends in Irenaeus scholarship are also reflected by something that would have been far less likely only fifty years ago: the diversity of church affiliation among the contributors. We include among ourselves scholars from the Eastern Orthodox, Roman Catholic, Anglican, Lutheran, and various Reformed and other Protestant traditions. How far this colors our different perspectives, we leave to the reader to judge. To say we believe Irenaeus would have approved is perhaps all the comment that is needed on how our portraits of him differ from those of some of his early editors.

Irenaeus and His Context

We begin with an examination by Paul Parvis of the first major portrait of Irenaeus, that of Eusebius of Caesarea around 300: hearer of the martyr Polycarp of Smyrna in Asia Minor, immigrant bishop of the largely immigrant community in Lyons in Gaul, writer of a number of works, witness to the formation of the New Testament, chiliast, and man of peace. Parvis largely accepts Eusebius's picture but tweaks and colors it, showing some of the ways in which Irenaeus's writings and life also differ from common modern perceptions of them.

Jared Secord, in an illuminating study, looks at the cultural geography displayed in Irenaeus's work. He demonstrates in the process just how Greek Irenaeus actually was and just how much of a foreigner he felt himself to be in Lyons, not because it was full of Celts but because it was so much more Latin than the Rome in which he had previously been living.

In the last chapter in this section, Allen Brent looks at length at the development of the early episcopacy in Rome and argues that Irenaeus's Roman succession-list cannot be considered a reliable witness to a tradition of monarchical episcopacy there. Building on previous scholarship, Brent takes the problem as far as 235, in several stages. Either Hegesippus or Irenaeus himself has compiled the Roman list on the basis of names attached to letters in the Roman archives, including the letter of Clement to the Corinthians and others of the same sort. (Irenaeus, Brent argues, misunderstood or else misrepresented the role of these officers, whose role would be better understood as that of Foreign Secretary to the Roman presbyterate, rather than president in any sense.) For Irenaeus, these names represented the same sort of succession list that would be implied in Diogenes Laertius's *Lives of the Philosophers*, guaranteeing that the teaching of the current head of the school was in clear and approved continuity with the teaching of its original founder. Their office was a teaching office rather than a ruling one. It is only with the building of the "papal mausoleum" in the Catacomb of

Callistus in 235, Brent argues, that we see the real ideology of a monarchical episcopate emerge in Rome.

Irenaeus and His Scriptural Traditions

Throughout his writings, Irenaeus reveals knowledge of various types of tradition, both oral and written. In that last category, the writings that formed the Jewish scriptures and those that were in the process of becoming the New Testament appear as a key resource in Irenaeus's thinking and theology. He is well known for being our earliest surviving witness to a fourfold gospel collection comprising the accounts written by Matthew, Mark, Luke, and John. However, his contribution to scriptural tradition is much greater than simply displaying awareness of what are now the four canonical Gospels. He bears more subtle witness to the contemporary status of the scriptures on the edge of the eventual New Testament canon, which only later fell definitively inside or outside of it: Hebrews, the *Shepherd of Hermas*, and 1 Clement. He witnesses to the dates and breadth of circulation of the scriptures of the Christian groups he designates as heresies, a study in their own right. He shows how both the Jewish scriptures and the emerging New Testament were read in his day and by the older generation whose teaching he remembered. He is an important witness both to the text of the New Testament, and to scribal practice in copying it. And in his love of and widespread use of imagery drawn from scripture, he began new traditions of interpretation that fed into later exegesis in sometimes quite surprising ways.

In the first essay in this section, Denis Minns discusses the form of the parable of the Two Sons (Matt. 21:28-32) known to Irenaeus. The textual tradition of the parable of the Two Sons is a famous textual conundrum, with three major divergent forms that disagree in the details of whether the first or second son agreed to go to the father's vineyard, coupled with differing assessments of which son actually carried out the will of the father. Two of the forms initially have the first son refusing to go to the vineyard but later repenting and deciding to go. This is the structure of the parable known to Irenaeus; however, Irenaeus does not explicitly state which of the sons is adjudged to have done the will of the father. As a result, most text critics assume he is more likely to have followed the form of the text that has Jesus' interlocutors answer sensibly that the first son did the father's will. The alternative is that Irenaeus is a witness to the form of text in Codex Bezae. This preserves the assessment that despite inaction and failure to go to the vineyard, it is the second son who actually does the will of the father. Such a form is seen typically either as a nonsensical form resulting from a textual corruption or as one that intentionally wished to characterize Jesus' opponents as perverse since they purposefully give the incorrect answer. However, discussing the last major section of book IV of *Adversus haereses* (IV.36.1—41.3), Minns notes that its aim is to prove the unity of the two testaments from the parables of Christ. Therefore, he observes, Irenaeus, in line with the interpretation of the parable of the Wicked Husbandman (Matt. 21:33-45) that immediately follows on from the Two Sons, argues that it, too, tells a story where the younger or more recent character supplants the former. Hence, Irenaeus must have had the parable in the form where the second son does the will of the father. Minns then delves into Irenaeus's exegesis of the parable and notes that he comments in relation to the contrition of the first son, "afterwards, when repentance availed him nothing." This suggests to Minns that Irenaeus's view was that the repentance of the first son either came too late or was defective in some way. Moreover, Minns argues that this view is entirely compatible with Irenaeus's wider understanding of the nature of human response to the call of God. The conclusions that are drawn from this study are, first, that Irenaeus is a witness to the form of the parable that is contained in Codex Bezae. Secondly, this form of the parable, which is seen as a corruption of one of the other two forms, must have occurred between the redaction of the Gospel and not much later than the middle of the second century. Thirdly, this reading of the form of the parable known to Irenaeus is consonant with the assessment that Codex Bezae displays an attitude of liberty toward the text and its revision. Minns's discussion highlights the valuable insights that can be derived through consideration of textual details combined with exegetical tendencies in the writings of Irenaeus.

Next, Jeffrey Bingham investigates the possibility that Irenaeus was a witness to the Letter to the Hebrews. His discussion opens with later patristic testimony that claims both that Irenaeus denied the Pauline authorship of Hebrews and that in a now no-longer extant work he composed a series of addresses drawing upon this same epistle. However, as Bingham documents, scholars have usually been less willing to see evidence for the use of Hebrews in his *Adversus haereses*. Bingham's purpose is to argue against and to overturn that understanding, which has emerged as something of a scholarly consensus. In place of such a view, Bingham does not suggest that Hebrews must therefore be understood as a fundamental scriptural text for Irenaeus. Instead, his claim is more subtle. Rather than arguing that Irenaeus revered Hebrews in the same way that he did the fourfold gospel collection and the letters of Paul, it is suggested that Irenaeus was dependent upon the language and teachings of Hebrews in various observable ways. After presenting a series of examples where this phenomenon might occur, a wider thesis is suggested to account for Irenaeus's somewhat ambivalent relationship with the Letter to the Hebrews. Bingham suggests that because Hebrews did not have the apostolic pedigree that Irenaeus viewed as so important for writings regarded as authoritative, he was hesitant to cite the epistle explicitly. Instead, the influence of Hebrews is to be detected at a deeper level, as it shapes his theology and ideology.

Karl Shuve considers Irenaeus's contribution to the later interpretative tradition of a rather different sort of scriptural text, the Song of Songs. He argues that despite the apparent neglect of the Song of Songs in the first two centuries of the Common Era, Irenaeus was fundamental in establishing the interpretative context that enabled later Christian exegetes to engage with this text. In the process of this argument, Shuve also wishes to challenge the scholarly assumption that the Song of Songs only became an artifact of interest in the third century, when Christian asceticism felt the need to develop metaphorical or allegorical interpretations of this most *un-ascetic* of texts. Shuve seeks to turn such an understanding of the rise in interest in the Song of Songs on its head. In opposition to the prevailing scholarly consensus, he argues that "the Song is best understood as emerging, quite organically, from a nuptial theological trajectory that affirms, rather than denies, the value of the body and sexuality." It is further suggested that Irenaeus is the first to affirm the Old Testament nuptial texts as being a typological patterning of Christ's redemptive activity. Thus, analogically, texts that speak of human marital union play a significant role in Irenaeus's discourse on ecclesiology and soteriology. Although Irenaeus does not himself make reference to the Song of Songs, Shuve argues that Irenaeus's "nuptial theology is developed primarily through the exposition of certain key Old Testament texts (Num. 12:10-14; Hos. 1; Isa. 54:1, 63:9)" that will be central to later exegesis of the Song. While nuptial theology does not appear with great frequency in Irenaeus's writings, partly because similar imagery is used by his Gnostic opponents, nonetheless the approach is seen as a methodological watershed that would provide a conceptual space in which the Song of Songs could be read by later Christian exegetes, beginning with Origen. For Shuve, therefore, it is right to see Irenaeus as laying the methodological foundation upon which all subsequent patristic exegesis of Song of Songs would stand.

Our next two papers debate the interesting question of the identity of the Elder of *Adversus haereses* IV.27-32, whose teaching, as outlined by Irenaeus, defends the believers of the Old Testament (the "former dispensation"), as well as God's dealings with them, from several sorts of attack, arguing that they too were saved by Christ. Irenaeus gives him no name but considerable status, calling him "a disciple of the Apostles," and describing his teaching at length. Sebastian Moll, from the perspective of his work on Marcion, questions Charles Hill's claim that this Elder must have been Polycarp. He argues, on the basis of Irenaeus's *Letter to Florinus*, from which an extract is given in Eusebius of Caesarea's *Church History*, that Irenaeus, being a "boy" (παῖς) at the time when he met Polycarp, could not have remembered his teaching as extensively as he remembers the Elder's. Moll argues that "boy" implies a "childlike age" (in Luke 2:42-43, for example, the twelve-year-old Jesus is called a παῖς). Moll further argues that the Elder's teaching as outlined by Irenaeus is as much anti-Valentinian as anti-Marcionite; that, given Irenaeus's age, the Elder, whose teaching he recalls so clearly that he must have heard him as an adult, must be a third-generation witness rather than someone who had seen the Apostles; and that it is hard to imagine why Irenaeus would not have given the Elder's name as Polycarp if he really were Polycarp, given that Polycarp is mentioned by name earlier in the work.

Hill agrees that the Elder's teaching is not simply anti-Marcionite, but aimed at other heresies as well, but argues that this does not exclude Polycarp as its author. He sets out the similarities between the *Letter to Florinus* and *Haer.* IV.27-32 in parallel columns. He dismisses the argument that the Elder must be third generation on the grounds that it assumes in advance that the Elder cannot be Polycarp, despite the fact that (as Moll had noted) the textual evidence presents him as a disciple of the Apostles. He then proceeds to discuss the ancient evidence as to what Irenaeus is likely to have meant by παῖς and by the parallel phrase "in my first age," as well as some modern studies on the pervasiveness of memories laid down between ages ten and twenty-five, and some ancient evidence on disciples memorizing the stories of their teacher. Hill posits that Irenaeus might have been seventeen or eighteen when he saw Florinus in company with Polycarp, and points out that Irenaeus could have carried on listening to Polycarp's teaching for a number of years afterwards. Finally, he argues that Irenaeus does not mention Polycarp's name because this is often his practice with post-apostolic teachers; he expected his readers to pick up the earlier allusion; and he did not want for modesty's sake to insist too frequently on his connection with the great martyr.

The next chapter in this section moves from looking at traditions that were a positive influence on Irenaeus—even if in a somewhat veiled manner—and instead looks at his reaction against "anti-traditions." Irenaeus was able to advocate holding fast to the apostolic writing, but the "flipside" of that assertion was the rejection of writings that did not meet his criterion for accepting such traditions as authoritative. Irenaeus devotes considerable space in his *Adversus haereses* to justifying the privileged standing of the fourfold gospel collection. In the process he rejects those who argue for a different collection of gospel writings, as well as those writings that are read in addition to the four gospels that he authorized. Irenaeus states that the heretics fall into one of two errors: either reading too many, or too few gospels (*Haer.* III.11.9). Foster surveys the *Adversus haereses* to determine which of the noncanonical gospel writings were likely to have been known by Irenaeus during the last quarter of the second century. While Irenaeus actually refutes that the competitor writings are truly gospels, the very fact that he has to mount such arguments suggests that others of his contemporaries did not share his view, and in fact had a very different understanding of what made a gospel a gospel. Irenaeus names some of those writings that he rejects. As Foster discusses, those include the *Gospel of Judas* and the Valentinian *Gospel of Truth*. In addition to these explicitly named texts, Irenaeus also cites a well-known tradition that occurs in a noncanonical gospel. This is the so-called alpha—beta logion that is now embedded in the *Infancy Gospel of Thomas*. Here, Foster suggests that it is more likely that Irenaeus came across this as a free-floating logion and not as part of that wider narrative. Also problematic are Irenaeus's references to the so-called Jewish-Christian gospels. Since these texts are only known from citations in early Christian writings, the accuracy of such quotations cannot be assessed. However, they are invaluable for providing access to otherwise unattested traditions. Lastly, this chapter looks at Irenaeus's knowledge of some of the writings that are found in the Nag Hammadi corpus. Foster concludes that Irenaeus was surprisingly well informed about the gospel texts and traditions being used by his opponents, and may have known more of these texts than it is now possible to detect. Thus, if Irenaeus's aim was to cast into oblivion such works regarded by his opponents as gospels, then he must be commended since for the most part he has succeeded!

In the second of his two chapters in this collection, Charles Hill illuminates the handling of gospel texts in the late second century through the lens of the earliest surviving manuscript of any part of Irenaeus's writings. The papyrus fragment under examination in this discussion, P.Oxy. 405, is of particular interest because it contains a citation of Matthew 3:16-17. There are a number of fascinating features and aspects of this scrap of text that results in its value far outstripping its size. First, the form of the text preserved in the citation is closer to that preserved in Codex Bezae. Secondly, Hill draws attention to the wedge-shaped marks, or *diplai*, that are used in the left margin to mark certain lines of the text, "where they are clearly being used to mark a quotation." However, after surveying other usages of the *diplai* in early Christian manuscripts, Hill notes that ordinarily they were not employed to indicate quotations. Interestingly, he states that he knows of no NT papyrus manuscript that uses *diplai* is this fashion, although the fourth-century parchment manuscript Codex Vaticanus does so. In this latter manuscript there is a systematic attempt to use these markers comprehensively throughout to mark OT quotations. Having cited Irenaeus's statements about his high regard for scripture and his exacting standards for scribal copyists, Hill suggests that "[i]t seems a natural outgrowth of such a doctrine of Scripture that certain measures should develop, even scribally, to signify it, to make it visible." Thus the earliest manuscript of Irenaeus's writings reveals in a physical way an insight into the very issues Irenaeus was keenly debating in his *Adversus haereses* at a more conceptual and theological level.

Irenaeus and His Theological Traditions

Michael Slusser begins the section on Irenaeus's theology with a challenge: What is the heart of Irenaeus's theology, the key that unlocks the whole of his thought? Sweeping aside other suggestions, such as recapitulation, Slusser argues that it is the interaction between God's greatness and God's love, *magnitudo* and *dilectio* in the surviving Latin translation. Irenaeus is in fact largely in agreement with his Gnostic opponents, Slusser argues, over the question of God's greatness, even though the Gnostics themselves are unable to admit the fact. But the reason why they are unable to admit the fact is precisely because they do not understand that greatness is not incompatible with love, and that the acts of love evident in creation and in the incarnation in the thought of what they call the "psychic Christians" do not compromise God's greatness, but show how unbounded God's power actually is.

Peter Widdicombe takes further the exploration of God's love in Irenaeus, by considering the ways in which Irenaeus speaks of the fatherhood of God. Widdicombe situates Irenaeus's theology of God's fatherhood in the wider patristic tradition, from Justin and Theophilus of Antioch before him through Origen to Athanasius. He argues that, although Irenaeus is not entirely consistent on the matter, and is prepared to use the term in slightly different ways in different arguments, on the whole his usage is quite distinctive and connected, above all, to the revelation by the Son that God is our Father, and we are God's adoptive children. Though he accepts the classical, philosophical tradition of God as "Father of all" as Justin and Theophilus had, and also to some extent the Jewish tradition of God as the Father of Israel (particularly in arguing against Marcion), these are not the traditions of divine fatherhood that interest him. Nor does he use the term, as Origen and Athanasius do, to discuss the immanent Trinity, the relationship between the Father and the Son in themselves. Instead, he is most interested in the new knowledge about God that the revelation of God's fatherhood transmits to us. He has a strongly Pauline sense of the good news as the revealing by the Son that God is not simply Creator and Lawgiver, Almighty and Lord, but loving Father. In this, Widdicombe argues, he is close to Origen, though Origen was to develop further the implications for the individual Christian's relationship with God.

Alistair Stewart examines Irenaeus's Rule of Truth as given in *Haer.* I.10.1, together with the context of his claim in *Haer.* I.9.4 that "whoever holds the Rule of

Truth immutable in himself, which he received through baptism, will acknowledge those names and sayings and parables which are indeed in Scripture, but will not acknowledge the blasphemous narrative" (which his opponents make out of them). Stewart argues that the traditional reading of this passage as evidence for a three-fold trinitarian questioning of baptismal candidates in Irenaeus's church is misplaced. Instead, he argues that the trinitarian section of the Rule would reflect catechetical instruction before baptism and a trinitarian formula of baptism in the name of Father, Son, and Holy Spirit, while the narrative christological confession at the end ("and the coming and the birth from the virgin and the passion and the resurrection from the dead and the bodily reception into the heavens of the beloved, our Lord Jesus Christ, and his coming again") reflects a christological confession that was to be made by the candidate herself immediately before baptism. Stewart concludes by suggesting that the confession of Christ specifically links back to the anti-Valentinian context: it is Christ who is the true meaning of scripture.

Sara Parvis looks at Irenaeus's implicit engagement with Gnosticism's appeal to educated women. The Gnostic myths and assemblies discussed by Irenaeus, on the face of it, had far more to offer women than the late second-century church: female divine principles, a creator Mother to the creator Father, a re-reading of the story of Eve by which eating the forbidden fruit was a wise action rather than a disaster, and, under Mark at least, some kind of liturgical role for women in the assembly. Parvis argues that Irenaeus is aware of the appeal of all of these, and carefully and sensitively counters them all in his work, maximizing room for women as far as possible within the tradition he understands himself to have received. He avoids the obvious move of criticizing women gods and female divine principles on the grounds of female inferiority, instead arguing that the roles of Sophia and Achamoth are logically impossible for other reasons. At the risk of creating serious theological difficulties for the tradition, he extends Paul's Adam/Christ paradigm to Eve and Mary. And he insists that women prophets are chosen by God and sanctioned by both scripture and tradition, going so far (Parvis argues) as to claim that those who reject them are committing the unforgivable sin against the Holy Spirit.

Stephen Presley's essay builds upon Michael Slusser's programmatic article "The Exegetical Roots of Trinitarian Theology" (1988), discussing Irenaeus's contribution to embryonic analytical trinitarian thought. Behind such analytical discussions, he notes, there is a prior exegetical discussion. In particular the focus on the concept of *prosōpon* in the interpretation of passages such as Gen. 1:26 and Psa. 110:1 is a cornerstone of this exegetical debate. While the prosopological method permeates the writings of many Christian authors of the second century, Presley asks why Irenaeus does "not more explicitly detail and utilize this method?" The answer Presley supplies is that Irenaeus's hesitancy to employ this method stems from his own polemical context. Specifically, Presley argues that Irenaeus recognized the potential this method had to play into the hands of his Gnostic opponents, for by discerning different voices in a given passage, they could validate suppositions about a multiplicity of heavenly characters speaking in scriptural passages. Irenaeus's response is not to dispense with the method in its entirety, but to step back from the method and to discuss the theological framework in which such a method could be applied, when there is a prior theological affirmation of belief in the only true God. Thus, Presley notes that Irenaeus limits the potentiality of the method so that "the only possible divine referent found in scripture is the one true God, and likewise any divine allusion must refer to either Father or the Son." Hence it is suggested that Irenaeus subordinates prosopological exegesis under his overarching theological framework, or *regula fidei*, that acknowledges the necessity of the prior commitment to the Father and Son as divine beings, to the exclusion of the Gnostic plethora of divine intermediaries. Consequently, for Presley, Irenaeus occupies a key place in the development of early trinitarian thought, particularly in regard to the concept of person.

Sophie Cartwright explores another distinctive aspect of Irenaeus's thought, his theology of the image of God, throwing it into relief by comparing it to the same doctrine in two fourth-century theologians whom he much influenced, Eustathius of Antioch and Marcellus of Ancyra. Like most patristic theologians, all of these writers understood scripture to teach both that Adam (and hence humanity in general) was created in the image of God, and that Christ is the image of the invisible God. Eustathius and Marcellus both followed Irenaeus's distinctive teaching that it is Adam's body specifically that is in the image of God and that Christ renews and perfects the image in Adam. Beyond this, however, the theological anthropology of the three differs in significant and mutually illuminating ways. For Irenaeus, Cartwright argues, Christ makes visible both what God is and what Adam is meant to be. This is because Adam already resembles God, even before the incarnation; humanity, indeed, "has an ontological affinity with God," being connected with God by both pattern and substance from its creation. On receiving the Holy Spirit, restored humanity becomes even more intimately connected to God, to the extent, she claims, of "entirely relinquishing the power of self-direction." For Marcellus, meanwhile, humanity is radically unlike the eternal God, and is in the image not of the eternal God but of God incarnate: Adam is modelled on perfect Adam. But the incarnation itself is temporary: although humanity can only be saved by being united to God, once the eschatological restoration has been achieved, humanity is left as the perfect creature, beloved of and saved by God, who yet, being a creature, continues to be radically unlike God. For Eustathius, meanwhile, it is the eternal Son who is the true image of God; Christ is image of God in a more attenuated sense, because of Eustathius' strongly divisive Christology. The Word is made visible through the "human being of God," and the Word, as true image, then makes known the whole Godhead. Eustathius thinks, like Irenaeus and Marcellus in different ways, that Adam's body is modelled on God, like a statue. But in Eustathius, the human soul in both Adam and Christ serves to keep the Word to some extent at a distance from its image.

Paul Parvis, again, in a typically learned and thoughtful survey of the seven major editions of *Against the Heresies*, looks at the way Irenaeus's work was claimed for various theological causes by its editors over the years, and Irenaeus himself to some extent remade in their image. Erasmus, in 1526, saw Irenaeus as a man of eloquence, learning, and scriptural piety, but above all a man of peace. The editions of the Reformer Gallasius in 1570 and the Franciscan Feuardent in 1575 were rather more interested in war. They were particularly interested in the heresiological aspect of the work, calling on Irenaeus's support against the presumed heresies of their own day. At the behest of Theodore Beza, Gallasius wrote extensive notes, including "admonition and censure" where Irenaeus's occasional incipient "impurity" left him in disagreement with Reformed thought; these notes themselves spurred Feuardent to respond with pro-Catholic ripostes, as well as the occasional encouragement to violence. Grabe, writing as an Anglican in Oxford in his edition of 1702, returns to a more irenic view of Irenaeus, whose aid he calls in support of a "middle way," looking toward primitive Christianity to reconcile modern doctrinal differences: he was no doubt only confirmed in this approach as he wrestled with the embattled notes of the two previous editors. Nonetheless, his Irenaeus was still too Protestant for Paris, and the Maurist Massuet responded with a major new edition in 1710, much politer and more urbane in his criticisms of his predecessor's edition than Feuardent had been but nonetheless firm in reclaiming Irenaeus for the Roman Catholic tradition. The final two editions, the establishment Anglican Harvey in 1857 and the Trappist monk Rousseau in 1965, bring us to the critical era. Parvis concludes by wondering what sort of Irenaeus our own age deserves.

Finally, Irenaeus M. C. Steenberg looks at Irenaeus's patristic context and legacy. He traces Irenaeus's knowledge of post-biblical writers before and during his own time, and considers his influence on subsequent patristic thought, East and West. On Irenaeus's legacy, he first sketches out evidence for the circulation and translation of Irenaeus's works, and then lists the explicit references to Irenaeus and his writings in the third, fourth, fifth, and later centuries, as well as direct, though unacknowledged, citations that have been identified from his works in various authors. Steenburg notes that Irenaeus, though widely referenced as a heresiologist, is oddly seldom referred to as theologian, despite the fact that his theology clearly influenced many of the great theologians of the fourth century, including Athanasius, Gregory of Nyssa, Gregory of Nazianzus, and Augustine, as well as later figures such as Maximus the Confessor. Steenburg proposes that, far from being a controversial figure in the fourth century, as some have argued, Irenaeus is not mentioned by name because his theology was too normal. It was simply viewed as "Christian theology," the gospel of Christ—which is what Irenaeus himself would have wanted.

PART ONE

Life

Irenaeus and His Context

CHAPTER ONE

Who Was Irenaeus?

An Introduction to the Man and His Work

PAUL PARVIS

Who was Irenaeus? This chapter will attempt to provide some sort of an answer to that rather complex question while, along the way, introducing some of the key literature that helps to articulate the study of Irenaeus.

We could try to answer it by looking at the bare bones of the little that is known of his life: he came from the East, was bishop of Lyons in the 180s, and wrote a monumental *Against the Heresies*. But that sort of an answer would not give us a handle on why he really matters—on why the question is of more than antiquarian interest in the first place.

Or we could give an answer in terms of his "achievement," which might involve us in talking about his role in the development of the very notions of orthodoxy and heresy or his contribution to a doctrine of "apostolic succession" or an understanding of the role of tradition in the life of the Church. But there are at least two problems there. One is the obvious fact that that sort of an approach means treating him as a sort of disembodied mind—"notions," "doctrine," "understanding"—rather than as one passionately engaged in the struggles and in the dramas of the world he lived in. And the other is the rather subtler danger of viewing him only from our end, as it were, for focusing on such "achievements" inevitably means privileging the problems and questions of later ages and that in turn means both belittling and distorting his thought by trying to wedge it into later categories. And the Irenaeus we are then left with is an inevitably divisive character because in the foreground as we look at him are issues that have caused and continue to cause division both within the Church and among the churches.[1]

So I would like to approach the question from another angle—by looking at the first more or less coherent account we have of Irenaeus and seeing how it does and how it does not fit the a priori questions we might be tempted to raise. That earliest account comes from the *Historia Ecclesiastica* of Eusebius of Caesarea, the first edition of which was produced shortly before the year 300.[2]

Eusebius tells us that Irenaeus (1) had in his youth been a "hearer" of Polycarp of Smyrna and (2) became bishop of Lyons in Gaul sometime around 180. He gives (3) a catalogue of Irenaeus's own writings, at least those "that have come to our knowledge" (*HE* V.26) and (4) an account of the books Irenaeus accepted as canonical. He is (5) suspicious of Irenaeus's views on chiliasm and the thousand-year reign of Christ but (6) knows him as a man of peace—which is, after all, what the name "Irenaeus" means— and as one who was active and influential in the ecclesiastical affairs of his day.

Those six points deserve to be looked at one at a time.

Polycarp of Smyrna

First, Polycarp. Irenaeus twice says that he knew Polycarp. In a letter that Eusebius quotes but which is otherwise lost to us, Irenaeus reminds the Florinus to whom it is addressed that "I saw you when I was still a boy, in lower Asia" and recounts how "I can speak of the place in which the blessed Polycarp used to sit and converse and how he would go out and come in and his manner of life and his bodily appearance and the talks he gave to the people and how he described his association with John and with the others who had seen the Lord and how he recalled their words" (*HE* V.20.5-6). That takes us back to the middle of the second century, if not slightly earlier, since Polycarp was martyred—burned alive in the arena in Smyrna—at the age of eighty-six on a date that appears to be 23 February 157.[3] Polycarp is important to Irenaeus because he thinks that through him he is himself linked to the apostolic age.[4]

And there we come to one of the central elements of Irenaean theology—the role of the bishop and succession from the apostles. For him the bishop is above all a teacher, a publicly accredited witness to the teaching of the apostles. It is easy for us to misunderstand that and to read him as if he were speaking of authority and some kind of juridical power.[5] He is not. While a later theology[6] came to affirm that the bishops *are* what the apostles *were*, Irenaeus wants to say that the bishops *teach* what the apostles *taught*. That can be clearly seen from his enumeration of the successive bishops of Rome in *Haer.* III.3.3.[7]

The Roman church, he thinks, was "founded and established by the two most glorious apostles Peter and Paul," and he lists the bishops from Linus to Eleutherus, who "now holds the episcopacy in the twelfth place from the apostles." There are twelve names in his list. In other words, Peter and Paul kicked off the succession at Rome but were not themselves bishops of Rome—indeed, there is no reason to think that he assumes they were "bishops" in any real sense at all. It is the job of the bishops to *teach* what the apostles *taught* rather than to *be* what the apostles *were*.

He thinks that he could in principle produce such a succession list for all the churches, but the only other example he even sketches in is Smyrna, where Polycarp, who "had been taught by the apostles and had conversed with many who had seen the Lord" was "established as bishop by apostles"—Polycarp, "whom we also saw when we were young" (*Haer.* III.3.4).

Eusebius dutifully copies Irenaeus's list of twelve names (*HE* V.6.1-5), but he does so without surprise. It has for him simply become self-evident that there should be in each of the major sees a chain of bishops leading back to the apostles.

But in selling the other part of his package—the role of the bishop as teacher— Irenaeus was in the end to be less successful. His model was based at least in part on the contemporary understanding of the "successions" in the schools of philosophy and medicine. The idea was that in each generation there had been a nameable individual who could be regarded as the official head of the school—Aristotelians, Stoics, Epicureans, and the like—and therefore as its official spokesperson.[8]

For Irenaeus, the bishop was an official spokesman—the nameable, identifiable individual you could go to in each city to find out what the apostles had taught. But even by the time of Eusebius that picture of the bishop as spokesman and witness was being displaced by a more juridical model, one based on the idea of a succession of authority. Hence the significance of the claim that the apostles had themselves been the first members of the various chains of episcopal succession: the bishops had in effect become what the apostles were.

Hence the importance of Polycarp for Irenaeus. It seems natural to infer as a corollary that Irenaeus was himself from Smyrna—the modern Izmir on the Aegean coast of Turkey—though he nowhere says so explicitly. Nor does Eusebius, who had little interest in anything like biography in the modern sense and who in any case would have had no source of information other than what he had read in Irenaeus himself.

It is in any event clear that Irenaeus was from the East. He thought and wrote in Greek and has links both personal and theological with Asia Minor.[9] But at some point he came west, from Smyrna in the Roman province of Asia to Lugdunum—the modern Lyons—capital of the province of Lugdunensis.

Lyons

Irenaeus never mentions Lyons either, though he does say that he dwells "among the Celts" and "busies" himself "for the most part with a barbaric tongue" (*Haer.* I. pref. 3).[10] The latter may be something of an exaggeration: the remark is made as part of a conventional apology for writing in a supposedly unpolished style.

The Lugdunum of Irenaeus's day was in fact quite a polished and cultured city—a Roman "colony" and, until the mid-third century, the largest city north of the Alps. It was the religious and economic hub of the whole of Gaul. There leading figures of all the Gallic provinces met annually to offer sacrifice at the altar of Rome and Augustus.

It was also a cosmopolitan city. What had initially brought Irenaeus there we do not know, but he was following a route taken by many others from the East.[11] His flock must have consisted largely, though not exclusively, of immigrants. It was a Greek-speaking community in a Latin-speaking city nestled in the midst of a Celtic-speaking countryside. They would in no small part have been outsiders, strangers in a strange land, alienated culturally as well as religiously from the life of the city around them. And they were, for that reason among others, mistrusted and despised.

Around the year 180 or very shortly before a vicious local persecution erupted. It began with mob violence that led to Christians being rounded up by the civic authorities and finally to a number of them being cruelly executed in the amphitheater by the Roman governor of the province.[12]

There is a detailed account of the persecution in the long and moving letter from "the slaves of Christ who sojourn in Vienne and Lyons to the brethren throughout Asia[13] and Phrygia who have the same faith and hope of redemption that we do," a document quoted at length by Eusebius in *HE* V.1.1—3.3. In the course of the persecution, the aged bishop Pothinos—"over ninety years of age" (V.1.29)—died in prison as a result of the maltreatment and torture to which he had been subjected. And he was succeeded by Irenaeus.

How Irenaeus escaped the persecution is unknown. It was, like all persecutions before the mid-third century, local, random, and haphazard. Perhaps in its earlier stages he was simply able to lie low. Perhaps he had friends in high places in the city. But before it was over, he seems to have been sent as an envoy to Eleutherus, bishop of Rome. Eusebius refers to a letter written by the confessors of Lyons and Vienne from prison, awaiting execution, in which they commend Irenaeus, the bearer of the letter and still a presbyter, "as one who is zealous for the covenant of Christ" (*HE* V.4.2).

Irenaeus mentions martyrdom several times, by which the Church is "often weakened though she at once experiences increase in her members and becomes whole" (*Haer.* IV.33.9). But it is a striking fact that from his writings we would know nothing of this savage little persecution in Lyons and Vienne. The community of which he became bishop must have been devastated—deprived of many of its leaders and living in fear of its neighbors. But there is not a hint of that in the pages of Irenaeus. There is instead optimism—a calm assurance and a quiet confidence in the working out of God's purposes in history.

That community was also rent by internal division. Within it he encountered a number of competing groups that can be loosely and imprecisely lumped together under the modern rubric of "gnosticism." Irenaeus's great work, which we call *Against the Heresies* and which he called *Refutation and Overthrow of Falsely-Named Knowledge*, was precisely an attempt to unmask and expose them.

Gnosticism has been the object of an enormous amount of scholarly discussion in recent decades, stimulated in part by the discovery in 1945–1946 of a large library of Gnostic texts in Coptic translation at Nag Hammadi in Upper Egypt.[14] As a result of that find, it is now possible to hear for the first time since antiquity the voices of those Irenaeus was trying to refute and to compare his account of what they were saying with their own. It seems to me that on the whole Irenaeus comes rather well out of the comparison (though it is—like everything to do with Gnosticism—a complex problem and very different views on the matter have been expressed).[15] On the whole, Irenaeus has a reasonably clear understanding of *what* the Gnostics are saying, though very little understanding of *why* they are saying it—and perhaps very little desire to understand. His purpose—so typically for antiquity—is refutation, not dialogue, and he has no sympathy at all for their project.

What was that project? The word *Gnosticism* is of course derived from *gnosis*, the stock, off-the-peg translation of which is "knowledge." But it is, I think, a mistake, though a mistake often made, to assume that the key to the various gnostic systems[16]— the unifying factor that somehow holds them together—is therefore a claim to esoteric knowledge, the possession of which will enable the gnostic in due course to pass from this world to the pure spiritual realm beyond.

One problem is that making that move leads to a privileging of the mythologies of the various gnostic groups in the sense of taking that mythology literally—as a sort of quasi-historical account—rather than as a poetic and indirect reflection on the nature of ultimate reality. That is in essence what Irenaeus does, and does very effectively. He begins his great refutation of the heresies with the version of gnostic myth associated with the school of Ptolemy, which was a spin-off of the highly influential system of Valentinian Gnosticism (*Haer.* I.1.1—8.5). There are, according to Ptolemy, thirty "aeons" that are at once separable cosmic entities and aspects of the fullness of divine being. As separable entities, they are arranged in quasi-sexual pairs and cascade down hierarchically from *Bythos* ("depth" or "abyss") at the top to *Sophia* ("Wisdom") at the bottom and as such play their various roles in the great drama of a pre-cosmic fall that leads to the tragic creation of our material world and the fragmentation and differentiation of spiritual being. But as aspects of divine reality, they together constitute the *pleroma* ("fullness") of divine being and each expresses or represents a facet of that mysterious and transcendent reality.

Irenaeus provides massive philosophical and scriptural refutation of the Gnostic myths, though he is also convinced that merely setting out their content will expose them as self-evident nonsense. And he can enjoy himself in the process, as when he parodies portentous-sounding Valentinian terminology with a myth of his own—the myth of the great primal aeon Gourd—inevitably reminiscent, for devotees of the cartoon strip *Peanuts*, of the Great Pumpkin whose return each Halloween was awaited so faithfully by Linus. In any event, Gourd with his companion Super Emptiness emits Cucumber and Melon, from whom all the lower melons descend. "If," Irenaeus asks tartly, "it's right to postulate names however you please, what's to stop us from using words"—like Gourd, Cucumber, and Melon—"that are far more plausible and actually in use and understood by everybody?" (*Haer.* I.11.4).

It is effective rhetoric and, as Irenaeus gets his teeth into parodying Valentinian language, actually quite funny. But a Valentinian would scarcely recognize it as getting at what he was in fact trying to say.

The problem is that the *gnosis* to which *gnostics* lay claim is really something much more like "insight" than simple factual or quasi-factual knowledge. The Gnostic came to an epiphanic understanding of his or her place in the grand scheme of things—a spark of the divine trapped in a material body in a material world that is both distasteful and ultimately meaningless and without purpose. It is a view of reality for the radically alienated, and it should perhaps occasion little surprise that it came to appeal to so many of the lonely and frightened men and women of the rapidly growing cities of the second century of our era.

The Writings of Irenaeus

Eusebius enumerates eight works of Irenaeus and quotes excerpts from four of them. (There is an annotated list—The Writings of Irenaeus—at the beginning of this volume.) Only two have come down to us and neither in the original Greek. His magnum opus, in five books, which we call *Against the Heresies* and which he called *Refutation and Overthrow of Falsely-Named Knowledge*, survives as a whole only in an ancient Latin version,[17] and even that is not quite complete. There are extensive fragments in Greek and Armenian, and the whole of books IV and V is preserved in a literal Armenian version, which is perhaps as old as the fifth century.[18] *Haer.* was probably written shortly after 180—say around 185.

The other work to survive is the *Demonstration of the Apostolic Preaching*, known to Eusebius (*HE* V.26) but unknown to modern scholars until the publication of an Armenian version in 1907. It is largely catechetical in character and focuses on types and prophecies of Christ in the Old Testament. It is impossible to pin down the date of composition, though it is clearly the later of the two works.[19]

Both surviving works are at least in part pastoral in nature and both are at least in part directed to the needs of Irenaeus's own community, and that is as true of *Against the Heresies* as it is of the *Demonstration*. It is important to emphasize that since *Haer.* is sometimes regarded as the first work of systematic theology. And it is true that it deals with a range of theological problems and doctrinal questions that had never before been presented with such coherence and in such depth. But it is far from systematic in structure and exposition, and there is much more scriptural exegesis than there is "abstract" discussion.

Irenaeus is convinced that the heretics, whether motivated by vainglory and arrogance or simply blind (*Haer.* III.3.2; IV.26.2), are bent on seducing—sometimes literally (I.13.7)—the simple faithful, and it is his purpose in *Against the Heresies* to try to prevent that. That shows through, for example, in a prayer inserted into the exposition of book III.

> And therefore I invoke you, O Lord, God of Abraham and God of Isaac and God of Jacob and Israel, the one who is the Father of our Lord Jesus Christ, the God who in the abundance of your mercy showed your good pleasure to us that we should know you—you, who made heaven and earth and rule over all things, who are the only true God, above whom there is no other god, you, who through our Lord Jesus Christ give us also the gift of the Holy Spirit—grant to everyone who reads this writing that he may know that you alone are God, and be strengthened in you, and keep away from every heretical and godless and impious opinion. (*Haer.* III.6.5)

Irenaeus's response to what he sees as the threat of "heretical and godless and impious opinion" is predicated on an unwavering conviction of the goodness of God and the goodness of the world he has made, in which and through which he acts in revelation and redemption. The whole history of humankind, from Adam and Eve on, is a single, coherent story that finds its focal point in Christ and that will find its culmination when he comes again.

It is a story of the initiative of God in gradually drawing to himself a people, of their education, and of their growing up. In the Garden, Adam and Eve were children; that is why they didn't have sex before the Fall—they were too young. But through the theophanies of the Old Testament, which were appearances of the Son, humankind gradually became "accustomed" to the presence of God, and God became "accustomed" to dwell with humankind. And at last there came "the Word of God, Jesus Christ our Lord, who because of his surpassing love became what we are that he might equip us to be that which he is" (*Haer.* V. pref.).

Christ "recapitulates" in himself the whole of this saving history, drawing all human experience together and summing it up, as it were, under one head—"coming through the whole dispensation and recapitulating all things in himself. But included in all things is humankind, moulded by God. And therefore he recapitulated humankind too in himself—the invisible made visible and the incomprehensible made comprehensible and the impassible made passible and the Word made man, recapitulating all things in himself" (*Haer.* III.16.6). That is why, according to Irenaeus, the Lucan genealogy (Luke 3:23-38) includes seventy-two generations, corresponding to the seventy-two peoples and languages into which humankind was thought to have been divided after Babel and so to the seventy-two (or seventy—there are textual variants) evangelists of Luke 10:1 and 17. The message Luke is sending is one of universality and comprehensiveness, "joining the end to the beginning and signifying that he is the one who recapitulated in himself all nations that had been dispersed after Adam and all tongues and generations of humankind together with Adam himself" (*Haer.* III.22.3).

That is also why Irenaeus (following, he thinks, John 8:57) insists that Jesus lived to be nearly fifty (*Haer.* II.22.6)—that is, he became, according to the reckoning of the ancients, an old man,[20]

> for he came to save all through himself, all, I mean, who through him are reborn to God—infants and toddlers and children and young people and the elderly. So he passed through every age—made an infant among infants, sanctifying them; a small child among small children, sanctifying those of that age and becoming for them an example of piety and righteousness and obedience; a young man among the young, becoming an example to the young and sanctifying them to the Lord. And so he also became an old man among the elderly, that he might be the perfect teacher in all things.
>
> And as a part of this drawing together of all things, "he came even unto death, that he might be 'the first-born from the dead, the one who is first in all things' (Col. 1:18), the prince of life, before all and preceding all." (II.22.4)

That is the story told in *Against the Heresies*, and it is on that work that Irenaeus's reputation depended, both in ancient and in modern times. It was the only work of Irenaeus known in the Latin West, and it was the only work to survive into the Byzantine world. The great ninth-century scholar and Patriarch of Constantinople, Photius, wrote for the benefit of his brother Tarasios a record of his voracious reading, and the entry on Irenaeus (codex 120 = 93b–94a) in the *Myrobiblion* or *Library*, written before 855, records only the *Haer.*, with a brief summary of the contents of the five books. That is, incidentally, the last certainly attested reference to an intact copy of Irenaeus in Greek.

Irenaeus and Scripture

One of Eusebius's aims in the *Historia Ecclesiastica* is to record the books cited as authoritative by "the ecclesiastical writers of various times" (III.3.3), and in V.8 he discusses Irenaeus. He cites Irenaeus on the origins of the Septuagint (V.8.10-15) and the four Gospels (V.8.2-4) and notes his use of I John and I Peter as well as the Apocalypse of John (V.8.5-7).

For Irenaeus, the scriptures of the Old Testament point to Christ while the scriptures of the New contain his teaching and the authoritative teaching of the apostles, and the two cohere. That is of vital importance for him, since one of his central concerns is to affirm, against "gnostic" views and against Marcion, the unity of the old and the new—the Father of Jesus Christ is the one who made heaven and earth and the God of the New Covenant is identical with the God of the Old.

He accepts, as was normal in the early church, the Greek version of the Old Testament—the Septuagint—as authoritative and inspired, which means that he accepts the longer, Greek canon instead of the shorter, Hebrew one, including what came to be designated the Apocrypha or deuterocanonical books. And he gives a version of the story of the providential origin of the Septuagint[21] when seventy elders from Jerusalem were sent to Ptolemy in Egypt and in isolation from one another miraculously produced seventy identical texts (*Haer.* III.21.2).

Irenaeus does not yet have a New Testament *canon*, in the strict sense of a closed list containing all (and only) the inspired books, but he emphatically does have a collection of authoritative books, books he refers to as "scripture", a collection that looks very like our developed New Testament canon, containing four Gospels, Acts, the letters of Paul,[22] 1 Peter, 1 John, and Revelation.[23] The number of Gospels is firmly pegged at four.[24] "Since there are four regions of the world in which we live and four universal winds and the Church has been spread over all the earth and the pillar and foundation of the Church is the Gospel and the Spirit of life, it is appropriate that it have four columns breathing out incorruptibility on all sides and kindling anew life for humankind" (III.11.8). In principle, the scriptures should suffice for teaching and instruction. In practice, though, there is a problem, for the "heretics" appeal to the same texts but, as Irenaeus sees it, distort their meaning. He uses (I.8.1) the analogy of a fine mosaic of the emperor which someone turns into the image of a dog or a wolf by prying loose the tesserae which make it up and rearranging them. The individual stones are the same, but a dog or a wolf is not what the emperor looks like.

How then do you know that you have the right picture? Here Irenaeus appeals to the notion of the Rule of Truth or Rule of Faith—where "rule" (*kanon* in Irenaeus's Greek) is being used, not as in the "rules of football" or the "rules of chess," but in the sense of a *ruler*, a straightedge, that will let you make sure a line is not crooked.

So Irenaeus thinks of the Rule of Truth as a sort of summary or condensation of what is taught in the scriptures. It is not something in competition with them nor does it stand over against them. Indeed, he can say that "we follow the one and only Lord as our teacher and have as a rule of truth his words" (*Haer.* IV.35.4). We might say that the relation of scripture to the rule of truth is rather like the relation of a jigsaw puzzle to the picture on the box. The picture is not a substitute for the full puzzle, but it does help you make sure you are putting the pieces together properly.

Concretely, the rule of truth is a sort of proto-creedal summary of the faith. It is not a fixed form of words but a set of propositions that Irenaeus articulates in roughly similar ways. He can, for example, wax eloquent about "barbarian tribes" who have no written scriptures in their own language but who "carefully guard the old tradition, believing in one God, the maker of heaven and earth and of all the things in them and in Christ Jesus, the Son of God, who because of his surpassing love for that which he had fashioned underwent birth from the Virgin, himself uniting in himself humankind to God, and who suffered under Pontius Pilate and rose and was taken up in glory—who will come in glory as the Saviour of those who are being saved and the judge of those who are being judged and send into eternal fire those who pervert the truth and who despise his Father and his own advent" (*Haer.* III.4.2).

Or, more lapidarily, he can speak of "a sound faith in one God almighty, from whom are all things, and a firm assent to the Son of God, Christ Jesus our Lord, and to the saving plan[25] through which the Son of God became man, and assent as well to the Spirit of God, who supplies the knowledge of the truth and who presents to humankind in each generation the saving plans of the Father and the Son, as the Father wills" (*Haer.* IV.33.7).[26] Scripture and the rule of truth, then, go together: both express and enshrine the teaching of the apostles. But there is a third mechanism as well—a third line of defense, as it were—for making sure you have the faith right since the apostles left successors in the churches, to whom "they handed on their own teaching role" (*Haer.* III.3.1). And there we come back to the position of the bishop and the notion of succession from the apostles.

> Even if there were a dispute on some small point, would it not be necessary to have recourse to the most ancient churches, in which the apostles dwelt, and to receive from them what is certain and clear on the question at issue? And what if the apostles had not even left us any writings at all, would it not be necessary to follow the structure of the tradition which they handed on to those to whom they entrusted the churches (*Haer.* III.4.1)?

So the scriptures are in principle sufficient for all our needs, and they have a richness and a complexity that can be explored in depth—as Irenaeus does throughout both *Adversus haereses* and the *Demonstration*—but the central truths they contain are transmitted by other means as well.

The Millennial Reign of Christ

There was one element of Irenaeus's thought that Eusebius deeply regretted. Eusebius was an enthusiastic admirer of the heavily Platonizing third-century Alexandrian exegete and theologian Origen, to whom most of the sixth book of the *Ecclesiastical History* is devoted, and his own theology can be described as in a Platonizing tradition. That meant, among other things, that he felt very uncomfortable when confronted with what he saw as an overly literal, overly physicalist view of the resurrection body and the Kingdom of God.

Such a view was associated with much of the earlier theological tradition, especially that connected with Asia Minor. One figure who comes in for particularly heavy criticism here is the early second-century elder Papias of Hierapolis. Papias, though a man of venerable antiquity, had recorded certain "strange teachings of the Saviour and some other things quite mythical in character. And among them he says that there will be a period of a thousand years after the resurrection from the dead when the Kingdom of Christ will subsist in bodily fashion on this very earth" (*HE* III.39.11-12).

This was, Eusebius tells us, a consequence of the fact that Papias was a man "of very little understanding, as one can conclude from his books," but sadly his antiquity had persuaded "ever so many of the ecclesiastical writers to adopt an opinion similar to his own," including even Irenaeus (III.39.13). This is probably one of the things Photius had in mind in the ninth century when he appended to his brief summary of the contents of *Haer.* the warning that in some of Irenaeus's writings "precision of truth with regard to the doctrines of the Church is defiled with spurious words—a thing which you must watch out for carefully" (*Bibliotheca*, codex 120 = 94a).

Irenaeus certainly did hold such views.[27] There will, he thinks, be a first resurrection of the just and an earthly Kingdom, "which is the beginning of incorruptibility, and through that Kingdom those who are worthy gradually become accustomed to receive God. . . . For it is right that they receive the fruits of endurance in that very creation in which they laboured or were afflicted, tested in every way and approved through their endurance, and that they be made alive in that very creation in which they were killed, and that they reign in that very creation in which they bore enslavement" (*Haer.* V.32.1).

That earthly Kingdom will last a thousand years. Christ taught that "those who have done good things will rise first, then so will those who are to be judged, as the book of Genesis has it that the sixth day—that is, the six-thousandth year—is the consummation of this age and then comes the seventh day of rest . . . that is, the seventh thousand year period of the Kingdom of the just, in which they will practice for incorruptibility, when the creation has been renewed for those who have been preserved for this" (V.36.3).

In that last sentence, Irenaeus may well have been thinking of his friends who had been so brutally killed in the amphitheatre in Lyons. It was, in any event, heady stuff. The former passage is preserved, as is the whole of the last five chapters of *Haer.*, in only one of the Latin manuscripts (*Vossianus lat.* F 33), while the latter is omitted even there and found only in the Armenian version. Eusebius was not the only one who disliked that kind of language. Later scribes felt they had to bowdlerize the text as well.

But we, from our perspective—excited by different things and frightened by different things—can see how that sort of millennial view simply underlines once again the importance of the body for Irenaeus. The real "me" is not, as various gnostic groups would have it, some spark of the divine imprisoned within my flesh, nor is it, as much of the Platonist tradition would have it, a *nous* more or less fortuitously attached to a physical shell. Men and women are, rather, bodily creatures.[28] So we were made and so we will remain. Irenaeus regularly refers to humankind as God's *plasma*—a thing he has formed—with an allusion to the verb used in the Septuagint text of Gen 2:7: "And God formed/moulded the human being, dust from the earth."

Irenaeus the Peacemaker

Eusebius says that Irenaeus was "appropriately named and a peacemaker by nature" (*HE* V.24.18). He is there talking about his intervention "in the name of the brethren throughout Gaul over whom he presided" (V.24.11) in the crisis provoked when Victor, bishop of Rome in the 180s, excommunicated the bishops of Asia who "thought it necessary to observe the festival of the saving Pasch on the fourteenth day of the month" (V.23.1)—in other words, to keep the connection between the crucifixion and the Jewish Passover.

Irenaeus was among those who in response wrote to Victor "on behalf of the peace of the churches" (V.24.18), and Eusebius cites two substantial fragments of the letter (V.24.12-13 and 14-17).[29] This tells us on the one hand something of Irenaeus's position as bishop of Lyons and on the other something of his character. But it also underlines his continuing connection with the churches and theology of Asia Minor.

Eusebius has another suggestive reference to that connection. The letter from the churches of Lyons and Vienne telling the tale of the persecution of 177 or so was, as we have seen, addressed to "the brethren throughout Asia and Phrygia who have the same faith in and the same hope of redemption that we do" (*HE* V.1.3). After his long extracts from the letter (V.1.1—3.3). Eusebius abruptly mentions "those around Phrygia who followed Montanus and Alcibiades and Theodotus"—that is, the beginnings of that ecstatic, charismatic, prophetic movement that came to be known as Montanism. After this brief and abrupt reference, Eusebius adds, "when there was disagreement about these matters, the brethren throughout Gaul again set out their own judgement, pious and most orthodox, about these things too, presenting also various letters from the martyrs who had been perfected among them, letters which they had written while they were still in prison to the brethren in Asia and Phrygia and also to Eleutherus, who was then bishop of Rome, acting as advocates for the peace of the churches" (*HE* V.3.4). Eusebius's next sentence (V.4.1-2) affirms that "the same martyrs" recommended Irenaeus, then still a presbyter, to Eleutherus and shows that he was the bearer of the letter.

Eusebius expresses no connection between these events, but there obviously was one. He is, as so often, being coy. Irenaeus must have taken the letter describing the persecution at least as far as Rome, and he took in the same bag various letters about the developing controversy over the New Prophecy, "Montanism."

For Eusebius, it is an open and shut case: Montanism is a heresy, and that's all there is to be said about it. But that leaves him with a dilemma—a dilemma from which he escapes by simply ignoring it. The martyrs, of whom he of course approves, were clearly sympathetic to the New Prophecy, or at least open to its influence. And the letter from the churches of Lyons and Vienne was, after all, addressed to the brethren of Asia and Phrygia—the home and heartland of the movement. And that sympathy was presumably shared by Irenaeus, the bearer of the letters.

So here once again we see Irenaeus working for the peace of the churches. And we also see his openness to the working of the Spirit in his own time.[30] This is a far cry from the ruthless heresy hunter and jackbooted authoritarian that he has sometimes been represented as.

We began with an identikit picture of Irenaeus—orthodoxy and heresy, bishops and apostolic succession. We can see the massive influence Eusebius has had in the formation of that picture, but we can also see in the things that Eusebius privileges a picture that is much more complex. We are, I hope, left with the picture of a man of broad sympathies and deep pastoral concern, firmly rooted in the traditions of his native Asia but immersed as well in the life and the problems of the church and the churches around him.

If we were to see in Irenaeus only a truculent polemicist or an authority figure with a hang-up about apostolic succession, we would do him a radical disservice. And if we were to take that line, we would also see him as an inevitably divisive character, for the simple reason that cluttering up the foreground would be issues that have caused and continue to cause disquiet among historians and dissent and division both within the Church and among the churches.

But if we take seriously the depth of his conviction that the Christian gospel is liberating as well as true and that it is for all men and women, we can see him as a figure of unity rather than of division. He proclaims the unity of God and the coherence of the world he has made, the unity of revelation and the integrity and meaning of human history, and—not least—the unity of all humankind as the men and women he has fashioned are called upon to grow up, together, in and into the presence of God.

CHAPTER TWO

The Cultural Geography of a Greek Christian

Irenaeus from Smyrna to Lyons

JARED SECORD

Seen within a broader context, Irenaeus is merely one among the thousands of Greeks—Christians and otherwise—who relocated themselves to Rome.[1] But Irenaeus stands out in this company because of his final destination: most of those who came before and after him went no further west and north than Rome itself, and not as far as Lyons, the crossroads of Roman Gaul.

Yet for all the uncommonness of Irenaeus's ultimate place of residence, he says virtually nothing about Lyons and very little about Gaul. Little attention has been paid to this silence, apart from the occasional frustrated comments of historians of Roman Gaul,[2] and the ingenious but misguided attempt by Jean Colin to relocate Irenaeus's episcopate to an obscure see in northern Asia Minor.[3] Suffice it to say, there is no reason to doubt that Irenaeus was a long-term resident of Lyons, but some explanation of his reticence about the city and the region as a whole is necessary.

The goal of this paper is to offer such an explanation, and to consider more broadly his perspective on the Mediterranean world and its geography. As I shall argue, Irenaeus's view on living in the West remained that of a Greek raised and educated in Asia Minor. He is deliberately vague in his references to Gaul, and he refers to it and the rest of the Mediterranean world in ways that would be comprehensible to an Eastern Greek who was only dimly aware of the geography of the West. The result is a strange mixture, simultaneously Christian *and* Greek in outlook: Irenaeus regards Gaul as a barbarian land on the Western periphery of the world, but he also emphasizes the unity of the church throughout the entire world and its peoples, even among those who do not speak Greek. This last element is particularly jarring with Irenaeus's own outlook on speaking a language other than Greek, and the paper will conclude by suggesting that he regarded even Latin as a barbarian language.

Irenaeus took with him to the West his Greek education, which he acquired likely in Smyrna, a major center of sophistic culture and teaching.[4] If his youth had been spent in Smyrna, he would have been a contemporary there of the sophist Aelius Aristides,[5] and there is good reason to believe that his teachers had much in common with the more philosophically inclined of the sophists.[6] His Greek learning is often put on display in the *Adversus haereses*, though in several cases the sources of his knowledge seem to be nothing more than doxographical handbooks, resources used by Christians and pagans alike.[7] Certainly, in matters concerning natural philosophy, Irenaeus's worldview is little different from that of his pagan contemporaries.[8]

A similarly common view is the basis for Irenaeus's perspective of the geography of the world. The frame of his map is provided by a commonplace of classical geography, viz., that the world has four chief regions and winds.[9] Irenaeus uses this fact as proof that there can be only four Gospels: "For there are four regions of the world in which we exist and four universal winds. And the church has spread out over all the earth, and the gospel is a pillar and foundation of the church as is the spirit of life. So it is natural that the church have four pillars breathing out incorruption everywhere and bringing new life to men."[10] In what follows, I shall fill in this map, starting in the East, and moving with a westward trajectory.

In the East, Irenaeus's geographical perspective picks up, as it were, where the Acts of the Apostles left off, with Christianity having spread to the world from Palestine.[11] But for Irenaeus, Jerusalem—by now Aelia Capitolina—is only the former starting point for the Christian movement, and it no longer holds a central position. Thus Jerusalem is likened to a twig no longer useful for bearing fruit, as in John 15: "For just as the twigs of vines are not made chiefly for themselves, but on account of the fruit growing on them, so when it ripens and is picked, the twigs are discarded and borne away [*a medio auferuntur*],[12] as they are no longer useful for bearing new fruit. So too with Jerusalem."[13] Jerusalem has already sown its seeds: "And with its fruit sown throughout the entire inhabited world, [Jerusalem]—which had once been very fruitful—is rightly abandoned, and taken away [ἐκ μέσου ἐγένετο]. From it Christ, according to the flesh, and the apostles had sprouted, but now it is no longer useful for bearing new fruit."[14] There was a sense of foreignness to the place of Jesus' ministry, as Irenaeus explains: "In a foreign land the people of Israel came into being in twelve tribes, since Christ too was to make the twelve supporting columns of the Church in a foreign land."[15] Reverence for Jerusalem was akin to living in the past, a charge that Irenaeus levels against the Ebionites, a group that still practices circumcision, follows the Mosaic law, and "adores Jerusalem as if it were the house of God."[16] Jerusalem and Palestine are now on the periphery of the Christian world, and regions to the west have trumped them in importance.

And from Jerusalem Irenaeus follows the paths of the apostles on their journeys west as they sow the seeds of a united church. The geographical narrative in Acts is particularly significant for Irenaeus, who emphasizes that Paul preaches the same message wherever he goes, no matter the audience. This process begins in Damascus, where Irenaeus paraphrases Acts 9:19-20: "In the synagogues in Damascus, Paul heralded Jesus with complete freedom of speech, saying that he is the Christ, the son of God."[17] Paul's speech *in the synagogues* is crucial, for Irenaeus can later find him saying much the same thing in Athens, where, Irenaeus emphasizes, there were no Jews present. Irenaeus concludes by finding Paul with Barnabas preaching the same message in Lystra, in the hinterlands of Asia Minor.[18] Despite the differences in education and language, the Christian message as taught by Paul was the same for Jews in Damascus, educated pagans in Athens, and rustic pagans in Lystra.

The movement west continues, and Irenaeus follows the apostles as they found churches in Rome, Ephesus, and Smyrna, the latter church providing Irenaeus with his own link to the apostles because of his association with Polycarp.[19] So we have a unified message of Christianity spread by Paul and the apostles, and maintained by their successors in a network of unified churches. These churches, says Irenaeus, are like islands afloat in the midst of the Empire: "These guarantees were made not only to the prophets and fathers, but also to the collected churches among the pagans. The Spirit calls these churches 'islands,' because they were founded in the midst of turbulence, and they endure the storms of blasphemy. They are also a safe port for those in danger and a refuge for those who love truth."[20]

This general view of the Christian church (in the singular) is related elsewhere with more geographic detail:

> Although it is scattered in the entire world [ἐν ὅλῳ τῷ κόσμῳ], the church, having received this preaching and this faith, keeps careful watch over it, as if it lived in one house. . . . The churches founded in the German provinces [ἐν Γερμανίαις] believe and pass down traditions no differently than the churches in the Iberian provinces [ἐν ταῖς Ἰβηρίαις], those in the Celtic provinces [ἐν Κελτοῖς], those throughout the eastern regions [κατὰ τὰς ἀνατολάς], those in Egypt [ἐν Αἰγύπτῳ], those in Libya [ἐν Λιβύῃ], and those throughout the middle regions of the world [αἱ κατὰ μέσα τοῦ κόσμου]. But just as the sun, the creation of God, is one and the same in the entire world [ἐν ὅλῳ τῷ κόσμῳ], so too does the preaching of the truth shine everywhere and illuminate all the men who wish to come into knowledge of the truth.[21]

The list moves around the four regions of the world, following classical convention, and the geographical divisions favored in handbooks of rhetoric. The German provinces are segregated in the North, the Iberian and Celtic are in the West, then the vaguely defined eastern regions, Egypt and Libya in the South, and finally the regions in the middle. Compare the instructions of Menander Rhetor, who offers advice about how to praise a country: "We estimate and judge the position of a country by its relation to land, sea, or sky. . . . Relation to the sky: is it in the west, east [ἐν ἀνατολαῖς], south, or north, or in the center [ἐν τῷ μέσῳ]?"[22]

The Greekness of the list is further demonstrated by Irenaeus's terminology for the Western regions, in notable contrast to the Roman labels used before him in a geographical excursus by Theophilus of Antioch, whose work he knew.[23] In Theophilus's list, the references are directly to the Roman provinces: "the so-called Gauls and Spains and Germanies [τὰς καλουμένας Γαλλείας καὶ Σπανίας καὶ Γερμανίας]."[24] *Germania* was interchangeable in Greek and Latin, but Irenaeus insists on referring to the provinces of Gaul and Spain with the preferred classical terminology of *Keltike* and *Iberia*.[25] In the process, he displays a more stubborn form of Hellenism than that of many of his Greek contemporaries, who at times gloss the term Iberia with Hispania,[26] and use the label Gaul without pause.[27]

Indeed, for a comparable use of the label ἐν Κελτοῖς we must turn to an author such as Philostratus, our chief source for the phenomenon of the "Second Sophistic," a term he invented.[28] Philostratus recognizes the potential difficulty eastern readers could have in distinguishing between Gaul and Galatia, so he identifies the sophist Favorinus of Arles as one of the "western Gauls [ἑσπερίων Γαλατῶν]" and the rhetor Aquila as from "Galatia of the East [Ἀκύλας ὁ ἐκ τῆς ἑῴου Γαλατίας]."[29] The term ἐν Κελτοῖς provides a way for Philostratus to remove any ambiguity between East and West. Thus he records differing reports concerning the location of a sophist's death: "Some say that Alexander died in the Celtic provinces [ἐν Κελτοῖς] . . . and others say that he died in Italy [ἐν Ἰταλίᾳ]."[30] Philostratus and Irenaeus speak the same geographical language.

So when Irenaeus locates himself for his readers, it surprises little that he does so with the phrase ἐν Κελτοῖς[31] and one almost parenthetical reference to the Rhone.[32] Such a level of vagueness is the norm for Greek authors who refer to Gaul, with the notable exception of specialized geographers. Typical references are to Massalia (modern Marseilles) or to a few other cities established as Greek colonies,[33] and to the Rhone.[34] The contrast in level of detail in accounts of Gaul between the Greek colonies in the south and the regions to the north is striking. Oppian, for instance, calls Massalia a holy city and its inhabitants the ancient residents of Phocaea, the metropolis that founded the city some eight centuries earlier![35] But, the rest of Gaul, in opposition to Massalia, is identified anachronistically as the region where the Celts dwell.[36] Sometimes the geographical focus on Gaul can even be so broad as to include reference to the Rhine,[37] suggesting that Western Europe north of the Alps was regarded as an amorphous area dotted with the occasional large river and a few Greek colonies.

Ultimately, then, little weight can be given to the phrase ἐν Κελτοῖς in support of the suggestion that Irenaeus preached "among the Celts."[38] Rather, seen in the larger context of Greek perspectives of Western Europe, Irenaeus is telling his readers that he lived on the course of the Rhone north of the Mediterranean, where the olive and fig trees gave out, vines produced grapes with difficulty, and there were no Greek colonies.[39] And, to avoid any confusion for readers unfamiliar with the details of western geography, he uses the term *Keltike* rather than Gaul.

To return now to the larger map, Irenaeus situates himself on the western periphery, to the east of which are the elusive "middle regions of the world" and the "eastern regions" (note the plurality). Given their company in the list of territories—they are balanced with all of Libya and Egypt in the south, for instance—both regions must be large. In other words, Irenaeus preferred brevity to detail when he used the phrases "eastern regions" (κατὰ τὰς ἀνατολὰς) and "middle regions of the world" (κατὰ μέσα τοῦ κόσμου). After all, these were precisely the areas where he could have engaged in the most detailed geographical lists of places, of the type especially common in Acts (for example, 2:9-11, 16:6-12). One can also compare the perspective of his contemporary Ptolemy in the *Tetrabiblos*, where the middle of the world is conceived of in broad terms. Ptolemy runs through the four quarters of the world and lists the regions that are "positioned around the middle of the entire inhabited world."[40] Some thirty-five such regions are named—including all of Asia Minor, Egypt, and much of the modern Middle East—situated around a center that seems to be located in the Mediterranean somewhere north of Egypt.[41] The middle of the world need not be small.

With all of this in mind, I suggest that Irenaeus's "middle regions of the world" encompass the apostolic churches of Rome, Ephesus, Smyrna, and Corinth (the only churches named in the entirety of the work). The boundaries are clearly enough demarcated: Europe west and north of the Alps forms one, Libya and Egypt another, and Jerusalem and vicinity a third. The main issue becomes deciding where to separate the eastern regions (κατὰ τὰς ἀνατολὰς) from the "middle regions of the world" (κατὰ μέσα τοῦ κόσμου). But just as middle is a relative term, so is east, and here I would suggest again that Irenaeus's perspective remained that of a resident of western Asia Minor. The "middle regions of the world" then include Italy, Greece, and at least the western coast of Asia Minor.[42] As should be no surprise, apostolic succession is the foundation for centrality in Irenaeus's world, and the result is a large center.

The location of this large center of the world is an area where Irenaeus has departed from his Greek contemporaries. To begin with, Irenaeus prefers the term *kosmos* to the less-inclusive *oikoumene*, with its classical implications of an inhabited world limited to Greek lands. Irenaeus's contemporaries almost invariably refer to the middle of the *oikoumene* rather than the *kosmos*, and they locate it in the east. Thus Aelius Aristides identifies the Aegean Sea as the middle of the *oikoumene*, Dio Chrysostom tells the Alexandrians that they are located almost in the middle of the *oikoumene*, and Galen places the middle region of the *oikoumene* on a line that runs east-west and passes through Cnidos and Cos in southern Asia Minor.[43] The Aegean and Asia Minor are still part of the middle of Irenaeus's world, but it has expanded farther west than his contemporaries would allow.

The expanded middle of Irenaeus's world is a consequence of the great opportunities for travel and communication during the Antonine Age. As he says, "the world [ὁ κόσμος] has peace because of the Romans so that we might walk on the roads without fear and sail wherever we please."[44] Our knowledge of Irenaeus's travels in this world is mostly lost, as is the case with his correspondence. But from the scraps of information that remain, we can still see the efforts he made to stay in touch with other churches and to collect and transmit literature.[45] Rome is part of the middle regions of the world, but it is not *the center*, and Christians exist and travel throughout the entire *kosmos*.

Leaving Rome nonetheless seems to have been a major transition for Irenaeus, despite his comments about the easy mobility provided for Christians by the empire. The *Haer.* itself seems to have been addressed to a fellow cleric at Rome whom Irenaeus (unfortunately) does not name or identify in any explicit way. But he does offer the hope that this recipient will find the work useful in his effort to lead the curious away from heretical doctrines, sufficient confirmation that he is addressing a cleric or at least a Christian teacher, most likely at Rome.[46]

Of this cleric or teacher, Irenaeus begs: "You will not expect from us, who reside in the Celtic provinces [τῶν ἐν Κελτοῖς διατριβόντων][47] and are busy most of the time with a barbarian language [βάρβαρον διάλεκτον], either the art of rhetoric which we did not learn, or the skill of a writer which we have not exercised, or embellishment of words or persuasion which we do not know."[48] Despite his claims, this is exactly the sort of comment one would expect from an author trained in rhetoric, and we should not be taken in by Irenaeus's false display of modesty.

Instead, what requires commentary is the βάρβαρον διάλεκτον with which Irenaeus is busy most of the time. It must be stated immediately that the word διάλεκτον has for Irenaeus the sense of "language" and not merely of a dialect within a language; he uses the word, for instance, to speak of the many different languages of the world, and also of Greek and Hebrew.[49] One must also note that Irenaeus divides the world up into the two classes of Greek and barbarian,[50] and speaks of faithful Christians who are nonetheless "barbarians in terms of our language [*ad sermonem nostrum barbari sunt*]."[51] Irenaeus maintains the classical linguistic sense of the word barbarian as a speaker of a language other than Greek.[52] There is no sign that his worldview includes a "third race" of Christians in addition to the traditional division of Greeks and barbarians.[53]

In light of this perspective, Latin is a possible candidate as the βάρβαρον διάλεκτον of which Irenaeus was speaking.[54] Other Greek authors had previously labeled the Romans as barbarians,[55] and a notable feature of the interaction between Greek scholars and their Roman patrons in the time of Augustus and the surrounding decades was a tendency to claim that Latin was merely a dialect of Greek.[56] This provides a sense of the linguistic anxiety regarding the status of Latin with respect to Greek, an anxiety that had largely faded by the second century, a time when most educated Romans spoke Greek fluently and there was less need for most educated Greeks to learn Latin.

This was even the situation at Rome, where it was quite possible for educated Greeks to function without having the need to speak any Latin. Plutarch, for instance, never had the time to learn Latin well while in Rome because he was too busy teaching in Greek![57] Galen, too, shows no signs of ever needing to speak Latin, and even writes about Rome as if it were a Greek city.[58] Such examples concerning the educated pagan elite could be multiplied at great length,[59] demonstrating both the commonness and the high status of Greek at Rome.

And Greek was also the most common spoken language among Christians at Rome.[60] In addition to the large body of Christian literature written at Rome in Greek, one can add ample testimony to the use of Greek by Christians from epigraphic evidence. The use of Greek for Christian epitaphs does not end until the fourth century, and Greek was used proportionately much more often in Christian epigraphy than in pagan, a fact that becomes significant when one considers that most of the Christian epitaphs in question were the work of amateurs, rather than of trained stone-carvers.[61] This demonstrates that Greek was the preferred "in-group" language of Christians at Rome, though Latin of course would be spoken by many of them too.[62] But Greek was the *sine qua non* for educated Christians at Rome, so many of whom came to the city from the East.[63] Greek was the language of instruction at the school of Justin Martyr at Rome, where Irenaeus was likely a student for a time.[64] Finally, one cannot forget that Irenaeus wrote to Christians at Rome and in the East alike in Greek, including the unnamed recipient of the *Haer.* at Rome.

Compared to the capital, Lyons was a Latin city. The amount of evidence available from Rome of course dwarfs that from Lyons, but some comparisons can still be made. Our literary sources for Lyons often provide more insight into the snobbery of the authors than the city's cultural attainments, but these authors still provide some evidence for the occasional presence of Greek actors and orators at Lyons, even as they disparage the city and its residents.[65] Epigraphy is a more promising area, as Lyons possesses a large corpus of inscriptions.[66] Greek appears rarely in these inscriptions,[67] and is often confined to short formulas, notably the phrase χαῖρε καὶ ὑγίαινε,[68] sometimes written in Latin script.[69] Rather than seeking mystical significance in this phrase, as many have done, Jean-Claude Decourt argues that this is a simple translation of a relatively banal Latin phrase: *ave et vale.*[70] These residents of Lyons, it seems, were merely attempting to display pretensions to Greek culture, as might be fitting for the city's more educated class.[71] This practice can be compared to the fashion for Greek epitaphs at Rome, thirty percent of which are in verse—a much higher proportion than *anywhere* else.[72] The educated classes at Rome display greater pretensions to Greek culture and are better able to demonstrate them than the educated at Lyons. And more people at Rome would have been able to read inscribed Greek verses than at Lyons.

The language in inscriptions, it must be admitted, says little about the language(s) spoken by the dedicator/ee. In this respect, it is not a matter of great significance that there are no inscriptions from Lyons in a Celtic language, or even a Celtic language written in Latin script.[73] Onomastics, however, can provide some additional insight, and here it is significant that Irenaeus's time in Lyons coincides with the peak of the Gallic epigraphic habit.[74] This period is also notable for an increasing number of people commemorated who lack the characteristic twofold or threefold pattern of Roman names and instead possess names in the "Celtic" style of a single name accompanied with a patronymic.[75] These dedicators/ees did not adopt Roman names for themselves, but they nonetheless participated in the Roman epigraphic habit, which necessarily involved the use of Latin.[76] This does not mean that they stopped speaking their native language, but it is still indicative of the increasing use of Latin among people whom we might expect to speak a Celtic language because of their names.

Many Greeks who came to Lyons are also commemorated in Latin.[77] A notable example is a bilingual inscription in Greek and Latin from the late second century that commemorates a trader (*negotiator*) from Syria named Thaemus Iulianus (Θαῖμος ὁ καὶ Ἰολιανὸς).[78] The bilingualism of the inscription is surely a reflection of his own bilingualism in Greek and Latin.[79] Thaemus was far from the only Eastern trader to come to Gaul,[80] and his example encourages us to think that the acquisition of some Latin was necessary for this profession. Latin could even serve as a means for communication between native Greek speakers and those who might speak a Celtic language within their households or in other settings.[81] And at Lyons, a Roman colony originally settled by veterans that also happened to be "the largest Roman administrative establishment north of the Alps,"[82] the number of these Celtic language settings must have been very few.

The application of this linguistic situation in Lyons to the case of Irenaeus suggests that he was busy most of the time with Latin and *not* with a Celtic language. The evidence concerning the martyrdoms at Lyons in 177 also suggests as much. Two of the martyrs were Greeks from Asia Minor,[83] but one of these—Attalus of Pergamum—addresses the crowd in Latin (τῆς Ῥωμαϊκῇ φωνῇ),[84] as does the deacon Sanctus from Vienne.[85] Overall, the names of the martyrs recorded by Eusebius are a mix of Greek and Roman, with few if any traces of Celtic.[86] And the activities of the

Christian community at Lyons seem to have been urban in character—the persecution began by banning them from the city's "houses, baths, and marketplaces (οἰκιῶν καὶ βαλανείων καὶ ἀγορᾶς)."[87] This was an urban church in a predominantly Latin-speaking city.

Indeed, if one persists in believing that Irenaeus preached "among the Celts" in a Celtic language, one would have to suggest, following Gustave Bardy, that this activity took place "bien loin de sa ville épiscopale."[88] The gaps in our knowledge of Irenaeus's biography might allow for such an activity, but the large body of his extant writings and the surviving traces of his no doubt voluminous body of correspondence are suggestive of a bookish existence. Irenaeus took great care in transcribing texts accurately,[89] and he shows a certain amount of pride in the collection of "heretical" writings he had managed to assemble.[90] He continued to receive texts from Rome,[91] and he made a great effort to disseminate his views on a variety of subjects to his fellow clerics.[92] He even displays some uncertainty about whether his opponents *really* do the "godless, lawless, and unspeakable things [τὰ ἄθεα, καὶ ἔκθεσμα, καὶ ἀπειρημένα]" they describe in their writings.[93] This much reading and writing took time, especially when we consider some of the other literary questions to which he devoted his energy. These include a study of Paul's use of *hyperbata*,[94] and of the possible numerological significance of the number of the beast.[95] And the longer that he stayed in Rome before coming to Lyons—he was still in Rome at the time of Polycarp's martyrdom, which likely occurred in the late 150s, but perhaps as late as 167[96]—the less time Irenaeus would have had to learn a Celtic language and preach "among the Celts."

Instead of this mission "among the Celts," which puts Irenaeus in the pagan countryside like Martin of Tours two centuries later, I would like to conclude by suggesting a different sort of mission to Gaul. Two propositions guide this suggestion: Christianity had to have been introduced to Gaul from outside, and the person or people who introduced it had to have been speakers of Greek. Native residents of Gaul certainly did become Christians, but there was still a need for the sort of (Greek) expertise that could come only from larger centers of Christian teaching, such as Rome. There is a clear precedent for this model in the practice described by Strabo of the Gauls welcoming and hiring Greek sophists and doctors to become residents of their cities and to work in them.[97] A Greek doctor, Alexander of Phrygia, was even one of the Christians martyred at Lyons.[98] In this sense, Irenaeus was perhaps a different sort of Greek expert encouraged or even invited to come to Lyons. How early he came to Lyons remains an open question, but one possible scenario for his invitation is as a response to the advancing age of Pothinus, the *episcopus* who would be martyred in 177 at the age of ninety years.[99] Irenaeus would have come to Lyons with an impressive pedigree thanks to his connections with the famous martyrs and teachers Polycarp and (most likely) Justin. At Lyons he learned Latin—or at least became a much more fluent speaker—and taught and preached in this language,[100] though no doubt in Greek too. He continued of course to write in Greek, though the Latin translation of the *Haer.* may well have been produced by the Christian community at Lyons soon after his death.[101] Seen in this light, Irenaeus becomes part of the "Latinization" of the church in the West.[102]

Still, as I have argued above, Irenaeus seems to have missed his time in what he called "the middle regions of the world." He was not entirely happy to be speaking Latin instead of Greek, and the perspective on the world he gained from the schools of Asia Minor remained entrenched in his mind, even as the Greek education he acquired there provided him with tools useful for the refutation of his opponents. Here in Lyons was a Christian who writes about Gaul and the western regions of the empire as if he were Philostratus, and who, on the one occasion when he deigns to mention the existence of the Latin language (a βάρβαρον διάλεκτον), displays more distaste for it than one finds expressed in any of his Hellenic contemporaries.[103]

But despite his unhappiness with some aspects of living in Lyons, Irenaeus still chose to reside on the western periphery of the world rather than in Rome or Asia Minor, something that cannot be said for almost all of these Hellenic contemporaries. His choice to leave Rome and not to return to Asia Minor must have been motivated in part by the example of Paul. As is reported in 1 Clement, a text Irenaeus knew well,[104] "[Paul] was a herald in the East [ἔν τε τῇ ἀνατολῇ] and the West [ἐν τῇ δύσει], and received the genuine glory of his faith. He taught the entire world righteousness and reached the limit of the West."[105] Irenaeus retraces Paul's travels in the third book of the *Haer.* (III.12.9, III.14.1), and he made a similar journey himself by heading north and west to Lyons. One cannot help but think that Irenaeus conceived of himself in some ways as continuing in Paul's footsteps. This element of Irenaeus's career is captured well by Theodoret of Cyrrhus centuries later, who summarizes his life in these terms: "Irenaeus, who benefited from the teaching of Polycarp, became a shining light of the Gauls of the West [Γαλατῶν δὲ τῶν ἑσπερίων]."[106] Beyond the principle of *successio apostolorum*, Irenaeus's choice to go to Gaul was a tangible enactment of the principle of *imitatio apostolorum*, and especially *imitatio Pauli*.

CHAPTER THREE

How Irenaeus Has Misled the Archaeologists

ALLEN BRENT

The anonymous author of the *Elenchos*, a work clearly in the literary genre of hereti-cal exposure in the tradition of the lost work of Justin, and of the surviving one of Irenaeus, describes the action of Zephyrinus regarding Callistus in the following terms: "Wishing to have him as an associate [ὡς συναράμενον αὐτὸν θέλων ἔχειν] for the direction of the clergy [πρὸς τὴν κατάστασιν τοῦ κλήρου], he honoured him to his own harm and to this end brought him back from Antheion and placed him in charge of the cemetery [εἰς τὸ κοιμητήριον κατέστησεν]."[1] Zephyrinus's immediate predecessor Victor (c. 190), in refusing to exchange the *fermentum* with Asiatic congregations in Rome, provoked according to Eusebius a rebuke from Irenaeus.[2]

Victor's act, though short lived, is hailed by Simonetti as the origin of a monarchical episcopate at Rome that replaced government previously by a presbyteral council. Vic-tor was succeeded by Zephyrinus, whose "associate" Callistus was. The "cemetery" over which the latter was put in charge has been identified, from de Rossi's time onward, with the catacomb that traditionally bears Callistus's name from the time of the Libe-rian *Depositio* (A.D. 354) onward, on the third mile of the via Appia Antica, followed by the medieval itineraries. But Callistus himself was not buried there, but rather in the cemetery of Callepodius on the via Aurelia. Some time before A.D. 235 an extensive building project was begun that involved a deepening of levels because the walls of the original nuclei were filled up with *loculi* that were obstacles to the opening of the transverse corridors. Thus the initial network had reached saturation point, and the new work was clearly a response to a desire to increase the capacity of the cemetery, in fact to some 1,100 tombs.[3]

On the basis of the note in the *Elenchos*, this new project has been attributed, as we shall see, to Callistus, with a plan conceived by him that was to result in the tomb of the popes from A.D. 235 onward. Thus Callistus can be said to reflect Victor's alleged proj-ect of creating a monarchical episcopate and seeking to centralize all Christian burial within one cemetery, however only partial its realization. And Irenaeus, but a few years previously, can be regarded, in his Episcopal succession list, as paving the way for such a development and legitimizing its grounds.

If Irenaeus is to be regarded as the ideologue of Victor's revolution, it seems strange that they should have clashed on the former's treatment of the Quartodeciman congregations. Admittedly, the later dispute between Stephen and Cyprian shows well a characteristic human behavior that one can accept a principle in theory though dissent from it in practice when the full enormity of what becomes possible from its application is felt. But there are further problems with reading Irenaeus's view of apostolic succession in this way. The assumption that Irenaeus is the ideologue of Victor's activity and of what is presupposed by the development of the catacomb by Callistus and that bears his name from the time is, as I will show, questionable.

My deconstruction of such a view may be summarized in a number of brief points that I will subsequently develop in greater detail:

1. The view that Irenaeus's Episcopal succession is modelled on a monarchical succession with supreme power handed on from St. Peter presupposes that his model is that of a chronographer charting the succession of kings, consuls, high priests along with consular and regnal dates, based upon Olympiads and other forms of parallel calendar dating. But the attempts of Ehrhardt and Telfer to identify Irenaeus's model as based upon succession lists of Jewish high priests mentioned by Josephus fails both on the basis of Irenaean theology of church order and on the fact that his list is undated and therefore unrelated to chronographical literature.

2. Irenaeus's view of succession is that of a teaching succession, and arises not from the study of chronography but from the general ideology of succession within Hellenistic philosophical schools. It was that scholastic model, combined with one piece of independent literary evidence that is available to us as well as to him, namely Clement's letter to the Corinthians, that produced his (and/or Hegesippus's) construction of Episcopal or presbyteral succession lists.

3. The creation of a papal mausoleum in the cemetery that bears Callistus's name for rulers of the Roman church therefore reflected a quite different ideology from that of Irenaeus, and from a quite later date (A.D. 235). Those that created what was a unique burial concept of a special mausoleum containing only the rulers of the community were influenced by the chronographic tradition that led them both to add dates to Irenaeus's undated list so as to create Episcopal reigns by analogy with pagan kings and Roman consuls.

4. Consequently, my conclusion will be that there is a sea change in the ideology of Episcopal authority between the age of Irenaeus and that of Pontian, grossly obscured by the assumptions that make the former the ideological supporter of Victor's monarchical project.

I now turn to a detailed examination of my case.

Irenaeus and Sacerdotal Succession Lists

In *Adversus haereses* III.3.2-3, Irenaeus presents his famous succession list of Roman bishops. He assures us, like Hegesippus before him, that there is a congruence of teaching between all major Christian centers.[4] The latter claims that while in Rome διαδοχὴν ἐποιησάμην μέχρις Ἀνικήτου. There are two ways of translating this sentence:

1. It can mean "I composed a succession list" of names "up until the time of Anicetus," in which case Irenaeus takes over from Hegessipus a named but undated succession list, or alternately,

2. It can mean "I established that there was a succession" without naming names.[5]

Certainly Hegesippus does not claim that he has a list of names of bishops for Corinth "up until the time when Primus was bishop of Corinth." If διαδοχὴν ἐποιησάμην means that he did compile a list of names for Rome, it is simply to demonstrate the coherence of doctrine between one generation and another and one geographically distant church from another: "In each succession [διαδοχῇ, or 'succession list'] and in each city the situation is as the law proclaims along with the prophets and the Lord."[6]

Certainly Eusebius believes that Hegesippus "when travelling as far as Rome mingled with many bishops" and regards the bishops of the second century as those of the fourth who acted as supreme teacher in their diocese that they governed monarchically, as shown also in the *Didascalia* and in the *Apostolic Constitutions*.[7] Eusebius, notoriously, believes that if monarch bishops reigned over their sees in the fourth century, then they would have done so from the first, and he is heir to a chronographic tradition that would so rank them. His description of structures of ecclesial authority in the distant past will always be suspect. But what of Irenaeus's testimony and his (or Hegesippus's) succession list? Do they suppose such a monarchical interpretation of the nature of Church Order?

It is now worth reflecting further on what was the model of Hegesippus and Irenaeus for constructing a succession list and what it might or might not have had to do with the chronographic tradition that emerges in a Christian form in the works of Julius Africanus, the writer of the Hippolytan Chronographia, the Chronographer of 354, and indeed Eusebius himself. Ehrhardt believed that it was such a chronographic model that lay at the basis of Irenaeus's construction of a succession list, regarding the origin of the Hegesippean concept in the succession list of Jewish high priests, described by Eusebius as "a catalogue [κατάλογον] . . . of the succession of the high priests [τῆς τῶν ἀρχιερέων διαδοχῆς]."[8] Though Eusebius had four Episcopal succession lists from which he compiled his Chronicon, (i) Jerusalem, (ii) Alexandria, (iii) Antioch, and (iv) Rome, (i) was the earliest and modelled on succession lists of Jewish high priests. The original of such lists was found in the book of Chronicles in the Old Testament, but continued by Jason of Cyrene and Nicolaus of Damascus for the Maccabaean succession and used by Josephus.[9] It was thus possible for Telfer to connect the origins of an Ignatian episcopacy that he believed to be monarchical with James and the Church of Jerusalem and the form of sacral-monarchical church order that continued there following his martyrdom and in succession to him.[10]

I have noted, however, a number of objections to this point of view.[11] My fundamental objection was the lack of any sacerdotal reference or emphasis in what Irenaeus says on apostolic succession. Telfer claimed at one point that "It is thus the sacerdotal character of the bishop which Irenaeus sees as passing from the order of the apostles to the order of bishops."[12] But in the passage on which he relies, Irenaeus is talking about "disciples" and not "apostles" and commenting upon the scene in the Gospels when Jesus was defending his disciples against the Pharisaic charge of plucking ears of corn on the Sabbath. By his action he had made "all the disciples of the Lord priests."[13]

Irenaeus is not commenting here on the apostolic succession but on Marcion's claim that Jesus' defense of his disciples in this passage reveals his rejection of the Old Testament law of a lesser god. Irenaeus's response is that Jesus in fact fulfills the law by making his disciples priests for the occasion, and they can therefore behave like priests on the Sabbath. When Irenaeus comments on the Eucharist as the "pure sacrifice" of Malachi, he does not conclude that it is the bishop's offering as a priest: he concludes that it is the church's offering.[14] Any notion that Irenaeus has before him as a model of apostolic succession a Jewish sacerdotal succession list is therefore ruled out. Irenaeus does not base his model upon a preexisting chronography but rather on that of the historiographical genre of Hellenistic philosophical schools.

It is clear from what both Irenaeus and Hegesippus say that they do not have general access to chronological succession lists, albeit without actual dates. Hegesippus did not claim to have established a succession or succession list for Corinth as opposed to the consistency over time of orthodox teaching. It was for Rome that he claimed, if this is what is meant, to have "composed a succession list." Eusebius was not to inherit any succession list for Corinth, and has no entry for the Primus that Hegesippus informs us "exercised the episcopal office." His only entry for someone named Primus is for the fourth bishop on his Alexandrian list (A.D. 107).[15]

Irenaeus had no list other than that for Rome. He accepted Hegesippus's general conclusion about other churches that "in each succession and in each city it is the case that the law is proclaimed along with the prophets and the Lord."[16] But he will draw an even more general conclusion from Hegesippus's declaration following his experience on a journey that included Corinth on his voyage to Rome: "There is present to be seen in every church throughout the whole world the manifest tradition of the apostles for all who wish to behold what is true."[17]

Thus Irenaeus was now able to go further. Hegesippus had been able to construct a succession list for Rome alone but in principle this had to be possible for any church in any place. Thus he continues: "We are able to call the roll [καταλέσαι] of those established as bishops [κατασταθέντας ἐπισκόπους] in the churches and their successors [διαδόχους] up until our time. . . . For they wished them to be in every respect perfect and blameless whom they left as their successors [διαδόχους], as they handed on to them their personal teaching position [τὸν ἴδιον αὐτῶν διδασκαλίας παραδιδόντες τόπον]."

But how in that case was Irenaeus able to construct such a list for Rome and with what model, given the lack of a chronography with dates?

How Irenaeus and Hegesippus Constructed Their List

Irenaeus and Hegesippus constructed their lists on the basis of the idea of a "succession" of philosophers and a "succession" of apostles. We can see that if we begin with Clement.

Irenaeus describes Clement as next but one after Linus, mentioned by the author of 2 Tim. 4:21 in a list of names undistinguished by any office, but now, Irenaeus adds, with the "ministry of episcopal oversight [τὴν τῆς ἐπισκοπῆς λειτουργίαν]," which both Peter and Paul had "placed in his hands [ἐνεχείρισαν]." After Linus succeeds Anacletus and then: "After the latter, in third place from the apostles, Clement received the inheritance of the episcopate [τὴν ἐπισκοπὴν κληροῦται]."[18] Why should we not accept Irenaeus's evidence quite independently from that of Eusebius?

The problem is that Irenaeus now associates the inheritor of the teaching office that is Clement with the extant letter of the Roman Church to the Corinthians. "At the time of Clement, when no small insurrection had arisen with the brethren in Corinth, the Church in Rome issued orders in a written letter of substance [ἐπέτειλεν . . . ἱκανωτάτην γραφήν] to the Corinthians that brought about peace . . ." From the preface of the letter that survives, we find that it is anonymous and simply claims to be written in the name of "the Church of God, which resides in Rome to the Church of God which resides in Corinth."[19]

Irenaeus clearly associates the letter with Clement, written "in his time" and by implication with his agreement but does not directly claim that he was its writer. It is the letter of Dionysius of Corinth cited by Eusebius that reveals Clement's authorship. In his letter to Soter, addressed as "blessed bishop" and to whom Irenaeus ascribes "twelfth place" in the succession list, Dionysius mentions the reading out in church of the letter "that was formerly sent to us through Clement [τὴν προτέραν ἡμῖν διὰ Κλήμεντος γραφεῖσαν]."[20] We conclude that the anonymous letter of the Church in Rome to that in Corinth was sent "through Clement," who wrote it not on his own authority but on that of the Roman community.

But what evidence do we find in that letter for Clement and for church order at his time, whether in Rome or in Corinth? It is in the light of such evidence that we will be in a position to evaluate both the claims of Irenaeus and those of Hegesippus. In the light of such evidence also, we shall be able to assess in what sense Dionysius of Corinth and Soter of Rome, cited by Eusebius,[21] or indeed Primus, cited by Hegesippus, could be said to hold Episcopal office. It will be the actual documentary evidence available to both Irenaeus and ourselves that will enable us to reconstruct the nature of their office and not a purely hypothetical chronographical list that would have needed to include a column for bishops as successors to high priests and in parallel with pagan kings and consuls.

Clement originally claimed to be writing on behalf of the Roman community to that of Corinth and not in exercise of his sole episcopal office. If he had claimed sole episcopal office, he would no doubt have sought to locate a counterpart in the church at Corinth, like Ignatius addressing Polycarp as sole bishop of Smyrna, as he claimed himself to be of Antioch, even though Polycarp is content to be a presbyter with his fellow presbyters, however personally distinguished was his name.[22] It is not possible to infer that though a plurality of presbyter-bishops administered the church at Corinth, nevertheless Clement was the single bishop and supreme teacher at Rome, in the kind of role that he appears to have in the later succession lists, including that of Irenaeus.

This point becomes even stronger when the letter goes on to make clear that there was no single bishop at Corinth in Clement's time: the blameless πρεσβύτεροι whom the Corinthians had expelled from office were a plurality, and were also called ἐπίσκοποι, in terms that were clearly practically interchangeable: both terms clearly emphasize different aspects of the same office. Like Irenaeus's ἐπίσκοποι, Clement's πρεσβύτεροι and ἐπίσκοποι have an "established office [ἱδρυμένος τόπος]" but not held individually, as in the case of Irenaeus, but rather exercised collectively.[23] The "strife [ἔρις] over the name of the bishop's office [ἐπὶ τοῦ ὀνόματος τῆς ἐπισκοπῆς]" was over a name that they bore generically.[24]

How then does it come about that Clement is identified by name in connection with the letter? Dionysius in his letter to Soter has already answered this question: the letter was sent διὰ Κλήμεντος, either written through him as secretary of the Roman community or of the Roman presbyterate, or carried by him as messenger.[25] Neither "secretary" nor "messenger" would characterize the sole Episcopal office of either an Irenaean bishop or of a later pope. But the term "secretary," if not "foreign secretary," well describes the role that Clement exercises in Hermas.

Hermas too mentions "presbyters" and "bishops" but no one single bishop, and thus in a document with dating possibilities between A.D. 110–140, we find corroborated the collective presbyteral government within the Roman community to which Clement's evidence has pointed. Regarding Clement's actual office, Hermas is instructed at one point to write down his vision in two identical books, one to Grapte to read out to the widows and orphans, but one to Clement. Clement's audience is to be an external one: he is to send his book "to the cities outside, for to him has been entrusted [ἐκείνῳ γὰρ ἐπιτέτραπται]" this ministry. Clement therefore is a kind of foreign secretary with the specific function of communicating with external churches. He is not sole bishop of Rome. Hermas is to read the contents of his vision: to this city accompanied by the presbyters who preside over the church [μετὰ τῶν πρεσβυτέρων τῶν προσταμένων τῆς ἐκκλησίας].[26]

When therefore Hegesippus, in Eusebius's quotation, speaks of Primus as "exercising episcopal office [Πρίμου ἐπισκοπεύοντος]" in Corinth,[27] it is highly improbable that he was regarded as supreme teacher in the later, Irenaean sense. Each presiding presbyter or bishop, together with Primus, could be described as ἐπισκοπεύων, as "exercising episcopal office" generically. His letters, if he wrote any, like those of Clement, can be ascribed to him as secretary of the Corinthian presbyterate. Or like Polycarp he can simply be a prominent name among his fellow presbyters. Hegesippus originally prefaced his claim to have "established a succession" with "remarks about the epistle of Clement to the Corinthians," though Eusebius has not recorded what his actual words were.[28] But clearly his construction of a Roman succession list that Irenaeus takes over was intrinsically bound up with the figure of Clement whose true office we have unravelled from his actual surviving letter.

We do not know what was Hegesippus's model in compiling such a list. But we do know what was that of Irenaeus. Clearly for him the office of bishop is the counterpart to the president of a philosophical school, like the *diadochoi* of Plato, Aristotle, Stoics, and Epicureans. Here was the guarantee that the true faith was taught uncontaminated by other influences. Not only was there to be a congruence between the "law, prophets and the Lord" proclaimed in every city and in every succession, but there needed to be a specific person inheriting the office with the right to teach. This was a model that Diogenes Laertius was to use around twenty years later, in his Lives of the Philosophers.

The object of this work was to show that the "wise men" of the golden age of Greece in the past constituted the exclusive origin of all Greek philosophical schools. Diogenes writes in an existing tradition in which writers such as Sotion (200–170 B.C.) and others wrote histories of philosophical ideas in terms of school with succession, and accordingly entitled their works as "successions of the philosophers" (διαδοχαὶ τῶν φιλοσόφων). The four great schools of his time, the Academic, the Stoic, the Peripatetic, and Epicurean, could be shown to descend in succession from their founders in logical succession with no Greek philosopher omitted. Thus Diogenes purported to prove that Hellenistic philosophy was a wholly Greek phenomenon uncontaminated by Indian or Egyptian influences, or indeed Latin ones.[29] He was thus very much part of the movement that was the Second Sophistic and that asserted Hellenistic cultural identity against imperial rule. Ignatius of Antioch had previously attempted to construct by analogy a similar Christian identity over against the Hellenistic culture of the Greek city-states of Asia Minor under Roman rule.[30]

But as Irenaeus was aware, the model of Greek philosophical school as a succession of teachers fitted only in some respects the church but not in others. Irenaeus at one point admits that the succession, the διαδοχή, was not to bishops alone but also to presbyters: "Again, whenever we make our appeal to the tradition from the apostles that is preserved through the successions of presbyters in the churches [ἐπὶ τὴν ἀπὸ τῶν ἀποστόλων παράδοσιν κατὰ τὰς διαδοχὰς τῶν πρεσβυτέρων ἐν ταῖς ἐκκλησίαις φυλασσομένην], they oppose the tradition, claiming that they are not only wiser than the presbyters but also than the apostles."[31] He is thus aware of the situation that had existed in both Clement of Rome and of the Shepherd in which bishops and presbyters formed a plurality and the Roman church was thus governed by a presbyterate. In some respects therefore previous bishops or presbyters could be said to share in a διαδοχή if they presented a similar coherence with the "law, prophets, and the Lord" that Hegesippus had observed, notwithstanding his failure to produce a named succession list for one διάδοχος at Corinth or anywhere else except perhaps Rome. But where was any single head like Speusippus who "succeeded [διεδέξατο]" to the headship of the Academy following Plato's death, and as διάδοχος inherited physical ownership of buildings such as the shrine of the Muses erected by Plato in the Academy, to which he added statues of the Charites?[32]

Theophrastus, successor of Aristotle, left a will, a version of which survives. Here he states of his estate in Stagira: "the garden, and the walk, and the houses adjoining the garden, all and sundry, I bequeath to such of my friends hereinafter named as may wish to study literature and philosophy there in common . . . on condition that no one alienates the property or devotes it to his own private use, but so that they hold it like a temple in joint possession. . . . Let the community consist of Hipparchus, Neleus, Strato, Callinus etc."[33] The Strato here named on the list was to succeed to the headship of the Peripatic school. That he as head had a special claim on the buildings is made clear in his own will that he leaves the school and the library (excluding his own books) "to Lyco, since the rest are too old and others too busy.

But it would be well if the others would co-operate with him."[34] It is not accidental that Lyco was formally chosen by the group as the διάδοχος.[35] The will Lyco clarifies exactly: "I leave the Peripatus to such of my friends who choose to make use of it, to Bulo, Callinus, Ariston, Amphion. . . . They shall put over it any such person as in their opinion will persevere with the work of the school, and will be most capable of extending it."[36] Clearly a διάδοχος of a philosophical school also had control over property.[37]

Irenaeus cannot parallel such ownership in the case of a president of a philosophical school with that of Christian πρεσβύτεροι or ἐπίσκοποι as διάδοχοι τῶν ἀποστόλων. This is because there is little evidence of any property held in common under the law: Roman Christians met in private houses as Lampe has described and justified in part by an analysis of the house-situation presupposed in the background of the Hippolytan *Apostolic Tradition*.[38] Undoubtedly, Justin Martyr had previously used the term "president" (used of a philosophical school) to designate the president of a Christian Eucharist. Justin's προεστώς presides over a congregation that gathers "above the baths of Myrtinus" and is understood by analogy with a philosophical school.[39] Indeed he had claimed as a teacher of Christianity to be the teacher of the true philosophy.[40] But Justin's group, as Lampe argued, was one group among a loose confederation of house churches, acknowledging their unity as Christians by the exchange of the *fermentum*, but each presided over by their particular πρεσβύτερος–ἐπίσκοπος–συνεστώς.[41] Could they all be διάδοχοι or did not the model require one διάδοχος? There was not here a clear fit between the scholastic model and the loose confederation of house churches.

Schism and the designation of "heresy" could not, given a church existing in the form of such house-groups, apply to a single community splitting, with the result that one of them physically leaves the sacred space and goes off to occupy another of its own in separation. There was no parallel here with Aristotle leaving Plato's academy and setting up on his own estate with its walkway for philosophical discussion, or the Stoic occupation of a Portico. The followers of Marcion or Valentinus did not "leave" in the sense that they departed from church buildings. Rather it was the case that they remained in their house-groups: their "leaving" was a case of their adopting a version of the faith that was not considered by the rest to be the διαδοχή ἀποστόλων.

Irenaeus's description of Valentinus could not be expressed more clearly when he says of him: "For he was the first from the so called Gnostic heresy to reshape the first principles of their school into his own character [τὰς ἀρχὰς εἰς ἴδιον χαρακτῆρα διδασκαλείου μεθαρμόσας]."[42] Valentinus "left" not by being formally expelled as an individual from the orthodox community but by reconfiguring the teaching of his group so that it became transformed into another tradition, another διαδοχή. Of Valentinus Irenaeus might have used the same description as did the Hippolytan writer later of Callistus, namely that the latter "founded a school [συνεστήσατο διδασκαλεῖον], having taught against the Church [κατὰ τῆς ἐκκλησίας διδάξας]."[43]

That writer fully acknowledged that it was possible for someone to be "called a Christian [λεγόμενος Χριστιανός]" and yet to "assemble (for worship) with a different person [παρ᾽ ἑτέρῳ τινὶ συναγόμενος]." It was when someone so gathering went over to Callistus's group for easy absolution from what the writer considered to be a heretical group whose διαδοχή was from Greek philosophy that he was taking "refuge in the school [σχολῇ] of Callistus" and not in the Catholic Church.⁴⁴ In this respect, the model of the διαδοχή of a philosophical school well fitted Irenaeus's purpose in drawing a boundary between heresy and orthodoxy.

But in another respect, the candidate for the title of διάδοχος over the διαδοχὴ τῶν ἀποστόλων proved for Irenaeus more elusive. He knew Justin Martyr's work against Marcion, and Justin's interpretation of his own role as Christian teacher as one of a συνεστώς of a philosophical school.⁴⁵ But Irenaeus could not place Justin's name on his episcopal succession list because, I maintain, had he done so, he would have been acknowledging only one group among many in the loose confederation of house churches. He needed another figure whose office was more than simply that of a presiding presbyter-bishop of one of the congregations forming the Church of Rome in the course of the first and second centuries. There was one such office holder, a member of the Roman presbyterate to whom was given by them an "entrusted ministry [ἐκείνῳ . . . ἐπιτέτραπται]" of writing to "the cities outside."

This example of Clement did not at first sight serve too well Irenaeus's purpose since clearly this figure was not described as ὁ προεστών like Justin over his own congregation. Furthermore, though Clement had written his copy of Hermas's vision to external churches, having received one of his two "little books," βιβλαρίδια, it was Hermas who was now to read his vision, with the charismatic authority of a prophet clearly acknowledged at this time, in the company of the presiding presbyters of the Roman church [μετὰ τῶν πρεσβυτέρων τῶν προσταμένων τῆς ἐκκλησίας].⁴⁶ But was Clement among those presbyters? No doubt we should conclude, in the light of what we shall shortly see was Soter's title, that the secretarial figure was a presbyter-bishop over one congregation but, having written the enclosing letter for the βιβλαρίδιον, he simply joined the ranks of the πρεσβύτεροι προσταμένοι, the "presiding elders/ presbyters." For Irenaeus this was awkward but he needed a list of names to make his application of the scholastic model credible and this was all that he had: it was better than nothing.

There were names on correspondence, cited by Eusebius, like that of Soter to whom Dionysius of Corinth addressed a letter. There he praised "your blessed bishop Soter," for the financial relief provided for those suffering persecution in the mines, and in so providing they had "preserved the long standing custom of the Romans." Indeed, the name of the presbyteral secretary whose letter accompanied such financial relief may have prefigured more outside Rome and been awarded greater importance than within Rome itself, and for this reason seemed more plausible to Irenaeus in constructing his succession list.

Soter in writing such a letter whose bearers also carried the material assistance is called "the blessed *episcopos*" (ὁ μακάριος ἐπίσκοπος).⁴⁷ But I would suggest that it is better to read these words in the sense in which they would be understood in the context of Clement's letter and the vision of Hermas rather than in that of Eusebius: the "blessed bishop" was one bishop among many but whose name was particularly gladdening given the resources accompanying the letter that he wrote on behalf of the whole community. Undoubtedly, as Lampe argued, the foreign secretary of the Roman community would receive the incoming correspondence to be circulated around the various house-groups. So the martyrs of Lyons sent their commendation of Irenaeus, called "presbyter" of his diocese, to Eleutherus.[48]

In Clement, *Corinthians*, whose contents Irenaeus clearly knew well, the author was anonymous, and made no reference to his possession of any office of sole bishop, let alone that of προεστώς. But nevertheless here was a figure that related to the presbyterate when it met together with "the whole church." The foreign secretary, writing to external churches on behalf of the presbyterate as a body, might appear to issue his own commands and exhortations, and Irenaeus could now well play up the role of this figure. He accordingly deprives Clement of his proper, secretarial anonymity in his determination to reconceptualize the nature and functions of his office so as to fit his scholastic model.

Unlike in the case of Justin, the secretary existed as the official spokesman to external churches with the entrusted ministry to write official letters to them apart from the local congregations from which they hailed. The evidence from Clement's *Corinthians*, once again, points to a presbyterate composed of the presbyter bishops of individual congregations who assembled together on some occasions as "the whole church." This was particularly the case when a presbyter-bishop was ordained, like Timothy, "through prophecy along with the imposition of hands of the presbyterate."[49] Paul's genuine 1 Corinthians points to how urban Christians met "as the whole church,"[50] perhaps by hiring a lecture room, for issues of discipline or to greet Gaius as "guest of the whole church."[51]

Clement specifically refers to the presbyter-bishops at Corinth as "having been appointed [κατασταθέντας] . . . with the whole church expressing their approval [συνευδοκησάσης τῆς ἐκκλησίας πάσης]."[52] Clearly, they were not appointed or ordained by one group alone in isolation, even though the act of ordination was not by the secretary alone but by all the presbyters coming from their individual congregations at a public meeting of the whole. This was why no presbyter who had "offered the gifts blamelessly" could be deposed by a single congregation or group of them, with the additional reason that the apostles had appointed the original presbyters. The practice of this kind of presbyteral ordination was clearly an aid to unity in the loose confederation of house-groups that constituted the Church of Rome for a least most of the second century.

We find this practice reflected behind the corrupt text of the Hippolytan *Apostolic Tradition*, the text of which has been incorporated into the *Apostolic Constitutions* and in the so-called *Canons of Hippolytus* and the *Testamentum Domini*. As it stands, the text reflects a situation in which a single bishop is being created over the whole community, but that this has required some revision of the original ordination rite: "Let a bishop who is chosen by all the people be ordained and, when he has been nominated and all have so resolved, let the people gather with the presbyterate and with those bishops who have made themselves present. With the consent of all, let them lay their hands upon him and let the presbyterate stand at their side in silence."[53] Here in Verona Latin (that in contrast with SAE omits references to deacons) clearly distinguishes between those who hold the office of bishop and those who form the presbyterate. One of the former is chosen to say the prayer of consecration and to lay hands on the candidate. But as Ratcliff pointed out, the instruction to the presbyters to remain silent is indicative that a rite is being edited and their original, spoken role is being edited out.[54] You write rubrics to instruct people to do things, and not simply to keep silence unless they needed to where they were accustomed to speaking. Originally, we may conclude that following what Clement described as the "approval of the whole church" the new presbyter-bishop was ordained, like Timothy, "through the imposition of hands of the presbyterate."

But on such an occasion, the secretary would be there with his fellow presbyters, particularly if the "whole church" had gathered together in some hired lecture hall to dispute an issue of faith. This is precisely the scene that is described after Irenaeus and the Victor whom he criticized as recorded in the Hippolytan *Refutation of All Heresies*. When the writer claims that Zephyrinus and Callistus had surreptitiously sided with Sabellius, and had denounced him and his group as "ditheists," it would have been every congregation in the confederation of house churches that so gathered. It would have been the secretary that kept the records, and, if as articulate as Callistus was with the ambition to transform his office into one of greater power, would have cast what was said and decided in his own mould.

This therefore was the figure, so clearly portrayed in Clement's own letter and in his description in Hermas, upon which Irenaeus (or Hegesippus) now alighted in his desire to make church order correspond to the διαδοχή of a philosophical school with a single διάδοχος or προεστώς with the right to preside over the transmission of the founder's teaching. Rome was the perfect example because in its archives it had not only Clement's letter that has survived but also others, no doubt more mundane, which have not. Since the archives would have contained the notes of the authorship of such letters on their copies, whether the secretary's name appeared on them or whether they were written anonymously in the name of "the whole church," Irenaeus or Hegesippus or both could now construct their διαδοχή ἀποστόλων by taking note of and constructing a list of those names in chronological order.

As I have said, Justin owned the title of προεστώς of a Christian congregation whilst Clement did not, with a role understood in a Hellenistic, scholastic sense. But his office was too local over a single congregation. But Irenaeus might see Clement's contemporary successor in the company of the assembled presbyterate when an extra-ordinary meeting "of the whole church" was gathered. Here the presbyter with secretarial office, who was the epistolary representative of the presbyterate to external churches, would "stand out [προεστώς]," from the rest with a better known name, like that of Polycarp, though for perhaps other reasons, or like Clement himself, as he stood listening to Hermas's reading out of his vision to the presiding presbyters of the church of Rome. It was this figure that Irenaeus was now to endow with the features of a διάδοχος in a Hellentistic philosophical school, according to the historiographic program of Diogenes Laertius and his predecessors in the genre of diadochic literature. As they had used the concept to establish the cultural coherence of Hellenistic philosophy and to remove from it all taint of barbarian corruption, so too could Irenaeus establish against Valentinus, Basilides, Marcion, and their associates the purity and culturally uncontaminated faith that had come down from the apostles and their teaching successors.

The one known figure of Clement on Irenaeus's succession list thus presents us with compelling evidence with which to penetrate the clouds of silence that surround the other names on his list, and to appreciate what in fact the original nature of their office was. There was no other list such as one might later find in the chronographic tradition, recording bishops in the *spatium historicum* of a *Chronicon* with parallel columns for consuls and Jewish high priests by means of which dates could be assigned for their Episcopal "reigns." Irenaeus, or Hegesippus before him, could compose such a list for Rome even though there was none at Corinth in which Primus could have been included: certainly Eusebius mentions no surviving letter of his. It was in Victor's time, as has been argued, that at least the first movement toward a monarch bishop took place when he sought to impose a common, Western date of Easter over Asiatic congregations in Rome. Victor's activity has been notoriously misrepresented by Eusebius who reads his sources in a grossly anachronistic light and reports that Victor excommunicated overseas dioceses like a fourth-century, Constantinian pope.[55] In fact, the focus of his activity in the late second century was Asiatic rite groups of Eastern origins keeping a Quartodeciman date for Easter within the fractionalized Roman Christian community itself.[56] Before his time, the only example with any evidence is of Clement, who acts in a secretarial role. Irenaeus knows of no other evidence than Clement, with the result that his innovatory imposition of a scholastic definition of the bishop as διάδοχος stands exposed.

Let us at this point summarize where our argument has taken us so far. Irenaeus, we have argued, was an innovator, imposing upon the presbyteral model of church order a scholastic concept only partially derivable from Justin before him, and quite at variance from that presupposed by the evidence of an extensive epistle of Clement himself, which Irenaeus admits to knowing. In producing an undated succession list, he was not influenced by any preceding chronographic tradition in which a succession list of Jewish High priests could be laid out in parallel with a list of Roman consuls and regarded as the predecessors of bishops: there are no dates in Irenaeus's list. Furthermore, his concept was a scholastic and not a sacerdotal one: he never finds it important to say that the presbyter or bishop is the person entrusted with offering "the church's offering."[57]

If therefore Irenaeus drew upon the historiographic tradition in which the successions of the philosophers was described and the Hellenic purity of what they taught established, then by what process did the chronographic tradition enter into the development of the succession lists? There was clearly a sea change in coming to regard Episcopal succession as monarchical rather than scholastic and in failing to grasp the character of that change, archaeologists have allowed themselves to be grossly misled regarding the nature of the Roman, Christian community at the end of the second and at the beginning of the third century.

It is to a discussion of how this has occurred that I now turn.

The Papal Mausoleum in the Catacomb of Callistus and Episcopal Power

An interpretation of the model of Irenaeus and Hegesippus as forerunners of the emergence under Victor of a monarchical episcopate in Rome has been, I believe, implicitly accepted by archaeologists in dating and interpreting the development under Callistus of the cemetery that bears his name. Simonetti maintains that Victor was the founder of the monarchical episcopate in a Roman church that was previously governed by a single presbytery. Within such a context, Irenaeus can be regarded as standing at the watershed, using the presbyter as well as bishop as a successor to the apostles. *Succession* in such a context must mean the successor of a monarch, like the successors of Alexander the Great, who were referred to as his διάδοχοι, or indeed, the sacerdotal successors of the Maccabees as priest-kings. Therefore, it might be concluded that Irenaeus, if not directly an ideologue of the monarchical episcopate, nevertheless played ideologically the role of a good fellow traveller in that direction.

I have already explained why I believe that the sacerdotal explanations of Ehrhardt and Telfer are misplaced in Irenaeus's case and scholastic ones more pertinent. But from de Rossi onward, despite Styger's considerable and warranted criticism of his famous predecessor, nevertheless regarded the dating of the considerable building work engaged in by the Roman community sometime in the course of the first half of the third century could be made more precise by reference to Callistus's pontificate and the alleged emergence of a monarchical succession in Rome to which Irenaeus's alleged model had pointed.

Styger had otherwise accomplished what Fiochi Nicolai and Guyon have described as "une veritable 'révolution copernicienne'" in the view of the original construction of the catacomb of Callistus that was the fruit of the original excavations of the brothers J. B. and M. S. de Rossi.[58] The high sections of the galleries of area I were in fact part of the original complex of the cemetery, and not the later constructions that they had been considered to have been. Styger's conclusions have been generally accepted in subsequent studies.[59]

But cubiculum L1, the so-called "tomb of the popes," remained for Styger nevertheless part of the original complex. Gallery L was constructed at the same time as A was begun, in accordance with the rules of *Ausgrabungstheorie* according to which transverse galleries are developed *pari passu* with those running lengthwise. But it is not simply Styger's archaeological analysis of the origins and construction of the catacomb that bears Callistus's name that has continued to survive, but also his historical interpretation and dating of the beginnings of the construction, and this has, in my opinion, been most unfortunate.

Styger, with the contemporary support of Fiochi Nicolai and Guyon, have all maintained that Callistus around A.D. 217 developed the original plan of the catacomb to be the burial place of the Roman Christian community.[60] Nicholai and Guyon point to the deepening of the level of gallery I[1] to that of galleries A and B, where I could form with them, when H, F, and J were added, a grid like network. But the real cause of this new phase of deepening the galleries was, for these two archaeologists, not simply that the first phase, gallery I[1], could be extended no further longitudinally beyond the boundary of the plot, but to excavate transverse galleries would have resulted in the demolition of existing tombs that lined those galleries. Rather there was an additional reason. The new excavation pointed to a desire to increase the number of burials that was in fact to amount to "the capacity to some 1,100 tombs." Thus they conclude: "the practice of collective inhumations was the real cause and that explains the fact that the deepening had the advantage of giving to the cemetery a far larger size than it had previously possessed."[61]

I must observe firstly that Nicholai and Guyon would have to concede that the role of Callistus in the creation of the later papal mausoleum and associated so called "cubicula of the sacraments" had been one of conceiving a plan that was only later fully executed: "The second excavation had proceeded for the same cause as the first and had followed the same logic and lead to the achievement, or nearly, of the plan in the form of a grid already in outline, thanks to the cutting of the three transverse galleries, H, F, G already indicated (fig 4). In this way . . . the fossores opened there the future entrances to the underground cemeteries."[62] But there is an important distinction that must be drawn between having a concept in one's mind tentatively and only partially formed in contrast with a "plan in the form of a grid already in outline." Both archaeologists assume the latter because they assume a single monarch bishop at Rome from the time of Victor having pastoral concern to respond to the desire of the whole community to be buried together.[63] But there are a number of considerations that must count against such a conclusion.

Callistus was not buried in the cemetery that has become associated with his name. His tomb, later monumentalized, has been excavated where the Liber Pontificalis located it, in the cemetery of Callepodius on the Via Aurelia. It is possible to argue that this occurred due to the particular circumstances of his martyrdom, which a late account tells was the result of his being "thrown from the window of his house (*per fenestram domus praeciptare*) and with a stone tied to his neck (*ligatoque ad collum eius saxo*), submerged in a well (*in puteum submergi*), and rubbish piled upon his head (*et in eo rudera cumulari*)."[64] But that late account, as I have argued elsewhere in detail, was not the result of any enduring record of events but rather a folk-memory in which the image of Callistus was associated with that of the emperor Elagabalus with the result that the death of the latter in a riot was paralleled in the imagined death of the former.[65] Liber Pontificalis I.17.12-13 implies, at all events, that he was buried in Trastevere on the Via Aurelia because that was where he had lived.

Without such an argument, and even with it, it is difficult to see why Callistus was not buried in Zephyrinus's cemetery on the via Appia Antica if he had laid the foundation for the concept of a general burial place for the whole community around the saints and martyrs who were also its leaders of a common community. At all events, his immediate successor was not buried there. Urban was buried in the cemetery of Praetextatus on the via Appia Antica.[66] There was therefore no Callistan model realized by himself and his immediate successor in Zephyrinus's cemetery over which he had been put in charge.

Moreover, as Rébillard has persuasively argued, the word τὸ κοιμητήριον ("the cemetery") in the brief passage that described Callistus's diaconal duties in the *Refutatio* has been read consistently but improperly as though the term could describe a large, general communal place of burial. Analyzed examples of the use of the word κοιμητήριον, whether in the singular or in the plural, reveal that it describes a tomb or tombs of the martyrs and not of the collective burial of the whole community.[67] Thus Rébillard can charge de Rossi with what the French call *antonomase*, that is to say, the regarding of a proper noun as though it were a general term. By this means he could suggest that the Callistus catacomb was at that time the sole cemetery administered by the Church of Rome, or that it was its principal cemetery. In reality, it applied to a single tomb, that of Zephyrinus's family, with some members of his community buried there, and which was to develop, not as the communal burial site of the whole community but as a place where the faithful wished to lie at rest with particular saints.[68]

Undoubtedly, a decade after Callistus's death, the catacomb on the via Appia Antica was to experience a radical reconstruction. That reconstruction must clearly be dated from the time when bishops of Rome in succession were to be buried in a special vault that was now under construction, namely the tomb of the popes in a mausoleum reserved for the leaders of the Roman community. Such a project was radically different from what Callistus could have ever envisaged, whose successor, Urban, no one saw any reason to bury there, nor was there any notion that he should be himself buried there. His successor, Pontianus the bishop, who died with presbyter Hippolytus in exile in Sardinia (A.D. 235), could hardly have arranged his own burial there—that was to be the work of Fabian, whose concept the papal tomb clearly was.

Pontian's death was followed by the election of his successor, Anteros, with a short period of office of one month and ten days (A.D. 236).[69] Then Fabian was to succeed him (A.D. 236), to whom the Chronographer of 354 attributes the division of Rome among the seven deacons into regions, and the ordering of the constructions of "many building works [*fabricas*] throughout the tombs [*per cimiteria*]."[70] The creation of the nucleus of the papal mausoleum in the Callistus catacomb was in all probability the design of Fabian. It was there that he buried his immediate predecessor, Anteros, placing his remains in the loculus sealed with the marble epitaph on which his name was engraved and affixed with his Episcopal title (EP.). He then added a loculus for the remains of Pontianus, similarly identified with an epitaph, brought back from Sardinia with those of presbyter Hippolytus whom he interred in the cemetery on the Via Tiburtina. Thus he could make provision for his own burial there with what was in process of becoming the papal crypt where together and apart from their community the leaders of the Roman church could be in turn buried.

The novelty of the design is witnessed by the fact that Cornelius, Fabian's immediate successor (A.D. 252), was buried neither in the crypt of the popes nor in the Callistus catacomb itself but in the Lucina region, which was a separate burial complex before the construction of the medieval pilgrim road that today has united the two. Was this because of the disputed character of Cornelius's office with his rival Novatian, or was it because the concept of a burial place apart for leaders of the community did not impress him? Certainly Novatian himself was buried in a grave excavated on the corner of where the Via Regina Margherita today stands opposite San Lorenzo fuori i muri. But though his grave was monumentalized[71] and was clearly a place of pilgrimage for his followers, there have not been discovered any epigraphs regarding the succession of twenty-four Novatian bishops corresponding to that number of catholic bishops of Rome from Cornelius to Celestine I. But any surprise at this fact follows from a false assumption that Novatian shared Fabian's new and unique design for a cemetery in which the leaders of the community were buried apart in their own crypt as an indication of their office.

But those who buried Cornelius's successor, Lucius (A.D. 255), well understood Fabian's design, as did also those who buried Stephen, and Xystus II martyred there as well as Eutychian. Gaius, Eusebius, and Miltiades, though not buried in the crypt of the popes itself, were buried in the catacomb itself, in separate cubilicula of their own. The catacomb of Priscilla was to become popular later where Marcellinus, Marcellus, and Liberius were laid to rest, with Julius I in Callepodius, Silvester in Balbina, and Damasus in his basilica on the via Ardiatina. It was from the time of Leo I that popes were laid to rest in Constantine's basilica on the Vatican Hillside around one claimant to be the tomb of St. Peter the Apostle. The Liber Pontificalis was to reassure us that the normal burial place of popes, from Peter to Victor, had been on the Vatican Hillside, but the practice had then been curiously interrupted until Leo's time.

The Vatican excavations have exposed the impossibility of this view where the Aedicula represents a putative tomb but there is no Papal crypt for where Linus, Anacletus, Cletus, and so on might have found their rest. St. Peter's today remains what it has conceivably always been, a martyr shrine to one individual apostle, with its circle of votive candles. It is not the resting place of large numbers of saints, as the catacombs came to be regarded in the Middle Ages.

What indeed was this new design of Fabian, that clearly was a new departure and not simply a continuation of what Callistus had definitely intended under the alleged inspiration of Irenaeus and his concept of apostolic succession? Borgolte has pointed out that the concept of a crypt for the leaders of the Roman, Christian community was unique in Roman burial practice; it had no real parallel in either Jewish or Roman pagan practice.[72] From where was such a concept derived? Jewish catacombs did not possess a separate crypt reserved exclusively for community leaders: ἀρχισυνάγωγοι were buried among their people. Roman aristocrats if unrelated were buried apart from one another and in their own family tombs along with members of their family and with their freedman who took their gentilicum. Indeed, this may have been why Cornelius was buried in Lucina, then still a separate burial complex, with a Latin rather than the Greek epitaph characteristic of tombs in the papal crypt in Callistus. The only real parallel is the mausoleum of Augustus where the emperor made provision for himself and his successors to be buried in a cemetery exclusively reserved for them and the celebration of his imperial power.

Fabian's concept of episcopal authority was therefore not that of Irenaeus. Fabian's Episcopal succession was monarchical in contrast to Irenaeus, who understood the διαδοχὴ ἀποστόλων in terms of a teaching succession within a Hellenistic philosophical school. I believe, furthermore, that Fabian's new concept is also witnessed in the entry at this point, and not earlier in Irenaeus, of the chronographic tradition into the monuments of Episcopal government. Irenaeus's list was an undated list, but what succeeded it, reaching a final form in the Chronographer of 354, had dates for the succession and deaths of bishops of Rome. The chronographic tradition has imposed on Irenaeus's original list of bishops and its continuation up until Pontian a quite artificial system of dating.

According to the dated list of the Chronographer of 354, each bishop before Pontian succeeds to the episcopate with his two contemporaneous consuls and dies at the point of another consular succession. For example:

1. Eleutheros died in the consulship of Paternus and Bradua (AD 185). His successor, Victor, succeeded him when Commodus and Glabrio became the next consuls (AD 186).

2. Zephyrinus lived "until the consulship of Praesens and Extricatus [AD 217]." Callistus succeeded him only when Antoninus and Adventus succeeded them (218).

3. Urban succeeded Callistus when Antoninus and Alexander left office (AD 222) and Maximus and Elianus succeeded them (AD 223).

But Pontian and his successors are given definite dates for their deaths, and so manage to die and be succeeded as bishops whilst consuls are still in office: bishops do not succeed consuls in parallel with each other. This process implies a radical transformation for the previous concept of Episcopal succession, as we shall now see in conclusion.

Fabian's Monarchical Episcopal Succession Is Neither Irenaeus's nor Victor's

In the imposition of dates upon Irenaeus's undated list, we are witnessing, I submit, for the first time the introduction of the chronographic tradition into Christian historiography. As Eusebius's *Chronicon* makes clear, the chronographic tradition set up parallel lists of pagan kings, Roman consuls, Hebrew monarchs, and Greek Olympiads side by side in order to try to establish the chronology of world history and, indeed, in Christian chronography, salvation history. Between such lists of names and dates there could be inserted the *spatium historicum*, which has left its mark on Eusebius's writing of his ecclesiastical history. Here the names of famous individuals or of significant events could be recounted with suitable anecdotes recounted, authors and their works briefly described, and dates of periods in which they "flourished" inferred from the parallel consular, regnal, or Olympiad dates. The continuator of Irenaeus's list could only deploy such a rough-and-ready method to establish dates for bishops before Pontianus and back to Peter. Having placed their names in the *spatium historicum*, he looked at the consuls in the columns at the side and fixed the deaths and subsequent succession of each bishop quite artificially with the beginning and end of consular reigns.

This being the case, two important conclusions follow in support of my argument that Irenaeus cannot be regarded with Callistus as the creator of the concept of monarchical episcopacy. The first is that the introduction of the chronographic tradition marked by the introduction of real dates from Pontianus onward can and should be read as part of Fabian's ideological concept reflected in the material fabric of the creation of the papal crypt. Popes have dates in their succession lists because monarchs have reigns that have dates in theirs, and that is important for the establishment of their legitimacy. Fabian's popes must have their own crypt in the way that Augustus's successors had their own mausoleum.

But a second conclusion for my argument now follows. If Pontianus and his successors with real dates mark an ideological change in the conception of episcopal authority, then that shift has not taken place with how Callistus's authority was conceived by his immediate successors. Neither Callistus nor his successor, Urbanus, are accorded real dates, but the artificial chronological method simply imposes consular dates with an assumed parallel. Had the pontificate of Callistus marked the success of an alleged episcopal monarchy established by Victor whose ideology Irenaeus had written with his concept of apostolic succession, then we should have expected real dates to have begun with his pontificate. The purpose, therefore, of Callistus's plan for the development of the catacomb that bears his name must have been, if not quite different from, at least more hazy and indefinite than that which Fabian was some fifteen years in the future to clarify and apply with precision.

The model for Irenaeus's succession list was therefore quite different from that which was to inform Fabian's Episcopal monarchy. It was, as we have argued, scholastic. To prove that there was a coherence in philosophical or theological teaching, you needed only to show that the school of the philosophers or of the apostles simply had an orderly succession of one philosopher or bishop to another: dates were not essential. Neither was an imperial mausoleum for monarchs to lie in state in succession to one another required for such a scholastic succession.

PART TWO

Scripture

Irenaeus and His Scriptural Traditions

CHAPTER FOUR

The Parable of the Two Sons (Matt. 21:28-32) in Irenaeus and Codex Bezae

Denis Minns

In his introductory essay in William Sanday's *Novum Testamentum Sancti Irenaei*, Alexander Souter remarks that as Irenaeus "is the earliest surviving writer of the Christian era who quotes the New Testament both extensively and accurately," "it is obvious that if we can secure the words of his New Testament text as he dictated them we shall be in possession of an extremely early type of text, whose claims to be in close connection with the original autographs will deserve examination."[1] Of course, the fact that so much of what Irenaeus wrote survives only in Latin, and to a lesser extent, Armenian, translation, adds considerably to the risk of contamination that is inherent in the transmission of the biblical text of any patristic author. It was the sorting out of some of those problems that was addressed so magisterially in *Novum Testamentum Sancti Irenaei*.

Westcott and Hort had judged that, both in the original Greek and in the Latin translation, the New Testament quotations in *Adversus haereses* were Western,[2] and Souter agreed that "even as two different things," they "are both Western texts."[3] The "Western text," has, of course, been subject to much criticism since Westcott and Hort: Kurt and Barbara Aland note that "hardly anyone today refers to this putative Western text without placing the term in quotation marks," as I have just done.[4] In the same place they assert that "it is quite inconceivable that the text of Codex Bezae Cantabrigiensis could have existed as early as the second century." C. B. Amphoux, on the other hand, holds that it is incontestible that the "modèle fundamental" of Irenaeus's Greek text of the New Testament was "une texte proche du Codex de Bèze."[5] The purpose of this paper will be to argue that, in one instance, the text known to Irenaeus was, in its essentials, that of Codex Bezae. It will be necessary to argue this, as the evidence is not immediately clear, and its interpretation has been disputed.

The textual tradition of Matthew 21:28-32 is notoriously complicated. Three main forms of the parable can be distinguished. Much scholarly argument has been devoted to the questions of which form is prior and how the other two arose from it. The three forms are enumerated differently by different scholars. I give them here with the abbreviated manuscript evidence as recorded by B. Metzger in *A Textual Commentary on the Greek New Testament*.[6]

I. The first son refuses but afterward repents and goes. The second son says "yes," but does nothing. The question "which of the two did the will of the father?" is answered "the first."

ℵ K W Π it[c, q] vg syr[c, p, h] *al*

II. The first son refuses but afterward repents and goes. The second son promises to go, but does not. The question "which of the two did the will of the father?" is answered "the second."

D it[a, b, d, e, ff², h, l] syr[s] al

III. The first son promises to go but does not. The second son refuses, but later repents and goes. The question "which of the two did the will of the father?" is answered "the second."

B *f*[13] 700 syr[pal] arm geo *al*

Though Tischendorf (*editio octava critica maior*) had cautiously limited himself to claiming Irenaeus as a witness only to the order of sons in form I, the third edition of the United Bible Societies *Greek New Testament* cites Irenaeus as a witness to form I as a whole. But Irenaeus does not say expressly which of the two sons did the Father's will and, so far as concerns the order of the sons, he is as much a witness to form II as to form I. Form II, although the most difficult, has found few champions. In general, it is either said to require the far-fetched assumption, first suggested, and that half-heartedly, by Jerome, that the chief priests and the elders gave an answer they knew to be untrue, or it is written off as a scribal blunder. In either case, it is regarded as a transitional stage in the evolution of form III from form I, or of form I from form III.[7]

Josef Schmid and Antonio Orbe argued that Irenaeus knew the parable in form II.[8] In Orbe's view, Irenaeus identified the first son, who said "no," and then repented, with the Jewish people, and the second son, who said "yes," but did not go into the vineyard, with the Gentiles—the Christian people of the New Testament. Philippe Bacq, however, claims that this "contredit formellement le texte de l'Evangile et la pensée d'Irénée," and that the exact opposite is true, that Irenaeus understood the first son to represent the Gentiles, who at first refused the call of God and were then converted, while the second son represents the Jews, who honor God with their lips "sans trouver la force de 'faire' (cf Rom 7:18) sa volonté."[9] It would appear that Bacq was unaware that the "text of the Gospel" was itself problematical. As to the "thought of Irenaeus," I believe that attention to the purpose the parable serves in the context of his argument and the exegetical comments he adds to the parable will show that it is to a high degree probable that Irenaeus's gospel-text showed the son who was said to have done the will of the father to be the second, who did not go into the vineyard (form II), and that it agreed with Codex Bezae also in omitting the negative in verse 32. I shall begin with the context of the parable in Irenaeus's argument.

Israel and the Gentiles: Which Son Is Which?

The third and last of the major sections of Book IV of *Adversus haereses* (IV.36.1—41.3) is devoted to the proof of the unity of the two testaments from the parables of Christ.[10] The parables in question are

1. The Wicked Husbandmen (Matt. 21:33-45)	*Haer.* IV.36.1-4;
2. The Great Supper (Matt. 22:1-14)	*Haer.* IV.36.5-6;
3. The Prodigal Son (Luke 15:11-32)	*Haer.* IV.36.7;
4. The Laborers in the Vineyard (Matt. 20:1-16)	*Haer.* IV.36.7;
5. The Pharisee and the Publican (Luke 18:9-14)	*Haer.* IV.36.8;
6. The Two Sons (Matt. 21:28-32)	*Haer.* IV.36.8;
7. The Barren Fig Tree (Luke 13:6-9)	*Haer.* IV.36.8;
8. The Tares (Matt. 13:24-30, 36-43)	*Haer.* IV.40.2—41.1.

In the first three parables, Irenaeus finds a clear progression from the Old Testament to the New. Thus, in the first, the tenants who killed the servants of the householder and his son are those to whom the vineyard was entrusted "by the lawgiving through Moses" (*Haer.* IV.36.2), while the other tenants to whom the vineyard is handed over represent the Church, the Gentiles who were outside the vineyard. In the second parable the king who gives the great feast is identified with God, whose city is Jerusalem. Those he invites first are the inhabitants of his city. When these repeatedly disobeyed the summons, the king destroyed their city and "called to the wedding feast of his son those from every path, that is, from all the Gentiles" (*Haer.* IV.36.5). In the third parable, the father does not give even a kid to his elder son but kills the fatted calf for the younger one, who had squandered his wealth among prostitutes, and bestows on him the best robe. Elsewhere, Irenaeus sees the killing of the fatted calf as a type of Christ's death, and the best robe as the gift of eternal life, or incorruptibility, lost in Adam but restored to humankind by Christ.[11]

In the fourth parable, a contrast between the people of the old dispensation and those of the new is not explicit, and the emphasis falls more heavily on the idea of successive invitations from the same God. Nevertheless, a progression from old dispensation to new can still be traced. Thus the sending of the workers into the vineyard at the middle hour (μετὰ τὴν μεσοχρονίαν) can be taken to represent the old dispensation, for at *Haer.* IV.25.1 Irenaeus says that circumcision and the law of works occupied the times intermediary (*media . . . tempora*) between the two ages of faith (Abraham and Christ), while those workers sent to the vineyard at the last hour are those to whom Christ was revealed in the last times.

In the fifth parable, Orbe suggests that the Pharisee is representative of those who rely on the Law, while the tax collector's *exhomologesis* is suggestive of Christian baptism.[12] In support of this, we might note that the prayer of the Pharisee is characterized by "self-glorification"—*extollentia*—and "boasting"—*iactantia*—which links him with the wicked laborers of the first parable, who are described as "contumacious and proud"—*contumeliosos et superbos*. In the seventh parable, the man who comes for three years to seek fruit from the fig tree signifies Christ's appeal to Israel through the prophets for the fruit of righteousness.

Why has Irenaeus included the Parable of the Two Sons in this series? It shows, he says, that there is one and the same God. It seems beyond doubt that he is assuming an allegorical interpretation in which the father typifies God and the two sons typify Israel and the Church. Earlier in Book IV (21.2-3), Irenaeus had, for exactly the same purpose, given in full just such an allegorical interpretation of Paul's account at Romans 9:10-13 of the election of Jacob in the womb. Rebecca's twin pregnancy, he says, was a prophecy of the two people, one elder, one younger, one slave, the other free, and yet both sons of the same father. Just as Jacob supplanted his elder brother and received the rights of the first born when Esau had spoken slightingly of them, just so the younger people accepted Christ, the first born, when the elder people had rejected him with the words "we have no king but Caesar" (John 19:15). In Christ the younger people stole from the Father the blessings of the elder people, just as Jacob stole the blessings of Esau.

Irenaeus's point is not simply that the two people are sons of the one God but that the younger supplants the elder. We have seen that in the series of parables discussed in *Haer.* IV.36 there is an underlying notion of progression from Old Covenant to New. If Irenaeus may be presumed to have intended the parable of the Two Sons to make the same point, the son to whom the father went first must represent Israel, and the son to whom the father went afterward must represent the Church. But if the second son represents the church, then Irenaeus's text of Matthew 21:31 must have identified the second son as the one who did the Father's will, and must thus have had the parable in form II. In form I, the church would have to be typified by the first son, which would not square with the pattern of progression from Old Covenant to New.

This conclusion gains support from the way Irenaeus links the two sons with the two groups approached by John the Baptist: first the chief priests and elders, secondly the tax collectors and prostitutes.[13] Irenaeus emphasizes the correspondence between the second son and the tax collectors and prostitutes. Just as in the parable of the Prodigal Son, it is the younger son who spent his wealth among prostitutes in a far land (the point is emphasized by Irenaeus) who is favored by his father; just as it is the tax collector who goes down to his house justified, so it is the second son, representative of tax collectors and prostitutes, who is said to have done the will of the Father. Just as the tax collector exceeds the Pharisee in prayer, and receives testimony from the Lord that he is justified, rather than the Pharisee, so the tax collectors and prostitutes precede the chief priests and the elders into the kingdom. Earlier, at *Haer.* IV.20.12, Irenaeus had said that the salvation of Rahab, the "Gentile prostitute who had confessed herself guilty of all sins" and who had received the three spies—"the Father, the Son, with the Holy Spirit"—had illustrated the Lord's saying that tax collectors and prostitutes precede the Pharisees into the kingdom of heaven.

Irenaeus's Exegesis of the Parable of the Two Sons

I turn now to a consideration of Irenaeus's exegetical comments on the behavior of the two sons. Irenaeus says of the first son that he repented "afterward, when repentance availed him nothing," and of the second son that he promised immediately "but did not go, because every human being is a liar, and while willing is easy, we are not able to accomplish what we will" (*velle quidem in promptu adiacet, non invenit autem perficere*). *Prima facie*, it seems as though Irenaeus's sympathies are with the second son rather than with the first, since the repentance of the first is said to be profitless, and the actual disobedience of the second son is excused by appeal to a universal law of human nature. This first impression is confirmed by closer analysis.

The notion that the first son repented "when repentance availed him nothing" can only make sense on the assumption either that the first son had lost his chance when the father went to the second son, or that there was something amiss with the quality of his repentance. If the first of these is Irenaeus's meaning, then we have a first son whose obedience is valueless, and a second son who does not obey at all, and in this case the only truthful answer to the question of Jesus at Matthew 21:31 would be "neither of the two." That is to say, the parable would be utterly without point. But, as J. Ramsey Michaels noted, while μεταμέλεσθαι "can be virtually synonymous with μετανοεῖν ['to repent'], it does not necessarily point to any decisive turning from one way of life to another," and when this verb is used of Judas at Matthew 27:3, it must mean a regret or remorse that is futile. If that was the meaning of the verb at Matthew 21:28-32, and if ἀπῆλθεν at verse 29 originally meant not that the son went into the vineyard, but simply that he went away (cf. Matt. 19:22; 22:5; 27:3), one could see why "the son of whom it is said μεταμεληθεὶς ἀπῆλθεν is *not* the son who 'did the will of his Father.'"[14] Irenaeus's use of μεταμέλεσθαι can be checked at only one other place, and there its use is entirely consistent with regret induced by a calamity that has befallen one: "Stesichorus was blinded for having reviled Helen in his poems, and then, after he repented [μεληθέντα αὐτόν/*penitentem*] and wrote the palinodes in which he celebrated her, he regained his sight" (*Haer.* I.23.2). Justin Martyr, speaking of the "consciousness" (αἴσθησι) to be experienced by the unjust when they are being punished says "and then they shall repent when they shall gain nothing" (τότε μετανοήσουσιν, ὅτε οὐδὲν ὠφελήσουσι) (*1 Apol.* 52.8-9).

Orbe correctly saw that Irenaeus's qualification of the repentance of the first son is derived from the interpretation of the parable in Matthew 21:32.[15] That is to say, Irenaeus has seen the link between parable and interpretation in the double use of the idea of repenting later. The late repentance of the first son symbolizes, according to Orbe, the repentance of the Jews after the fall of Jerusalem: a repentance that is late and inefficacious, because it does not involve faith—in fact, no true repentance at all, but merely the lamenting of the distress that has befallen them. However, Orbe creates several difficulties for his case by accepting the most widely attested reading at Matthew 21:32, with the negative οὐδέ before μετεμελήθητε: "but even after you saw it, you did not repent and believe him." Riggenbach had similarly supposed that Irenaeus's text had οὐδὲ μετεμελήθητε, and he chided Irenaeus for doing violence to the text in deriving from the negative the supposition that the first son's remorse came too late, and was therefore fruitless.[16] However, if this is what Irenaeus did, he must have understood Matthew 21:32 to mean "but you, having seen, did not repent afterward so as to believe him," and not, as Orbe would have it "but you, having seen, repented afterwards, but did not repent in such as way as to believe him."[17] Otherwise, Irenaeus would have to be supposed to be taking ὕστερον in different senses in each case: it will be equivalent to "too late" in Matthew 21:29 and equivalent to "later" or "afterward" in Matthew 21:32. In fact, however, if οὐδέ is to stand, then the first son and the chief priests and elders are not compared, but contrasted, since the latter are said not to have repented. Moreover, the repentance spoken of in Matthew 21:32 *will* in this case be equivalent to faith, and therefore cannot be compared with the profitless repentance of the first son. All these difficulties would evaporate if, with Josef Schmid,[18] we assumed that Irenaeus's biblical text, in common with most witnesses for form II, did not have οὐδέ at Matt. 21:32, and was understood to mean "you repented too late to believe him." That is how J. Ramsey Michaels proposed to understand that verse, but he was embarrassed by the lack of exact parallels to the use of ὕστερον ("later") which it requires.[19] Irenaeus's exegesis of *postea* as meaning "when it profited him nothing" (*quando nihil profuit ei*) suggests that he understood ὕστερον to be functioning in just this way, and that he understood this word to be the clue to the exact comparison between the first son and the chief priests and elders: both repent, but too late—*quando nihil profuit . . . paenitentia*.

All commentators are agreed that in his comments on the behavior of the second son, Irenaeus appeals to Rom. 7:18ff: "I can will what is right, but I cannot do it, for I do not do the good I want, but the evil I do not want is what I do." Irenaeus takes Paul to be speaking here of a universal law of human experience ("every human being is a liar"—cf. LXX Psalm 115:2 [116:11])—the inability to do the good one wills, an inability grounded not in the mind but in the members, an inability, moreover, which amounts to a lack of liberty (cf. Rom 7:23). Now, if all of this is to be applied to the second son in explanation of his behavior, it is very difficult to see how that son could be taken by Irenaeus to represent Israel. For, if that was Irenaeus's meaning, what would have been the point of his qualifying remarks, even if they were not excusatory but merely explanatory? If, as Philippe Bacq argues, Irenaeus's point was that Israel was never converted, why should he explain this in terms of a universal law, when, according to the same explanation, the Gentiles (here the first son) are not bound by this law, since they do in fact repent? Again, why should Irenaeus introduce such an explanation (flawed as it is) so shortly before a lengthy excursus designed in part to prove "the ancient law of liberty," to prove, that is, that what Israel did not do it could have done? It is not a question of their not being able to effect what they willed, but of their not willing, and this is made abundantly clear by the text with which Irenaeus introduces this excursus: "how often have I willed to gather your sons, and you would not?" (Matt. 23:37, *Haer.* IV.37.1). That Jesus could address this remark to Jerusalem is, as Irenaeus tells us in the course of the excursus, a sign that human beings are autonomous and free-willed (*Haer.* IV.37.5).

This analysis of Irenaeus's exegetical comments on the behavior of the two sons yields the same conclusion as our investigation of the function of the parable in the general context of his argument: that Irenaeus favored the second son, who said "yes," but did not in fact go into the vineyard. This can only be explained on the assumption that his gospel-text identified this son as the one who was said to have done the father's will: a circumstance sufficiently paradoxical to prompt Irenaeus to suggest an explanation. But the explanation is no more than suggested. Nevertheless, the failure of the second son to fulfil what he had willingly undertaken can be explained in terms of a distinction found elsewhere in Irenaeus between heeding a divine calling and producing the fruits of righteousness.

As Philippe Bacq rightly observes, in *Adversus haereses* IV.36 Irenaeus has a two-fold objective: the parables "décrivent le drame historique du refus d'Israël. Mais il souligne aussi, par un série de paroles claires du Seigneur, l'actualité de ce drame qui se joue, aujourd'hui encore, dans l'Église: ceux qui refusent l'enseignement des prophètes subiront une condamnation semblable à celle d'Israël, plus sévère même depuis que le Seigneur en personne est venu appeler l'homme au salut."[20] These two themes correspond to two heterodox views Irenaeus seeks to combat: first, that the Old Testament and the New belong each to a different God; secondly, that human beings are good or evil by nature rather than by choice.[21] The identity of the demand for the fruit of righteousness in both Old and New Testaments indicates the one God responsible for both, and that the fruit is asked for itself implies the freedom of human beings to meet or refuse this request.

Often when speaking of the response of Israel, and occasionally when speaking of the response of the Church, Irenaeus gives the impression that unfruitfulness is identical with disobedience and unbelief, and fruitfulness identical with belief and obedience. Thus, in his exegesis of the parable of the Wicked Husbandmen, these are described as arrogant and proud and unfruitful and killers of the Lord and unbelievers, while those to whom the vineyard is later entrusted are described as giving back the fruits at the proper time with all obedience (*Haer.* IV.36.1; cf. 36.2 and 36.4). Similarly, the refusal of faith implied by Matthew 23:37-38 is said to be equivalent to the failure of the fig tree to produce fruit (Luke 13:7, *Haer.* IV.36.8). Despite this apparent equivalence of believing and producing fruit, Irenaeus also suggests that there is a distinction between faith and works. Thus, in the excursus on freedom of the will he says: "and the Lord safeguarded the liberty and autonomy of human kind not only in works but also in faith" (*Haer.* IV.37.5). Such a distinction operates throughout *Haer.* IV.36, when Irenaeus speaks of the need for Christians to produce good works. Thus the collection of sayings added to the discussion of the parable of the Wicked Husbandmen are said to have been spoken by the Lord to his disciples "preparing *us* to be good workers" (*Haer.* IV.36.3). The story of the man without a wedding garment (Matthew 22:11-14) appended to the parable of the Great Feast is taken to be a demonstration of the distinction between accepting the invitation offered by Christ and producing the works of righteousness:

> He also showed that, as well as being called, we should be adorned with the works of righteousness, so that the Spirit of God might rest on us; for this is the wedding garment, of which the Apostle said "we wish not to be unclothed, but to be further clothed, so that what is mortal might be swallowed up by what is immortal" (2 Cor. 5:4). But those who are, indeed, called to God's banquet, and because of their evil behaviour do not receive the holy Spirit, will, he says, be thrown into outer darkness, plainly showing that it is the same King who called the *faithful* from every place to the wedding feast of his Son and gave the banquet of incorruptibility, who will command to be thrown into outer darkness the one who does not have a wedding garment, that is who is contemptuous. (*Haer.* IV.36.6)

Such a distinction between faith and works may even be found in Irenaeus's exegesis of the parable of the Wicked Husbandmen. For Irenaeus sees in this parable an indication of a lapse of time between the handing over of the vineyard to the laborers and the demand for the fruit of righteousness. This lapse of time allows for a period of preparation before the fruit is called for (cf. Matt. 21:34). In fact, this parable is presented as a brief résumé of the history of salvation. The digging of the wine press is seen as the *preparation* of a "receptacle for the prophetic spirit." Irenaeus sees in this feature a reference to the sending of the preexilic prophets. It is only with the post-exilic prophets that the fruit of righteousness is actually demanded, and it is then that the laborers are said not to believe and to have the vineyard taken from them, to be handed over to other laborers, who will bear fruit *in their own time* (*Haer.* IV.36.2). Irenaeus repeats these last words three times in the course of his exegesis of this parable, and it is clear that he takes them to imply a period of time between the handing over of the vineyard to those who were outside it (and the digging of a wine press throughout the world) and the time for the fruit to be handed over. As the collection of eschatological sayings that Irenaeus presents in explanation of "in their own time" makes plain, this time is in fact the day of judgement, when the Word of God will give the Spirit to those who believe in him, and cause the unfruitful fig tree instantly to wither (*Haer.* IV.36.4).

This distinction between vocation and fruitfulness lies beneath Irenaeus's comments on the parable of the Two Sons. To answer the call and to produce the fruit are both in our power, but we need exhortation to fruitfulness even after we have given the assent of faith (*Haer.* IV. 37.2-4). The need for this exhortation is not grounded in human incapacity but precisely in human freedom: "If then it were not in our power to do or not to do something, on what grounds did the Apostle, and much more the Lord himself, counsel us to do some things and not to do other things" (*Haer.* IV.37.4). Moreover, because we are free our obedience to God is difficult: it can be achieved only after contest and struggle, and just this makes the reward of obedience even more to be sought after (*Haer.* IV.37.6-7). Irenaeus takes it for granted that humankind will suffer setbacks in the course of this struggle, the more so since it is a struggle with Satan (*Haer.* IV.40.3). But God is tolerant of these setbacks, and indeed, the direct experience of evil they entail strengthens the apprehension of the good, and the resolve to adhere to it in obedience to God (*Haer.* IV.37.7; 39.1; 40.3). For Irenaeus, human freedom itself implies some measure of divine tolerance of human apostasy. This is not to say that producing the fruit of righteousness is not of the highest importance for Irenaeus, but simply that, by divine dispensation, this fruitfulness need not follow immediately upon the confession of faith. It is to be achieved at the due time. Irenaeus's leniency toward the second son in the parable is thus entirely compatible with the understanding he develops in this section of *Adversus haereses*, of the nature of a human being's response to the call of God.

Irenaeus's employment of the parable of the Two Sons suggests, therefore that he knew it essentially in the form in which it is preserved by Codex Bezae. It was the second son who said "yes" but did not go into the vineyard; that son was identified as the one who was said to have done his father's will, and in verse 32, the negative οὐδέ was not found before μεταμελήθητε. If form II of the parable of the Two Sons is a later corruption of form I or form III, that corruption must have taken place between the redaction of the Gospel and not much later than the middle of the second century, when Irenaeus encountered the corrupted text.

When the oddity of Irenaeus's exegesis of this parable first piqued my curiosity, now nearly thirty years ago, I shared Souter's supposition, referred to at the beginning of this paper, that if Irenaeus's biblical text could be secured it might bring us closer than later witnesses to the original form of the text. That remains a possibility, but one of the gains of revisiting this subject has been the discovery that more recent scholarship of the text of Codex Bezae itself has revealed an "attitude of liberty with respect to the text, displayed by an anonymous second-century διορθώτης who obviously felt free to revise the text of the gospel."[22]

CHAPTER FIVE

Irenaeus and Hebrews

D. Jeffrey Bingham

In the sixth century, Stephanus Gobarus stated that Irenaeus (along with Hippolytus) denied the Pauline authorship of the Letter to the Hebrews.[1] A couple of centuries before, Eusebius had written that Irenaeus had quoted from the Letter in a no longer extant work. He had said that "[Irenaeus composed] a collection of addresses on various subjects, in which he mentions the Epistle to the Hebrews and the 'Wisdom of Solomon,' quoting several passages from them."[2] That Irenaeus knew the Letter and that he used it in his ministry should not surprise us. Already at the end of the first century in Rome, Clement "subtly, but unmistakably," to use the words of Luke Timothy Johnson, employed the thought and language of Hebrews (for example, *1 Clement* 36.1-5).[3] The notion of subtle usage is helpful. B. W. Bacon counted "forty-seven [!] 'echoes,'" and states that Hebrews is "the model for whole paragraphs" of *1 Clement*, but found no "reference" to the Letter.[4] Of Clement's use of Hebrews, Eusebius wrote:

> In it he gives many thoughts from the Epistle to the Hebrews and even quotes verbally when using certain passages from it: thus most clearly establishing the fact that the treatise was no recent thing. For this reason it has seemed right and reasonable to reckon it among the other letters of the apostle. For, Paul having communicated in writing with the Hebrews in their native tongue, some say that the evangelist Luke, others that Clement himself, translated the writing. The latter statement is more probably true; because both the Epistle of Clement and that to the Hebrews maintain the same character from the point of view of style, and because the thoughts in each of the two treatises are not divergent.[5]

Hebrews in Rome

Such an early attestation to the prominent place of Hebrews in Clement's thought has been recognized by modern scholarship. D. A. Hagner wrote that "Clement's acquaintance with and dependence upon the Epistle to the Hebrews is acknowledged by nearly everyone."[6] He goes on to conclude, after a thorough analysis of Clement's use of the Letter, that "It seems certain then that Clement read, loved, was taught by, and made use of the Epistle to the Hebrews in writing his pastoral letter to the Church of Corinth. . . . Clement, faced with the need of writing to the Corinthian Church, found in the Epistle to the Hebrews a veritable mine of ideas and phraseology which were found to be not only convincing in themselves, but which seemed ready-made for, or perfectly adaptable to, his own purposes."[7]

The position of A. F. Gregory is a bit different. He recognizes, following Elling-worth's argument, that Clement is at places dependent on Hebrews, but wishes also to note the likelihood of independence and common relation of both Hebrews and *1 Clement* to another, common source. He says, after acknowledging the certain use of Hebrews by Clement in *1 Clement* 36.1-5, "Yet the pattern of striking parallels and possible allusions, but only limited verbal identity, means that it is difficult to exclude altogether the possibility that Clement and the author of the letter to the Hebrews might each have drawn on a common source or tradition. It may be best to conclude, as Paul Ellingworth demonstrates, that it is possible to affirm both the independence of Clement's thought from that of Hebrews at a number of critical points, yet not to question the general consensus of the literary dependence of *1 Clement* on Hebrews."[8]

Gerd Theissen, on the other hand, takes the argument to an extreme. He insists that *1 Clement* 36:1-6 is not dependent upon Heb. 1:1-14 but derives only from a common tradition shared between them.[9] However, G. L. Cockerill has, in my view, success-fully challenged Theissen's conclusions. He argues that while there is common tradi-tional material, *1 Clement* also evidences in places derivation from and paraphrase of Hebrews.[10] H. W. Attridge also believes that for *1 Clement* 36.2-6 "it is impossible to assume anything but literary dependence."[11] Clare K. Rothschild agrees that Clement depended on Hebrews.[12]

With current scholarship recognizing the validity of Eusebius's testimony regard-ing Clement and Hebrews, there is no reason to doubt the historian's comments con-cerning Irenaeus and Hebrews. Irenaeus in a work or works no longer extant quoted from several passages in the Letter in his own pastoral-polemical task.

Westcott also thought that there were "several coincidences of expression" between Hebrews and the *Shepherd of Hermas* "sufficient to show that Hermas also was acquainted with it."[13] The recent essay by Joseph Verheyden has not done anything to raise confidence in Wescott's view of Hermas's acquaintance with Hebrews.[14] He seems to allow for Hermas's use of Matthew and 1 Corinthians.[15]

But other contemporary scholarship seems to take for granted the use of Hebrews by *Hermas*, although perhaps in a more restrained manner than Westcott. Raymond Brown and John Meier, for instance, argue that both Clement and *Hermas* "although using the wording of Hebrews move in an almost opposite thought-direction."[16] Yet, Rome still from 96 through the entire second century "remains the main witness for an awareness of Hebrews."[17] The Epistle was "received by the Roman church but never enthusiastically appropriated."[18] In other words, Rome knew Paul had not written Hebrews; the author was merely a respected "second-generation Christian authority," so "Hebrews was not Scripture by the Roman criterion" of apostolic origin.[19] Therefore, because of the qualified respect with which Rome (Clement, *Hermas*) held Hebrews, it felt free to modify its teachings in its own theological construction. Clement, then, softens the strong rejection of the Levitical priesthood and cult present in Hebrews while *Hermas* softens the position of Hebrews on no forgiveness of sins after baptism. Rome did this, Brown and Meier say, because "Rome did not like extreme positions."[20]

Whether or not the acceptance the Letter had received in Rome influenced Irenaeus's comfort with quoting it we do not know. Nor can we say what use the Asians in the late first and second century made of it. But one note is worth making. Brown and Meier insist that Rome modified Hebrews in its employment of the writing. It could be that rather than blatant modification and alteration of the thought of the Epistle, Clement and *Hermas* were engaged in interpretation of it. In other words, they might not understand their own work to be a change from Hebrews, but rather a proper reading of it. As we encounter Irenaeus's own engagement with Hebrews, we will witness uses and readings not necessarily expected by the modern critic. Such readings should not necessarily be assumed to be conflicts with the theology of Hebrews. They might be interpretations of the text believed by Irenaeus to be inherent within the text and the rule of faith.

Modern Reflections on Irenaeus and Hebrews

Nevertheless, despite the reasonable basis for believing Eusebius's testimony that Irenaeus quoted Hebrews in works that are now lost, and the early evidence for Rome's own use of the Epistle, scholars have been less willing to see the Letter making its mark in *Adversus haereses*. Some do acknowledge a partial citation of Heb. 1:3 in book 2 and some allusions to the Epistle scattered elsewhere in Irenaeus's main work.[21] In the nineteenth century, for example, we may note A. Camerlynck and W. W. Harvey. Camerlynck saw allusions to Heb. 1:3; 1:13; 3:5; 10:1 (*Haer.* II.28.2; II.28.7; II.30.9; III.6.5; IV.11.4), being especially confident about Heb. 1:13, while Harvey saw allusions to ten passages: Heb. 1:3; 2:10; 3:5; 7:28; 8:1; 10:1; 10:26-31; 11:5; 11:13; 13:15.[22] But, Camerlynck ultimately concluded that although Hebrews should have provided a "veritable arsenal" for Irenaeus's polemic, it did not. Irenaeus knew and read Hebrews, but because of his belief that it was not from Paul's hand, he did not employ it.[23] Even though Harvey recognized those several echoes, he remarked that *Adversus haereses* "contains no clear quotations from this epistle."[24] Views minimizing the connection between Hebrews and Irenaeus abound.

Camerlynck's summary of other opinions in the nineteenth century seems to show even less willingness to recognize Irenaeus's interest in Hebrews. Cornely (1885) believes any allusions to have little weight and Werner (1889) sees them as dubious.[25] It is difficult to find twentieth-century, and more contemporary, confidence in Irenaeus's use of Hebrews in his extant writings. Most deny it a place in his "canon." The place of the Epistle in Irenaeus's constructive theology is minimized. For instance, Hoh allows for only four indirect citations, but he questions even these.[26] F. R. M. Hitchcock thought that Irenaeus quite possibly knew Hebrews, but notes only four or five allusions (1:3; [2:5, translation of Enoch?]; 3:6; 13:10; 10:1/ *Haer.* II.30.9; [3.6.4]; IV.18.6; IV.5.1; IV.11.4) and postulates that he was "reluctant to use" the epistle because of Montanist appeal to Heb. 6:4-5.[27] C. H. Turner recognizes no citations from the Letter and although he sets forth occasions in which the language of Irenaeus may echo Hebrews (Heb. 1:3; 3:5; 4:4-10; 6:1; 10:1; 10:26ff; 11:5; 11:5-6; 11:13/*Haer.* II.30.9; III.6.5; IV.15.2; II.2.5; IV.16.1; III.12.13; IV.11.4; IV.28.2; IV.13.1; IV.16.2; V.5.1; V.32.2), he is quick many times to point out other textual parallels.[28] André Benoit finds all the allusions identified by Harvey to be "vague and remote."[29] The bishop had read Hebrews, Benoit thinks, but he did not believe it had the same authority as apostolic texts. This is why Irenaeus did not mention the Letter. *Adversus haereses* is devoted to proving the Christian faith based upon the apostolic teaching.[30] Irenaeus is content, therefore, only to make indefinite allusions to it. Rothschild is also content to see incidental citations/allusions in Irenaeus.[31] Schneemelcher recognizes the Scriptural status the four Gospels, Acts, and thirteen Pauline epistles held for Irenaeus. He notes also the high appraisal, similar to the place of honor he gave to Paul's writings, that Irenaeus gives 1 Peter and 1 and 2 John. Hebrews, he says, however, "is not so highly esteemed."[32] Norbert Brox notes that it is one of the few books that are "missing in him" but which are found in the canon of the fourth century church.[33] Citing Eusebius he says, "Irenaeus knew Hebrews, but apparently outside the church's Canon."[34]

Robert Grant's position shows a change from his early thought on Irenaeus to his later understanding. At first, Grant saw minimal reference to the Letter. Later, he would explicitly deny that it was a text in Irenaeus's New Testament canon and that it appears in his extant works. He writes in one place that "The views of Irenaeus (*c.* 180) are not altogether clear. He certainly alludes to Hebrews (1:3) when he says that the Father created everything 'by the Word of his power' (*Haer.* 2, 30, 9); but this is the only clear allusion in his writings, and he speaks of the Christian 'altar in the heavens' (4, 18, 6) in such a way as to show that he is not relying on what Hebrews has to say on the subject."[35] However, in other places he says that Irenaeus "knew most of the New Testament rather well," but his collection of New Testament books "did not include Hebrews" and furthermore that "There are no real traces of Hebrews in his works."[36] Luke Timothy Johnson, who was optimistic about Clement's use of the Letter, joins this last opinion of Grant's and writes that "there are no references to it in any of his extant writings."[37]

In this chapter, an analysis of Irenaeus's knowledge and use of Hebrews, I hope to begin a challenge to such opinions. I don't intend here to insist that Irenaeus revered Hebrews as a sacred text, the same way in which he sees the Spirit speaking through the prophets, the evangelists, and Paul. But I do wish to demonstrate that his thought appears to be dependent in important degrees upon its language and teaching. Perhaps Gobarus, Camerlynck, and Benoit were correct and he knew that the bishop rejected it as being from Paul's hand and that this caused him to use it more subtly in his argument against the Gnostics and Marcionites. His concern must have been overwhelming; otherwise, it is difficult to explain why the voice of such a text is reduced almost entirely to a whisper. For merely one example of the potential power of Hebrews in the debate against his opponents, we need only recall what E. C. Blackman pointed out sixty-two years ago: Heb. 1:1 was a text that could be called forth to demonstrate that "Marcion's isolation of the Redeemer from the World-creator was not difficult to refute."[38] Perhaps Hitchcock is right and the bishop refused to use it because of the Montanist appeal to Heb. 6:4-5.[39] Or we might speculate that he muted its presence because of an attraction the "prophetic" contents of Hebrews held for the Montanists or other prophets.[40] Or perhaps there is another cause. But, nevertheless, here we will see that whatever its place in his concept of sacred, inspired texts, Hebrews was important for his theological construction. It did serve, *contra* Camerlynck, as a mine of riches for his polemic.

Irenaeus and Hebrews[41]
Hebrews 1:2-3: The Omnipotent Creator

It is in his refutation of the Valentinian theses concerning the final consummation and the Demiurge (*Haer.* II.29-30) that we find Irenaeus's first reading of the Letter to the Hebrews. In the particular portion (*Haer.* II.30.1-9) of his argument into which he inserts the wording of Hebrews, he is arguing against the Valentinian notion that the Demiurge has a psychic nature, a nature of a quality between matter and spiritual, and which is then inferior to the nature of the spiritual Valentinians themselves. His concluding point is that reason shows that even the Valentinians must ultimately confess that the Demiurge is the creator and former of all things, which makes him superior, not inferior, to themselves, for he is also their creation.

At this point Irenaeus presents a beautiful statement on the Catholic perspective concerning the creator. In it he inserts a partial citation of Heb. 1:3 to teach that "by the word of his power" he created all things:

> If . . . He made all things freely, and by his own power, and arranged and finished them, and His will is the substance of all things, then He is discovered to be the one, only God who created all things, who alone is Omnipotent, and who is the only Father founding and forming all things, visible and invisible, such as may be perceived by our senses and such as cannot, heavenly and earthly, "*by the word of His power,*" [Heb. 1:3] and He has fitted and arranged all things by His wisdom, while He contains all things, but He Himself can be contained by no one: He is the Former, He the Builder, He the Discoverer, He the Creator, He the Lord of all; and there is no one besides Him or above Him.[42]

I have stopped this remarkable theological statement short as it goes on for several more lines. In those lines, the bishop of Lyons contrasts the God of the church to the Valentinian concept of the Demiurge, emphasizing that the Father creates through His Word and wisdom, and that this Father is the God of the patriarchs, the law, the prophets, Christ, the apostles, and the church. He is revealed through the Son who eternally coexists with him.

What is important for our understanding of this early Christian father's reading of Hebrews is that the only biblical text quoted within this magisterial reflection on God is a portion of Hebrews 1:3: "by the word of his power [*verbo virtutis suae*]."[43] Irenaeus takes from this text two key theological themes that appear in his grand confession and that are taken explicitly from the biblical text's language. First, we see the idea of the exclusivity and supremacy of God's power in creation. From this text he derives his language within his doctrinal summary that affirms that God "by his own power [*ex sua potestiale*]" made, arranged, and finished all things.[44] Of this same biblical text he was thinking when earlier, as he was working his way up to the conclusion of his theological statement, he asked rhetorically, who can number all those things that have been constituted "by the power of God" (*per virtutem Dei*).[45]

In addition to his argument for the immensity of God's power while he anticipates his citation of Hebrews 1:3, he also takes to heart the passage's language concerning the word (*verbum*) of God's power. This, of course, he reads christologically, as he reads references to wisdom, pneumatologically. Both appear in his grand theological statement. God creates by his Word and arranges all things by his Wisdom (*Sapientia*).[46] Later in the conclusion, this becomes "He is the Creator who made all things by Himself, that is, through [*per*] His Word [*verbum*] and His Wisdom [*Sapientiam*].[47] In the same conclusion, his Word is further identified as his Son (*Filius*).[48] This suggests that Irenaeus is thinking not only of Hebrews 1:3, but also verse 2, which says that God has spoken through his Son.[49]

Hebrews 1:2-3 performs for Irenaeus as a text that teaches the all-sufficiency of the creative power of the Father by means of or through the agency of his Word, his Son. In this way, Heb. 1:2-3 ranks with biblical texts like Psalm 32 [33]:6 and John 1:3 that Irenaeus elsewhere joins together to teach that the rule of truth announces that "There is one God All-Powerful [*omnipotens*], who created all things through his Word [*verbum*]."[50] What the Psalmist and John provide in testimony to the Father's creation of *all things* through the Word, Son, the author of Hebrews provides in testimony to the *Almightiness* of the Word's, Son's creative agency, for it is the Word, or Son, of the Father's power who creates.

We must not think that Hebrews 1:2-3 functions alone in this context, however: It joins a host of other biblical testimonies that together provide Irenaeus with a network, a cento, if you like, of Bible words. Together with the words from Hebrews we find also words from Eph. 1:21; Exod. 20:11; Ps. 145 (144):6; Acts 4:24; 14:15; Gen. 2:7-8; Matt. 22:32; 2 Cor. 1:3; 11:31; Eph. 1:3; 3:14; Col. 1:3; and 1 Pet. 1:3. Such centos are typical of Irenaeus. Through them—through his explicit linkage of biblical texts that in his mind are obviously associated and connected and that testify to the rule of truth—he demonstrates the proper connection of the scriptures. The Valentinians, he thinks, lack propriety in their own centos, their own arrangement of Scripture's pieces.[51]

Hebrews 1:8-9: The Exclusivity of the Father and Son

We may also be able to recognize a further role for the first chapter of the Letter in Irenaeus's polemic. In his third book, he argues that the titles "God" and "Lord" have only been given by the Lord, the Spirit, or the Apostles appropriately to the Father and his Son. There, we may find a reference to Hebrews 1:8-9 and the immediate context. The argument in both *Adversus haereses* III.6.1 and Hebrews 1 is similar. Hebrews, through a collection of Old Testament passages, is arguing that the application of the titles "Son," "God," and "Lord" is restricted to Jesus (Heb. 1:5 [Ps. 2:7]; Heb. 1:8, 13 [Ps. 45 [44]; 6 [7]: 110 [109]:1]; Heb. 1:10 [Ps. 102 [101]: 25 [26]; Heb. 3:1). The scriptures, or more pointedly, God, has never applied them to angels. In the same manner, Irenaeus, also through a network of texts, is arguing that the titles "God" and "Lord" have only been used "definitely and absolutely" by the Father for the Son, the Spirit, or for both (Ps. 110:1; Ps. 45:6; Ps. 82:1; 50:1, 3). The scripture, where it doesn't record the Father speaking, Irenaeus insists, has used them only of the Son (Gen. 19:24). He emphasizes, particularly, that when the Spirit employs the titles "God" and "Lord" he restricts application to the Son. However, the title "gods" can be applied to the church, to those who have received the adoption by grace (Ps. 82:1; Ps. 50:1, 3; Isa. 65:1; Ps. 82:6; Rom. 8:15). Only Psalm 45:6 and Psalm 110:1 occur in the sets of Old Testament texts employed by both Hebrews and Irenaeus.

Although Irenaeus might have put his cento of Old Testament texts together completely on his own, or might have had access to some early *testimonia*, the similarity of concentration on the proper application of the same titles, as well as five other considerations, suggest dependence upon Hebrews 1. First, we know that in *Adversus haereses* II.28.7, when he cites Psalm 110:1, the presentation in Hebrews is in his mind. When he cites it, he reflects the idea of Hebrews 1:13 when he says that it was to the Word "alone" to whom he said the words of the Psalm. He reflects in his own thought the teaching of the Hebrews text when it says, "But to what angel has he ever said?" This is the language of exclusivity. Camerlynck is especially impressed by the similarity and sees here clear "dependence" upon the Epistle.[52] Second, we already know of his explicit reading of Hebrews 1:2-3. Third, Hebrews 1 is contrasting the titles "God," "Son," and "Lord" to *angels*. Angels, the Letter argues, do not receive these titles from God. Irenaeus, similarly, is contrasting the titles "God" and "Lord" to the adopted children of God, the members of the church, those he sees the Spirit naming as "gods." Also, however, further down in his argument (III.6.1-5), he will also demonstrate that the term "gods" is also applied to those who are "no gods at all." The Father and Son are to be contrasted to the church in terms of supremacy, as the angels are different from the Son. On the other hand, the false gods, the idols, are to be contrasted in terms of reality. Fourth, the same types of rhetorical questions occur in both Hebrews and Irenaeus. In Hebrews we find: "For to what angel did God ever say?" as Psalm 2 is read and, "But to what angel has he ever said?" as Psalm 110 is read (Heb. 1:5, 13). In Irenaeus we find, "who is meant by God?" between the reading of Psalm 50:1 and 50:3 and "But of what gods [does he speak]?" just prior to the reading of Psalm 82:6. Finally, both the Letter and Irenaeus make explicit reference to the Father and Son. Hebrews 1:5 has the titles from Psalm 2:7 and 2 Samuel 7:14 (1 Chron. 17:13) and in Hebrews 1:8 where "son" occurs in interpretation of the title "God" in Psalm 45:6. Irenaeus has the same titles in the immediate context without biblical references, but like Hebrews 1, uses both titles in interpretation of the titles "Lord" and "God."[53] Again, we should point out that the bishop employs individual texts in centos that he composes. He rarely reads a text independently. His biblical reading is always canonical. Here, it seems, though the entire cento is his own, that he composes it under the influence of Hebrews 1. Probably, his attention to Psalm 2 is drawn by Hebrews 1:8-9.

Hebrews 3:5: Moses and the One God

Because Irenaeus apparently borrows the language of Hebrews 3:14, it now becomes possible for us to appreciate a broader appeal to the third chapter of the Letter. It might also be that when he characterizes Moses as the "faithful servant and a prophet of God" (II.2.5), he is reading toward the beginning of the chapter in verse 5. There the Letter reads: "Now Moses was faithful in God's house as a servant, to testify to the things that would be spoken later." It might also be that he has Numbers 12:7 and Joshua 14:7 as his source, but there, although the attributes of "servant" and "faithful" are said to be true of Moses, the context of Numbers 12:6-8 contrasts Moses with a prophet, which is an office Irenaeus attributes to him. Numbers says that to prophets, the LORD manifests himself in visions and dreams, but to Moses he speaks "face to face." However, in Hebrews 3:5, Moses is characterized as a prophet, as one who testified "to those things that were spoken later." This suggests that the text of Hebrews, which does not carry forth the contrast between Moses and the Lord's prophets, is the text upon which Irenaeus was gazing.

The language of Numbers 12 and Hebrews 3 occurs again later in *Adversus haereses* III.6.5, where Irenaeus writes that Moses is spoken of by the Spirit as "the faithful Moses, the attendant and servant of God."[54] But once again, it seems that the text that influences Irenaeus's words is Hebrews 3. In his polemic, the bishop is concerned with arguing the difference between gods and the one God, idols and God the Father, the creator of all things by his Son. To this effect he cites Galatians 4:8-9, 2 Thessalonians 2:4, and 1 Corinthians 8:4-6. The last of these three passages states that there is "one God, the Father, of whom are all things . . . and one Lord Jesus Christ, by whom are all things." Here he argues that all things, τὰ πάντα, derive only from the creator and his agent and no one else. Therefore, there is only one God the Father and one Lord Jesus Christ. The argument against other gods is made by demonstrating the unique identity of the creator and his Son. He then quotes Moses twice, from Deuteronomy 4:19 and 5:8, to make the point that one should not make idols of created things, "of whatsoever things (πάντος) are in heaven, earth, and the waters." Hebrews 3:4, the verse that immediately precedes the one under consideration, reads "that the builder of all things, [τὰ] πάντα, is God." The context of Hebrews 3 serves the polemic of Irenaeus better than that of Numbers 12. It also seems that Heb. 3:5 is silently part of the cento of texts that includes the ones of Paul and Deuteronomy. The case for Irenaeus's use of Hebrews 3:5, on the basis of context, seems a bit stronger than the case Hagner was able to make for Clement of Rome. In his treatment of Clement, he concluded that Clement was "very possibly dependent upon Heb. 3."[55] Once again, as with Hebrews 1:3, it seems the Letter comes to the aid of the polemicist as he presents the catholic faith concerning the creation, the creator, the Father, and his agent, his Son.

Hebrews 5:8-9: Christ, Mary, and the Amendment

It is to the category of salvation that we now turn. In particular we will see how Hebrews 5:9 helps him build his concept of Mary's recapitulation of Eve and of Eve's descendants. In the argument in which the presence of Hebrews 5 can be seen, Irenaeus is arguing that the end is connected to the beginning within the fabric of salvation history. "Our Lord," he states, in his flesh, his humanity, his finitude and suffering, is traced back to Adam over seventy-two generations "connecting the end with the beginning."[56] Adam, for Irenaeus, after Romans 5:14, is "the figure of him that was to come," for the Word of God had predestined that the first human, of animal nature, would be saved by the second human of spiritual nature.

This view of redemptive history so clear in the figures of Adam and Christ sets the pattern for understanding other biblical figures, for recognizing other connections inherent within the history of salvation. So, in *Adversus haereses* III.22.4, Irenaeus begins, "In accordance with this design, Mary the Virgin is found obedient. . . . But Eve was disobedient. . . . . [and] having become disobedient was made the cause of death, both to herself and to the entire human race."[57] Here Irenaeus makes another connection based on the one between Adam and Christ. But now it is the two virgin women, Mary and Eve, and the connection is not one of redemption, but of disobedience and death. In the same way in which the sorrowful nature of Adam passed to all of his descendants, Eve passes death along also; her disobedience is the cause of death to all of these. But Irenaeus goes on to argue that the reverse is true as well. "So also," he continues, "did Mary, having a man betrothed [to her] and being nevertheless a virgin, by yielding obedience, *become the cause of salvation, both to herself and the whole human race.*"[58]

Irenaeus will pick up this theme of "recapitulation of disobedience" through obedience again in *Haer.* V.19.1. There he says that Adam's disobedience at the tree "receives amendment by the correction" of the First-begotten, and Eve's virginal disobedience is balanced by Mary's virginal obedience.[59] Mary, he says, became the "patroness" (*Advocata*) of Eve so that the human race is rescued by a virgin as well.[60]

Having seen the theme of balance, advocacy, amendment, and correction through the connectedness of the Irenaean economies, we need to return to the language of *Haer.* III.22.4. There Eve was said to have "become the cause of salvation, both to herself and the whole human race." Here we can see how Irenaeus has read, employed, and extended the words of Hebrews 5:8-9. There we read: Although he was a Son, he learned *obedience* through what he suffered; and being made perfect he *became the source of eternal salvation to all* who *obey* him.

In Irenaeus's thought we see that he seems to have taken the language of cause and effect and obedience/perfection applied strictly to Jesus in Hebrews, and through his theme of connections applied it also to Mary, so that she becomes also the "cause of salvation" to all. For Irenaeus, Adam is not the only figure that needs to be corrected, and Christ is not the only one who corrects, for the Lord accomplishes "recapitulation of so comprehensive a dispensation."[61] The Lord makes the recapitulation, but employs a variety of figures in the comprehensiveness of that recapitulation. So, for Irenaeus, the cause and effect of the amendment performed by Christ for Adam and his obedient descendants, whom we see in Hebrews 5:8-9, must be extended to Mary and the amendment of Eve and her obedient children.

Bertrand de Margerie hears the same allusion to Hebrews 5:9 in Irenaeus, an allusion he characterizes as "universally acknowledged."[62] In his understanding, Irenaeus's reflection on Hebrews "signifies that Mary participates in the salvific obedience of Christ on the cross and has participated in it ever since the Annunciation, receiving from her Son the grace of obedience—obedience to him—in view of the salvation of the human race."[63] Mary, then, becomes one of those who "obey him," by means of grace, and one who thereby uniquely joins him in the recovery of the lost. De Margerie goes on to say that Mary "received from him [Christ] the power to contribute in a unique way—by consenting to become his mother—to the salvation of the whole human race."[64]

So now we have seen how Hebrews has helped inform Irenaeus's presentation of redemptive history as he addresses his opponents. The entire reference to the reversal brought about by Christ and Mary began with the bishop concerned to explain the reality of Christ's flesh, the actuality of his share in Mary's flesh, his true taking from her of her flesh. He did not just pass through her as through a tube. In one dimension, then, the reversal of Eve through Mary, brought about in history, structures not only Irenaeus's soteriology, but also his Christology. Mary's participation in the amendment with Christ puts forth also Christ's participation with Mary in her substance. They both bring about reversal of two erring humans, by virtue of the fact that both of them are obedient *humans*. They share. He shares her flesh; She shares in the work of reversal. There is co-participation. He participates in her humanity; she participates, by grace, in the making of recapitulation. They share in obedience as they share in flesh. Hebrews has appeared linked to both the notion of recapitulation in history and also to the authenticity of the historical actual fleshiness of Christ.

Hebrews 5:15: The Immaturity of Humanity

We next see how the Epistle seems also to be linked to Irenaeus's anthropology. In particular, it is linked to a very unique portion of his doctrine of humanity: his peculiar idea of the immaturity of humanity, a creature created to grow, mature, and develop within economies and a history designed to facilitate such maturation.

The discussion leading up to his apparent allusion to Hebrews begins with a question: "If, however, anyone says, 'what then?' could not God have exhibited humanity as perfect from the beginning?"[65] His response initially takes this line: All things are possible to God. He is always the same. But created things are inferior to him. They, unlike God, are not uncreated. As created, then, they are initially imperfect. A mother has it in her power to give food, meats, stews, firm vegetables to her infant, but does not, for her child is unable to receive it. Likewise, God could have made humans perfect from the beginning, but humanity being infantile in its creatureliness could not have received it. So, it is in this way that we should understand the first advent of the Lord. He came not with the glory with which he might have come, but in a fashion that we were capable of beholding. And then in Irenaeus's own words we read: "He, who was the perfect bread of the Father, offered himself to us as milk [because we were] as infants."[66] That is, as it were, we nursed "from the breast of his flesh," so that by this "course of milk nourishment" we might "become accustomed to eat and drink the Word of God," and might be able to receive and "contain" the Spirit, the "bread of immortality."[67]

In his continuing discussion of the topic, Irenaeus cites 1 Cor. 3:2: "And on this account does Paul declare to the Corinthians, 'I have fed you with milk, not with meat, for you were not ready for it.' That is, you have indeed learned about the advent of our Lord as human, nevertheless, because of your infirmity, the Spirit of the Father has not yet rested upon you."

Because of the sin of the Corinthians, they did not have the Spirit; they were not spiritual. So, Irenaeus says, "the apostle had the power to give them strong meat," that is the Holy Spirit, "but they were not capable of receiving it, because," and now we hear the presence of Heb. 5:14, "they had feeble and untrained faculties [ἀγύμναστα ἔχειν τὰ αἰσθητήρια]."[68] Hebrews 5:14 and its context parallels 1 Cor. 3:2 in specific ways. Both are rebukes to the immature. Both address the unfortunate need to restrict the hearers to the consumption of milk and not meat or solid food. Hebrews 5:12c reads: "You need milk not solid food," and 5:13 makes clear that the one fed milk is a child. And then 5:14 states: "But solid food is for the mature, for those who have their faculties trained (τὰ αἰσθητήρια γεγυμνασμένα) by practice to distinguish good from evil." It is important to note, since Irenaeus interprets the Corinthian poverty as the absence of the Spirit of the Father, that a few verses later in Hebrews 6:4, "partakers of the Holy Spirit" are mentioned.

Apparently, Irenaeus only borrows the specific language concerning "faculties" and "(un)trained" from Hebrews. However, his mind has joined the two passages together because of the commonality of language and topics shared by 1 Cor. 3:2 and Heb. 5:14. Whereas he cites 1 Corinthians, the presence of terminology from Hebrews indicates that he is thinking of both texts. They form a cento that informs his concept of humanity's immaturity. This concept, of course, is contrasted to the perfection and absence of deficiency in the creator. Rousseau, we might note, in his notes to the critical edition, also sees the allusion to Heb. 5:14. Because of the presence of its language and the parallel contexts and topics, he believes that it is "certain" that the bishop is alluding to the Epistle.[69]

Hebrews 8:5: Typologies and Economies

Now, as we move from chapter five of Hebrews to the eighth chapter, we find material that is attractive to Irenaeus as he expresses the hermeneutical framework for his understanding of the relationship between the two economies, between prophecy and fulfillment, between Law and grace, the earthly and the heavenly. Specifically, his eyes are fixed on Heb. 8:5. In the context we find that the author is discussing the true high priest of the order of Melchizedek and the true sanctuary, the true tent erected not by humans but by the Lord. Earthly priests ("now if he were on earth [γῆς]") and the earthly sanctuary of the old covenant, which was not faultless as the new covenant is, the epistle says are to be distinguished from the true ones. The earthly things, Hebrews 8:5 records, "serve as a copy and shadow [σκιᾷ] of the heavenly [ἐπουρανίων] sanctuary; for when Moses was about to erect the tent, he was instructed by God, saying 'See that you make everything according to the pattern [τύπον] that was shown you on the mountain'" (Ex. 25:40).

We read of Irenaeus describing perhaps the Jews as those who deny that the prophets announced the one and the same Jesus Christ and who deny that the Son taught the same Father proclaimed by the prophets. In his mind they are "scoffers," "those not subject to God" and those who "follow outward purifications for the praise of men."[70] To these he goes on to say, God has "assigned everlasting perdition." But he develops more fully what he considers to be their false worship. The "outward purifications" they follow he describes as "observances" that "had been given as a type of future things" ("things to come," τῶν μελλόντων). "The law," he says, and here he makes recourse to Hebrews 8:5, was "describing and outlining [σκιαγραφήσαντος] eternal things by the temporal and the heavenly by the earthly [*terrenis caelestia*; τῶν ἐπιγείων τὰ οὐράνια]."[71] One can also hear here the language of Heb. 10:1, which speaks of the law as "a shadow of the good things to come" (σκιὰν . . . τῶν μελλόντων).

In the bishop's understanding, there are those who do not recognize the connection between the prophets, Jesus Christ, and the Father. They remain tied to "the Old Testament dispensation" without believing in the "greater gift of grace" or "a fuller [measure of] grace and greater gifts" brought by Jesus in his advent. They have not moved in their worship beyond the outlines, the shadow, the temporal, the earthly.[72] Origen, in Alexandria, of course, spoke of the "Jewish cultus" as the "image and shadow of heavenly things" on the basis of Hebrews 8:5.[73] Here, we already find a similar construction present in Lyons in the second century.

We see the same connection at least two more times in *Adversus haereses*. In *Haer.* IV.14.3, he cites Exod. 25:40, which also appears in Heb. 8:5, and 1 Cor. 10:4, 11. But it appears that he is thinking of Hebrews over Exodus or at least in addition to it. Again, the language of the earthly and heavenly, present in Heb. 8:4-5, occurs in his argument. Irenaeus says that God in the old economy was "calling" the people of that economy "by secondary things to primary ones, that is, by the figurative to the true, by the temporal to the eternal, by the carnal to the spiritual, by *the earthly to the celestial*" (*terrena ad caelestia*; ἐπιγείων εἰς τὰ οὐράνια).[74] As in *Haer.* IV.11.3-4, the language of the "greater," "fuller" new economy is here as well with the contrast between "secondary" and "primary," and this language echoes the terminology of Hebrews 8, that of a "more excellent" ministry, a "better" covenant, "better promises", and a "new covenant" versus one that was not "faultless" and that was "obsolete" (Heb. 8:6-8, 13). In the same way in which we have already seen the bishop join Heb. 5:14 with 1 Corinthians 3:2 in a cento, where the Corinthian text is cited and the Hebrew text is present in allusion, we see here the linking of an allusion to Hebrews 8:5 with the citation of other passages from 1 Corinthians (10:4, 11).

Another allusion to the same context of Hebrews 8:5 appears in one of Irenaeus's rebukes concerning inappropriate hermeneutical practices. In *Haer.* IV.19.1, he acknowledges that the Old Covenant modes of worship were received "in a figure as was shown to Moses." And he states that it was appropriate that "earthly things" (ἐπίγεια; *terrena*) should be types of "heavenly things" (τῶν ἐπουρανίων; *caelestia).*[75] But he scolds the person and has in mind his opponents, who might incorrectly imagine that the "heavenly and spiritual things" are in themselves types of a "Pleroma" or another Father.[76] The typology has an end. This is his point again in *Haer.* V.35.2 where he again refers to Exodus 25:40/Hebrews 8:5. Here, in the midst of his argument for a literal new, eschatological resurrection, kingdom, Jerusalem, and earth, he insists that such things are not to be "understood in reference to super-celestial matters," for none of these literal elements of his eschatological hope "is capable of being allegorized."

In the immediate context, a host of texts occur in support of his literal hermeneutic. Revelation 20:11-15; Matt. 25:4; Rev. 21:1-4; Isa. 65:17, 18; 1 Cor. 7:31; Matt. 26:35

all solidify his position in his mind. They place a limit on the manner in which the typology taught in Exod. 25:40/Heb. 8:5 may be understood. For Irenaeus, Hebrews 8:5 provides a way to comprehend the differences in economies, dispensations, and covenants. It informs a paradigm for understanding the differences between old, new, and eschatological. But it must be read in linkage to other biblical passages that complement it and that place limitations of catholicity on the typology it presents.

Hebrews 11: Faith, Promise, and Resurrection

We find also in *Adversus haereses* the bishop probably alluding to other material from Hebrews that now we shall mention only briefly. He may have Heb. 11:4 (and Matt. 23:35) in mind as he discusses the sin of Cain and speaks of Able as just (*iustus*; δίκαιος).[77] Hebrews 11:5-7, Wis. 4:10, and Sir. 44:16 might inform his discussion of Enoch and Noah and those faithful ones "before Abraham," as our Bishop says. They pleased (*placens*; εὐαρεστήσας) God by faith and demonstrated salvation without circumcision or the Law of Moses.[78] Furthermore, he may, as A. Orbe suggests, have his eye on these same texts as he reads Genesis 5:24 and discusses the surety of bodily resurrection demonstrated when God bodily translated (*translatus*; μετετέθη) Enoch.[79] Both Hebrews and Wisdom of Solomon could have inspired his reading of Enoch. We might speculate, then, that this gives us a clue as to how we are to understand Eusebius's statement about Irenaeus's extensive citation of these two books in that work no longer extant.[80] Could it be that in that work, Irenaeus treated, at length, portions of Hebrews (at least elements of the eleventh chapter) and linked them interpretively to Wisdom (at least chapter 4)?[81] Maybe this book was a theological treatise largely supported by centos composed of material from Hebrews and Wisdom.[82]

Irenaeus's treatment of Hebrews 11 is not exhausted in what he does with verses 4-7, and *Haer*. V.32.1-2 figures prominently.[83] Hebrews 11:8-9, 10, 13 (along with Heb. 4:1; 6:12; 10:36) seem to be behind his discussions of Abraham. Irenaeus presents him as a stranger and pilgrim (*peregrinor*; *peregrinatio*; *peregrinus et advena*; ξένος; πάροικος καὶ παρεπίδημος) in this world, who lived by faith. However, the patriarch did not receive the inheritance (*hereditas*; κληρονομίαν) of the land (*terra*; γῆν), promised (*promitto*; ἐπαγγέλλομαι) by God. Instead, Irenaeus makes clear, what God promised would only be received (*recipio*; ἀπολαμβάνω [Heb. 11:39 has: κομίζω]) at the resurrection. He used Abraham in this way to argue for the one God, the prefiguration of both covenants in that one patriarch and the blessed hope of resurrection. Furthermore, the language of Hebrews 11:19 makes a probable appearance as well. It speaks of the patriarch's faith in God as the one who can raise humanity from the dead (ἐκ νεκρῶν ἐγείρειν). When Irenaeus writes of him (God) who raises (*suscito*; ἐγείροντος) mortal flesh from the dead (*a mortuis*; ἐκ νεκρῶν), he uses the terminology of Hebrews.[84]

Other Occurrences of Hebrews in *Adversus haereses*

Finally, we glance at two appearances of Hebrews in book three. First, at the beginning of his third book we hear what appears to be a whisper of Heb. 3:14. As he concludes the first chapter of book three, where he insists that the evangelists transmitted the teaching of "one only God, Creator of heaven and earth" and of "one only Christ, the

Son of God," he employs a unique term to describe the church's evangelists who endure in the catholic faith. In Heb. 3:14, the author of the letter refers to those who hold their "first confidence firm to the end" as those who "share [μέτοχοι] in Christ." Now in *Adversus haereses* III.1.2, he says that those who disagree with the truths of one God and one Son of God, that is, in his mind, the Valentinians, despise "those who share [*participes*; μετόχους] in the Lord."[85] For the bishop of Lyons, it seems that it is those who have written the Gospel in four versions who remained firm and who are those who share in Christ. To despise their teaching is to despise Christ and the Father and to render one condemned. The evangelists "share" in Christ because they have been given the power of the Gospel.[86] It is they who transmit the truth and of whom the Lord spoke in Luke 10:16: "He who hears you hears me, and he who rejects you rejects me, and he who rejects me rejects him who sent me."[87] The evangelists share in the Lord in the sense that, however the heretics respond to their teaching, that is the same way they respond to the Son and the Father. Here then, it appears, is Irenaeus's reading of Heb. 3:14 in connection to Luke 10:16.

Second, we have what seems to be a reference to Heb. 13:12 in one place where Irenaeus speaks of Christ's death.[88] Heb. 13:12, in speaking of the suffering of Jesus, declares that it took place outside the gate. The purpose of this suffering was "to sanctify [ἁγιάζω] the people [λαός] through his own blood [διὰ τοῦ ἰδίου αἵματος]." Irenaeus describes Jesus Christ as redeeming the church from apostasy by his own blood (*sanguine suo*; τῷ αἵματι αὐτοῦ) so that it might be a sanctified (*sanctifico*; ἁγιάζω) people (*populus*; λαός).

Conclusion

At this point, I think, we have provided sufficient warrant for our claim. Hebrews, though Irenaeus scarcely cites it in *Adversus haereses*, is present in allusion in significant ways. It informs important, paradigmatic theological theses in Irenaeus's response to his opponents.

It is important to note that in this argument for the use of Hebrews in Irenaeus, most evidence has not come from the presence of explicit citations. However, although he does not cite remarkable portions of Hebrews, he unobtrusively inserts its language, argument, and conceptions. He has appropriated the text's language and ideas and made them his own through memory, association, and argument. It flows from his pen as if it were his own creation. Allusions, rather than signifying an absence of citation, and therefore a minimal role for a text, actually signify the opposite. Scripture has become such a part of thought and life through memory and rumination that it shows itself without pomp. But this is what we would expect from a culture in which both orality and the written word function centrally. Jan Vansina said it best:

> As opposed to all other sources, oral tradition consists of information existing in memory. It is in memory most of the time, and only now and then are those parts recalled which the needs of the moment require. This information forms a vast pool, one that encompasses the whole inherited culture—*for culture is what is in the mind.*[89]

Allusions, rather than indicating the incidental function of scripture, indicate its normative place. But they witness to something else as well. Allusions are selected from a pool, and selection is interpretation that "occurs mainly for social reasons."[90] These social, or cultural profiles "correspond to the *present* view of reality and of the world."[91] Therefore, allusions reflect what a culture currently believes to be paramount. Allusions are windows into prominent communal values. They are also windows into the whole pool of tradition for "even the smallest word or phrase . . . refers in some degree to the whole and to the authority that the whole commands."[92]

Irenaeus's use of Hebrews demonstrates, then, the presence of a text, the language and ideology of which has seeped selectively and quietly into his polemic. Its presence is not, apparently, as easily recognized as it was to Eusebius in the collection of Irenaeus's writings with which he was familiar but which are no longer available to us. But present, in *Adversus haereses*, it seems to be, nevertheless. Its presence, perhaps, is not more obvious because Irenaeus rejected its Pauline authorship and therefore, in polemic against the Gnostics and Marcionites, he feels the need to be subtle. This seems also to hold true for Tertullian, who believed that Barnabas wrote Hebrews and in *On Modesty* (20.2) cites Heb. 6:4-8, but who, in *Adv. Marc.*, does not provide a defense for the apostolicity of Hebrews, although he defends all of Paul's epistles.[93] He never cites nor appears to allude to Hebrews in *Adversus Valentinianos* and never cites the Letter in his *Adversus Marcionem*, although there appear to be recognizable allusions to at least Heb. 1:14 and 4:12.[94] Tertullian appears to use it in a subtle way, typical of Irenaeus, perhaps because Marcion did not recognize Hebrews as apostolic.[95] In anti-Valentinian and anti-Marcionite polemic, catholic authors do not seem to make obvious use of Hebrews. But it does inform Tertullian and Irenaeus in their polemics.

Suffice it now to conclude that although perhaps in a different manner than Eusebius knew it, *Adversus haereses* also provides evidence of the important place of Hebrews in the theological work of the bishop of Lyons. Perhaps hesitant to explicitly cite it in this polemical work, because of his argument's tie to the apostolic tradition, he, regardless, has its language and ideology in his mind. It informs his concept of Catholicity and his response to those who think it appropriate to depart from it.

CHAPTER SIX

Irenaeus's Contribution to Early Christian Interpretation of the Song of Songs

Karl Shuve

The title of this chapter may strike the reader as odd, for Irenaeus neither cited nor alluded to the Song of Songs—at least as far as our extant evidence goes. What I hope to demonstrate, however, is that the bishop of Lyons had an important role to play in establishing the contextual framework according to which the Song would be interpreted by subsequent Christian exegetes. In so doing, I am contesting a trend in contemporary scholarship that attributes the rise in early Christian interest in the Song, which began in the early third century, to a growing ascetic impulse that sought to erase, through various interpretive strategies, the literal force of Old Testament nuptial texts.[1]

The Rise of Song Interpretation

Through the first two centuries of the Common Era, the Song of Songs was not cited by any Christian authors. It is virtually alone among the biblical books in this regard. Beginning with a citation of a single verse (Song 4:8) in Tertullian's *Adversus Marcionem* (IV.11.8), the landscape begins to change as we approach the third century. Hippolytus is the first to write a commentary on the Song of Songs, although this survives complete only in two Georgian manuscripts, which are based upon an Armenian translation of the original Greek.[2] It is Origen, however, who, as he so often does, defines the terms according to which the Song will be read for centuries. He penned no fewer than three works on the subject—a lost commentary from his youth, and a commentary and two homilies dating to his time in Athens and Caesarea[3]—in each instance reading the Song as a dramatic enactment of the desirous longing of the corporate church and individual soul for the saving union with the Word of God.[4] Victorinus of Poetovio is the only other third-century writer to compose a commentary on the Song,[5] but he is followed in the fourth and fifth centuries by Gregory of Nyssa, Nilus of Ancyra, Theodoret of Cyrrhus, Gregory of Elvira, and Apponius.[6]

How can this increase in the prominence of the Song in early Christian discourse be explained? Much of the attention has, unsurprisingly, focused on Origen. And, again unsurprisingly, much of it has been critical and tinged with cynicism.[7] Indeed, remarking on the subject of Origen and sex requires little nuance or deftness of touch. What else, other than an allegorical reading, would we expect from a man who, according to Eusebius, castrated himself in a youthful fit of piety?[8] As Stephen Moore has argued, "the Song simply could not be what it seemed to be. That would have been unthinkable. . . .The allegorical interpretations of the Song sprang from disinclination, discomfort, or downright disgust on the part of pious male exegetes."[9] The growing ascetic majority, so the argument goes, constructed a reading of the Song meant to undermine—rather than uphold—the goodness of marriage and sexual union.

Origen—and, by extension, the tradition—has had his share of defenders. Most recently, J. Christopher King has mounted an elaborate theological defense, focusing upon Origen's nuptial theology[10] and his hermeneutic of the "bodiless" text.[11] He proposes that Origen maintains a "symbolic coherence" between earthly union and its "corresponding spiritual reality."[12] But lacking in King is any sort of *historical* defense of allegorical exegesis of the Song.[13] That is, to what extent did allegorical readings arise out of the matrix of first- and second-century Christian thought? What images might have been conjured in the minds of early Christian readers (and hearers) by the story of a courtship between a young king and his bride-to-be?

I argue that the early Christian allegorization of the Song is best understood as emerging, quite organically, from a nuptial theological trajectory that affirms, rather than denies, the value of the body and sexuality. I rely on David Dawson's observation that the "plain" sense of a given text is not an objectively available level of meaning but is rather a construct conditioned by the cultural expectations of the community in which it is read, to argue that spiritual readings of the Song reflect a deeply engrained understanding of the theological significance of nuptial imagery and not a fear of the erotic.[14]

In this account, Irenaeus can be said to make a significant contribution to the patristic tradition of Song exegesis, even though he never cited the text and wrote his *Adversus haereses* decades before the first commentaries were composed. From as early as the deutero-Pauline epistle to the Ephesians (5:22-31), the union of Christ and the church has been explained on analogy with the union of man and woman in marriage. But it is not until Irenaeus, as we shall see, that the analogy of human marriage plays a significant role in ecclesiological and soteriological discourse. Irenaeus, moreover, is the first to provide a typological pattern according to which Old Testament nuptial texts are read as a prophetic witness to Christ's redemptive act toward a sinful people. He does this not to repress or downplay the corporeal dimension of marriage, but quite the opposite, to argue for the essential goodness of embodied existence against an anti-material spirituality. We shall begin by examining the use of nuptial imagery in the Apostolic Fathers and Justin Martyr, before turning to Irenaeus.

The Apostolic Fathers and Justin Martyr

We have only one rather elusive example in the Apostolic Fathers of nuptial theology, in the pseudonymous *2 Clement*.[15] This homily blends, rather awkwardly, two key (deutero-)Pauline images—the church as the body of Christ and the male-female union as sign of the union of Christ and the church: "I do not suppose that you are ignorant that the living Church is the body of Christ [ὅτι ἐκκλήσια ζῶσα σῶμά ἐστιν Χριστοῦ], for the Scripture says, 'God created man male and female [ἐποίησεν ὁ θεὸς τὸν ἄνθρωπον ἄρσεν καὶ θηλῦ] (cf. Gen. 1:27).' The male is Christ; the female is the Church."[16] The final line echoes the allegorical proclamation of Ephesians 5:32, although put far more discretely and with Genesis 1:27 as the base text rather than Genesis 2:24, which explicitly speaks of the joining together of the man and woman. The preacher attempts to resolve the tension between these two images by associating the female with the flesh, which is Christ's body—"showing us that if any of us guard her in the flesh and do not corrupt her [ἐὰν τις ἡμῶν τηρήσῃ αὐτὴν ἐν τῇ σαρκὶ καὶ μὴ φθείρῃ], he will receive her back again in the Holy Spirit."[17] The payoff of this ecclesiological excursus is an appeal for the restraint of the desires of the body, as Paul Parvis has recently argued,[18] rather than the glorification of the properly ordered marriage as a signifier for the union of Christ and church, which is the case in Ephesians 5:21-32. This passage is not unimportant, though, for it attests the growing matrix of Old Testament nuptial texts that come to be employed in ecclesiological discourse.

One could perhaps also point to the enigmatic *Shepherd of Hermas* as relevant to the present discussion. At the start of the text, Hermas, after being accused by his former mistress before the heavenly court, encounters "an old woman, in a great shining garment, holding a book in her hands."[19] Mistaking her for the Sibyl, Hermas is visited by another heavenly agent, who informs him that this woman was in fact the church, "created first of all things [πάντων πρώτη ἐκτίσθη]."[20] This text demonstrates that in the early second century the church could be personified as a woman, but it is notable that any strictly nuptial or erotic dimension is lacking, even though as the visions progress the woman becomes more comely and beautiful.

Justin Martyr shies away from employing nuptial imagery when speaking of the church, although he is the first Christian, after the author of the epistle to the Hebrews (cf. 1:8-9), to cite Psalm (LXX) 44, the royal/messianic wedding song. He does this six times in the *Dialogue with Trypho*,[21] and in each instance he offers a christological reading (38.3-5; 56.14; 63.4; 76.7; 86.3; 126.1). This Psalm has an obvious appeal to Justin, for the quite straightforward reason that its protagonist is referred to as Χριστός and θεός (44:7). Justin invokes this Psalm when chastising Trypho at the end of the *Dialogue* for being ignorant of the one whom David calls "Christ and the God who is to be adored [Χριστὸς καὶ θεὸς προσκυνητός]."[22] In only one instance does he give an ecclesiological reading of this Psalm, and notably he identifies the church with the daughter and not the queen: "The Word of God speaks to those who believe in him . . . as to a daughter [ὡς θυγατρί]—to the Church established by and sharing in his name" (63.4).[23] The king's desire (ἐπιθυμέω) for the beauty of the daughter receives no comment. Although Justin cannot himself be said to articulate any kind of nuptial theology, the christological interpretation of Psalm 44, which he advances in a number of instances throughout the *Dialogue*, sets an important pattern for the interpretation of marriages in the Old Testament.

Irenaeus and Nuptial Theology

It is, however, only with Irenaeus that we can begin to speak of an ecclesiology and soteriology that takes into account the analogy of the union of man and woman in marriage. This nuptial theology is developed primarily through the exposition of certain key Old Testament texts (Num. 12:10-14; Hos. 1; Is. 54:1, 63:9). In the *Adversus haereses*, Irenaeus plays on the theme of the church as sinful bride who is sanctified by her husband (IV.20.12). In the *Demonstration of the Apostolic Preaching*, he develops the image of the church as the once-sterile but now-fecund mother delivering children for Christ (94).

Admittedly, Irenaeus does not frequently resort to nuptial imagery. In the *Adversus haereses*, we find only a handful of uses of "bridegroom" or "bride," νυμφίος/*sponsus* or or νύμφη/*sponsa*/*uxor*, in a theological or cosmological context. These can be further sub-divided into two categories: those that occur in his descriptions of the "Gnostic" systems (e.g., I.7.1, 5; I.8.4; I.9.1; I.11.5; I.13.3; I.30.12) and those that occur in his attempts to construct an orthodox Christian response to these Gnostic claims (e.g., II.27.2; IV.20.12; V.9.4; V.35.2). The obvious problem for Irenaeus in his exposition of a nuptial theology is that the "heretics," on his account, also use such language to depict the redemption of the cosmos and the salvation of the elect. Indeed, this may well account for Justin's hesitancy in using such imagery. According to the Valentinians, for example, when Achamoth ends her exile in the intermediate realm, she espouses the Saviour and transforms the Pleroma into a "nuptial chamber" (*nymphonem*), into which the "spiritual seed" (*spiritales*), who have "taken off their souls" [*exspoliatos animas*] and become "intelligent spirits" (*spiritus intellectuales*), may now enter.[24] Nuptial imagery here points to the future dissolution of the material realm, to which the soul is considered to belong, and the full initiation of those who have taken off entirely their created nature into the mysteries of the cosmos. It is particularly problematic for Irenaeus that the Valentinians justify these claims by reference to Paul: "And they say that Paul speaks about the consorts within the Pleroma [*coniugationes quae sunt intra Pleroma*] showing them in one. For concerning union in this life [*de ea enim coniugatione quae est secundum hanc vitam*] he says, writing, 'This is a great mystery, but I speak about Christ and the Church.'"[25] This is the only instance in the *Adversus haereses* where any portion of Ephesians 5:21-32 is cited, and it is interesting that Irenaeus does not attempt to contrast an ecclesiological reading of the text with the cosmological reading he imputes to the Valentinians. Neither is there a citation of this text in the *Demonstration*.

Indeed, Irenaeus never explicitly attempts to contrast his own nuptial theology with these competing "heretical" accounts. But when he employs nuptial imagery in a theological context, it is to express a positive valuation of the created world and to demonstrate the continuity between the gospel of Christ and the revelation of the Creator. Even though marital union points toward, and almost becomes absorbed in, a spiritual reality, its use in anti-heretical polemic ensures that it remains firmly embedded in a body-affirming discourse. This is a point often lost on commentators keen to see repression as the primary motivating factor in allegorical readings of marriage in the Hebrew Bible.

There are two main passages in the *Adversus haereses* where Irenaeus uses nuptial imagery to speak of the church and the redemption of humanity. We shall begin with the less extensive and more elliptical account in V.9.4. Irenaeus's aim in this passage is to argue against the assertion that the Pauline phrase "flesh and blood are not able to inherit the kingdom of God (1 Cor. 15:50)" means that the "creation of God is not saved [*non salvari plasmationem Dei*]."[26] Irenaeus proceeds to articulate an anthropology that contrasts flesh and spirit, placing the soul as intermediary between the two. The soul, he admits, that panders to the lust of the flesh is drawn down into baseness and cannot be saved. But the soul that participates in the Spirit has "the infirmity of the flesh absorbed by the strength of the Spirit, and such a one is not carnal, but spiritual, on account of communion with the Spirit [*absorbeatur infirmitas carnis a fortitudine Spiritus, et esse eum qui sit talis non iam carnalem, sed spiritalem, propter Spiritus communionem*]."[27] Not content to let the argument rest, however, Irenaeus proceeds to offer a linguistic argument, based upon the use of the active voice in the Pauline text: "For if it is necessary to speak precisely, the flesh does not inherit, but is inherited [*non possidet sed possidetur caro*]."[28] Irenaeus says that the Spirit delights in the temple—a periphrasis for the flesh—in the same way as a bridegroom does his bride. The bride does not wed, she *is* wed; the flesh does not inherit the kingdom, it is in fact taken into the kingdom *for* an inheritance (V.9.4). The analogy of marital union is here secondary, employed in the service of both anthropology and soteriology.

The far more lengthy and developed exposition comes in IV.20.12, and it is here that Irenaeus's contribution is most significant. This particular passage is situated in the context of an exhaustive attempt to demonstrate that the same prophets who revealed knowledge of the Creator God also disclosed the future redemption of humanity through Christ (IV.20.1ff). Having listed numerous prophetic visions of the coming of Christ, Irenaeus turns to the prophetic foreshadowing of Christ's coming "in works that were undertaken by the prophets [*in operationibus usus est prophetis*]."[29] The first two *operationes*/ἔργα that Irenaeus cites are Hosea's marriage to the prostitute and Moses' union with the Ethiopian woman. In both instances, the men serve as types of Christ and the women, outsiders of ill-repute, signify the Gentiles.

In the case of Hosea and the prostitute, Irenaeus emphasizes that it is her *communicatio*/κοινωνία with the prophet that sanctifies her and that her redemption acts as a sign of the salvation of the Gentiles in Christ: "God was pleased to receive the church that had been sanctified by union [*communicatione*] with His son, just as she had been sanctified by union [*communicatione*] with the prophet."[30] We see Irenaeus here making a clever play on words. Κοινωνία almost certainly the Greek word behind *communicatio*, has the general meaning of union, fellowship, or association, but it can carry both the more specific meanings of marriage to someone (cf. Aristotle, *Pol.* 1334b) and, in Christian writing from the New Testament, of the believer's participation in Christ (cf. 1 Cor. 1:9), which Irenaeus here juxtaposes. We no longer, as in Justin, have a simple identification of the bridegroom with Christ but a more robust ecclesiological and soteriological reading that reflects upon the dynamics of the marriage itself. Irenaeus, moreover, does not allow the corporeal dimension of Hosea's marriage to be swallowed up entirely in a typological reading of the story; rather, he claims that the soteriological dynamics that underlie the account continue to be played out anywhere faithful men marry faithless women, concluding, "And on account of this Paul says that the faithless wife [*infidelem mulierem*] is sanctified by her faithful husband [*viro fideli*]."[31] Thus his nuptial theology does not only provide a framework for interpreting texts, but social structures more broadly.

A similar logic informs his typological reading of the marriage of Moses to the Ethiopian woman in Num. 12:10-14. Irenaeus emphasizes that in taking her as a wife (*accipiebat uxorem*) and making her an Israelite (*quam ipse Israelitidem fecit*), Moses foreshows (*praesignificans*) the grafting of the "wild olive tree" into the "culti-vated one,"[32] that is, the incorporation of the Gentiles into the elect nation of Israel. Being more explicit, he says, "Through the marriage of Moses the marriage of the Logos was revealed [*ostendebantur*] and through the Ethiopian bride the Church from among the Gentiles became manifest [*manifestabatur*]."[33] Human marriage once again becomes a profound symbol of redemption and communion with the divine. The story of Moses and the Ethiopian is, however, quite different in that it is not presented in the biblical text as a prophetic enactment of God's redemptive union with his people. It is only on analogy with the story of Hosea that such an ecclesiological reading is given. Irenaeus establishes Hosea as the lens, as it were, through which other Old Testament narratives of marriage and courtship are to be read. The next time we encounter an interpretation of Moses' marriage to the Ethio-pian woman—nearly half a century later in Origen's *Homilies on Numbers* and *Homi-lies and Commentary on the Song of Songs*—the need for any such explicitly stated analogy has dropped out. The hermeneutical principle is assumed: human marriage signifies God's redemptive act toward his people.

We find a rather different take on the nuptial theme in the *Demonstration*. Once again, the relevant passage comes in the context of a lengthy list of typological readings of the prophets pertaining to the salvation of the Gentiles (86ff.). The incarnation of the Word, says Irenaeus, marked a turning point for the Gentiles, who at that moment experience a "change of hearts [*mutatio cordium*]."[34] Irenaeus then juxtaposes the ste-rility of the church—a term that he uses interchangeably with Gentiles—before the incarnation with its fecundity afterward: "Isaiah demonstrated saying, 'Rejoice, barren one, who did not bear children'—the barren one is the Church, who never in earlier times presented sons to God—'Cry out and shout, you who did not labour, since the many sons of the desolate one are more than she who had a husband (Isa. 54:1).'"[35] He also juxtaposes the spouse of the church, who is Christ, with the spouse of the "first assembly [*prima synagoga*],"[36] which is the Law. Specifically of importance is Irenaeus's emphasis that the church consorts with Christ directly, rather than by the mediation of the prophets: "For it was neither Moses the legate nor Elijah the messenger, but the Lord himself who has saved us." This becomes a stock theme in exegesis of Song of Songs 1:1 from Origen onward.[37]

Irenaeus and Origen

Irenaeus, as I have attempted to demonstrate, is the first "orthodox" Christian writer to make any sustained use of the nuptial analogy in expressing his ecclesiology and soteriology. In so doing, he opened the door, if only partially, to the possibility that an enigmatic poem about a desiring bride and a virile bridegroom might have theological significance for the Christian community. But, it is possible to speak more concretely than this. Irenaeus's direct contribution to the early Christian tradition of Song exegesis was to provide a typological pattern according to which Old Testament narratives of marriage and courtship were to be read. And, far from being an attempt to repress the corporeal, sexual, and social dimensions of marriage, Irenaeus develops this typological pattern to uphold the essential goodness of embodied existence. Just as Hosea's *historical* marriage to the prostitute constituted a prophetic witness to God's redemptive act toward a sinful people, so too did Moses' *historical* marriage to the Ethiopian signify his inclusion of an excluded people.

This typological pattern of marriage as a prophetic witness provides the key to a more sympathetic—and, I would argue, historically attuned—reading of Origen's massively influential *Homilies* and *Commentary on the Song of Songs*. For the moment, however, probing the one direct link between the *Adversus haereses* and the *Commentary on the Song of Songs* will suffice—the typological reading of Moses' marriage to the Ethiopian woman in Numbers 12. Since Origen provides his fullest exposition of the passage in the *Commentary*, that will be the locus of our analysis. At the start of Book Two, Origen offers an interpretation of Song 1:5, "I am black but beautiful," words attributed to the Bride. His remarks sit uneasily with a twenty-first century audience. She is a Gentile, and her blackness, taken to mean ugliness, stems from her ignorance of "the teaching of the patriarchs."[38] Her beauty is juxtaposed with this blackness, coming through faith in Christ, which restores the original imprint of the divine image. For Origen, however, this verse is not fully intelligible apart from the other Old Testament texts that "foreshadow" this mystery. He expounds at length four passages: Numbers 12, 2 Kings 10, Psalm 67, and Jeremiah 37. At the head of this list, notably, is the story of Moses' marriage to the Ethiopian, which Origen begins: "Therefore, in Numbers we find Moses taking [*accipere*] an Ethiopian wife, who is *dark* and *black* [*fuscam videlicet vel nigram*]."[39] Origen, in his erudition, goes on at much greater length than Irenaeus, discoursing about Aaron and Mary's jealousy and the favor shown to Moses after the marriage; he writes, "Mary, who is a type [*formam*] of the abandoned synagogue [*synagogae derelictae*] and Aaron, who is the image [*tenebat imaginem*] of the priesthood according to the flesh [*sacerdotii carnalis*], seeing their kingdom taken away from them and given to a people [*genti*] bearing its fruits [cf. Matt. 21:43], say: *Has God spoken to Moses alone? Has he not also spoken to us* [Num. 12:2]?"[40] But, in its essentials, the Irenaean reading is preserved: "It seems to me that they [i.e., Mary and Aaron] understood the thing Moses had done more as a mystery [*secundum mysterium*], and they saw Moses—that is, the spiritual Law [*spiritalis Lex*]—entering into marriage and union [*in nuptias et coniugium*] with the Church that is gathered together from among the Gentiles."[41] Moses' historical marriage to the Ethiopian has prophetic significance regarding the inclusion of the Gentiles into the people of God, which Aaron and Mary are able immediately to identify. The marriage of the black and beautiful bride of the Song to Christ, it is true, has no "historical" dimension—the union of Christ the bridegroom and the church the bride is immediately transparent to the literal sense. But to have any genuine meaning, Origen must relate it to actual flesh-and-blood unions, which, in their corporeality point to spiritual reality.

My aim in this paper is a modest one. I do not wish to conflate Irenaeus's and Origen's attitudes toward embodied existence, nor am I arguing that Irenaeus exercised a decisive influence over Origen's exegesis. I have, however, hoped to demonstrate that the distance between these two important early Christian theologians is not, perhaps, as wide as is often thought, and that as much as Origen was a brilliant innovator in his biblical interpretation, his debts to his predecessors—here, Irenaeus—are patent. Moreover, I trust that I have shown that Irenaeus had an important role to play in building the foundation onto which the edifice of the patristic exegesis of the Song of Songs would rest.

CHAPTER SEVEN

The Man with No Name

Who Is the Elder in Irenaeus's Adversus haereses IV?

SEBASTIAN MOLL

In *Adversus haereses* IV.27-32, Irenaeus repeatedly refers to the teachings of a certain elder. Despite the fact that the teachings of this man seem to be of high importance to Irenaeus, he omits revealing his name. This omission on Irenaeus's part has given rise to much speculation regarding the identity of his source, starting as early as in the 1575 edition of Irenaeus's works by François Feuardent. For some time, however, the books on this issue appeared to be closed. Scholars started to content themselves with the anonymity of this elder as no satisfying solution could be found—until recently, when Charles Hill tried to demonstrate that this anonymous individual can be nobody else but Polycarp of Smyrna and thus renewed the debate.[1] The complexity of Hill's work makes it impossible to portray his thesis in full here, but there is one passage in his book that, from my perspective, sums up the key elements of his argument quite well:

> We must now observe that it is precisely in this letter to Florinus, on the sole sovereignty of God and against the notion of God being the creator of evil, a work written to refute some version of Marcionism, a work which parallels so closely the teaching of the elder in *Haer.* 4.27-32, that Irenaeus gives his well-known description of Polycarp. It is this letter in which Irenaeus claims to have heard Polycarp on many occasions and to have listened so attentively that he could still reproduce many of his teacher's actual words (*HE* 5.20.4)! Simply stated, in *Haer.* 4.27-32 Irenaeus recounts from memory the anti-Marcionite, oral teaching of a respected "presbyter, a disciple of apostles" (4.32.1), and in the letter to Florinus, a letter devoted to the very same aspects of Marcion's teaching, Irenaeus claims he could remember much of the oral teaching of Polycarp of Smyrna, whom he calls "that blessed and apostolic presbyter" (*HE* 5.20.7). I submit that it would be too great a coincidence if these two apostolic presbyters were not the same individual, namely, Polycarp of Smyrna.[2]

In this passage we can find the three elements that Polycarp and the elder in *Haer.* 4.27-32 have, according to Hill, in common, and which thus suggest the identity of the two:

1. Irenaeus was in close personal contact to them to the point that he can literally reproduce their teachings from memory;

2. their teaching is anti-Marcionite;

3. they are immediate disciples of the Apostles.

Hill's Theory Reconsidered

Let us now take a closer look at the validity of these arguments.

1. In the letter to Florinus, to which Hill refers, Irenaeus informs us about his relation to Polycarp:

> For, while I was yet a boy, I saw thee in Lower Asia with Polycarp, distinguishing thyself in the royal court, and endeavouring to gain his approbation. For I have a more vivid recollection of what occurred at that time than of recent events (inasmuch as the experiences of childhood, keeping pace with the growth of the soul, become incorporated with it); so that I can even describe the place where the blessed Polycarp used to sit and discourse—his going out, too, and his coming in—his general mode of life and personal appearance, together with the discourses which he delivered to the people; also how he would speak of his familiar intercourse with John, and with the rest of those who had seen the Lord; and how he would call their words to remembrance. Whatsoever things he had heard from them respecting the Lord, both with regard to His miracles and His teaching, Polycarp having thus received [information] from the eye-witnesses of the Word of life, would recount them all in harmony with the Scriptures. These things, through God's mercy which was upon me, I then listened to attentively, and treasured them up not on paper, but in my heart; and I am continually, by God's grace, revolving these things accurately in my mind. (*HE* V.20.5-7)[3]

As far as the elder in *Haer.* V.27-32 is concerned, Irenaeus is actually quoting from his teachings in the said passages, and there is no particular reason to doubt the authenticity of these statements. As for Polycarp, however, Irenaeus does not provide us with such proof of his mnemonic ability; in other words, in this case we have to rely simply on his (repeated) assertion that he is able to recollect Polycarp's teachings. In fact, it may be doubted whether this constant (self-) affirmation really helps the credibility of his claim. Several features seem to question it.[4] First of all, Irenaeus was very young when he met Polycarp. Both the "while I was yet a boy" (παῖς ἔτι ὤν) in the letter as well as the "in my early youth" (ἐν τῇ πρώτῃ ἡμῶν ἡλικίᾳ) in *Haer.* III.3.4 suggest a childlike age rather than that of a young man. We would have to postulate an enormous degree of comprehension for young Irenaeus, if we were to assume that he was not only able to understand the teachings of Polycarp in the first place, but also to keep them in his mind until he wrote *Adversus haereses*—about forty years later. It is in accordance with this observation that all the things Irenaeus actually reports about Polycarp in the letter to Florinus (or elsewhere) are nothing but very general information and do not reveal any personal remembrance of Polycarp's teachings on Irenaeus's part, much less provide a literal quote from them. All in all it must, therefore, be doubted whether Irenaeus's recollection of Polycarp's words was in fact as excellent as he claims and as excellent as it would have to be in order to identify him with the elder.

2. "I recognize thee as first-born of Satan!" This was Polycarp's reply to Marcion's wish for recognition—at least according to the testimony of Irenaeus.[5] Once again, however, this story does not bear the image of personal remembrance on Irenaeus's part; it has rather the character of an anecdote. While that does not necessarily mean that the meeting between Polycarp and Marcion never took place, we find ourselves— regarding the question of an anti-Marcionite stance within Polycarp's teaching—con- fronted with the same problem as before, the problem of Irenaeus not providing any literal remains of it. As far as the above mentioned letter to Florinus is concerned, the information that can be derived from its fragment is very limited.[6] Hill believes that the theme of this letter "On the Sole Sovereignty of God or That God is not the Author of Evils" identifies it as an anti-Marcionite writing, as Florinus held the opinion "that there were two Sovereignties or Gods, not one, and that one of them, the God of the OT Scriptures, was the author of evils."[7] However, this last piece of information, the identification of the author of evils and the Old Testament God, which would indeed sound very much like Marcionite doctrine, is not to be found in the fragment and thus constitutes an amendment by Hill. There can hardly be any doubt that Polycarp was opposed to Marcionite doctrine, but there is no textual evidence that would inform us about any particular anti-Marcionite writing or discourse.[8]

The teachings of the elder in *Haer.* IV.27-32, on the other hand, have been handed down literally and are considered by many scholars to be directed against Marcion.[9] That there is an anti-heretical motive in these chapters is beyond doubt; however, no heretic or heretical movement is mentioned by name. What is the content of this anti- heretical teaching? It is basically an apology for the Old Testament with the intention to demonstrate that the two Testaments speak of one and the same God. Certainly, this does sound like a treatise against Marcion, and there is no point in denying that these sections are directed against him, *too*.[10] However, defending the cruelties described in the Old Testament was not just an object for those fighting against Marcion. When Origen explains the allegorical meaning of the battles of Joshua, for instance, he explic- itly addresses Marcion, Valentinus, and Basilides.[11] Thus, these other heretics could also be envisaged in the elder's preaching. In fact, there are certain lines that seem to indicate a Valentinian opponent: "All those are found to be unlearned, audacious and also shameless who, because of the transgressions of those who lived in earlier times and because of the disobedience of a great number (of them), say that one God was the God of those, the maker of the world, originated from deficiency,[12] but that the other God was the Father declared by Christ, the one all of them [the heretics] have (alleg- edly) conceived in spirit" (*Haer.* IV.27.4).[13]

Three elements in this passage are both typical for (Irenaeus's portrait of) the Valentinians and atypical for the doctrine of Marcion. There is firstly the idea of the Demiurge originating from deficiency that correlates with the Valentinian myth that the origin of the Demiurge is the result of a fallen aeon,[14] whereas Marcion never expressed any such theory about his origin, nor did he establish a mythological system as such. The second element is the idea that the heretics (and only they) have received the second God in spirit. It is a crucial element of the Valentinian Gnosis that only a few chosen ones, the Pneumatics, have access to the complete knowledge (*Gnosis*) about God,[15] whereas Marcion does not preach any form of election of a certain group of people, nor that some higher form of knowledge is required to be saved. The most important feature, however, which suggests an opponent other than Marcion is the general theme of this passage, the critique of people who bring forth reproaches against Old Testament individuals, something Marcion never did. When we compare *Haer.* IV.27-32 with Tertullian's defense of the Old Testament in opposition to Marcion (mainly to be found in the second book of *Adversus Marcionem*), we find parallels for the story of the hardening of Pharaoh's heart[16] and of the Hebrews' robbery of gold and silver from the Egyptians,[17] but not for the rebukes against David, Solomon, or Lot and his daughters, to which the above quoted passage refers. The latter group consists of rebukes against the behavior of certain Old Testament individuals, the former presents accusations against the God of the Old Testament.[18] Concerning the stealing of the silver and golden vessels for instance, neither Irenaeus/the elder nor Tertullian report that their opponent would blame the Hebrews for stealing but instead that he blames their God for ordering them to do so. In fact, there is no passage in all the Fathers that would ever suggest that Marcion reproached any Old Testament figure for doing something bad, but always their God. It seems therefore that only chapters 28–30 of *Adversus haereses* IV (containing both the justification of the hardening of Pharaoh's heart and the robbery of the Egyptians) are directed against the arch-heretic. This view is confirmed by other elements found in these chapters. When the elder states that the heretics oppose the things Christ did for the salvation of those who received him to all the evil that was inflicted by the Old Testament God on those who disobeyed him,[19] not only does this sound very much like a Marcionite antithesis, but the Greek term ἀντιτιθέντας itself forms an "allusion transparente"[20] to Marcion's work.

In sum, if, in the case of Polycarp and the elder, we were dealing with two purely anti-Marcionite teachers with similar arguments, this may be considered in favor of the identity of the two. The mere fact, however, that they were both opposed to heresy in general is certainly not enough to substantiate this claim.

3. In early Christianity (and beyond), Polycarp of Smyrna is unanimously considered to be an immediate disciple of the apostle John. Regarding the "status" of the elder, however, there is an uncertainty as to whether the original Greek text spoke of an immediate witness of the apostles or of someone who had heard from those who had seen the apostles.[21] From a purely text-critical point of view, one may lean toward the immediate disciple. Still, the overall situation indicates a third generation witness. Irenaeus explicitly states that he heard the teachings he refers to from the elder himself, and it seems most unlikely that Irenaeus had personal contact with a man of the generation of the immediate disciples,[22] at least not in a way that would allow for him to recall his teachings so precisely (see above). This seems to be confirmed by the fact that in all the other passages in which Irenaeus refers to those elders who were disciples of the apostles,[23] he never claims to have had any personal contact with them.

All three alleged similarities between Polycarp of Smyrna and the elder in *Haer.* IV.27-32 have thus proven to be hints at best, which can by no means be considered as proof of their identity. Apart from all this, there is, of course, still the obvious objection against Hill's theory, the question why in the world Irenaeus would fail to mention Polycarp's name, given that a reference to this authority would so enormously strengthen his argument. Hill addresses this "conundrum" in his book,[24] and I would concede that if there was strong evidence for the identity of the elder and Polycarp, the mere fact that Irenaeus does not mention his name would not be strong enough to contest that identity. However, with no conclusive evidence in favor of their identity, the omission of Polycarp's name makes this hypothesis even less likely.

What's in a Name?

The wish to fill certain black holes within the history of Church, and thus the wish to identify anonymous characters within it, is more than understandable. Still, the mere wish must never be father to the thought. One methodological problem in these cases seems to be the (unfounded) premise that the person we attempt to identify must be someone we know from another context.[25] In fact, if this premise was valid, of all characters we know from this particular era, I would consider Polycarp to be the most likely candidate. As a result we could even, in a manner of speaking, say that the elder is either Polycarp or someone we simply do not know. I vote for the second option. Still, even if Irenaeus's source in *Haer.* IV.27-32 is not the bishop of Smyrna, it remains a very important source for our understanding of second-century heresy, given that the elder was in all probability a third-generation Christian, and thus a likely contemporary of men such as Marcion or Valentinus. Unless new evidence is found, however, he may remain forever the man without name.

CHAPTER EIGHT

The Man Who Needed No Introduction

A Response to Sebastian Moll

Charles E. Hill

Further attention to Irenaeus and the anonymous elder he quotes in *Against Heresies* IV.27-32 is much welcomed. The testimony jointly given by these two second-century figures reflects the earliest response to Marcion that we possess, and provides information about other related controversies of the day. The material is therefore worthy of renewed consideration and of any serious attempt at further refinement in our understanding of it. I am happy, then, for Sebastian Moll's contribution in this volume, for it advances the discussion on at least one point. He claims that part, at least, of the presbyter's polemics could not have been directed against Marcion, for the latter's attack on the God of the Jewish Scriptures did not ever include a denigration of any of the Old Testament figures like David or Solomon. The proposal merits further discussion.[1] The thrust of Moll's essay, however, is to argue against the identification of Irenaeus's presbyter and Polycarp. I am grateful to the editors for the opportunity to offer here a response, to supplement what I said in *Lost Teaching* and, I hope, to clarify why, despite Moll's objections, I am persuaded that the presbyter is indeed Polycarp.

Moll correctly identifies (though also simplifies) three common elements that I argued united the presbyter and Polycarp: Irenaeus had close personal contact with each and claims he can repeat from memory, or actually does repeat from memory, teachings they gave; each delivered anti-Marcionite teaching; each was an immediate disciples of apostles. Moll then lays out objections to each of these three common elements, and then adds a fourth objection which he thinks has no independent value but which supports the other three. I propose to say something about all four, but for practical and stylistic reasons, not in the same order. Objections two and three may be treated more briefly, the other two will require more space.

Strictly Anti-Marcion?

Moll's second objection is that neither the presbyter of *Haer.* IV.27-32 nor Polycarp (as described in the letter to Florinus, or elsewhere) can be shown to have opposed a purely Marcionite error and with similar arguments, but only heresy in general. Therefore they cannot be identified. But I do not see how it matters if indeed the presbyter is addressing a wider range of heretical ideas related to but not limited to the Marcionite system. This in fact is what I argued in *Lost Teaching* was actually the case.[2] We may disagree about the extent to which the presbyter's teaching as remembered and expounded by Irenaeus had reference to other teachers besides Marcion.[3] But even if only some of the presbyter's arguments are aimed directly against Marcion, these arguments do go to the heart of the issue that formed the theme of the letter to Florinus: *On the Sole Sovereignty (of God) or That God is not the Author of Evils.* This title could just as well serve as a title for the presbyter material in *Haer.* IV.27–32. And the case for the identity of Polycarp and the presbyter rests not only on the common anti-Marcionite character of their teaching. The argument, as it relates to the letter to Florinus, is that this letter and the section *Haer.* IV.27–32 share several characteristics that make it look like Polycarp and the presbyter are the same person, as one may see in Table 1.

Table 1. Similarities between the *Letter to Florinus and Haer. IV.27-32*

Letter to Florinus, On the Sole Sovereignty, or That God is not the Author of Evils (HE V.20.4-8)	*Against Heresies IV.27-32*
Written to deal with a (mainly) Marcionite problem.	Written to deal with a (mainly) Marcionite problem.
Apparent aim: to show that there is but one true God and to defend that God from charges that he is the author of evils.	Apparent aim: to show that there is but one true God and to defend that God from charges that he is himself immoral and the author of evils.
Emphasis on the importance of following the teaching of the church's presbyters.	Emphasis (cf. chs. 26, 32) on the importance of following the teaching of the church's presbyters.
Reference to the teaching of a particular presbyter, Polycarp, who had been taught by apostles.	Reference to the teaching of a particular presbyter, unnamed, who had been taught by apostles.
Irenaeus claims he can remember things Polycarp said he heard from apostles.	Irenaeus on one occasion repeats from memory something that the presbyter heard from apostles.
Irenaeus claims he can speak of the discourses Polycarp made to the crowds.	Irenaeus repeats from memory teaching the presbyter used to give in public.
Irenaeus calls Polycarp "the blessed and apostolic presbyter."	Irenaeus calls the presbyter "the presbyter, the disciple of apostles" (32.1).
Reference to Florinus faring illustriously "in the royal court."[4]	Reference to Christians "in the royal court."

Unlikely Apostolic Connections

In making his third objection, Moll seems to accept that the text of *Haer.* IV.27-32 denotes the presbyter's personal association with apostles.[5] He says, however, that the overall situation indicates instead that the elder belonged to the next generation and did not himself know any apostles (this would mean that the overall situation contradicts and trumps the text). What is it about the overall situation that indicates this? We are only told that it "seems most unlikely" that this elder would have been an immediate disciple of apostles. It is only unlikely if we first presume that the elder is not Polycarp, for Irenaeus has already told the reader (III.3.4) that Polycarp had learned from apostles. The only stated confirmation for this unlikelihood is "the fact that in all the other passages in which Irenaeus refers to those elders who were disciples of the apostles,[6] he never claims to have had any personal contact with them." With this I would agree entirely. And that is why this passage is different, and why it correlates with what Irenaeus says elsewhere about Polycarp and does not correlate with what he says about the plural "elders" he mentions in other places. Those places where he refers to the teaching of "the elders," and does not speak of any personal associations with them, are places where he is either definitely (V.33.3; *Proof* 61) or most likely (II.22.5; V.5.1; V.36.1-2) dependent on Papias,[7] and not dependent on him personally but on his books. On the other hand, in those places where Irenaeus does claim to be one link away from the apostles (*Haer.* III.3; *Flor.*), that link is Polycarp.

Consequently, I do not see that objections two or three carry any real weight against the proposed identification of Polycarp and the presbyter. What about one and four?

Irenaeus's "Childhood Memories"

Moll's first objection is that the presbyter whose teaching Irenaeus recounted so well in Book IV could not have been Polycarp, because Irenaeus was too young at the time when he was acquainted with Polycarp to have understood and remembered so much. As evidence that Irenaeus's memory was not as good as he claimed it was, Moll states that "all the things which Irenaeus actually reports about Polycarp in the letter to Florinus (or elsewhere) are nothing but very general information, which do not reveal any personal remembrance of Polycarp's teachings on Irenaeus's part, much less provide a literal quote from them." First, I would have to disagree; the things Irenaeus says he remembers about Polycarp in the letter to Florinus as quoted by Moll in his essay (to which I refer the reader), seem to me to go well beyond the category of "very general information." Second, we do have what looks like a fairly literal quote in a portion of the fragment not quoted by Moll: "O good God, for what times hast thou reserved me, that I should endure these things?"

Third, the kind of "personal remembrance of Polycarp's teaching" Moll is asking for is exactly what I argue exists in *Haer.* IV.27-32. This is teaching that Irenaeus remembered from somebody. And it sounds a lot like the kind of thing he had in mind when he told Florinus, "I used to listen eagerly to these things [which Polycarp taught] even then by the mercy of God given to me, making notes of them not on papyrus but in my heart. And always by the grace of God truly do I ruminate on them."

Now to the issue of Irenaeus's age. Moll says Irenaeus's words "presume a 'childlike age' incapable of understanding and remembering what Polycarp taught." This is even though Irenaeus immediately goes on to claim forthrightly that he *was* able to understand and remember what Polycarp taught. Moll is hardly alone in questioning the credibility of Irenaeus's recollections of Polycarp based on Irenaeus's tender years. Because one part of Irenaeus's testimony concerns Polycarp's alleged contact with the apostle John, the registering of doubts about the accuracy of Irenaeus's "childhood memories" has been almost a stock element in many commentaries on the Gospel of John.[8] While some are content to pronounce his youthful reminiscences "vivid but confused," others seem inclined to charge Irenaeus with deliberate fabrication.[9]

Before addressing the issue of Irenaeus's age and memory directly, it is interesting to note the one-way direction of thought here. Why is it that, when it comes to his reports about Polycarp, the only time Irenaeus may be trusted to tell the unvarnished truth is when he mentioned his age? How do we know, for instance, that the other things he reported are not "true" and that it was not his youthful inexperience which he exaggerated for effect, as when Solomon declared he was "only a little child"[10] when he asked God for wisdom, though he had already taken a wife? Or, to take a less cynical approach, why is it that the only part of Irenaeus's memory which was somehow able to escape the ravages of time was the part that stored information about his age? But what I hope to show here is that there is really no need to question the credibility of Irenaeus's testimony, or his ability to learn, based on his reported age.

a. There are two places in Irenaeus's extant works where he says something about his age at the time when he knew Polycarp. One is in his letter to Florinus, where he uses the word παῖς (boy; child) to describe himself. Moll is in line with many who assume that this must mean someone very young indeed.

In our parlance, childhood is usually perceived as ending at about the time when adolescence starts, or when a person becomes a teenager. But this is not necessarily how it was in Irenaeus's day. Various schemes of "ages" or life stages are discoverable in various authors (I have come across three-age, four-age, five-age, six-age, seven-age, and ten-age schemes). A scheme attributed to Hippocrates, by Philo (*On the Creation of the World* 105) posits a new stage of life every seven years, the age of the παῖς seen as beginning at seven and lasting to fourteen.[11] Pythagoras, on the other hand, according to Diogenes Laertios (*Life of Pythagoras* 8.10), used the word παῖς for boys up to twenty years, though this may have been Pythagoras's schematic judgment, not "actual social practice."[12] Indeed, artificial systems like these and others were, as Wiedemann says, "philosophical ideas toyed with by intellectuals; they perhaps led to interesting speculation about the 'ideal' age, but had no application to real life."[13] He continues, "It is difficult to believe that any of them led people to believe that some other division was more important than that between the child and the adult capable of bearing arms."[14] And that transition, among both Greeks and Romans, took place at the age of seventeen or eighteen. From at least the fifth century B.C.E., Leinieks indicates, "An Athenian almost certainly ceased to be a παῖς and became a νεανίσκος when he reached the age of emancipation at eighteen."[15] And for the Romans, Wiedemann says, "the crucial division between child and adult was at seventeen: the age at which a male could learn to fight."[16]

If one were to insist that Irenaeus was a παῖς for the entire time he knew Polycarp, I think it fair to point out that there seems to be nothing he reports of the presbyter in *Haer.* IV.27-32 which a boy of, let's say, sixteen to eighteen is not capable of learning and remembering. This is the case particularly if the learned material was reviewed regularly, as Irenaeus says it was. At the time when he saw Florinus in lower Asia, Irenaeus was, as a παῖς, at least astute enough to pick up that Florinus, a young Roman official, was trying to make a favorable impression on Polycarp. This is not, I would suggest, the insight of an eight- or ten-year-old. A youth of sixteen to eighteen, on the other hand, might well be attentive to such things. It is likewise with his description of Florinus as at the time "faring illustriously in the royal court" (λαμπρῶς πράσσοντα ἐν τῇ βασιλικῇ αὐλῇ). How many eight- or ten-year-olds pay attention to the civic achievements of visiting minor officials? This sort of awareness is at least more appropriate for someone who was himself about to enter into public life or had already done so. Irenaeus's contemporaries in Rome normally did this sometime between the ages of thirteen and eighteen,[17] most often at the Festival of Liber every March 17, when they exchanged the childhood *toga praetexta* for the *toga virilis*, marking "a transition from boy to youth"[18] and "the beginning of the young man's public life."[19]

Boys in their late teenage years may have a very high capacity for learning and memorization. They may also be animated by deep admiration for a respected, even celebrated, elder statesman of their communities. It requires no great stretch to imagine that both traits might have been found in the young Irenaeus.

b. I think it should be remembered that the subject that called forth Irenaeus's use of the word παῖς in the *Letter to Florinus* was not his experience with Polycarp but his acquaintance with Florinus. Obviously he knew Polycarp at the time when he says he was a παῖς and observed Florinus trying to impress the bishop, but he never remotely implies that his acquaintance with the two men ended at just the same time. Still speaking of his remembrance of Florinus, but as he begins to transition to relating what he remembered of Polycarp, Irenaeus uses a slightly different turn of phrase: "For, the things learned from childhood [ἐκ παίδων] grow up together with the soul, becoming one with it." He is reporting to Florinus what he learned not simply "as a child" or at a point "in childhood" but, "from childhood," which is something potentially quite different. Justin, for instance, boasts that men and women "who have been Christ's disciples from childhood [ἐκ παίδων], remain pure at the age of sixty or seventy years" (*1 Apol.* 15.6). Here ἐκ παίδων speaks of an ongoing and continuous experience (discipleship) that only began in childhood, not a brief experience that ended there. Similarly, Genesis 46:34, where Joseph instructs his brothers to say to Pharaoh, "you shall say, 'Your servants have been keepers of livestock from our youth [ἐκ παίδων] even until now, both we and our ancestors.'"[20] Things happening "from childhood" start in childhood, but they do not end there. Irenaeus certainly means to say that he was learning things from and about Polycarp while he was still a παῖς (probably a late teen), at the time he was taking notice of Florinus's efforts to gain Polycarp's approval. But the expression ἐκ παίδων does not place an upper limit on the time when he was learning these things from and about Polycarp.

c. When Irenaeus has occasion to speak of his acquaintance with Polycarp apart from any thought of Florinus in *Haer.* III.3.4, he does not use the word παῖς (despite Kirsopp Lake's translation in the Loeb edition). Instead, he says he was "in my first age" (ἐν τῇ πρώτῃ ἡμῶν ἡλικίᾳ; *in prima nostra aetate*). What does he mean by this?

Philo used the expression πρώτῃ ἡλικίᾳ ("first age") fairly often, usually to describe someone old enough to take instruction of various kinds. On two occasions, however, he associates the expression with a definite age. First, in *On Joseph* he says that Joseph the patriarch was immersed in civil affairs "from his first age [ἐκ πρώτης ἡλικίας]," and this pertains to activities Joseph embarked upon at age seventeen, and not before (*On Joseph* 1–2). Elsewhere (*Jos.* 270), he says that at age seventeen Joseph was just entering the age of a youth (μειράκιον),[21] that is, he was just passing beyond the age of a παῖς. Second, in *On the Embassy to Gaius* 87, Philo expresses horror at the actions of the young emperor Gaius, who had his cousin Tiberius Gemellus murdered when the latter was "in the prime of first age" (ἐν ἀκμῇ τῆς πρώτης ἡλικίας). He also says that Gemellus was "just emerging from childhood and becoming a youth [εἰς μειράκιον]" (*Embassy* 23). Although Philo does not tell us exactly how old the youth was, it is recorded that Gemellus was born 10 October 19 c.e. and was killed late in 37 or early in 38 and thus had just turned eighteen.[22]

Based on the usage of Philo, Irenaeus's ἐν τῇ πρώτῃ ἡμῶν ἡλικίᾳ might have been seventeen or eighteen years old, or older. For Philo clearly does not conceive of "the first age" as limited to the stage of childhood. And there is good reason to think that Irenaeus didn't either. *LSJ* defines the phrase "in the prime of life, manhood," citing an example from Pindar (ἐν ἁλικίᾳ πρώτᾳ, *Nemean Odes* 9.42), which pertains to a period well past the age of a παῖς. Support for understanding Irenaeus in this way comes from his own statements in *Against Heresies* Book II, where he had employed a five-stage scheme for human life. The Greek, unfortunately, does not survive here, but the Latin progression of *infans, parvulus, puer*,[23] *juvenis, senior* (II.24.4; II.24.4), probably translates βρέφος (or νήπιος?), νήπιος (or παιδίον?), παῖς, νεανίας, πρεσβύτερος.[24] Also unfortunate, for our purposes, is that Irenaeus does not define these stages by years. One could translate ἐν τῇ πρώτῃ ἡμῶν ἡλικίᾳ in III.3.4 as "in our first age," but this cannot be equated with the first of the five stages listed in Book II (*infans*). For, besides resulting in an absurdity, it would be contradicted by his letter to Florinus, where he indicates he was a παῖς (likely also the word translated *puer* in the list above), two stages beyond *infans*, when Polycarp was quite active.

An insight into his thought comes from his discussion in the same context (II.22.5), where, provoked by the views of his Valentinian opponents, he mounts a valiant effort to prove that Jesus lived beyond the age of forty. Here too the Greek does not survive and the Latin is difficult. With Luke's notice in mind (Luke 3:23), that Jesus was beginning to be about thirty years old when he came to be baptized, Irenaeus says, "Now, all will agree that the age of 'thirty years' belongs to the first age of natural youth [*aetas prima indolis est iuvenis*], and this extends as far as the fortieth year; moreover, from the fortieth and fiftieth year it declines into the age of an elder [*in aetatem seniorem*]" (*Haer.* II.22.5).[25]

The main transition with which Irenaeus is concerned here seems to be that of *iuvenis* to *senior*, a transition that starts at age forty, when one begins the decline toward old age. If, as his opponents allege, Jesus had died only one year after he received baptism, he would have been still in the first age of life. As it is (so he argues), Jesus passed beyond the age of forty (in fact, was closer to fifty), beyond the "first age of natural youth," and so could legitimately be said to have encountered, and thereby to have sanctified, all the stages of human life (*infans, parvulus, puer, juvenis, senior*). It seems that before the age of forty, one is still in the prime (first age) of natural youth. After that are one's "declining years."

Once we understand this, it becomes clear that when in Book III Irenaeus says that he was ἐν τῇ πρώτῃ ἡμῶν ἡλικίᾳ when he knew Polycarp, he is simply saying that he was then in the prime of his life (by implication, something he had since passed). And this prime seems to be more or less identifiable with the stage of a *iuvenis* or νεανίας,[26] which, in Irenaeus's view, began after boyhood and ended at the age of forty. Thus, all one can say for certain from his use of this expression of his age in III.3.4 is that Irenaeus was under forty when he knew Polycarp. It may well be that in the spectrum of life's prime years, Irenaeus was closer to the age of a παῖς than to that of a πρεσβύτερος when his contact with Polycarp ended, but to say this we would have to depend on other considerations, not strictly on the age terminology he uses to describe himself.

d. I pointed out in *Lost Teaching* that an interesting comparison can be made between what Irenaeus says of himself and what Philostratus says about the disciples of Dionysius of Miletus, who flourished under Hadrian.

> How was it then that his pupils had a peculiar gift for memory? It was because the declamations of Dionysius gave them a pleasure of which they could never have enough, and he was compelled to repeat them very often, since he knew that they were delighted to hear them. And so the more ready-witted of these youths (νέων) used to engrave them on their minds, and when, by long practice rather than by sheer memory, they had thoroughly grasped them, they used to recite them to the rest; and hence they came to be called "the memory-artists," and men who made it into an art.[27]

The delight of Dionysius's youthful students is reminiscent of Irenaeus's words, "The presbyter used to delight us by recounting certain matters like these . . ." (*Haer.* IV.31.1). The engraving on the minds of these students reminds us of Irenaeus's notations "not on papyrus but on my heart" (*Ep. Flor.*). The repeated recitations of the Dionysian disciples are not unlike Irenaeus's "And always by the grace of God truly do I ruminate on them" (*Ep. Flor.*). I would not claim that Irenaeus was a memory artist, but it was probably, as Philostratus said, by practice rather than sheer memory that Irenaeus was able to maintain his recollection over the years. We also see evidence of a mnemonic device in one of the fragments of the elder's teaching.[28] Philostratus's account serves as a reminder that the eagerness of the young Irenaeus to retain the oral teaching of a revered teacher is not out of the ordinary for his time and place.

e. Finally, there may be something to be gained from the modern psychological study of memory, and what is called by some researchers "the reminiscence bump." Summarizing the results of many studies, Ulric Neisser and Lisa K. Libby observe that when tested by the method of *open recall*, in which subjects are allowed to choose to tell their own memories, "middle-aged and older adults produce disproportionate numbers of memories from adolescence and early adulthood: roughly, from ages

10 to 25. . . . This pattern, now called the *reminiscence bump*, also emerges in free life narratives. . . . It is not limited to episodic memory: in every cognitive domain, 'things learned early in adulthood are remembered best.'"[29] Not only are they remembered best, but events occurring during adolescence and early adulthood tend to be deemed more important. "The empirical observation is that people remember, and report as important, public events that happened in their late teens or early twenties."[30] Theories from different areas of psychology have been advanced to account for the repeatedly corroborated findings. An accounting based on "cognitive abilities or their neural substrates" concludes that "laboratory tests of processing speed and standardized tests of memory and intelligence support the basic claim of a rapid increase in cognitive abilities of several kinds until early adulthood followed by a slower decline."[31] A theory of identity formation would say, "events from this period will be more likely to be organized and incorporated into an overall story or view of the self and thus benefit mnemonically from all the advantages of such schematic organization as well as from increased spaced rehearsal."[32] Irenaeus's own theory to explain why "I remember the events of those days more clearly than those which happened recently" deserves to be placed alongside these: "for the things learned from childhood grow up together with the soul, becoming one with it" (*HE* V.20.6). Memory studies also confirm that memories are preserved best when there are repeated reviews or rehearsals of them.[33] Irenaeus attests, "I used to listen eagerly to these things [which Polycarp taught] even then by the mercy of God given to me, making notes of them not on papyrus but in my heart. And always by the grace of God truly do I ruminate on them" (*HE* V.20.7).

It would seem, then, that a great deal of skepticism about Irenaeus's memory and testimony based on his alleged tender age when he knew Polycarp has been misplaced. This in itself does not, of course, mean that anything he says he remembers should not be subjected to further scrutiny; it simply means that references to Irenaeus's "childhood" should no longer be regarded as sufficient cause to dismiss what he says about Polycarp. Nor should his statements about his age be used to judge adversely the possibility that the remembered words of the presbyter were the words of Polycarp. Irenaeus was probably in his mid or late teenage years when he was observing Florinus's movements in Smyrna. And his contact with Polycarp almost certainly extended into his early twenties, if not longer. This is precisely the period of life in which, modern psychology says, human memory operates best, from which autobiographical memories are best retained and remain most vivid into middle and old age. Moreover, Irenaeus always placed a high value on what had grown up with his soul concerning Polycarp, and maintained those memories, which included some verbal teaching, by frequent review.

Why Didn't Irenaeus Give the Man with No Name a Name?

Moll's final objection against identifying the unnamed presbyter of *Haer.* IV.27-32 with Polycarp is, as he puts it, "the obvious objection . . . the question why in the world Irenaeus would fail to mention Polycarp's name, given that a reference to this authority would so enormously strengthen his argument." But how do we know that he thought it would strengthen his argument, or that he thought his argument needed strengthening?

In any case, the short answer, I think, to the question of why Irenaeus did not name the presbyter's name is that he didn't have to. I will add that, in my opinion, he also gives the impression that he thought it might transgress his notion of modesty to do so.[34] His readers knew very well what apostolic presbyter Irenaeus had known. If I am right that the *Letter to Florinus* had been sent to Rome (not only to Florinus, but certainly to others as well, at least the Roman church) before Book IV was finished, then many of Irenaeus's readers would have been quite familiar with Irenaeus's connection with the apostolic presbyter Polycarp from the words of that letter.

But we do not need to rely upon the readers' acquaintance with that letter, however probable it might be. Readers of *Against Heresies* itself would have known of this connection because they would have read about it in Book III. And if they had for some reason forgotten about it, Irenaeus gently but definitely reminds them. It is important to observe (something I failed to observe in *Lost Teaching*) that the excerpts from the presbyter in *Haer.* IV.27.1—32.1 occur in a larger framework of 26.2—32.1. And at both the beginning and at the end of this framework, Irenaeus refers the reader back to Book III, to the very place where he had mentioned his own acquaintance with a particular presbyter who had learned from apostles.

In IV.26.2, Irenaeus charges, "it is incumbent to obey the presbyters of the church—those who, as I have shown [*sicut ostendimus*], possess the succession from the apostles." Who were those presbyters who possessed the succession from the apostles, and where had Irenaeus shown that they possessed it? "*As I have shown*" is a reference back to the "succession lists" in III.2–4, Irenaeus's classic treatment of, and also his last mention of, the succession of the presbyters. There he had "shown" that the "tradition that originates from the apostles" is "preserved by the succession of presbyters in the churches" (III.2.2). There he delivered the presbyteral succession of only two churches, the church in Rome and the church in Smyrna (Ephesus receives a brief reference as well). And, of course, it is there where he introduced Polycarp, who "was not only instructed by apostles, and conversed with many who had seen Christ, but was also, by apostles in Asia, appointed bishop of the Church in Smyrna, whom I saw in the prime of my life. . . . [Polycarp] having always taught the things he had learned from the apostles, which the church has handed down" (III.3.4). In other words, in IV.26.2, as he prepares for an extended section in which he will expound the teaching he personally received from an apostolic presbyter, Irenaeus refers his readers back to the very section in Book III where he had mentioned his personal connection to Polycarp, an apostolic presbyter. When he then begins IV.27.1 with the words "as I heard from a certain presbyter, who heard it from the apostles whom he had seen," it is hard to imagine that Irenaeus did not fully expect his readers to catch his unpretentious but fairly obvious reference to Polycarp.

Finally, after recounting all his tradition from the presbyter in the section IV.27.1—32.1, he concludes IV.32.1 with one more reminder of the importance of reading "the scriptures in company with those who are presbyters in the Church, among whom is the apostolic doctrine, as I have pointed out [*quemadmodum demonstravimus*]." Here then is another reference back to his discussion in the opening chapters of Book III where he had mentioned his acquaintance with Polycarp.[35] For the attentive reader, the upshot is clear. If one wants to read scripture in company with the presbyters with whom is the apostolic teaching, one can hardly do better than to read Irenaeus's books! But Irenaeus accomplishes this without having to invoke Polycarp's name again, but instead by framing his exposition of Polycarp's teaching with references back to the place where he had revealed his association with that apostolic elder.

Irenaeus's omission of Polycarp's name is perhaps not so mysterious.

Conclusion

It is not simply that Polycarp is the best candidate to be identified with the presbyter, among those whose names we know. It is that if the presbyter is not Polycarp, we shall have found his twin. The omission of Polycarp's name from the section IV.27-32 is now, I think, not hard to understand. The reader of *Against Heresies* already knows his name. What would be much harder to understand is why Irenaeus would never (here or elsewhere) have mentioned the name of *another* presbyter he had known, a presbyter who like Polycarp had learned from apostles, who like Polycarp lived long enough to address a Marcionite problem, and some of whose teaching Irenaeus had learned by heart, as he had Polycarp's.

Despite his very considerable contributions in exegesis, theology, and church life, Irenaeus saw himself very much as a conduit, as one part in a line of succession from the apostles. For him, this line was very important, and it was very short. The apostles of Jesus had deposited the faith into the safe coffers of the church, and Polycarp was one of those who had personally received the transfer. However we might assess Irenaeus's construction of things, the prospect of retrieving from Irenaeus more of Polycarp's teaching is an opportunity to increase our contact with a time and situation in early Christianity for which we have all too little, contemporary information. Irenaeus's rehearsal of what he learned from his "apostolic presbyter" can expand our understanding of Irenaeus and Polycarp, of Marcion, of Cerinthus, and of the intriguing nexus of social, theological, and ecclesiastical matters they all played their parts in shaping.

CHAPTER NINE

Irenaeus and the Noncanonical Gospels

PAUL FOSTER

Famously, Irenaeus is known as the earliest certain witness to the fourfold canon of Gospels contained in the New Testament. In book III of his *Adversus haereses*, Irenaeus not only states that there are four Gospels, but by using natural analogies he implies that "four" is the fitting number since this provides a stable basis because it allows the church equipped with "the gospel and the spirit of life" to bring life to humanity.[1] As he states, "It is not possible that the Gospels can be either more or fewer in number than they are. For, since there are four zones of the world in which we live, and four principal winds, while the church is scattered throughout all the world, and 'the pillar and ground' of the church is the gospel and the spirit of life; it is fitting that she should have four pillars, breathing out immortality on every side, and vivifying men afresh" (*Haer.* III.11.8). Irenaeus then rails against those "who destroy the form of the gospel" by either adding to its number or by accepting fewer gospels. Representative of the latter group, Irenaeus explicitly names Marcion, whom he accuses of "rejecting the entire gospel," as well as the Montanists, who are charged with setting "aside at once both the gospel and the prophetic Spirit." On the other hand, those with additional gospel texts are seen as arrogantly claiming "to have discovered more than is of the truth" (*Haer.* III.11.9). In the immediate context, only the disciples of Valentinus are singled out as recklessly adding their own compositions alongside the fourfold gospel, with the writing the *Gospel of Truth* named. This last statement reveals at least part of Irenaeus's motivation for introducing his statements about the gospel known in its fourfold form. Also, he tantalizingly reveals knowledge of other texts that are known as gospels, but which he himself rejects since they do not stem from the apostles. Apart from this *Gospel of Truth*, Irenaeus also names or alludes to a number of other gospel texts in his writings. This discussion will investigate which noncanonical gospels appear to be known by Irenaeus, and it will also consider the nature and degree of that knowledge which he appears to exhibit concerning such writings.

Survey of Possible Noncanonical Gospel Texts Known by Irenaeus

The purposes of Irenaeus's *Adversus haereses* are perhaps more complex than the author declares in his preface to volume one. Nonetheless, it can be stated, based upon the self-professed statements of Irenaeus, that one of the work's most explicit and transparent purposes is to refute those whom he accuses of propagating heresy. A key way this is achieved is by attacking the writings used by individuals or groups to support their own alternative theological viewpoints. This is stated in the Preface to book one of the work, where Irenaeus opines that those who set the truth aside "bring in lying words and vain genealogies" (*Haer.* I.1.1). This expression does not necessarily reveal dependence on alternative texts, but later in the Preface he states that such people "falsify the oracles of God" (*Haer.* I.1.1). This, far less ambiguously, appears to denote the use of alternative, disputed, or modified texts. The negative portrayal of such writings resurfaces at various points in *Adversus haereses*, but Irenaeus allows only a few glimpses into the various writings he considered so repugnant.

The *Gospel of Judas*

Among the noncanonical writings that Irenaeus cites by name using the term "gospel," the first text to be mentioned in this way is the Gospel of Judas. Until May 2006, the actual contents of a text bearing this name were unknown.[2] At that date, the *National Geographic* issue for the month, along with accompanying television documentary and two book length publications, made known a text with this title.[3] Prior to this, there were only short descriptions provided by patristic authors. Irenaeus is in fact the earliest extant writer to have made reference to a work with this title. He provides the following account of the work:

> Others again declare that Cain derived his being from the Power above, and acknowledge that Esau, Korah, the Sodomites, and all such persons, are related to themselves. On this account, they add, they have been assailed by the Creator, yet no one of them has suffered injury. For Sophia was in the habit of carrying off that which belonged to her from them to herself. They declare that Judas the traitor was thoroughly acquainted with these things, and that he alone, knowing the truth as no others did, accomplished the mystery of the betrayal; by him all things, both earthly and heavenly, were thus thrown into confusion. They produce a fictitious history of this kind, which they style the Gospel of Judas. (*Haer.* I.31.1)

Since the publication of the text, similarities with and differences from this description furnished by Irenaeus have been described and commented upon.[4] April DeConick notes one of the most striking differences between text and description. Whereas Irenaeus attributes the text to a group that declared itself to be descended from Cain, Esau, Korah, and the Sodomites, the text of the *Gospel of Judas* traces its descent to the great Seth. Obviously, the four ancestral figures Irenaeus states as being linked to the group behind the *Gospel of Judas* do not form the type of pedigree that many would be likely to claim. This leads DeConick to suggest that Irenaeus has constructed an anti-genealogy to undermine the group and the text. Thus she states, "Since the people who wrote the *Gospel of Judas* understood themselves to be descendants of the great Seth, not Cain or any of the others whom Irenaeus names, this suggests to me that the genealogy is fictitious, serving only to undermine the Gospel's credibility."[5]

Irenaeus portrays the *Gospel of Judas* as representing a Judas who perceives the true significance of the act of his betrayal, which is different from the depiction of the betrayal in the canonical narratives. In effect, he accuses those who hold to the perspectives of this document as valorizing Judas, rather than representing him according to the canonical perspective as a person who betrayed Jesus for financial gain. This raises a number of complex issues concerning the identification of the *Gospel of Judas* text known to Irenaeus with the recently published text bearing the same name. First, one must ask whether the newly discovered text presents Judas in a heroic fashion; secondly, if not, whether Irenaeus could have understood the text that way (either intentionally or mistakenly); and finally, whether Irenaeus knew this text directly and had read some of its contents, or if he only had second-hand knowledge of the existence of this text.

When the *Gospel of Judas* was initially published, it was read as supporting the notion that Judas was an anti-hero. Wurst cites the following passage from the *Gospel of Judas* in support of such an understanding: "But you will exceed all of them. For you will sacrifice the man that clothes me" (Tchacos, page 56). He draws the implication that "Jesus teaches Judas that he will have his part to play in the history of salvation. . . . Judas's task is to sacrifice the body of Jesus. For what reason is not preserved, but we may guess that by this sacrifice the inner spirit of Jesus is liberated."[6] This interpretation has, however, been strongly contested. After reassessing the translation of the text, DeConick convincingly argues that Judas is not commended but rather is condemned. Her translation of the passage in question is that Jesus says to Judas, "You will do *worse* than all of them, for the man that clothes me, you will sacrifice him."[7] Regardless of which side of the debate one finds convincing, the possibility remains that Irenaeus either intentionally misrepresented the text as promoting a type of Judas-devotion based on a complex cosmology that rejected the material world, or alternatively and perhaps more likely, misunderstood the text's subversive parody of the type of apostolic Christianity that Irenaeus and others represented.[8]

Caution must be exhibited in assessing whether or not Irenaeus had directly read portions of this text. This is due to the lack of evidence. Although the title is given, no direct citations are provided and there is little description on the contents of the text. In fact, the description relates more to the beliefs of the "Cainites" than outlining the contents of the *Gospel of Judas*. Notwithstanding this, some of the things the group is charged with believing appear to be found in the recently published text. Judas is certainly the central figure in both the description provided by Irenaeus and the *Gospel of Judas*, and the protagonist's betrayal of Jesus is seen by both as having cosmic ramifications. Admittedly, these are only brief similarities, but they do lead DeConick to state that Irenaeus's "description is a highly accurate account of the manuscript we possess."[9] It seems, therefore, highly likely that the text known to Irenaeus was indeed at least a related version of the same text that has come down to modern readers bearing the same name.[10] However, the evidence base is simply too narrow to determine with any degree of certainty whether Irenaeus had read this text for himself, or if he only had a description of its contents mediated to him by others.

The *Gospel of Truth*

Perhaps the principal group of opponents to whom Irenaeus responds is the Valentinians. As was mentioned briefly in the introduction, the reference to the fourfold gospel is mentioned directly in contradistinction to the tendency of certain parties to use additional texts, such as the named *Gospel of Truth*. Repeatedly, Irenaeus refers to the school or the followers of Valentinus, and he attributes the *Gospel of Truth* to disciples who follow the teachings of Valentinus. In this context he states, "But those who are from Valentinus, being, on the other hand, altogether reckless, while they put forth their own compositions, boast that they possess more Gospels than there really are. Indeed, they have arrived at such a pitch of audacity, as to entitle their comparatively recent writing 'the Gospel of Truth,' though it agrees in nothing with the Gospels of the Apostles, so that they have really no Gospel which is not full of blasphemy" (*Haer.* III.11.9). Here Irenaeus divulges little knowledge of the actual contents of this document. Instead, he labels it as being full of blasphemy, and states that it was composed by "those who are from Valentinus," rather than it having been written by Valentinus himself.[11] While no extant text from antiquity is explicitly titled the "Gospel of Truth" in either a prescript or subscript, the third tractate of codex 1 from Nag Hammadi opens with the words "The gospel of truth is joy for those who have received from the Father of truth the grace of knowing him" (NHC I,3: 16.31). Although not directly a title, this is suggestive of a work that may have been known by such a name. Consequently, this Nag Hammadi tractate has been identified as the work to which Irenaeus refers. From this perspective, Thomassen argues, "the probability that there existed two independent works, one entitled 'The Gospel of Truth' and the other accidentally beginning with the same words, and both of them 'gnostic,' must be regarded as very slim indeed."[12]

It must, however, be acknowledged that the text from Nag Hammadi does not self-identify itself as a Valentinian work. Nonetheless, as Attridge and MacRae note, "certain key themes and perspectives characteristic of Valentinian theology, such as the principle that knowledge of the Father destroys ignorance (18.10-11; 24.30-32), are emphasized."[13] The cosmological and theological perspectives discussed in this text are, nevertheless, not as complex as some of the schemas and thought structures found in other Valentinian texts. This may plausibly lead to the supposition that this tractate was either an early work in that stream of tradition, or that it was self-consciously designed as an introduction to Valentinian ideas, or perhaps both possibilities are correct.[14] If indeed this were designed as a work introducing Valentinian understandings of Christianity, then presumably the text may then have been easily accessible to Irenaeus and other Christian readers in the second half of the second century. Yet as was stated in relation to the discussion concerning the *Gospel of Judas*, there may exist significant differences between the text form discovered at Nag Hammadi and that known to Irenaeus. This is not only because the Nag Hammadi text is available as a Lycopolitan "subakhmîmic"

Coptic version, whereas presumably Valentinian adherents where reading the text in Greek. More significantly, it must be noted that the "fragments of a Sahidic version of *Gos. Truth* found in NHC XII . . . seem to differ in several places from the text of NHC I."[15] While it may be debated whether the small fragments from NHC XII represent an earlier version of the text or not, they at least suggest that more than one recension of the text was in circulation. These factors need to be borne in mind when making statements about Irenaeus's knowledge of the *Gospel of Truth* on the basis of the shared perspectives on the essentials of Valentinian teaching.

Irenaeus reports that the Valentinians "affirm it was that the 'Saviour'—for they do not please to call Him 'Lord'—did no work in public during the space of thirty years" (*Haer.* 1.1.3). This preferred christological title accords with the usage in the *Gospel of Truth*, "through the power of the Word that came forth from the pleroma, the one who is in the thought and the mind of the Father, that is, the one who is addressed as the Saviour, (that) being the name of the work he is to perform for the redemption of those who were ignorant of the Father" (*Gos. Truth*, NHC I,3: 16.34—17.1).

Although an interesting parallel, this feature is hardly unique to the *Gospel of Truth*, with the term "savior" being widespread as the preferred title in a number of Nag Hammadi tractates. Irenaeus also shows a detailed knowledge of the emanation of the Aeons. The cosmological scheme he describes speaks of thirty aeons which are divided "into an Ogdoad, a Decad, and a Duodecad" (*Haer.* I.1.3). However, Irenaeus states that this advanced cosmology is known to only the "professing teachers" of the movements. Therefore, it is unsurprising that this hidden knowledge is not revealed in the *Gospel of Truth*, which may be some kind of introductory or "evangelistic" sermonic text. By contrast, reference to terms such as "Duodecad" and "Decad" is a feature of other texts such as *A Valentinian Exposition* (NHC XI,2: 22.1-30.38),[16] and also in a Sethian text, the so-called "Untitled Text" of the Bruce Codex, which refers to the Decad.[17]

Since Irenaeus possesses more detailed knowledge of the protology, cosmology, and soteriology of Valentinianism than is provided in the *Gospel of Truth*, it is apparent that he had other sources of knowledge, either written or orally transmitted to him. Furthermore, since he does not directly cite from the text of the *Gospel of Truth*, nor does he betray knowledge of any concept that is unique to that text, the case for definitive dependence is far from being absolutely certain. Nonetheless, he does use the title *Gospel of Truth*, which echoes the opening line of the text in NHC 1,3. This is highly suggestive, by itself, of the possibility that Irenaeus had knowledge of some text-form of this writing. Whether he had direct access to a written copy of the text, or had learned of it through a secondhand mechanism, is unclear.

The Alpha-Beta Logion and the *Infancy Gospel of Thomas*

After describing the cosmological speculations of the Valentinians, Irenaeus recounts the teachings of one Marcus and his followers. The latter group are described as having an impact on the local area of the Rhône valley of which Lyons was a major city standing at the confluence of the Rhône and Saône rivers (*Haer.* I.13.7). One of the key aspects of the teaching of the Marcosians, attributed to them by Irenaeus, is their mystical interpretation of letters and the use of gematria to find hidden meaning in various significant terms.[18] It is unsurprising that Irenaeus places the story of the Alpha-Beta logion after the description of the Marcosians' use of gematria, and in fact attributes this story to the same group, since to his mind it is illustrative of how such a hermeneutical approach perverts the true characterization of Jesus as found in the fourfold gospel.

Thus, in conjunction with attacking the hermeneutical methods of the Marcosians, Irenaeus also accuses them of circulating spurious writings "which they themselves have forged to bewilder the minds of foolish men" (*Haer.* I.20.1). He then cites the example of the Alpha-Beta logion: "Among other things, they bring forward that false and wicked story which relates that our Lord, when He was a boy learning His letters, on the teacher saying to Him, as is usual, 'Pronounce Alpha,' replied as He was instructed, 'Alpha.' But when, again, the teacher bade Him say, 'Beta,' the Lord replied, 'You first tell me what Alpha is, and then I will tell you what Beta is.' This they expound as meaning that He alone knew the Unknown, which He revealed under its type Alpha" (*Haer.* I.20.1). A close parallel to this story also occurs twice in the *Infancy Gospel of Thomas* (6.3 and 14.2), although Irenaeus's form of the story is closer to the version found in *Inf. Thom.* 14.2.[19] The version in *Inf. Thom.* 14.2 is the shorter of the two forms found in the *Infancy Gospel of Thomas*. It has fewer novelistic details, but focuses more on the mysterious power of letters than the version preserved in *Inf. Thom.* 6.3. The shorter form has Jesus respond in the following manner to the attempt of the teacher to instruct him in letters, "'If you are indeed a schoolmaster and you know perfectly well the letters, then tell me the meaning of the alpha and I will tell you of the beta.' And the schoolmaster became irritated and struck him on the head. And the boy Jesus cursed him and instantly he fainted and fell upon his face" (*Inf. Thom.* 14.2).

A number of possibilities exist that could explain the process through which Irenaeus had come to know this story. First, it is possible that Irenaeus read a continuous text that was close to one of the four major recensions of the *Infancy Gospel of Thomas*,[20] but attributed this text to, or knew of its use by the Marcosians because of its interest in the magical properties of letters. Secondly, it is possible that this text was also contained in another no longer extant text used by the Marcosians. Thirdly, the text could have circulated independently of any larger narrative, either in written form or orally, and Irenaeus either learnt of the text in connection with the Marcosians, or made that connection himself. The fact that the story is used twice in the *Infancy Gospel of Thomas* in what appear to be both a primitive and an expanded yet slightly softened form, may suggest that this story had a prehistory before its incorporation into the *Infancy Gospel of Thomas*. On this basis, the hypothesis that is slightly favored over the other alternatives is that Irenaeus came across this story as a free floating tradition, either in written or oral form, but independent of a larger narrative context. He either knew that the Marcosians used this text to justify their magical interpretation of letters, or Irenaeus saw this link himself and attributed the text to this group.

The Jewish-Christian Gospels

As a group, the so-called Jewish-Christian Gospels pose a number of problems that are not shared by other texts discussed here. First, there is no text, or at least no continuous text, or even fragments from a once continuous text. Instead, all that survives are a few brief citations preserved in the writings of early Christian writers who tend to be hostile both to these gospel texts and to those groups whom they associate with these writings. Secondly, the fragments are cited by different authors preserving these fragments using different forms of reference to the titles of the works from which they are excerpted. It is, therefore, an issue to decide which fragments belong to the same text and also to determine how many texts should be identified under the umbrella term Jewish-Christian Gospels.[21]

Irenaeus makes reference to the group known as the Ebionites, with whom the text given the name by modern scholars the *Gospel of the Ebionites* is associated (although the actual title it carried in antiquity is unknown). Irenaeus makes four statements about the Ebionites in his writings. First, he reports their exclusive use of the Gospel of Matthew, and rejection of Paul (*Haer.* I.26.2). Secondly, this sole usage of Matthew is reiterated in book III (*Haer.* III.11.7) and this is stated as being the cause of the group's "false suppositions with regard to the Lord." Thirdly, he accuses them of perverting the scriptures by rendering Matt. 1:23 (cf. Isa. 7:14) as "behold a young woman will conceive a son," rather than translating παρθένος as "virgin" (*Haer.* III.21.1). Fourthly, his last comment in relation to the Ebionites is a more expansive description of their failure to hold to a full incarnational theology, relating to interpretations of details in the Matthean and Lukan infancy narratives which are seen as being erroreous.

> Vain also are the Ebionites, who do not receive by faith into their soul the union of God and man, but who remain in the old leaven of [the natural] birth, and who do not choose to understand that the Holy Ghost came upon Mary, and the power of the Most High did overshadow her: wherefore also what was generated is a holy thing, and the Son of the Most High God the Father of all, who effected the incarnation of this being, and showed forth a new [kind of] generation; that as by the former generation we inherited death, so by this new generation we might inherit life. (*Haer.* V.1.3)

This is not explicitly stated here as being a denial of virgin birth but rather describes a lack of acceptance of the notion of divine power being operative in the conception of Jesus. By implication, of course, if divine agency is removed, the consequence is to see the conception of Jesus occurring naturally. Taken together, these four statements led Vielhauer and Strecker to conclude that, "when in other places he says that they had eliminated the virgin birth (III 21.1; V 1.3), it is clear that the gospel used by them cannot have been the canonical Mt, and that Irenaeus had not himself seen this book; otherwise he would not have been able to identify it with Mt."[22]

However, the strong conclusion they draw may be an overstatement of the evidence. The final two references to the Ebionites do not say that they "eliminate the virgin birth." In *Haer.* III.21.1, the issue is one of interpretation and appears to be based upon the more accurate renderings of the Greek text of Isaiah 7:14 which bring it into line with Hebrew *Vorlage*. Irenaeus mentions the recensions of the LXX prepared by both Theodotion and Aquila: "Some allege, among those now presuming to expound the Scripture, 'Behold, a young woman shall conceive, and bring forth a son,' as Theodotion the

Ephesian has interpreted, and Aquila of Pontus, both Jewish proselytes. The Ebionites, following these, assert that He was begotten by Joseph" (*Haer.* III.21.1). Similarly, the final reference claims that the Ebionites did not hold the same interpretation as Irenaeus, concerning elements of the birth story attested by both Luke and Matthew. The implication that the Ebionites had eliminated the virgin birth and consequently were not using canonical Matthew does not necessarily follow from Irenaeus's statements. Moreover, despite claims made in some quarters that see Irenaeus as the earliest witness to the *Gospel of the Ebionites*, it must be stated that he never uses that or any other title in connection with a gospel text used by this group apart from the Gospel of Matthew. Their interpretation of the birth of Jesus as not being by a virgin is attributed to an interpretation based on recent recensions of the LXX, not on a claim of rejection of Matthew. Thus, contrary to some expressed scholarly opinions, Irenaeus does not cast any light on the text that has become known as the *Gospel of the Ebionites*.

Irenaeus and the Nag Hammadi Writings

In many ways, the title to this section is anachronistic since many of the texts from Nag Hammadi had not been composed at the time when Irenaeus wrote. However, a number of them contain earlier traditions that may pre-date Irenaeus's composition of the *Adversus haereses*, and a few of the texts (perhaps in earlier recensions) might be sources for his knowledge of "gnostic" thought systems. The *Apocryphon of John* is correctly identified as a work of fundamental importance among the Nag Hammadi writings and more widely as a key text representing the fundamental ideas of Sethianism. As is well known, the text survives in four copies, three in the Nag Hammadi corpus and one in the Berlin Codex. Pearson summarizes the nature of the textual evidence in the following way. "Two different recensions are reflected in these copies, a longer one (NHC II,*1*; IV,*1*) and a shorter one (NHC III,*1*; BG *2*). The versions in Codices III and IV are very fragmentary."[23]

Book I of *Adversus haereses* contains a detailed refutation of various forms of Valentinianism. This variety, or "inconsistency," as Irenaeus styles it, is seen as representative of the falseness of a self-contradictory system. In chapters 23–28 of book I, Irenaeus moves away from the topic of "Gnosticism" and tackles a range of other belief systems that he deems to be deviant. Then in chapter 29, he returns to a discussion of "Gnosticism," not of the Valentinian variety but of a type illustrative of the "multitude of Gnostics [who] have sprung up." The similarity between the mythical system described in this chapter and the one more fully outlined in the *Apocryphon of John* has long been noted. Based on the form of the text in the Berlin Codex, in 1907 Carl Schmidt published a comparison between the contents of the *Apocryphon of John* and Irenaeus's exposition of the cosmological system discussed in *Adversus haereses* I.29. Schmidt advanced the convincing suggestion that the former was the source for the latter.[24]

It is helpful to set out the main elements in Irenaeus's shorter description and to compare features in the *Apocryphon of John* that parallel those elements. At this stage, no pre-judgments will be made concerning which recension of the *Apocryphon of John* is most likely to have been known to Irenaeus. The parallels will simply be documented and then it will be considered whether the evidence is sufficient to allow any further conclusions to be drawn. As a preliminary remark, it is useful to bear in mind (and to test) Pearson's observation in relation to this text that "[t]he first part, containing the revelation discourse, may have originally been a separate unit. It is precisely this material that is parallel to Irenaeus's paraphrase of a text used by the Gnostics (*Against Heresies* 1.29)."[25]

Irenaeus opens his account of this Gnostic myth by recounting the existence of "a certain Aeon who never grows old, and exists in a virgin spirit: him they style Barbelos" (*Haer.* I.29.1). In the *Apocryphon of John*, after the narrative framework that introduces John the son of Zebedee and the circumstances that led to the revelatory discourse, John enquires concerning the meaning of the savior's words, when he declared "this aeon to which you will go is of the type of the imperishable aeon" (*Ap. John*, NHC II,1; 1.27-28).[26] It is not till later in the *Apocryphon of John* that one reads that the name of this aeon is Barbelo, from whom comes forth a virginal spirit who is the visible manifestation and glory of Barbelo (*Ap. John* 4.27—5.11). Next Irenaeus introduces the figure of the father and describes his wish for self-revelation. "They declare that somewhere or other there exists a certain father who cannot be named, and that he was desirous to reveal himself to this Barbelos" (*Haer.* I.29.1). In the *Apocrphon*, the existence of the Monad is revealed to John, above which is nothing else. This Monad exists "as God and Father of everything," and in a classic example of apophatic theology this figure is described as "illimitable," "unsearchable," "immeasurable," "invisible," "ineffable," and "unnameable since there is no one prior to him to give him a name" (*Ap. John* 3.7-18).[27] Next Irenaeus describes a series of emanations, many of which are paralleled in the text of the *Apocryphon*, in one way or another. Thus, according to Irenaeus, "incorruption is called forth from the father" whereas in the *Apocryphon*, in only slightly different terms, the father "exists as incorruption" (*Ap. John* 2.30).

Next there follows a complex description provided by Irenaeus of his understanding of the myth of the generation of Christ. This will be seen to be largely in agreement with the major elements in the *Apocryphon*.

> Barbelos, glorying in these, and contemplating their greatness, and in conception [thus formed], rejoicing in this greatness, generated light similar to it. They declare that this was the beginning both of light and of the generation of all things; and that the Father, beholding this light, anointed it with his own benignity, that it might be rendered perfect. Moreover, they maintain that this was Christ, who again, according to them, requested that Nous should be given him as an assistant; and Nous came forth accordingly. Besides these, the Father sent forth Logos. The conjunctions of Ennoca and Logos, and of Aphtharsia and Christ, will thus be formed; while Zoe Aionios was united to Thelema, and Nous to Prognosis. These, then, magnified the great light and Barbelos. (*Haer.* I.29.1)

In the *Apocryphon*, Barbelo also plays a key role in the bringing forth of a spark of light, which is "an only-begotten child." In the highly confusing description that follows, it appears Barbelo is the one who anoints it with goodness until it becomes perfect. A fellow worker, which is the mind (i.e., Nous) is requested for the only-begotten child. The Nous is emanated, and glorifies both Christ and Barbelo. It is then stated that "because of the word, Christ the divine autogenes created everything" (*Ap. John* 7.10-11).

Here then, the three beings which form the primal triad, that is the Father, Barbelo the Mother, and Autogenes (the self-generated son), are clearly known and described by both authors.[28] However, Irenaeus presents a summary of this protological myth and, as one would expect, this is not an altogether sympathetic reading that would attempt to understand the system on its own terms. Thus, in Irenaeus, there is no clear description of the emanation of Barbelo as a feminine reflection of the self-thought of the Father. Nor is the distinction in the emergence of the Son set forth, whereby the Son emerges as a result of Barbelo's vision of the Father.[29]

Instead, Irenaeus describes the role of Autogenes in a number of statements he presents as the essence of the group's teaching on the origin of this being. First, he states, "They also affirm that Autogenes was afterward sent forth from Ennoea and Logos, to be a representation of the great light, and that he was greatly honored, all things being rendered subject unto him. Along with him was sent forth Aletheia, and a conjunction was formed between Autogenes and Aletheia" (*Haer.* I.29.2). This close link between Autogenes and Aletheia ("truth"), is also found in the *Apocryphon*. This figure is named as "the divine Autogenes of truth" (*Ap. John* 7.24) and a couple of lines later it is noted that the truth dwells in Autogenes (*Ap. John* 7.26). In terms of the series of emanations, it is then noted that adherents to this thought-world "declare that from the Light, which is Christ, and from Aphtharsia, four luminaries were sent forth to surround Autogenes; and again from Thelema and Zoe Aionios four other emissions took place, to wait upon these four luminaries; and these they name Charis (grace), Thelesis (will), Synesis (understanding), and Phronesis (prudence)" (*Haer.* I.29.2). In the *Apocryphon*, in place of the pairing of *thelēma* (will) and *zoē aiōnios* (eternal life), there is a triad: will, thought, and life. Therefore, Irenaeus appears to have dropped one member of this triadic list, or alternatively, perhaps it was expanded at a later stage. The four emissions named by Irenaeus as "grace, will, understanding and prudence" are in the *Apocryphon* collectively termed "the four powers, understanding, grace, perception, and prudence" (*Ap. John* 8.2-4). Once again, there is some minor variation in terminology, but it is apparent that the overall schema referred to in both texts is the same. The emanation of these beings is not recognized by Irenaeus as the author of the *Apocryphon* represents it: that is, as ultimately an expression of the plenitude of the Father which transcends notions of limitations of being. In this way, the cosmos is not totally distanced from the Monad, yet its physicality cannot impact on the Father. As Waldstein describes the outlook, "the cosmos is not something outside the Father and additional to him, the Father's desire and knowledge of himself contains his desire and knowledge of all, including the cosmos."[30]

The final aspect of Irenaeus's portrayal of the role of Autogenes that is mentioned here is his generation of the perfect man. He states, "Autogenes moreover produces a perfect and true man, whom they also call Adamas" (*Haer.* I.29.3). This Adamas exists in the realm between the primal triad and the lower world, where the corresponding earthly Adam dwells deprived of light and exposed to death (*Ap. John* 20.25; 21.4).[31]

Adamas is mentioned but once in the *Apocryphon*, "And from the foreknowledge of the perfect mind, through the revelation of the will of the invisible Spirit and the will of the Autogenes, <the> perfect Man (appeared), the first revelation, and the truth. It is he whom the virginal Spirit called Pigera-Adamas, and he placed him over the first aeon with the mighty one, the Autogenes, the Christ, by the first light Armozel; and with him are his powers" (*Ap. John* 8.27-35). Interestingly, although Irenaeus identifies the role of Adamas as a key element in the cosmological system he describes, the actual name is not used with great frequency in the *Apocrphon*. Instead, that text uses the term "the perfect man" on four occasions, apparently to designate the same figure.

The final paragraph in chapter 29 of book I is in some ways a miscellany of elements that Irenaeus recalls or deems worthy of comment concerning this system. The opening line summarizes the origin of the Holy Spirit: "they maintain, that from the first angel, who stands by the side of Monogenes, the Holy Spirit has been sent forth, whom they also term Sophia and Prunicus" (*Haer.* I.29.4). This protological account of the Holy Spirit accords with elements found throughout the *Apocryphon*, but again does not preserve all elements to be found in that text.

Pearson's assessment that parallels between *Adversus haereses* I.29 and the *Apocryphon of John* occur within the first part of that text is generally correct. This is the section of the revelation discourse, and in fact many of the parallels are drawn from the first part of that revelation discourse (*Ap. John* 1.1—9.24). Whether the implication automatically follows that Irenaeus may have been using a shorter form of the text is dubious, especially as the ten questions of the dialogue section (*Ap. John* 13.13—31.25) do have some parallels with *Haer.* I.30, where Seth is a named character.[32]

Since Irenaeus gives a general outline of the cosmological system for the purpose of discrediting it, he does not provide close enough parallels to determine if he was indebted to any specific text form of the *Apocryphon*. Nor can one be entirely certain that he was citing the cosmic myth from this text either directly or by memory. Yet, notwithstanding these caveats, the key features of the system in the *Apocryphon* and those outlined by Irenaeus abound in shared features. There can be no doubt that the same cosmology stands behind both descriptions, and there is a reasonably high likelihood that Irenaeus used a text similar to that of the *Apocryphon* as the source of his information. However, Grant may be correct, based on the fact that Irenaeus shows no apparent knowledge of the names of the 365 angels responsible for the parts of the human body or of the descent of the Pronoia to the lower darkness which are contained in the longer version of the text, that Irenaeus "almost certainly used the shorter Greek *Apocryhon*."[33] Nonetheless, two factors should be acknowledged. First, that Irenaeus leaves out many of the elements found in the Berlin Codex since he is summarizing the main ideas of the text. Also secondly, although some text form of the *Apocryphon* almost certainly circulated in Greek, there is no way of proving that this was the form preserved in the Berlin Codex. Thus, while there is strong evidence to suggest that the underlying myth of the *Apocryphon* and *Adversus haereses* 1.29 came from a common source, and that it is likely that the source of *Adversus haereses* 1.29 was some form of the *Apocryphon of John*, beyond this other conclusions are ultimately speculative.

Conclusion

Irenaeus clearly sets out his self-declared purpose for writing his five-volume work in the preface to volume one. He states his assessment that "certain men have set the truth aside," and in response he outlines his agenda. Believing that "error, indeed, is never set forth in its naked deformity, lest, being thus exposed, it should at once be detected," he sets out to write an exposé of such errors in order that "men may no longer be drawn away by the plausible system of these heretics." This task was not undertaken in ignorance. There is no doubt that Irenaeus knew much concerning the belief systems of his opponents. Whether what he knew totally corresponded to what he wrote may be debated, and at the very least it must be acknowledged that Irenaeus wrote in such a manner so as to portray his opponents' beliefs in an unfavorable light. His work was no neutral assessment, rather it is written with the passion of a polemicist—albeit a rather well-informed one.

This brief survey has tried to assess which written "gospel-like" sources Irenaeus may have known. He shows clear knowledge of the four canonical Gospels, which he sees as the basis of knowledge of the truth. As was described, he is the earliest extant source that explicitly acknowledges the fourfold gospel canon, although (perhaps ironically, at least for Irenaeus), implicitly Tatian's *Diatesseron* may witness the fourfold canon maybe a decade earlier.[34] The focus of the discussion has been, however, not on the sources that Irenaeus affirms as being free from error, but on those texts from which he may have gained knowledge of the belief systems that he seeks to refute. Two gospel-type sources are explicitly named, the *Gospel of Judas* and the *Gospel of Truth*. In terms of genre, one can sympathize with the reasons why Irenaeus saw these as being so different from the four texts he accepted as being "gospels." The *Gospel of Judas* is a revelatory discourse, in which the Saviour reveals the mysteries of the Sethian understanding of the cosmos. The similarities between the recently discovered *Gospel of Judas* and Irenaeus's description of a text with the same name suggests that a Greek version of the same text that has come down to modern readers was known to Irenaeus.

On the other hand, it was more difficult to conclude with certainty anything concerning Irenaeus's knowledge of the *Gospel of Truth*. Whereas he knew of a text bearing that title, modern readers know only of a text that speaks of the "gospel of truth," in its opening line, as a source of joy to those who apprehend it. However, these words are not written either as a titular prescript or superscript. Nonetheless, such evidence was seen as suggestive of the hypothesis that Irenaeus knew a form of the same text that was discovered at Nag Hammadi. Yet, because there are no direct citations from this text, and because Irenaeus appears to conjoin elements that might have been found in this text with more advanced descriptions of Valentinian cosmology, it cannot be determined whether he gained information concerning the beliefs of Valentinus and his followers directly from the text, or whether he objected to this sermon-like tractate, because it circulated widely to attract potential adherents to the movement.

The Alpha-Beta logion was known to Irenaeus in a form that was closest to its second, shorter version contained in the Greek A recension of the *Infancy Gospel of Thomas*. That multiple forms were incorporated into the same text strongly suggests that this pericope had a prehistory before it was integrated into the *Infancy Gospel of Thomas.* Irenaeus states that he knew this text was used by the Marcosians as a dominical justification for their own use of gematria to interpret scripture. There is, however, no evidence to lend support to the idea that Irenaeus knew the actual text of the *Infancy Gospel of Thomas.* In fact, the more likely hypothesis is that he knew this pericope independently of and possibly prior to the composition of that narrative of the childhood years of Jesus.

Claims that Irenaeus knew the *Gospel of the Ebionites* were seen to have little basis in the statements made in the *Adversus haereses* itself, and, moreover, there is no support for that theory to be derived from the remaining fragments cited by other early Christian writers. Irenaeus describes the fact that the Ebionites used the Gospel of Matthew alone, although he disputes their interpretation of the theology of the birth of Jesus. Rather, Irenaeus's statements of the group's use of the Gospel of Matthew make sense as they stand, and there is no need for recourse to the theory that he had mistaken Matthew for the *Gospel of the Ebionites.*[35]

Although not titled as being a gospel, the *Apocryphon of John* (not unlike the *Gospel of Truth*) sets out the soteriological and cosmological beliefs of the group that adhered to its teachings. The weight of shared details between this text and the description of the belief system that centered on representing the Godhead as a triad of Father, Barbelo, and Autogenes, along with the variation emanations leaves no doubt that the same cosmological system is being described. The most plausible hypothesis for the occurrence of these shared elements is that Irenaeus was dependent on some literary form of the *Apocryphon of John.*

In answer to the question concerning the extent of Irenaeus's knowledge of the literary "gospel-like" traditions of his opponents, it may be concluded that he was relatively well informed. He may have known of texts that are no longer extant and consequently for which modern scholars can no longer detect the degree of Irenaeus's dependence, since he does not name these sources. In terms of clearly detectable literary dependence on "gospel" texts, the recently discovered *Gospel of Judas* alone may be identified. Moreover, Irenaeus undoubtedly knows of the *Apocryphon of John* (or a text closely related to the revelatory discourse contained in that text), but it is probably stretching the definition and genre of "gospel" to include this text in the category of "gospels." While the thought world of the *Gospel of Truth* is not entirely dissimilar to the *Apocryphon of John*, however, in distinction from the *Apocryphon*, Irenaeus himself knows it under a title using the word "gospel." It is uncertain whether he knew this text by reputation, or whether he had read its actual contents. Finally, other texts such as the *Gospel of the Ebionites* and the *Infancy Gospel of Thomas* are unlikely to have been known to Irenaeus. Thus, while Irenaeus may have known of far more noncanonical gospel texts than we can identify, he betrays little knowledge of this possibility. If his aim was to cast such works known as gospels outside his cherished fourfold gospel canon into oblivion, then he must be commended since for the most part he has succeeded!

CHAPTER TEN

Irenaeus, the Scribes, and the Scriptures

Papyrological and Theological Observations

from P.Oxy. 405

CHARLES E. HILL

As a reader and as a writer, Irenaeus was well aware of the problem of scribal imperfection in the production of books. Eusebius preserves for us a colophon Irenaeus placed at the end of his *On the Ogdoad* probably written around the year 190,[1] which illustrates the gravity of textual corruption and Irenaeus's efforts to ensure faithful transmission: "I adjure [ὁρκίζω] you, who shall copy out this book [τὸν μεταγραψόμενον], by our Lord Jesus Christ, by his glorious advent when he comes to judge the living and the dead, that you compare [ἀντιβάλῃς] what you shall transcribe [ὅ μετεγράψω] and correct [κατορθώσῃς] it with this copy [ἀντίγραφον] from which you shall transcribe [μετεγράψω], with all care [ἐπιμελῶν], and you shall likewise transcribe [μεταγράψειν] this oath and put it in the copy" (*On the Ogdoad*, Eusebius, *HE* V.20.2).

Irenaeus's attitude toward the copying of scriptural texts was certainly no less stringent than this, a fact borne out by another famous comment about the copying of the book of Revelation. Mentioning a scribal fault[2] by means of which, intentionally or unintentionally, the number 666 in Rev. 13:18 was changed to 616, Irenaeus reminds the reader, "there shall be no light punishment [inflicted] upon him who either adds or subtracts anything from the Scripture," alluding to the curse laid on copyists by the author of the book of Revelation in Rev. 22:18-19 (*Haer.* V.30.1). Irenaeus was thus aware of the varying scribal quality of scriptural books then circulating. Some copies of Revelation, he says, were both "ancient" and "most approved" or (perhaps better) "most excellent,"[3] others evidently not.[4]

There is thus no mistaking Irenaeus's ideal of copying texts of scripture, at least in continuous manuscripts. In Irenaeus's day, however, and for a long time both before and after, scripture did not necessarily come through the *citation* process quite intact. Like all literary borrowings, borrowings from scripture too were subjected to minor modification to fit the quoting author's context, or perhaps to highlight a point the quoting author thought was latent in the text. Exact reproduction was evidently not the necessary concomitant of a regard even for the sacredness of the material quoted.[5]

In the often adversarial writings of Irenaeus, however, in which contested interpretations often hung on words, even letters, we see perhaps a greater care in getting the text right than in any Christian writer before him. He is, as Souter said, "the earliest surviving writer of the Christian era who quotes the New Testament both extensively and accurately."[6] The secondary use of scriptural texts by Irenaeus and some of his Valentinian opponents, and in other authors engaged in exegesis, is becoming more scrupulously exact. A stable text, or at least the perception of one, is the presupposition of this kind of citation practice and of the kind of scribal activity encouraged by Irenaeus. The Alands say "It is not until 180 (in Irenaeus) that signs of an established text appear."[7] Despite his awareness of certain textual corruptions, Irenaeus seems to believe that he possessed a text which had been preserved for him in its essential integrity, speaking as he does of "the unfeigned preservation [*custoditio*], coming down to us, of the scriptures, with a complete collection allowing for neither addition nor subtraction" (*Haer.* IV.33.8).[8]

P.Oxy. 405

Appropriately enough, the care for textual preservation and the high regard for scripture exemplified in Irenaeus's literary output is in an interesting way symbolized in the earliest known fragment of his work. P.Oxy. 405 (van Haelst 671), consisting of fragments of a papyrus roll containing parts of *Against Heresies* III.9.3, was first published in 1903. At that time, Grenfell and Hunt could say that "it is probably the oldest Christian fragment yet published."[9] This of course is no longer the case, though P. Oxy. 405 can still claim the distinction of being the oldest Christian fragment yet published that contains a New Testament quotation.

Written in what C. H. Roberts calls "a handsome professional hand,"[10] the fragment has also gained notoriety for its being so close chronologically to its original. Book III of *Against Heresies* was written sometime in the 180s, and Roberts was very confident that P.Oxy. 405 should be dated to the late second century.[11] In his memorable words the manuscript "reached Oxyrhynchus not long after the ink was dry on the author's manuscript."[12] Peter Rodgers thinks, "It is not impossible that Irenaeus himself had written the fragment."[13] If P.Oxy. 405 did not actually originate in Lyons (penned by Irenaeus himself or not), the manuscript surely will be a first, or at latest, second-generation copy of one which did originate there under Irenaeus's own direction or supervision.

Finally, P.Oxy. 405 has been of interest to New Testament text-critical scholars because its quotation of Matthew 3:16-17 is closer to the form of text in Codex Bezae than even the reputedly faithful Latin translation of *Haer.* allows, for it reveals, among other things, the reading, "you are my beloved Son," rather than, "This is my beloved Son."

But P.Oxy. 405 reveals another very interesting and potentially significant scribal phenomenon which has received almost no attention, namely, the wedge-shaped marks, or "*diplai*," in the left margin, each corresponding to a line of text.[14]

This is the first occurrence in a Christian text of the marginal *siglum* known as a *diple*. But what do they signify?

Illustration 1. P.Oxy. 405 containing Irenaeus's quotation of Matt. 3:16-17. Reproduced by permission of the Syndics of Cambridge University Library.

The Diple as Literary *Siglum*

Kathleen McNamee notes that the *diple*, like other *sigla*, had been used in literary texts at least since the second century BCE.[15] In the Homeric tradition, it was often used to mark a place in a text to which a separated commentary (ὑπομνήματα) corresponded.[16] But McNamee calls the *diple* "a general-purpose symbol"[17] and notes (in her Table 2) that it is used to mark division in the text, to mark a quotation, to indicate an error, a variant, a marginal note, and that sometimes its meaning is uncertain.[18]

The Diplai in P. Oxy. 405 and Other Christian Literature

In P.Oxy. 405, *diplai* are clearly being used to mark a quotation, as Grenfell and Hunt noted in their original report.[19] But how common was the practice of using the *diple* to mark quotations? In 1992, according to McNamee, there were "roughly three hundred Greek literary papyri from Egypt in which sigla appear in the margin or between the lines."[20] Of these three hundred, McNamee finds thirty-three that use the *diple*, and of these thirty-three only twelve use the *diple* as a marker of quotations. Clearly, these twelve must represent a very small minority of the Egyptian literary texts that contain quotations, showing that the marking of quotations was rather exceptional. Of the twelve manuscripts that use the *diple* to mark a quotation, the earliest are from the second century, which contributes five.[21]

The use of *diplai*, or any other marginal markings, to indicate quotations was thus not the norm. And P.Oxy. 405 turns out to be not only possibly the earliest Christian example but among the earliest of all examples. Of other surviving Christian theological works from the early period, many, such as the Mss of *The Shepherd* of Hermas, do not contain quotations *per se*. Others do contain quotations but no marginal markings.[22]

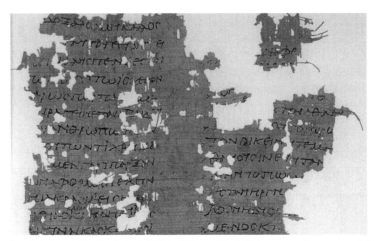

Illustration 2. P. Oxy. 53.3699 (LDAB 4859), Philosophical Dialogue, perhaps part of Aristotle's *Protrepticus*, second century, papyrus roll, identified by McNamee as one of the early examples of the use of marginal *diplai* for quotation. Image courtesy of the Egypt Exploration Society and Imaging Papyri Project, Oxford.

I have, however, so far come across six more, non-biblical Christian manuscripts from the seventh century or earlier that use the *diplai*. They are:

P.Mich. xviii.764, a two-column papyrus roll, dated by the editor to the second or third century,[23] so, very much contemporary with P.Oxy. 405. It is a fragment of an unidentified homily or treatise. The left margin of the right-hand column contains *diplai* marking citations of Jeremiah 18:3-6 and 1 Corinthians 3:13.[24]

Paris Bib. Nat. P.Gr. 1120, a late third-century,[25] two-column papyrus codex found at Coptos, Egypt, containing two of Philo's works.[26] As Roberts pointed out, it is clearly a Christian copy of Philo, as shown by the *nomina sacra* abbreviations for God, Son, Father, Spirit, and Lord.[27] It appears from the transcription that the scribe abandoned the effort to mark quotations after a few leaves in each treatise, and the editor remarks that in the second treatise, where the writing is more rapid, the sign is rounded in the shape of a comma.[28] Interestingly, this is the codex of Philo which contained as stuffing for its cover the fragments of Luke now known to New Testament textual critics as P⁴.[29]

A papyrus fragment given the Gregory-Aland number P⁷, variously dated anywhere from the late third to the sixth century.[30] This is actually not a New Testament manuscript but an unknown work which contains a quotation of Luke 4:1-2, marked with marginal *diplai*.[31]

A sixth-century papyrus codex of Hilary of Poitiers' *De Trinitate*, marked evidently later in the sixth century by Dulcitius of Aquino (Vienna, Nationalbibliothek, MS lat. 2160).[32]

A late sixth- or early seventh-century papyrus copy of Origen's *Dialogue with Heraclides* found at Toura (van Haelst 683, cf. 684) which uses the *diple* to mark Old Testament and New Testament texts.[33]

Pap. Louvre E 10295 (van Haelst 638 (2)), a sixth- or seventh-century copy of Cyril of Alexandria's *On the Adoration and the Worship in Spirit and Truth* found at El Deirin in the Fayum.[34]

I have, so far, found no New Testament papyrus manuscript that uses *diplai* to mark quotations.[35] The first Biblical manuscript I know of which does so, also the only one of the period that does so consistently, is Codex Vaticanus (early to middle fourth-century). The *diplai* belong to the original hand[36] (scribe B, who penned the New Testament), as is visible, for example, at John 7:42, where the scribe presumed there was a citation of the Old Testament (in reality there is not).[37] There the *diple* is much fainter than the writing of the text, preserving the original hand which was not overwritten by a later hand, as were the letters in the text.[38] It is clear that this scribe's attempt was to use *diplai* comprehensively throughout the New Testament. The last surviving page of Codex Vaticanus contains Hebrews 8, where the quotation of Jeremiah 31 takes nearly a whole column of text, each line of which is carefully marked by a *diple* in the margin.

"Scribe A" of Codex Sinaiticus also knows the practice. Milne and Skeat say, "It seems indeed that the Eusebian apparatus and the paragraphi are both part of a thorough-going revision of the manuscript by A, for in these same early pages of Matthew accents and breathings have been carefully supplied, quotations from the Old Testament marked with arrow-heads (and, in the earlier cases, the name of the book as well), and a number of corrections in a minute hand . . . inserted. The Old Testament quotation-marks cease after the third page (N.T. 2), the accents and breathings in the middle of the fifth" (NT 3, col. 3, l. 10).[39]

The *diplai* return at the beginning of Romans, but do not extend throughout the book or the Pauline corpus, then again they appear at the beginning of Acts[41] and once again fade out. In addition, there are two instances in 1 Peter (2:22; 3:10).

Codex Alexandrinus[42] uses the *diplai* but shows us some irregularities in the Gospels. In its present state, it contains only the last part of Matthew, but from where it begins, at 25:6, there are no *diplai* marking the Old Testament citations. In Mark, only five citations are marked, all in chapters 10–12, and using an irregular form: a dot followed by a small *diple* (Illustration 5) and sometimes followed by an obel (Illustration 6).[43]

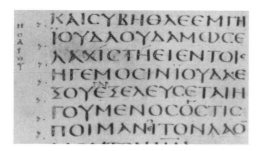

Illustration 3. Codex Sinaiticus (q. 74, f. 1v), Matthew 2:6 citing Micah 5:2. Note scribal mistake in attribution to HCAIOY. What look like dots following the *diplai* are actually line pricks.[40]

Illustration 4. Codex Alexandrinus 39a, Mark 12:29-30 citing Deuteronomy 6:4-5, dotted *diple*.[44]

Illustration 5. Codex Alexandrinus 17a, Mark 11:9-10 citing Psalm 118:25, stigmatized dotted *diple*.[45]

In Luke, only three Old Testament citations are marked,[46] all, though, with the simple *diple*, in John only one (at 12:37-40), using the dotted *diple*. Despite the sparseness and irregularity of the markings in the Gospels, beginning with the citation of Psalm 69:26 in Acts 1:20, the rest of the codex, containing Acts, the Catholic Epistles, the Pauline epistles (including Hebrews), Revelation and the two Clementine epistles show a regular use of the "standard" form of marginal quotation *diplai* for scriptural quotations, although *2 Clement* does not have them.[47] The use or nonuse of the *diplai* does not seem to distinguish the various scribes[48] but could be related to the underlying textual complexions of the exemplars used, as I will note later.

Illustration 6. Codex Alexandrinus, 82a, Acts 1:20 citing Psalm 69:26.[49]

I have not observed any such use of marginal markings in Codex Washingtoniensis or Codex Bezae.[50] I have not been able to obtain any images of Codex Ephraemi, the fifth-century palimpsest written over in the twelfth century with the works of Ephraim the Syrian. But Ulrich Schmidt, who has looked at photos of the manuscript, has reported that the New Testament portion does contain marginal *diplai* marking the Old Testament citations.[51]

The quotation *diplai* resurface in at least two related, ninth-century, Greco-Latin interlinear uncials, Codex Sangallensis (Δ) and Codex Boernerianus (G^P), thought to be companion volumes penned by Irish monks at Bobbio.[52] Sangallensis (Δ) contains the four Gospels,[53] Boernerianus (G^P) the Pauline corpus.[54]

From a limited survey of photographic reproductions of later New Testament manuscripts, it would appear that the practice never became standard in the copying of New Testament texts but was continued in some manuscripts throughout the textual tradition.[55]

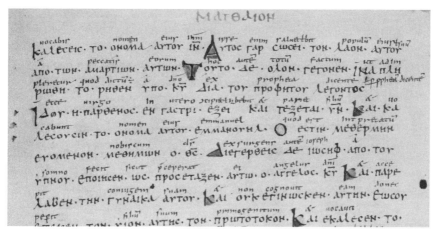

Illustration 7. Codex Sangallensis, Matthew 1:23 citing Isaiah 7:14. Note the coloring-in of the *diplai*.[56]

Were the Marks Original to Irenaeus (or His Scribe)?

Arguing against their originality would be the fact that the next earliest known fragments of *Against Heresies*, the Jena fragments, from a very fragmentary third- or fourth-century roll (portions of *Haer.* V.3.2—13.2) found at Apollonopolis, P. Jena. Inv. 18 and 21,[57] do not have them.[58]

Illustration 8. Jena Fragment, column three, lines 6-7, containing *Haer.* V.5.1 and Irenaeus's quotation of 1 Thessalonians 5:23.[59] Papyrussammlung Jena (Germany): P. Jen. Irenaeus.

One might easily imagine, however, that by book V this scribe, like the scribes of the Philo treatises mentioned above and of Sinaiticus, might have simply given up. Also, the Jena fragments display a less careful hand than P.Oxy. 405.[60] Perhaps this scribe did not have the skill or the interest required to produce a more scholarly volume such as P.Oxy. 405.

On the other hand, the earliest and perhaps textually most important of the Latin manuscripts of *Against Heresies*, Codex Claromontanus of the ninth century, does use marginal markings, though of a somewhat different shape, more like an elongated "s."[61]

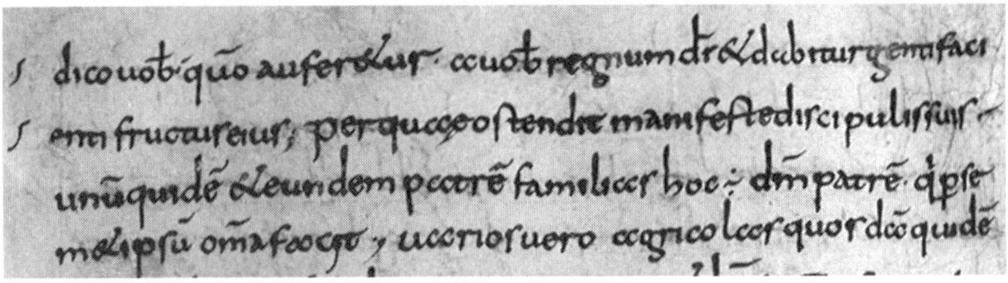

Illustration 9. Codex Claromontanus, *Haer.* IV.36.1 citing Matthew 21:43.[62]

Moreover, as observed above, P.Oxy. 405 has been dated so close to the original writing of *Against Heresies* book III that it is at least a real possibility that it was produced in Lyons. If so, the *diplai* would almost certainly reflect Irenaeus's own intention (Rodgers, we recall, suggests Irenaeus himself as scribe).

Diplae Sacrae?

In any case, it is significant that the author or the scribe of P.Oxy. 405 (whether Irenaeus himself or another) is very conscious that Irenaeus is at this point in the manuscript quoting a literary text. Do the *diplai* tell us anything more? In particular, would the scribe have marked Irenaeus's quotations of the writings of Ptolemy the Valentinian, or pagan authors, or only quotations of what Irenaeus (or the scribe) regarded as scripture? It is a pity that no more of the manuscript survives, from which alone we might be able to gain a definitive answer to this question. But the surrounding evidence may help us form a reasonably solid provisional answer.

The only discussion of this phenomenon from antiquity which I have to this point discovered is that of Isidore of Seville (560–636) in his *Etymologies* I.21.13[63] compiled between 615 and the early 630s. In his section on critical marks, he says of the *diple*, "Our scribes place this in books of churchmen to separate or to make clear the citations of Sacred Scriptures."[64] Isidore links the *diple* to the marking of quotations of Sacred Scripture, and mentions no other forms of literature. How does this accord with our evidence?

Most closely contemporary with Irenaeus is P.Mich. 764, in which *diplai* marking the citations of both Jeremiah 18:3-6 and 1 Corinthains 3:13 are visible. The fragment contains no other quotations of non-biblical materials, but it is at least noteworthy that 1 Corinthians, a New Testament text, is marked in the same context as an Old Testament text. The *diplai* in the margin of the Philo codex Paris Bib. Nat. P.Gr. 1120 mark scriptural citations but apparently not citations from other sources. The first treatise in this codex, *Who is the Heir of Divine Things*, contains a few short quotations of non-scriptural sayings, most notably his citation of the comic poets ("If a slave is always dumb, he is scarcely worth a crumb: let him, freely told, boldly speak"),[65] is unmarked by a *diple* where in the same context three citations of Genesis are so marked.[66]

In Vaticanus,[67] Paul's citation of two pagan writers in his speech at the Areopagus in Acts 17:28 provides an interesting case. Though he does not mark Paul's quotation of Epimenedes,[68] the scribe does mark in the same verse Paul's brief citation of Aratus. This would seem at first glance to show that the scribe at least once used the *diple* for a non-scriptural citation. But the introductory formula in Vaticanus, along with several later witnesses, reads here not "As even some of your (καθ᾽ ὑμᾶς) poets have said" but "As even some of our (καθ᾽ ἡμᾶς) poets have said."[69] Thus, it would appear that the scribe thought Paul was quoting a Jewish, scriptural poet.

Titus does not survive in Vaticanus for us to check the quotation of Epimenides in Titus 1:12. Jude's quotation of *1 Enoch* at Jude 14–15, however, provides another interesting case. The scribe uses the *diple* at the beginning of the quote but stops about halfway through. Did the scribe deem *1 Enoch* a "semi- or deutero-canonical" book, worthy of only "half-quotes"? Or did he or she realize halfway through that the text being copied was not a scriptural text and abort?[70] The latter of these two options seems the most likely for a fourth-century Christian scribe.[71] In any case, if we accept that the marking of the Aratus citation in Acts 17:28 was done on the faulty assumption that Paul was citing a scriptural poet, we may say that the scribe of Vaticanus intends the *diple* to mark only scriptural texts.

Codex Alexandrinus offers another lucid example. The scribe clearly does *not* use *diplai* for Paul's citations of two pagan authors at Acts 17:28 (the text of A has καθ᾽ ὑμᾶς not καθ᾽ ἡμᾶς), nor for the citation of Enoch in Jude 14–15, nor for the citation of Epimenides in Titus 1:12.[72] Undoubtedly it was the intention of the scribe or scribes of Alexandrinus, or its archetype, to mark only Scriptural citations.

Similarly, the scribe of Boernerianus (Paul) does not use the *diple* at Titus 1:12, again, presumably because Epimenides is not a Scriptural author.

At least in manuscripts where we can make the distinction, then, Isidore's comment proves true. Early Christian scribes adopted this *siglum* for marking quotations of Holy Scripture. Apart from Vaticanus's probably unwitting marking of Aratus in Acts and its partial marking of *1 Enoch* in Jude, we have uncovered no instance of a Christian scribe (or scribe of a Christian text) marking non-scriptural quotations—this pertains even to the Christian copy of Philo mentioned above.

If we may presume that this was the case also with P.Oxy. 405, it will be even more significant that its *diplai* mark not an Old Testament but a New Testament writing, the Gospel according to Matthew. This would mean the scribe is using the *diple* to mark Matthew's scriptural status. We already know from the contents of Irenaeus's writings that he considered Matthew's Gospel, like the other three Gospels, to be scripture.[73] So if indeed the *diplai* are an indicator of scriptural status, this would not tell us anything new about Irenaeus, or, presumably, about many of his early readers.

The adoption of this new scribal convention to mark scriptural status would, however, be quite significant, as it would parallel a better known and more pervasive scribal convention, the *nomina sacra*.[74] As the *nomina sacra* apparently mark out certain names as holy, the marginal *diple* marks certain texts as holy, according to the testimony of Isidore of Seville, and consistent with the evidence collected so far. P.Oxy. 405 uses both scribal conventions, and is probably the oldest manuscript we have which does so.[75]

Conclusion

Irenaeus tells us he was "most properly assured that the Scriptures are indeed perfect, since they were spoken by the Word of God and His Spirit" (II.28.2).[76] For him, the Gospels according to Matthew, Mark, Luke, and John were among these perfect and divinely authored scriptures (II.27.2, etc.). It seems a natural outgrowth of such a doctrine of scripture that certain measures should develop, even scribally, to signify it, to make it visible. The physical properties of P.Oxy. 405 show us two ways in which this was done. First, this copy of Irenaeus's writing is made on a roll. As Roberts and many others have observed, Christians used the codex for their scriptural writings. Larry Hurtado says, "there is no New Testament text copied on an unused roll among second- or third-century Christian manuscripts."[77] Second, the words of scripture contained in this roll are distinguished from the words of Irenaeus by *diplai* in the margin. Some Christian scribes, whether on their own or on the instruction of their clients, employed this *siglum* to enact visually what, one might say, was expected to take place in the mind or heart of the reader (perhaps of the next copyist as well, as per *On the Ogdoad*!), a setting-apart of certain words by quite literally "pointing them out." Thus these scribes initiated a practice which, while it never achieved the universal usage of the *nomina sacra*, was continued in parts of the Christian scribal tradition. We might say it is perpetuated today in our present critical editions of the New Testament by italicizing the Old Testament citations in the Nestle-Aland text and by putting them in bold type in the UBS text.

The quotation *diplai* in P.Oxy. 405 also "point" us to what seems an untapped source of information about scribal practices and beliefs. Every layer of scribal activity provides another opportunity for mistakes, and this one is no exception. We have seen inadvertent non-dipling, perhaps inadvertent or ill-advised dipling, and erroneous marking of the sources (ΗΣΑΙΟΥ where we should have had ΜΙΧΑΙΟΥ in Sinaiticus, q. 74, f. 1v).

In manuscripts in which they are used, quotation *diplai* can provide an avenue of access to the scribe's, or the scribe's community's, conception of canon. That is, the scribe, or someone instructing the scribe, has to decide which quotations to mark and which not to mark. We have noted the treatments of *1 Enoch* in Vaticanus and Alexandrinus. Another example is the citation of an unknown prophetic writing in *1 Clement* 23.3, "Far from us be that which is written, 'Wretched are they who are of a double mind, and of a doubting heart; who say, These things we have heard even in the times of our fathers; but, behold, we have grown old, and none of them has happened unto us.'" The scribe of Alexandrinus does not mark this text with *diplai*, even though Scriptural texts are marked in the same context. The presence of the *diplai* in P.Oxy. 405 (as well as in P.Mich. 764 mentioned above), if they may be assumed to function like all other *diplai* in early Christian writings, are thus significant evidence against the thesis espoused by some that no ideas of canonicity existed among Christians before the fourth century.

The marking of scriptural quotations in some manuscripts also provides one more way of linking certain manuscripts to others and thus can also help us with the transmission history of documents and with textual criticism. For instance, in Codex Alexandrinus it seems we can say that this scribal activity was also a copying activity, and not the independent, interpretative activity of the individual scribe. We have observed the irregularities of Alexandrinus in the Gospels, where *diplai* are used only sparsely, and sometimes in an unusual form. Since this variance is evidently not due to a change of scribes, it would seem that it is attributable to a difference in the exemplars used. Now, it is well known that the Gospel text in Alexandrinus is of a different quality from the rest of the New Testament. Metzger and Ehrman say of Alexandrinus, "In the Gospels it is the oldest example of the Byzantine type of text . . . In the rest of the New Testament (which may have been copied by the scribe from a different exemplar from that employed for the text of the Gospels), it ranks along with B and ℵ as representative of the Alexandrian type of text."[78] The varying form and occurrence of dipling provides an independent conclusion that confirms the hypothesis based on textual complexion that different exemplars were used by the scribes. That is, the "Byzantine" exemplar(s) for the Gospels did not contain *diplai* (at least not consistently) but the "Alexandrian" exemplar(s) for Acts, Paul, and the Catholic Epistles and 1 Clement (Revelation contains no Old Testament quotations) did contain them. The evidence of the *diplai* also raises the possibility that *1 Clement* and *2 Clement* may not have existed together in the scribe's exemplar.

How appropriate that such textual and canonical issues should arise from our earliest known text of Irenaeus. Not only is he, as Souter said, "the earliest surviving writer of the Christian era who quotes the New Testament both extensively and accurately."[79] The earliest surviving fragment of his work opens up for us a unique and previously obscured scribal window on issues of text, canon, and theology in the late second century, issues for which Irenaeus himself is so justly famous.

PART THREE

Legacy

Irenaeus and His Theological Traditions

CHAPTER ELEVEN

The Heart of Irenaeus's Theology

Michael Slusser

The title of this chapter is meant to provoke. After all, many scholars and many books have described Irenaeus's theology and located the heart of his thought in other places. Recapitulation is probably the theological idea most frequently proposed as the central theme for Irenaeus. Even if I did not harbor the suspicion that Irenaeus learned about recapitulation from Justin Martyr,[1] I would consider *magnitudo* and *dilectio* to be at the heart of Irenaeus's theology. Two other authors have hinted at the argument that I am about to make, but they have not carried it out in full. Joseph Caillot proposes "the distance between God the creator and created humanity" as a kind of unifying thread throughout Irenaeus's work, and he resolves that distance by the union effected by Jesus Christ.[2] Yoshifumi Torisu in a recent book addresses my theme, although only briefly, since he is mainly occupied with trinitarian doctrine.[3] Neither author places enough emphasis on love as the central factor in true knowledge of God, true gnosis.

Critical to my argument is the way that Irenaeus sees the matter at dispute between himself and the Gnostics against whom he is writing. As he presents it, the Gnostics accuse the ecclesiastical Christians (the church people, as I shall call them), who are not spiritual but merely psychic, of worshiping a limited being, the creator Demiurge, instead of God. These psychic Christians do not know any better. They are ignorant, knowing nothing of the infinite and eternal God, the God above the Demiurge, the high God about whom the Gnostics speak and to which they claim to be related in their spiritual nature.[4] The Valentinians "speak to the crowd regarding those who are from the church, whom they call ordinary church people, and by their speeches they take in very simple people and deceive them, by imitating our mode of address, into frequenting their classes. These then ask us why, although they think many things the same as we do, we arbitrarily refrain from communicating with them, and why, although they say the same things and hold the same doctrine, we call them heretics."[5] The alleged knowledge of the Gnostics and the alleged ignorance of the psychic Christians set the parameters of the argument in *Adversus haereses*.

The way in which Irenaeus portrays God's transcendence is similar to the terms that he ascribes to the Gnostics. The heart of his difference from them lies not on the side of the divine transcendence but rather on how God can nevertheless be known. The Gnostics claim that some people, those who are "spiritual," may be capable of such knowledge through their connection with Sophia and through the rescue effort launched on her behalf from the other Aeons of the Pleroma. In contrast, Irenaeus proposes that knowledge of God is available to all, not because God lacks transcendence but because of God's love. The divine transcendence, while it constitutes an unbridgeable chasm from our side, offers no obstacle to God when God wills to give vision, life, and union to creatures.

Irenaeus appeals to two axioms, one from philosophy and the other from scripture, in spelling out what is fitting for God (θεοπρεπές).[6] The first is from the pre-Socratic philosopher Xenophanes (Diels B24), which Irenaeus has amplified from other Platonist sources.[7] The key phrase from Xenophanes is "The whole (of God) sees, the whole thinks, the whole hears"; there is a simplicity and simultaneity about the deity that can only be so described, if one compares it to the way in which creaturely agency flows from distinct, complementary faculties. Irenaeus uses the axiom to underline the transcendence of the Godhead and he expands on it in different contexts.[8] Robert Grant says, "In Irenaeus's opinion this statement is a universally valid axiom of theology. The second quotation is introduced by the words *quemadmodum adest religiosis ac piis dicere de deo*. The third is stated thus: *qui dicit eum totum visionem et totum auditum . . . non peccat*. And the fourth correlates it with biblical doctrine: *sicut ex scripturis dicimus*. This is to say that the teaching of Xenophanes is one of the pillars of the theology of Irenaeus."[9]

The other axiom, the one that he claims as scriptural, is actually from *The Shepherd* of Hermas, *mand.* 1.[10] In *Adversus haereses* IV.20.2, Irenaeus says, "Well, therefore, did scripture declare, 'First of all, believe that God is one, who created and completed all things and made out of that which was not that all things might be, who contains all things, and is contained by no one.'" Rowan Greer says "that the formula 'God contains all things, but is uncontained' supplies a simple and concise definition of Irenaeus's theological premise. The details of his doctrinal position may all be derived from the one formula."[11]

As William Schoedel points out in his fascinating study of this second axiom, it is one that the Valentinians were willing to accept, at least according to the first lines of *haer.* I.1.1[12]: their Propator was invisible and no being could contain him.[13] A few lines later, Irenaeus tells us that Mind (Nous), born of the Propator and Silence, like and equal to the one who had put him forth, alone could encompass the greatness of the Father (*haer.* I.1.1).[14] Mind alone could see him and rejoice in the Father's immeasurable greatness, thinking how he might convey this greatness to the other Aeons, how great the Father is, without beginning and unable to be contained or comprehended (*haer.* I.2.1). That is rather close, even uncomfortably so, to the Great Church's understanding of the relation of the Word to the Father as Irenaeus presents it: "all saw the Father in the Son, for the Father is the invisible of the Son, the Son the visible of the Father" (*haer.* IV.6.6.).[15] We shall return to those opening descriptions of the Pleroma at the end of this paper.

When the late Richard A. Norris spoke about the unity and transcendence of God as Irenaeus and the Gnostics addressed it, he did it in philosophical terms. He emphasized, "He [Irenaeus] repeats over and over again that God is *without limits*. The true God is himself the Pleroma, 'the Fullness' of all things. As such, he is contained by nothing, yet himself contains whatever exists." In Norris's view, since Irenaeus was fighting a teaching that held "the irreconcilability of divine Being with material existence," he was "in search . . . of a way of asserting the transcendent majesty of God which will not seem to exclude him from the world." The notion of limitlessness, "not merely that God cannot be measured, but also that nothing sets a limit to his power and presence," in Norris's view is "precisely what assures his direct and intimate *relation* with every creature."[16] A good case can be made that only a strong doctrine of divine transcendence can make divine immanence possible, but I am not convinced that Irenaeus has that in mind. In addition, Norris's phrase "will not seem to exclude him from the world" could undermine that transcendence. Norris's philosophical angle of approach looks for a metaphysical solution to conflict with the Gnostics. I think that this obscures Irenaeus's real agenda, which goes beyond metaphysics and portrays God in terms of love and will.

When Irenaeus comes to provide a basis for creaturely knowledge of God, he does not appeal to divine infinity or to limitlessness, however great a role those concepts played in his fencing with his Gnostic opponents. He appeals, rather, to a divine initiative that overrides the insuperable metaphysical obstacle constituted by God's incomprehensibility and *magnitudo*. That initiative is usually, but not always, rendered in the old Latin translation by *dilectio*. Let us look at the principal passages where those two stand in contrast.

The first is in *haer.* II.13.4. Using the first axiom above, the one from Xenophanes, Irenaeus has just described how the Father of all—a term widespread in early Christian usage for God the creator—is above human emotions and conflicts. He continues,

> [God] is, however, even beyond these things and for these reasons indescribable. "Intelligence" encompassing all things [*capax omnium*] will well and truly be said [of God], but not in a way like human intelligence; and "Light" will most properly be said, but nothing like the light with which we are familiar. Likewise in all other respects the Father of all will in nothing be like our human littleness. He is spoken of in these terms according to love [*secundum dilectionem*]; according to greatness [*secundum magnitudinem*], however, he is understood to be above them.

This is a passage where both of the axioms that I introduced at the start of this paper appear alongside the terms on which I wish to focus. *Magnitudo* in the Latin translation of *Against heresies* generally represents the Greek μέγεθος, according to Bruno Reynders' *Lexique comparée*.[17] The case of *dilectio* is not so simple. Where there is Greek with which to compare the Latin, it is ἀγάπη in all cases but one, but those are usually biblical passages. The best parallel in which there is Greek is in *haer.* V.17.1: "He [i.e., God] is the Creator, who according to love [ἀγάπην] is Father, but according to power, Lord, according to wisdom, our creator and fashioner." Going back now to the passage we have just seen in *haer.* II.13.4, one might well suppose a Greek φιλανθρωπία as the basis, but that word does not appear in any of the fragmentary remains of Irenaeus's Greek. Adelin Rousseau, in his retroversion, takes the Greek to be ἀγάπη.[18] For my argument, it is enough that the early translator used *dilectio*.

Our second instance comes a little later at *haer.* II.17.11, where Irenaeus questions why his opponents assert that their Father delayed in making known his unknowability, when that could have been done much earlier.

> Why did the aeons rest and receive perfect knowledge when they learned that the Father is uncontainable and incomprehensible? They could have had this knowledge before they got into passions, for the greatness [*magnitudo*] of the Father would not have been diminished if they had known from the beginning that the Father is uncontainable and incomprehensible. For if he was unknown on account of his immense greatness [*magnitudinem*], he ought also out of immense love [*dilectionem*][19] have preserved impassible those who were born from him, since nothing stood in the way, but it even would have been more useful had they known from the beginning that the Father is uncontainable and incomprehensible.

Granted, Irenaeus here is arguing dialectically against his opponents' hypothesis, not giving his own doctrine of God. It is an ironic argument. He is placing ideas in their minds that apparently are not there, and suggesting that they should have been there, and even more should have been in the mind of their alleged Father.

Our third passage is close to the end of Book Three, *haer.* III.24.2. Irenaeus is already into his concluding peroration asserting the Church's better claim to be the source of knowledge about God. The terms that he uses are his own ideas, not ones that he is attributing (however ironically) to his opponents. Irenaeus has just accused his opponents of constantly looking and never being able to find; he continues,

> For they blaspheme the Maker, that is, the one who is truly God, who furnishes "finding." They think they have found another god above God, or another fullness or another economy. And for that reason the light that comes from God will not enlighten them, because they have dishonored and scorned God, thinking him insignificant because, on account of his love [*dilectionem*] and immense benevolence [*benignitatem*] he came into human knowledge—not knowledge according to greatness [*magnitudinem*], nor according to substance, for no one has measured or touched it, but in this respect: that we may know that the one who made and fashioned and breathed the breath of life into them and sustains us through creation, making all things secure by his word and joining them together by his wisdom, is the only true God.

His opponents, Irenaeus says, would prefer to dream of an Epicurean-style god who would never be caught communicating with the human race or taking care of the world. The only way that his opponents can conceive of a transcendent god is by isolating him so completely from the created world that he is barred from creating it, caring for it, or communicating with rational creatures. The Gnostics' low opinion of the creator God worshiped by the church people goes hand in hand with their scorn for a God who would love as the church people say that God loves. There is no doubt here about Irenaeus's own position: The creator is the true God, who is unknowable in terms of greatness, but who so loves creatures as to find a way to be known by them. This is pure Irenaeus, with the possible exception of the use of the term *substantia*. Here it implies materiality, since it could be measured and touched; it may be a term that he is borrowing from Gnostic usage.

By the famous chapter 20 of Book IV, Irenaeus is completely involved in presenting his Christian alternative, while he continues—as he always will—to assert the intrinsic greatness and immeasurability of God. Right from the beginning of *haer.* IV.20.1, he combines the *magnitudo/dilectio* pairing with the second axiom mentioned above, the one that says that God contains all things while remaining uncontained. "Therefore according to greatness [*secundum magnitudinem*] there is no knowing God, for it is impossible for the Father to be measured. But according to his love [*secundum dilectionem*]—for this is what leads us through his word to God—those who obey him are always learning that God is so great [*tantus*], and that it is he who through himself established and chose and adorned and contains[20] all things—including in 'all things' us and this world of ours. And we therefore were created along with those things contained by him." I think that the "him" in "when we obey him" refers to God's Word. The equation of Word and Son is made explicitly at the start of *haer.* IV.20.3, where likewise Wisdom, as it appears in Proverbs, is equated with the Spirit.

In any case, it is clear that, for Irenaeus, the creator is the transcendent God and love can bring about results that would be strictly inconceivable in terms of God's greatness alone. At the beginning of *haer.* IV.20.4, Word and Wisdom are integrated into what by now we recognize as one of Irenaeus's favorite ways of speaking:

> Therefore there is one God, who made and finished all things by Word and Wisdom. But this is the Creator [*Demiurgus*], who also entrusted this world to the human race, who according to greatness [*secundum magnitudinem*], indeed, is unknown to all of his creatures (for no one has searched out his height, neither of the ancients nor of those who are alive today); but according to love [*secundum dilectionem*] he is always known through him through whom he established all things. This is his Word, our Lord Jesus Christ, who in the last times became a human being among human beings, in order to join the end to the beginning, that is, humanity to God.

How does the knowledge of God that is possible "according to love" become available? Through the Word of God, through whom God establishes all things. On the face of it, this could be the kind of natural knowledge of God that can be obtained by inference from the works of creation, a knowledge *that* there is God. Making such knowledge available, austere and minimal though it be, might itself be a loving act. But that is why Irenaeus continues with the Lord Jesus Christ as the Word made flesh. That very Word gave the prophets the power to foretell the whole plan of God by which we might "serve him in holiness and justice all our days" (Luke 1:75).

Irenaeus continues in *haer.* IV.20.5 in the direction suggested by his mention of the prophets, where he notes that

> the prophets foretold that God would be seen by human beings—as the Lord said, "Blessed are the clean of heart, for they shall see God" (Matt. 5:8). But according to his greatness [*magnitudinem*] and inexpressible glory, "no one will see God, and live." For the Father cannot be contained. But according to love [*dilectionem*] and humanity,[21] and because he can do all things, to those who love him he grants even this, namely, to see God, which is what the prophets prophesied, because "things impossible to human beings are possible to God." A human being cannot see God on its own. But he voluntarily will be visible to human beings, to whom he wills and when he wills and how he wills.

This is not merely knowledge *that* there is a divine creator, but something much more generous: a way to see this God. Not only a way to see God and live—which the prophets said was impossible to human beings—but a complete inversion of their warning: where before, no one could see God and live, now, the vision of God is life for human beings[22] (*haer.* IV.20.7). The vision of God which is metaphysically impossible *secundum magnitudinem*, and which the prophets themselves (who could see better than most) warned would be fatal if by any chance it occurred, is granted *secundum dilectionem*; and *dilectio* here refers not just to God's benevolent love for people but the love with which people love God back, a relationship of love. A completely new range of possibilities arises in the heart of love, possibilities inconceivable in the realm of metaphysics. This knowledge in and according to love is, for Irenaeus, the true knowledge of God, the true Gnosis, and it is the church people who know about it and live by it.

Let us return to what Irenaeus tells us about the Gnostic Pleroma and the unfortunate Sophia. Back in *haer.* II.6.1, Irenaeus had questioned how, in the hypothetical spiritual Pleroma, God could have remained unknown: "He could indeed be invisible to them according to eminence [*eminentiam*], but hardly unknown, on account of providence [*providentiam*]." Like many of Irenaeus's remarks in Book Two, this one has an ironic edge; while the other Aeons ahould have had some sense of the invisible Father from the order of their Pleroma, that order was not planned out well enough so as to forestall the fall of Sophia. This is not exactly our dialectic of greatness and love, but it resembles it in form and may be how Irenaeus could describe that dialectic when love is not available.

Early in his exposition of Gnostic doctrines (*haer.* I.2.1-2), Irenaeus says that Mind (or Nous), who alone knew the Father, wanted to "communicate the Father's greatness" to the rest.

> But at the Father's wish, Silence restrained him, because she wanted them all to rise to a notion and a desire of seeking their aforesaid Propator. And indeed

the rest of the Aeons likewise silently yearned to see the ultimate source of their seed and to know their root that has no beginning.

But the last and youngest Aeon of the Dodecad that was emitted by Man and Church, namely, Wisdom, was much more impetuous and suffered passion without being joined with her partner Theletos. This [passion] started among those around Mind and Truth but ended up with this misled [Aeon], allegedly out of love but really audacity, on account of not being able to have fellowship with the perfect Father, as Mind does. The passion was searching for the Father, for she wanted (they say) to comprehend his greatness [*magnitudinem*]. Then she was unable, because the deed was impossible, and was in very great anguish on account of the greatness of the abyss, and the Father's untraceability, and her affection [στοργήν] for him.

The account goes on, but I shall pause here, because the factors most relevant to the argument of this paper are in what I have quoted. The Father's greatness and height and incomprehensibility are certainly there, but the closest thing to love lies in Wisdom's daring but doomed desire to know God. Her ambition may have been noble in its way, but it all goes for naught, because the Gnostic Father has greatness but no love. As Irenaeus charges in *haer.* II.17.10, the Gnostics have made the Father's greatness and power the cause of the ignorance of the rest of the Aeons, and hence the author of evils.

Observe Irenaeus's strategy in attacking the Gnostic view of things. He does not say that they are wrong about the transcendence of the true, the high God; on the contrary, he exalts that transcendence in language like theirs. The Gnostics cannot claim to proclaim a higher, purer divinity than the church people have. But Irenaeus insists that those attributes of transcendence apply to the creator Demiurge, who is therefore *the* high God, and no divinity beyond the creator can be posited that would be still more transcendent. On the transcendence of the creator versus the transcendence of the Pleroma, that is, on God's *magnitudo*, church people and Gnostics play to a draw. The reason why the church people outstrip the Gnostics in their knowledge of God is that they know that God is also loving and recognize and believe the works of that love.

All the rest of Irenaeus's wonderful theology, whether he came up with it himself, learned it from Justin, or came by it some other way, makes its full sense only in terms of this overarching vision. Knowledge of the creator God is possible to ordinary creatures, not because the creator is a puny, less than spiritual being, but because the immeasurably great creator God loves everything in creation and therefore gives that knowledge even to us human beings through the Word made flesh and the Spirit of wisdom, according to the measure of the divine love.

CHAPTER TWELVE

Irenaeus and the Knowledge of God as Father

Text and Context

PETER WIDDICOMBE

In both *Adversus haereses* and *The Demonstration of the Apostolic Preaching*, Irenaeus uses the word *Father* to refer to God with great frequency.[1] It is a commonplace of his theological vocabulary, and it is fundamental to his theology that it be understood that the creator God of the Old Testament and the Father of Christ of the New Testament were one and the same. But did he have a conception of the fatherhood of God? Indeed, did the word have *any* particular theological significance for him? The question is not patient of a certain answer. He nowhere engages in a discussion of the meaning of the word or why he thinks it appropriate to use it of God, and the bulk of the evidence suggests that he used it unselfconsciously as a synonym for such divine titles as "God," "creator," and "Lord." There are, however, glimpses in Irenaeus's writings of what would become hallmarks of third- and fourth-century reflection on the idea of divine fatherhood, a reflection that, beginning with Origen and reaching doctrinal shape with Athanasius, would eventuate in the idea of divine fatherhood being seen as fundamental to the doctrine of the Trinity and the doctrine of salvation. These glimpses mainly have to do with the knowledge that God is Father and with how human beings come to that knowledge. They occur in a few passages scattered throughout both *Haer.* and *Dem.* They suggest that something more is going on in Irenaeus's use of fatherhood language than is to be found in the writings of his Christian predecessors, something more that shows the potential in the second century for what was to come in the later Christian tradition.

Irenaeus lived in a world in which for Greek, Jew, and Christian alike it was taken for granted that God was to be referred to as Father, and this was no less true of those against whom he directed *Haer.* He was heir to what earlier studies on the fatherhood of God in Western thought tended to regard as two distinct traditions of referring to God as Father. Schrenk and Quell, in their well-known entries on πατήρ and related words in the *TWNT*,[2] and Jeremias, in various studies,[3] identified two families of traditions of referring to God as Father—the Greek and the Judeo-Christian—which they sharply contrasted with each other. The Greek conception they characterized as cosmic and genealogical, and the biblical as historical and elective. The presence of the former they thought indicated in Greek literature by the occurrence of some form of the phrase *Father of all* from *Timaeus* 28c.[4] The latter, the biblical, they thought indicated by the occurrence of some form of the absolute phrase *the Father*, which, together with the phrases, *my Father*, and *your Father*, they regarded as typical of New Testament usage.[5] The phrase *Father of all* occurs once in the Bible at Ephesians 4:6.

As Justin had before him, Irenaeus refers to God as Father using both types of phrases interchangeably.[6] He quotes texts from the Old Testament, the Synoptic Gospels, and the Pauline epistles in which God is referred to as Father, as had Justin, but in contrast to his predecessor, there is no doubt that Irenaeus knew the Gospel of John, and many of his New Testament quotations in which God is referred to as Father come from it.[7] Irenaeus also quotes Ephesians 4:6 on a number of occasions, a verse not quoted by Justin.

Although Irenaeus quotes material from the *Timaeus*,[8] Homer, and other Greek texts, unlike Justin, he does not quote *Timaeus* 28c or any other passage from a Greek text in which God is referred to as Father. Indeed, Irenaeus's use of Ephesians 4:6 renders the division of fatherhood usage into the two traditions, Greek and biblical, not especially helpful for analyzing Irenaeus's use of the word Father for God, although it should be borne in mind that the *Father of all* phrase occurs seldom in the writings of Origen and not at all in those of Athanasius, for whom God is Father strictly of the Son and those who have been adopted as sons.[9] In none of the instances in which Irenaeus cites biblical verses in which God is referred to as "Father" does he comment on the occurrence of the word *Father*. As Irenaeus portrays his opponents' views in *Haer.*, they too referred to God as "Father" in the same manner as he, using both types of phrase and quoting biblical verses in which God is called "Father." They no more than he questioned the appropriateness of ascribing the appellation to God. Their disagreement lay in the identity of the one to whom the word applied.

Irenaeus does not discuss the question of whether and how language applies to God. The attributes he assigns to the God who is to be referred to as "Father" are those commonly used by the Middle Platonists to characterize divine transcendence and among them is that God is "indescribable." In *Haer.* II.13.3, charging his opponents with attributing human "emotions and passions" to God, Irenaeus claims that the "Father of all" is at a great remove from such things, for God is "simple, not composite, without diversity of members, completely similar and equal to himself, inasmuch as he is all intellect, all spirit, all intellection, all thought, all Word, all hearing, all eye, all light, and entirely the source of all good things." Irenaeus then sums up the argument by concluding that God "is above this and therefore is indescribable [*inenarrabilis*]."[10] In *Haer.* IV.20.5, he describes God's "goodness" as "indescribable" (*inenarrabilis*, ἀνεξήγητος); and in the following section, he links "indescribable" with "invisible," the latter being one of his favorite ways of characterizing God. The one "who works all in all," he explains, "is invisible [*invisibilis*] and indescribable [*inenarrabilis*] as to his greatness and his power, to all beings made by him."[11] On the other hand, however, Irenaeus can also maintain that God has "titles." In *Haer.* II.35.3, in the course of arguing that the "diverse words" (*diuersas dictiones*) used for God in the Old Testament, such as Sabaoth and Adonai, all refer to one and the same being, Irenaeus gives a list of other "titles" (*nuncupationes*) that also apply to that same being, the "Father of all," together with the "Lord of Powers," "God Almighty," the "Most High," the "creator," and the "maker," being among them.[12]

Ireneaus, however, never makes either the indescribability of, or the grounds for assigning titles to, the divine nature a matter of analysis, nor does he address the question of the relationship between them. Unlike Justin before him (and Origen after),[13] Irenaeus appears to have seen no tension between the two. For Justin, for instance, the occurrence of the word *name* in the baptismal injunction required explanation in the light of God's ineffability,[14] whereas Irenaeus says nothing about the question when he quotes the injunction.[15]

Justin's understanding of the relation between God, being, and language reflects Middle Platonist speculation about divine ineffability.[16] Justin explains that the first God, by definition, can have nothing before him. But inasmuch as naming presupposes the priority of the one who does the naming, such terms as Father, God, creator, and Lord cannot refer to God's essence but can only be derived from God's activities,[17] a contention that appears elsewhere among second-century Christian writers and may reflect the influence of the analogical principle formulated by Alcinous.[18] The principle states that some things may be predicated of God in as much as he is their source and cause. Justin does not explain what he thinks gives rise to the predications for any of the divine names he lists, but Theophilus does, with a rather longer list of thirteen titles. With reference to the title "Father," he says that when one speaks of God as "Father," one speaks "of him as all things," and that God is "Father because he is before all things."[19]

But we see nothing of such discussions in the writings of Irenaeus. When we turn to the passages in which Irenaeus comments on the knowledge that God is Father, what we see suggests that he placed the ascription of the word *Father* for God on another footing. The knowledge that God is Father comes not through the activities of God but uniquely through the revelation of the Son and adoption as sons.

Irenaeus's comments occur in four passages, three in *Haer.* and one in *Dem.* What Irenaeus says has to be treated with caution, however, as his concern in all three passages is neither with issues of epistemological method nor with the question of what is signified about the divine nature by the word *Father*. In the first passage, *Haer.* II.6.1, Irenaeus makes a distinction between, on the one hand, what can be known about God by anyone through the observation of the providential ordering of the world and, on the other, the knowledge that can come only through the revelation of the Son. The lordship of God can be known through the former, that God is Father seemingly only through the latter. To make his case, he quotes Matthew 11:27 (Luke 10:22). After having explained that as God's "invisible essence is mighty, it confers on all a great intelligence and perception of his sovereign and omnipotent supereminence," he goes on to observe that "accordingly, although 'no one knows the Father except the Son, nor the Son except the Father, and those to whom the Son will reveal him' (Matthew 11:27), nevertheless, all beings know this invisible reality itself, because reason, implanted in their minds, moves them and reveals to them that there is one God, Lord of all things."[20] That the Son is the unique vehicle for the revelation that the creator God and the Father of Christ are one and the same is fundamental to Irenaeus's argument in *Haer.*, of course. But here in II.6.1, he appears to be suggesting that the knowledge *that* God is "Father," in contrast to the knowledge of others of his titles, is unique to the revelation of the Son.

The statement in the second passage, in *Haer.* IV.6.6, is more schematic. It occurs in the course of Irenaeus's response to what he perceives to be Marcion's misinterpretation of Matthew 11:27 (Luke 10:22).[21] In the passage, Irenaeus makes it clear that the revelation by the Son that God is Father is not something that takes place only through the incarnation, but that the Son had revealed it earlier through the Law and the Prophets. According to Irenaeus, Marcion cited the verse in the form, "No one knew (*cognovit*) the Father, but the Son," rather than in the form, "No one knows (*cognoscit*) the Father, but the Son," the latter of which he approves.[22] The Father, then, in Marcion's view, was not known until the incarnation,[23] and, as the God of the Old Testament was known before then, *that* God could not have been the Father of Christ. In his riposte, Irenaeus argues that the Word did not make the Father known first through the incarnation; rather, he had revealed the Father earlier through the Law and the Prophets.[24] But, and this is the point that is of particular concern for the present study, it is a knowledge that comes specifically through the Son, who, Irenaeus observes, did not come into existence at the time of the incarnation.[25] He maintains that by the creation, "the Word reveals God the Creator [*Conditorem Deum*]"; by the world, "the Lord the Maker of the world [*Fabricatorem mundi Dominum*]"; by the handiwork, "the Artificer of the handiwork [*eum qui plasmaverit artificem*]"; and "by the Son, the Father who generated the Son [*per Filum eum Patrem qui generavit Filium*]." Irenaeus goes to on to make it clear that while all these impress themselves on human beings in a similar way, not everyone believes in a similar way.[26] Presumably, he feared lest the distinctions he had made in how God is known lead some to confuse epistemology with ontology and thus undermine his fundamental point: the fact that not all have believed that God is Father should not be taken to mean that that one and the same God is not Father.

Irenaeus again distinguishes between the knowledge that the Gentiles and Jews have of God and the knowledge of the Christians in *Dem.* 8. This time the distinction is based not directly on the uniqueness of Christ as the revealer of that knowledge, although he does refer to the idea in the preceding section, but rather on what the three groups know about God. The critical factor is "adoption as sons" (which is true also in the fourth passage, from *Haer.* IV.16.5, which will be taken up below). Irenaeus begins section 8 with an affirmation directed against the Gnostics and Marcion: the "Father," the one called by the Spirit "Most High" and "Almighty" and "Lord of Hosts," is also the "creator." This God, Irenaeus observes, is "merciful, compassionate, good, righteous, the God of all—both of the Jews and of the Gentiles and of the faithful." But the three groups do not know God in the same way. For, "to the faithful he is as Father, since in the last times he opened the testament of the adoption as sons"; while to the Jews, he is "Lord and Lawgiver," and through the giving of the Law, they learned that God is "Maker and Fashioner"; and to the Gentiles, he is "Creator and Almighty."[27] In contrast to his discussion in *Haer.* IV.6.6, Irenaeus is not concerned this time to ensure that it be understood that God was also known as Father in the Old Testament. The attributing of the knowledge of divine fatherhood "in the last times" to adoption may well have inhibited him from doing so. While this might lead us to conclude that his desire to link the knowledge of God as Father with the new dispensation brought about by the incarnation was so great that he was willing to risk the possibility that it might be concluded that the God of the Old Testament was not the Father of the New Testament, the explanation might be simpler. It may just reflect the fact that the description of God as Father is not something about which he thinks systematically.

But we should note that Irenaeus is not wholly consistent in attributing the knowledge that God is Father specifically to the revelation of the Son. In *Haer.* III.25.1, he appears to contradict the claim. There he says that those Gentiles who exercised at least a measure of moral discipline, who were not given to superstition and the worship of idols, and who had a sense, however slight, of divine providence, "were led to call the Maker of this universe the Father, who exercises providence over all things and arranges the affairs of our world [*conuersi sunt ut dicerent Fabricatorem huius uniuersitatis Patrem omnium prouidentem et disponentem secundum nos mundum*]"; and no reference is made in the passage to Christ. [28]

But what is it that the term *Father* tells us about the divine nature in distinction from the other divine titles? Irenaeus never comments on the question in a sustained way, but there are a number of passages in which he gives a fleeting indication of his answer. That answer, which we do not find in Theophilus or Justin, is that the description of God as Father has to do with love.

In the course of his explanation in *Haer.* V.17.1 that it was to one and the same Father who was also the God of Adam that humankind was disobedient and the Son obedient, Irenaeus assigns particular attributes to particular divine titles, "Father" among them. "This same being," he remarks, "is the Creator, who according to his love is Father, but according to his power, he is Lord, and according to his wisdom, our Maker and Artificer [*Demiurgus qui secundum dilectionem quidem Pater est, secundum autem virtutem Dominus, secundum autem sapientiam Factor et Plasmator noster;* ὁ Δημιουργός, ὁ κατὰ μὲν τὴν ἀγάπην Πατήρ, κατὰ δὲ τὴν δύναμιν Κύριος, κατὰ δὲ τὴν σοφίαν Ποιητὴς καὶ Πλάστης ἡμῶν], by transgressing whose commandments, we became his enemies." Through the incarnation, Christ has restored us to "friendship" (*amicitia*; φιλία) with the Father.[29] In *Dem.* 2–3, he again links "power" with "Lord" and "love" with "Father," in a statement about the believer's response to God. Irenaeus warns that lest we "receive the poison" of the teaching of the "heretics," we must adhere strictly to "the rule of faith," and "perform the commandments of God, believing in God and fearing him, for he is Lord, and loving him, for he is Father."

Irenaeus never engages in an explanation of why he links descriptions of God as Lord with fear and as Father with love, but it may be connected with his understanding of the relationship between the law of the old covenant and that of the new, ushered in by Christ, an understanding that reflects the influence of Paul's discussion in Gal. 4:1—5:1 and Rom. 8:14-15. In *Dem.* 8, following his statement that the Jews knew God as "Lord and Lawgiver," he says that when humankind "forgot, abandoned, and rebelled against God, he brought them into slavery by means of the Law." In *Haer.*

IV.13.4, he links servitude with the Mosaic law and contrasts it with friendship. He argues that those who were under the old covenant were "slaves," but under the new covenant, in which one assents to love God and neighbor, the Word "set those free who were subject to him." This Irenaeus thinks evidenced by Christ's statement to his disciples in John 15:15, "I no longer call you slaves, for the slave does not know what his lord does; but I have called you friends, for everything I have heard from the Father, I have made known to you."[30]

A little later, in *Haer.* IV.16.5, Irenaeus essays to explain why the Ten Commandments were not abrogated by the coming of Christ. Unlike the particular statutes laid down for the Jews, which created "bondage," the Decalogue, which teaches love of God and love of neighbor, are "natural and liberal and common to all." Christ cancelled the former "by his covenant of liberty," while "amplifying" the latter, and "granting to men generously and without grudging, by means of adoption, to know God the Father [*per adoptionem Patrem scire Deum*], and to love [*diligere*] him with their whole heart and to follow his Word without deviation." Christ also granted an increased feeling of veneration for God, for, Irenaeus explains, drawing on common human experience, "sons should have more veneration than slaves, and greater love for their father [*filios enim plus timere oportet quam servos et majorem dilectionem habere in patrem*]."[31]

In *Haer.* III.19.1, Irenaeus links the idea of the freedom that comes through adoption with incorruption and immortality, using another verse from the Gospel of John, this time 8:36. Inasmuch as Christ said, "If the Son shall make you free, you shall be free indeed," those who have not been "joined to Christ" remain in the "bondage of the old disobedience," not having received the "gift of adoption" and are in a "state of death," whereas those who have received adoption "have been united to incorruptibility and immortality."[32] Again, in these passages with their focus on adoption, Irenaeus does not go on to point out that God was also known as Father in the Old Testament.

As has been noted already, these statements concerning God as Lord, the law, servitude, and fear, on the one hand, and God as Father, love, adoption, and friendship, on the other, are scattered throughout *Haer.* and *Dem.* and are never brought together systematically, although several of the elements are present in *Dem.* 3–8. He never acknowledges Paul's influence on his thinking about the matter, although he may well have thought that self-evident; and he never cites Paul's phrase "Abba, Father" from Gal. 4:6 and Rom. 8:15 in the immediate contexts of these statements, although he does elsewhere in his writings. Nevertheless, the occurrence of such statements as these, however inchoate, marks a signal moment in the history of Christian reflection on the description of God as Father. They do not appear in the writings of Justin, who seems unaware of the idea of adoption as sons, never quotes either Gal. 4:6 or Rom. 8:15 in any context, and makes no reference to the Johaninne notion of friendship with God.

Conversely, however, such statements feature prominently in the writings of Origen, who makes them fundamental to his conception of salvation. Origen draws deliberately on the adoption imagery of Paul, cites Gal. 4:6 and Rom. 8:15 frequently, and cites a collage of verses from the Gospel of John, 15:15 prominent among them. In terms similar to those of Irenaeus, but in a dense and complex way, Origen concludes that as the believer comes to know God as Father and not just as Lord, the believer's relationship with the Father is transformed from one of fear to one of love. Referring to John 15:15 and Rom. 8:15, for instance, Origen says that Jesus becomes the friend of those who initially as slaves feared him as Lord;[33] and he can sum up his thinking about the matter by concluding simply that it is only when one loves Jesus that God becomes one's Father.[34] This, for Origen, culminates in the ability to call God "Father" in prayer, the most intimate form of communication with God. It is for this reason that Christ taught the disciples to pray using the words "our Father" in the Lord's Prayer,[35] words that Irenaeus neither quotes nor discusses, although he does allude to the Lord's Prayer.[36] Such an intense focus on the affective aspect of the relationship between the believer and the Son, and thus the Father, we do not see in the writings of Irenaeus, but in his conjoining of the word *Father* with the language of "love," we do see its beginnings.

Adoption as sons, according to Irenaeus, is brought about through participation in the Word. In two passages, he makes this explicit. In *Haer.* III.18.7, he says that it was incumbent on the "Mediator," by virtue of his relationship with both God and humankind, to bring both to "friendship and concord" (*amicitia et concordia*, φιλία καὶ ὁμόνοια), for it is only through the "fellowship" (*communio*) that we receive from God that we can "participate in the adoption of sons." It is for this reason that Christ assumed flesh and passed through every stage of life.[37] In *Haer.* III.19.1, we find Irenaeus positing something of a formula of exchange between "Son" and "sonship through adoption." Irenaeus explains that the purpose for which the "Word became man" and "the Son of God became the Son of man" was that man, "having been joined [*commixtus*] to the Word and receiving adoption, might become the son of God."[38]

Irenaeus does not quite make a parallel between "Son" and "adopted sons" in the manner later writers would do. Irenaeus does not say that it is because the Son is *Son* that we may become sons—we are "joined" to the "Word," not the "Son."[39] Nor does he say that it is specifically divine fatherhood that this "joining" through adoption allows the believer to know. Nevertheless, it is clear that those who believe in Christ do become sons and Irenaeus is prepared to include the adopted with the Father and the Son, as those who are called gods in Psalm 81:1. Earlier, in *Haer.* III.6.1, he had explained that Psalm 81:1, "God stood in the congregation of gods, he judges in the midst of the gods," "speaks of the Father and the Son and those who have received the adoption, for they are the church." Those to whom Psalm 81:6 (LXX), "I have said, you are gods and all sons of the Most High," is addressed are those "without doubt, who have received the grace of adoption, by which 'we cry, Abba, Father.'"[40]

What Irenaeus thought was entailed in this standing with the Father and the Son, however, is not patent. It has been argued that what Irenaeus understood by the word "adoption" was "establishment as a son,"[41] and it is clear that he did not intend to suggest that human beings were dehominized and made the ontological equal of the Son (and the Father).[42] In *Haer.* IV.41.2-3,[43] Irenaeus, following, as he says, one of his predecessors (whom he does not identify), explains that the word *son* has two meanings, son "according to nature" and "son according to teaching." According to nature, "son" applies both to the offspring and to the work of the creator, the difference between the two being that the former is by generation and the latter is made. Thus, all human beings are sons of God inasmuch as they were created by God, but if they follow right teaching and remain in filial obedience to God, they become sons of God in a deeper sense. Through disobedience, however, this sonship can be lost and the sons of God can become sons of the Devil. It is only through conversion and repentance that the unfaithful son can return to the status of son of God. Adoptive sonship, then, entails filial obedience. The love of the believer for God may well have something to do with this—Irenaeus makes it clear that moral discipline enables the believer to increase in love for God.[44]

There are, however, two passages in *Haer.* that suggest that adoption as sons as the basis for the knowledge of God as Father may not be the end of the story for Irenaeus. In them, he makes comments that raise questions about how and, indeed, whether, he thought that the adopted sons will continue to know God as Father in heaven. In *Haer.* IV.20.5, he indicates that there is a progression in how God is seen both in this life and from this life to the next. To those who love him, God grants the power "to see" him. God was first seen prophetically through the Spirit, then adoptively through the Son, and he shall be seen "paternally [*paternaliter*] in the kingdom of heaven," the Spirit preparing the believer in the Son of God, and the Son leading them to the Father, who confers incorruption and eternal life on them, which, as Irenaeus explains, results from seeing God.[45] What is involved in "paternal" seeing is not clear, but Irenaeus appears to be suggesting that this seeing is superior to the seeing that the believer has through adoption.

Perhaps Irenaeus intends us to understand that adoption as sons is something that pertains only to this life and not to the next, where the knowledge of God as Father will be unmediated. But is he also implying that to know God as Father is the highest reach in the believer's knowledge of God? Perhaps, but his comments in the second passage, in *Haer.* V.8.1, seem to point in the opposite direction. There Irenaeus explains that while the faithful await the resurrection, they are given a "part" (*pars*) of the Spirit, which Paul also terms a "pledge" (*pignus*), to help prepare them in this life for the life of incorruption. This pledge is what allows Christians to cry "Abba, Father." But, in a statement that suggests the possibility that he thought both that the ability to call God Father is extraordinary and that it will give way to something better, Irenaeus concludes that if we can cry "Abba, Father" having only the "pledge," imagine what we shall be able to do when, seeing God face to face, we shall be given the "entire" (*universus*) grace of the Spirit and are made into the image and likeness of God. Then everyone who is raised "shall burst out into a continuous hymn of triumph, glorifying him who raised them from the dead and gave the gift of eternal life."[46] Quite what this means is not certain, but the apparent implication is that there will be an addressing of God in heaven that is superior to the addressing of God as Father that the Christian now makes to God. In the writings of later theologians such as Origen and Athanasius, we do not find even a hint that the calling of God "Father" might ultimately be left behind. The question did not arise for them. Salvation for Origen lay in the recognition that God is Father.

Thus, in the end those who become "perfect sons" will know the Father "as now only the Son knows the Father."[47] But we should not press our author too hard. The topic of the knowledge of God as Father is not his concern in the passage. Whatever it means for Irenaeus for those adopted as sons to stand in church as gods together with the Father and the Son, he does not spell it out in terms of divine fatherhood. This may reflect in part the fact that in the passages where he distinguishes the description of God as Father from other descriptions, Irenaeus is mainly concerned with the human being's knowledge of God and not with the divine nature itself and the relationships within it. He says nothing about the Father-Son relation that turns on the description of God as Father. He does not use the description, for instance, to argue for the eternal generation of the Son, as Origen and Athanasius were to do, nor seemingly does it lead him to think about the Father-Son relation in affective terms as it did them.

That Origen, and then Athanasius, thought of God as Father and Son in the way they did reflects in large part the way in which they read the Gospel of John. Irenaeus, by contrast, tends to use verses from the Fourth Gospel such as 1:18, "No one has ever seen God; the only Son who is in the bosom of the Father, he has made him known," not to address the immanent life of the Trinity, but rather to address its economic expression. He repeatedly cites it, in much the same way as he does Matthew 11:27 (Luke 10:22), to help establish his fundamental concern to demonstrate that Christ uniquely reveals the one God who is both creator and Father.[48]

But this should not surprise us. It is with the economic activity of God that Irenaeus is mainly concerned throughout his theology and there is, accordingly, little sense of an intimate, immanent life of God into which the believer may be drawn. As we have seen, in his few references to the knowledge that God is Father, Irenaeus's focus lies on the human perception of the divine and, to the extent that there is an affective element to that, his focus lies on the transformation of the human experience of God. But, however infrequent his references to knowing God, and however brief and not joined-up his comments about this knowledge, what they tell us is that there is no doubt that the Pauline imagery of adoption and the Johannine of Christ as friend left their impress on his understanding of salvation. For the Bishop of Lyon, whatever the nature of the believer's encounter with God in heaven, we can conclude that the revelation of God in Christ effected a transformation in the believer's knowledge of God, a transformation which allowed one in this life at least to encounter God no longer as Lord and in fear but as Father and in love.

CHAPTER THIRTEEN

"The Rule of Truth . . . which He Received through Baptism" (*Haer.* I.9.4)

Catechesis, Ritual, and Exegesis in Irenaeus's Gaul

Alistair Stewart

This chapter explores the relationship between baptismal ritual and catechesis in Irenaeus's context in the light of his statement that the rule of truth is received through baptism. For whereas it is entirely possible that this statement is a confusion of baptismal ritual with catechumenal process (it is taken as axiomatic that the rule of faith was the basis for catechetical direction),[1] the possibility that there is a link between the substance of the material delivered in catechesis and the baptismal ritual itself might give some clue to the nature and development of credal declarations. The statement that the rule of faith is received in baptism is made in the context of a discussion of Valentinian reading of scripture; those who are baptized in this manner, says Irenaeus, are able properly to understand the Scriptures. Against this heretical misreading of the Scriptures, then, is set the rule of faith, which is then stated.[2] This particular statement is interesting because its fundamental trinitarian shape is followed by a christological supplement.

> Although the church is extended over the entire inhabited world up to the boundaries of the earth, she has received both from the apostles and from their disciples the faith that there is one God, the Father Almighty "who made the heaven and the earth and the sea and all that is in them", and in one Jesus Christ the Son of God made flesh for our salvation and one Holy Spirit which has proclaimed through the prophets the dispensations (οἰκονομία) and the coming and the birth from the virgin and the passion and the resurrection from the dead and the bodily reception into the heavens of the beloved, our Lord Jesus Christ, and his coming again from the heavens in the glory of the Father for the consummation of all things and the resurrection of all flesh of the whole of humanity. (*Haer.* I.10.1)

In examining Irenaeus's statement here I intend to suggest the following:
a. that the catechetical process known to Irenaeus involved some form of *traditio* or "handing on" to the candidate of a credal formula;

b. that the *traditio* was directed not to repeating a trinitarian credal statement at baptismal interrogation, but to a christological confession and that this is reflected in Irenaeus' citation of the rule of faith, *regula fidei*, at this point;

c. that this christological confession took place at the *syntaxis*—the formal pre-baptismal profession of faith—and constituted the credal affirmation of Irenaeus's baptismal rite.

Scholarly orthodoxy anticipates that the earliest forms of baptismal profession were interrogatory and trinitarian; this has prevented us from reading this text in its plain sense. It is hard to see where this orthodoxy has come from, though in the Anglophone world the finger of suspicion would seem to point to Carpenter;[3] that this orthodoxy is widespread, however, will be illustrated when we deal with Kelly's treatment of Irenaeus.

The *Traditio*

The first indisputable evidence for a rite of *traditio* is from the latter part of the third century. In a letter to his Diocese, preserved by Athanasius in an appendix to his *De decretis*, Eusebius states that he presented the creed of Caesarea as defense of his orthodoxy, "as we have received from the bishops who preceded us, both in catechesis and when we received baptism [ἐν τῇ κατηχήσει καὶ ὅτε τὸ λουτρὸν ἐλαμβάνομεν]."[4] The catechetically received creed is employed somehow in the baptismal rite. Is the same, we must ask, true of the rite known to Irenaeus approximately a century earlier? In particular, if the rule of faith, the *regula fidei*, had a role in catechesis, it is possible that some communication of the *regula* might be part of baptismal ritual; this, after all, is what Irenaeus is saying. Since the context is the knowledge of the scriptures that is held by and bestowed upon the faithful Christian, this is clearly delivery *to* rather than *from* the candidate, either as part of the baptismal rite or as part of the complex of catechumenal rites, or both.

The christological postscript to the statement of the *regula fidei* here has clear similarities to the christological sequence of other creeds. Thus we may compare the second part of the baptismal creed found in *Traditio apostolica:*[5]

Irenaeus	"Hippolytus"
and the coming and the	Christ Jesus, the son of God,
birth from the virgin	who was born of the Holy Spirit and
	Mary the virgin
and the passion	and was crucified under Pontius Pilate
	and was dead [and buried]
and the resurrection from the dead	and rose on the third day alive from
	the dead
and the bodily reception into the heavens of	and ascended in the heavens
the beloved, our Lord Jesus Christ,	and sits at the right hand of the Father
and his coming again from the heavens in the	and will come to judge the living and
glory of the Father for the consummation of	the dead.
all things	

However, if the *regula fidei* is to be considered in some sense a credal statement, we need to refer to the objection raised by Smulders to any relationship between the *regula fidei* and baptismal ritual. Namely, the fact that there is more than one form of the rule of faith, and that many of these are binitarian rather than trinitarian.[6] As such, he rejects any relationship between the *regula* and the baptismal creed, and is followed in this by Westra.[7] It is certainly the case that there are forms of the *regula* which are not trinitarian; indeed, we may note that Irenaeus's own writings contain a number of binitarian forms.[8] As such, we cannot say that the rule of faith generated a threefold baptismal interrogation, or indeed that there is any relationship between a threefold interrogation and the rule.[9] Two-membered rules exist alongside three-membered. However, given that we might root Irenaeus in Smryrnean Christianity, we may particularly note another binitarian çredal formula from Smyrna, namely in the confession of the elders of *Contra Noetum*.[10] In using the term *binitarian*, however, we should be clear that we are not talking of a technical binitarianism, but rather of what Hall has identified within the work of Melito, namely, a typically Asian Christocentric monotheism.[11] Thus the existence of two-membered versions of the rule of faith may in itself be a clue to the direction of development within the rules, namely, that they reflect christologically centered statements of faith such as that found, again in Smyrna, in Polycarp's writing.[12] The existence of a christological confession at baptism is thus the next point that needs to be established. For the moment, however, we may observe that there is instruction received in the course of the catechumenate that relates directly to baptismal ritual and that might reasonably be called a *traditio*.[13] The creed, according to Eusebius, was received both in catechesis and in the baptismal ritual. The same seems to have been the case in Irenaeus's practice, even if it is hard, for the moment, to see what that meant in fact.

Christological Confessions at Baptism

There is evidence of christological confessions at baptism in the Western text of Acts, in which the Ethiopian eunuch makes a confession that "Jesus Christ is the Son of God" before being baptized,[14] and in a ps-Hippolytean homily on the *Theophany* that states that the candidate at baptism "confesses that Christ is God."[15] We may also note the rite of commitment to Christ found in Antioch at the time of Chrystostom, as well as being reflected in the *Apostolic Constitutions*.[16] Finally, I argue elsewhere that such a confession is mentioned in Pliny's report of Bithynian Christians who sing a hymn *secum invicem* ("among themselves" or "in turn") to Christ as to a God.[17] I may suggest that this in turn explains the form of the *regula* given here. For what is odd about this rule is that the Christology is not part of the second section of a threefold rule but is an appendix to the triadic formula; this may be explained by suggesting that the rule is given in a form reflecting catechetical instruction and then is followed by a version of the christological confession made in baptism. Kelly notes that we have "an ingenious conflation of a short, neatly balanced trinitarian confession with a more detailed and circumstantial christology."[18] We suggest that the christological section is joined on to the trinitarian *regula fidei* here because this is an expanded form of the christological statement that was made at baptism, having been delivered in catechesis. Thus when Kelly suggests that "it has all the air of having once existed as an independent one-clause confession,"[19] the evidence for christological affirmations in baptism indicates that his instincts here are sound. Whereas this evidence, apart from the debatable instance in Pliny, is from the third century or later, we may nonetheless note the old suggestion of Haussleiter that, deriving from the original mission within forming Judaism, the christological confession is primary in the development of credal forms, and may thus derive from the original Christian proclamation.[20]

In recognizing the christological confession as distinct, we may escape from Smulders's strictures, as from the similar point made pertinently by Bradshaw, namely, that we should be careful not to assume that all catechetical material is to be found repeated in the baptismal rite.[21] The trinitarian *regula*, we may suggest, is a reflection of catechesis but the peculiar manner in which the christological section is appended reflects the baptismal ritual known to Irenaeus.

Interrogation or Declaration?

It is here that we must pause to consider a significant issue. For if there is a christological declaration as part of this rite, then this runs counter to the underlying assumption in credal research that interrogatory creeds preceded declaratory creeds.[22] Of this I am far from sure; rather, in agreement with Bradshaw on broad lines, even if with some difference in detail, I suggest that there are two distinct forms, one of which knew a threefold interrogation in the waters, the other of which involved a renunciation and a confession by the waters.[23] However, the assumption that a creed must be trinitarian and interrogatory, delivered in the waters, has skewed the reading of Irenaeus here.

Credal research is largely dominated by the influence of Lietzmann. Building on the work of Holl and Harnack, Lietzmann argued that the Roman creed was constructed from the fusion of two formulae, a christological sequence and a basic trinitarian creed.[24] In support of his argument, Lietzmann notes instances of credal statements in which a brief trinitarian formula is supplemented by more extensive christological material provided as a postscript. Among these we may note that this passage in Irenaeus appears. Beyond Irenaeus, Lietzmann notes a confession of Alexander of Alexandria (*apud* Theodoret, *HE* I.4.46) and a confession of Apollinaris.[25] Lietzmann's explanation is that the christological content of the creeds had been separately generated and that original trinitarian creeds were only subsequently filled out with this additional material. We may perhaps put aside the fourth century confessions as, since they are motivated by christological controversy, it is possible that their postscripts are explanatory glosses on what has gone before, but this cannot be said of Irenaeus. However, rather than being a trinitarian creed that was subsequently expanded with christological material we may suggest, on the basis of the argument already presented, that we have a christological confession generated by baptismal ritual and that this is preceded by a trinitarian statement that has been generated entirely independently, namely catechetically. Lietzmann does not, to my knowledge, identify the source of the christological sequence; here it is suggested that the sequence is generated baptismally. This in turn means that the Roman creed is not the product of a trinitarian creed supplemented with a christological confession but rather that, if there is a relationship between the three-part Roman creed and the christological sequence, the reverse is true, namely, that a christological confession has been supplemented in order to form a threefold interrogation.[26]

Before turning to Irenaeus, we may note other examples of the manner in which the assumption that baptismal creeds are necessarily trinitarian and interrogatory has skewed the reading of eastern liturgical sources. The baptismal rites lying behind the Jerusalem *Catecheses mystagogicae* know a renunciation and a profession—*apotaxis* and *syntaxis*—taking place immediately before baptism,[27] the *syntaxis* consisting of a trinitarian declaratory creed whereas a second, interrogatory, credal assertion then takes place within the water.[28] Whereas the complex of *apotaxis* and *syntaxis* here may be an importation from another rite, it is also possible that the interrogatory creed is an accretion which has come about as the *apotaxis-syntaxis* has been moved away from the waters. The prevailing assumption, however, is that the interrogatory creed is original.[29]

Similarly, it is suggested that in the rites known to Chrysostom in Antioch there was an interrogatory creed. Wenger alludes to a passage in the fortieth *Homilia in I Cor.* in which Chrysostom states that "when we are to baptize we command them to say [κελευόντες εἰπεῖν] 'I believe in the resurrection of the dead' and they are baptized on the basis of this faith,"[30] and he is followed by Finn in suggesting that this is a response to an interrogatory creed.[31] However, the statement that they are "commanded to say" the words is more indicative of a declaration. Although we cannot say whether this is an allusion to a declaration of faith at the *syntaxis* or to the *redditio symboli* when the candidate formally repeated the newly learned credal formula (we confront here the problem, yet again, of knowing whether a reference to a creed relates to pre-baptismal catechesis and its associated ritual or to the act of baptism itself),[32] this homily is Antiochene; the fact that the baptizer in Antioch employs a baptismal formula[33] makes it likely that baptism was accompanied by a declaratory creed, since were baptism administered on the basis of interrogation, as in the West, then a formula is unnecessary.[34] The situation with regard to Constantinople is equally unclear; however, the evidence of a later period likewise points away from any interrogatory formula, as there is no absolutely no basis in the writings of Proclus of Constantinople to assert, as do Finn and Wenger, that the formula of baptismal profession "is a question and answer dialogue."[35] Rather, the candidate makes a statement, a confession that *she* has learned in the course of catechesis.[36]

The Evidence of Irenaeus

Thus to turn to Irenaeus, we may observe the classic discussion of Kelly. He begins by noting two statements from the *Demonstration*. "First of all it bids us bear in mind that we have received baptism for the remission of sins in the name of God the Father, and in the name of Jesus Christ the Son of God, who was incarnate and rose again, and in the Holy Spirit of God"[37] and the statement that "the baptism of our regeneration proceeds through three points, God the Father bestowing upon us regeneration through his Son by the Holy Spirit."[38] Finally, Kelly notes Irenaeus's restatement of the three points of baptism in *Dem.* 6. From this he deduces a threefold series of baptismal questions:

Doest thou believe in God the Father?

Doest thou believe in Jesus Christ the Son of God who was incarnate and died and rose again?

Doest thou believe in the Holy Spirit of God?[39]

The basis for this is a further statement of the rule of faith from *Dem.* 6. Kelly writes: "Manifestly this is not the baptismal creed. It is rather a kind of short commentary on it. It gives the gist of the pre-baptismal catechetical instruction and illustrates how it was modelled on the pattern of the baptismal questions."[40] Power makes similar statements regarding this passage, so stating that belief in God the Father is "the first article professed by the candidate"[41] and "the principal point for the liturgy of baptism is its connection with the rule of faith. The creed, as handed down by the apostolic tradition, is proclaimed in the baptismal rite."[42] It certainly seems to be the case that there is a connection between catechesis and baptismal ritual though Power is (perhaps wisely) less than clear about what he considers to be the nature of the connection.

In testing Kelly's hypothesis that the rule represented here reflects an interrogation, we may note that no mention is actually made of interrogation. Whereas Kelly states that "the clear implication of his (Irenaeus's) language is that he knew a series of baptismal questions," there is no such implication, unless one assumes the interrogation as given. On the other hand, it does seem that there is a link between the trinitarian form of the regula as given here and some kind of trinitarian form (if not formula) of baptism, as witnessed in *Didache* 7.1 and in Matthew 28:19. This we may deduce from the clear statement at *Dem.* 3 that baptism is received "in the name of God the Father, and in the name of Jesus Christ . . . " However, nothing is said regarding baptismal interrogation, or indeed of a baptismal profession of trinitarian faith. Indeed, the statement that baptism is "In the name . . . " sounds as if it might represent a baptismal formula. A baptismal formula, we may suggest, is possible if there is no interrogation, and if the statement of faith by the candidate had preceded the moment of baptism. This is certainly the case in later rites in which a confession of faith is made prior to baptism and baptism itself is then delivered with a formula whilst the candidate is silent.

It is thus possible that the candidate makes a declaration rather than simply answers questions. Here we may note again the statement that the faith is "received" in the baptismal ritual. If a historian might be allowed to engage his imagination, we may see the manner in which this takes place from the clue left by Chrysostom in his statement that the candidates are instructed to make a declaration. The candidate, we suggest, receives the faith as part of the baptismal ritual by being instructed or prompted to make a declaration of faith, a declaration, we may suggest, that is christological and is reflected in the christological supplement to the *regula fidei* given here.

The *Syntaxis*

In later baptismal rituals there are two points at which declarations of faith might be found, namely at the *syntaxis* before baptism and at the moment of baptism itself in baptismal interrogation. However, although the *syntaxis* in later rites is found as a rite distinct from the baptism itself, there is evidence that the *syntaxis* had originally taken place by the water, that in some circles at least this formed the baptismal declaration of faith, and that this statement, as suggested already, was christological. This is particularly prominent in Syrian rites. Again I refer to ps-Hippolytus's *De Theophania* where a christological confession that is closely joined to renunciation takes place immediately before baptism. Thus rather than assuming that there must be interrogations, simply because the earliest evidence points to interrogations, we may observe that there is ample evidence of early declarations, taking place immediately prior to baptism, and may then further suggest that a declaration prior to baptism might have been the form known to Irenaeus, and that it is to be found at the *syntaxis*. This in turn implies that the complex of *apotaxis-syntaxis*—renunciation and profession—is a relatively early development in some baptismal rituals. Here we may allude to a suggestion of Rordorf that a rite of this sort might have been known as early as the first century. His argument is essentially that the marked eschatological dualism of the rite points to an origin in early Judaism, and suggests, moreover, that the two-ways instruction, to which the *Didache* bears witness, might well give rise to such a ritual.[43]

Having already argued for a christological confession as part of the rite of *syntaxis* in some rites, we may here allude to the Armenian baptismal rite, employed by Lietzmann as a crown witness for his theory of the separate development for the christological sequence. The most primitive form preserved in the manuscripts is a simple trinitarian interrogation: "Do you believe in the Father? Do you believe in the Son? Do you believe in the Holy Spirit?" This simple trinitarian formula is supplemented in later manuscripts by a series of other questions relating to the salvific activity of Christ. "Do you believe in the birth of Christ? Do you believe in the baptism of Christ?"[44] There is a point of comparison with Irenaeus in that the christological material is a postscript to the trinitarian form. We must stress, however, that this is at the rite of *syntaxis* rather than at the baptism itself.

The reason for stressing that this occurs at the *syntaxis* rather than at the baptismal interrogation is that this points up the possible origin of the christological sequence. Namely, that whereas in western rites there is a threefold interrogation, and so a trinitarian-shaped creed developed, in Syrian rites the baptism is not so closely linked to the statement of faith, but rather the statement of faith, originally simply christological, preceded the baptism itself. We should not confuse the interrogatory rites of the West with eastern rites as the two are entirely distinct. Although there is a widespread assumption that interrogation is an earlier form than any rite involving a statement of faith, there is ample evidence that the two forms are equally ancient. The statement of faith, however, was joined to a renunciation. The situation is directly comparable to *Haer.* I.10.1.

Thus I suggest the *regula fidei* here is said, by Irenaeus, to have been delivered in baptism because its strong christological element is a reflection on the christological confession which formed the *syntaxis*, and on the basis of which baptism was delivered. It is also delivered in catechesis, and herein the trinitarian form of the *regula fidei* is represented.

Conclusions

The Development of the *Traditio*

When we come to the time of Eusebius, perhaps as much as a century later than Ire-naeus, we meet the phenomenon of a trinitarian and declaratory baptismal creed. We reject von Campenhausen's claim here that Eusebius was presenting a private creed after the manner of a disputation simply because Eusebius states that it was received in baptism whereas von Campenhausen's primary intent is to argue that no such thing existed at the time.[45] Nonetheless, we may accept von Campenhausen's more general point that a credal statement does not necessarily mean a creed that is fixed in wording. In particular, as Eusebius states that this creed has been learnt from the scriptures, we may accept that it is a more general reflection of catechesis, with a general similarity to the *regula fidei*. As such we may not be absolutely sure that this is a creed like those of a later period that has fixity in wording. However, the trinitarian shape is significant as is the incorporation of an extended christological sequence into the creed. Insofar as Eusebius states that it is received in catechesis, we may recognize that there is a reflec-tion of the instruction received but that also there is a repetition of a trinitarian state-ment of belief within the baptismal ritual, presumably at the *syntaxis*.[46] Here we may suggest that there is a development of what would subsequently become more wide-spread, namely, the substitution of a trinitarian statement of belief for a christological confession.[47] We may suggest, moreover, that the candidate's declaration (sic) is still prompted, and for that reason is said, still, to be received in the course of the baptismal ritual. Thus there is no *redditio symboli* beyond the repetition of the creed in the bap-tismal rite; such a ritual, it would so appear, within the complex of catechumenal rites, came about due to the growing weight placed upon precise doctrinal formulations in the course of the fourth century.

Baptism as a Source of Exegesis in Irenaeus's Theology

Having a picture of the ritual presupposed by Irenaeus, we may return to the context of Irenaeus's statement regarding the baptismal reception of the *regula fidei*.

In this part of *Adversus haereses*, he is arguing against Valentinian interpretation of scripture. It is the rule of truth, he suggests, which is the hermeneutical key to under-standing the scriptures, the rule of faith received in baptism. It is in doing so that he comes to concentrate on the role of Jesus as incarnate Word and Savior.[48] Thus when he comes to present the rule of truth, he supplements this with a christological section and it is this christological confession which, I suggest, is derived from the baptismal rite. However, the reason for its being appended is the earlier discussion, concentrat-ing on Christ as the true meaning of the scriptures, as Christ is the word delivered to the candidate within the baptismal ritual and so confessed. This is the same statement that is made more fully and explicitly in *Demonstration 7*, again a statement relating directly to a repetition of the *regula fidei*: it is through the baptismal water that we receive the Spirit, and the Spirit leads us to understanding of the Word, Jesus Christ, enfleshed and spoken in the scriptures.

CHAPTER FOURTEEN

Irenaeus, Women, and Tradition

SARA PARVIS

Questions of gender have from time to time been identified as key to Gnostic thought and writing. For Elaine Pagels, gender was central to Gnosticism's implicit critique of patriarchal Christianity.[1] For many other scholars, images of the feminine have continued to be a refreshing part of what Gnosticism had to offer.[2] As feminism has been replaced by gender studies in scholarly attention, this interest has continued. It has recently been argued by Jonathan Cahana that the rationale of Gnosticism can best be made sense of as a form of queering of ancient theological and social gender norms.[3]

It should be noted that there have also been voices on the other side. Michael Williams, in his seminal and wide-ranging study *Rethinking "Gnosticism": An Argument for Dismantling a Dubious Category*, has questioned whether the relative prominence of feminine imagery in "Gnostic" texts is much more than simply a sign of their greater accommodation to ancient religious norms than the more hardline, "deviant" Jewish and Christian traditions.[4] He also argues that "Gnostic" exegesis is not appropriately characterized as the exegesis of "value reversal" (what would be called "queering" in contemporary parlance).[5]

Whether notions of gender are quite as central to Gnostic, or biblical demiurgic,[6] traditions in general as Pagels and Cahana imply, Irenaeus is clearly aware that the alternative traditions he is dealing with appeal to women in particular, and in a number of different ways. I want to argue here that one of the subtexts of Irenaeus's *The Refutation of Knowledge Falsely So Called* (*Adversus haereses*) is a defense of the space for women within mainstream Christianity. Indeed, I shall argue, it is a double defense: both an articulation of the space that Irenaeus claims already exists for women in the mainstream Christian community, and a sanctioning of it by the strongest sanctions he is able to bring to bear.

It is easy to argue that the Gnostics, as they appear in Irenaeus's work, have better news to offer women than he does, both in the second century and now. First, in contrast to the apparently male creator God of Judaism and Christianity, the highest divine beings in the Gnostic myths described by Irenaeus come in male and female pairs.[7] The male God of the Old Testament is still there as creator, and still says "I am God, and besides me there is no other," but this is only because he is not very bright, and is unaware that the better quality aspects of creation are actually the work of his mother.[8] Second, earthly women are not the ones who have created the theological problem. Eve, in transgressing Ialdabaoth's (the creator God's) commandment, is the victim of a divine power-struggle between Ialdabaoth and his mother, and although her action has immediately unpleasant consequences (in this version of the myth), the fruit that she persuades Adam to eat teaches them both to know the Power who is above all things.[9] Thirdly, women can hold positions of power in the Gnostic churches, at least among the group that is led by Irenaeus's contemporary Marcus. Women are called on to give thanks over the mixed cup, and to prophesy.[10]

But it is just as easy to argue that this Gnostic news is not as good for women as it seems. The highest God of all the aeons is still, after all, male.[11] The evils of the world are still caused, ultimately, by a female—the youngest aeon, Sophia, who conceives an unrealistic desire to know the highest aeon.[12] And, if there is any truth in Irenaeus's account, Marcus and perhaps also his associates traded in sexual and financial exploitation in return for his attentions to women.[13]

I will leave more detailed discussion of Gnostic views of gender, of the female and of women to Gnosticism scholars. For the remainder of this paper, I want to look at how Irenaeus responds to the three areas of implicit appeal to women I have identified in Gnosticism as he presents it: feminine images of the divine, the theological exculpation of Eve, and female ministry in the church.

All that Irenaeus is prepared to say about the Divine comes from the tradition he believes himself to have received: the books of scripture from the old and new dispensations which he regards as authoritative, and the straight edge represented by the Rule of Truth which teaches him how to adjust the sayings of scripture against one another. The straight edge, given to Christians at baptism, is belief in one God, Father almighty, and in one Jesus Christ the Son of God (I.3.6); the Holy Spirit is included in other versions of the Rule which Irenaeus uses. On the basis of this, he allows two feminine principles room in his theology: Wisdom and the church.

Wisdom (Sophia), of course, is a key term in the thought of Irenaeus's opponents. In Ptolemy's thought, she is the youngest of the thirty aeons, the one who triggers the events leading to creation. For this reason, there is perhaps a certain nervousness in Irenaeus's handling of this figure. But Wisdom takes part in or assists at creation in a number of Old Covenant writings, and as such Irenaeus accepts her as part of the tradition. According to his straight edge, she must be identifiable either with Father or Son or Holy Spirit. Other theologians would identify her with the Son, the Word of God; Irenaeus identifies her with the Holy Spirit.[14]

The Holy Spirit would be grammatically feminine in Hebrew or Syriac, but in Irenaeus's own Greek she is neuter, and in the Latin of the city where he lives, masculine. Mostly, he keeps to the term *Spirit*, or *Holy Spirit*, rather than *Wisdom* (or, indeed, *Paraclete*), except where drawing specifically on the Old Covenant scripture passages that use the term *Wisdom*, and he does nothing to develop any feminine quality in speaking either of Wisdom or the Holy Spirit. But God the Father is meanwhile often described in terms reminiscent of a mother, nourishing newly made humanity, caring for it and having pity on it.[15] Irenaeus's God the Father may not be quite as masculine as he seems (though of course gender characteristics are notoriously fluid, particularly in a society influenced by a multiplicity of cultures such as the Roman Empire of the second century). Where Irenaeus does allow a feminine principle to be directly colored by feminine imagery, and particularly the maternal imagery of breastfeeding, is in speaking of the church.[16] However, once again, this is driven by scripture from both covenants, specifically Paul (Galatians 4:26, "The Jerusalem above is free, and she is our mother") and Isaiah (66:10-11, "Rejoice with Jerusalem and be glad for her . . . that you may suck and be satisfied with her consoling breasts").

None of this need be explained by an attempt on Irenaeus's part to respond to Gnostic feminine imagery with "orthodox" feminine imagery: it may all have been firmly fixed in Irenaeus's thought through simple scripture exegesis before he ever heard of Ptolemy or Valentinus. But he does leave room for women to take that imagery further if they want to, so long as they assort it with scripture and the straight edge.

As regards Irenaeus's direct response to divine feminine imagery in the Gnostics, the evidence is more intriguing, though also oblique. What is particularly notable here is that he never criticizes the notion of a female God, creator, or principle per se, which would have been easy to do from various second-century cultural perspectives, scriptural and philosophical.

Instead, his arguments against the female gods and female principles are all objections to something other than the fact that they are female. His arguments against the pleroma are arguments from unity. The male and female aeons would inevitably be united, he argues, because Abyss and Silence, Thought and Truth and the rest cannot exist apart from one another.[17] Sophia, in particular, could not have separated herself off from her partner, Will.[18] Instead, they must all be one and indivisible, as befits a true God.

Irenaeus does not target Sophia and Achamoth for being female, as he easily could have done. Instead, he argues that Sophia's actions are incompatible with her nature: nothing that she is supposed to have done is appropriate to Wisdom.[19] He makes fun of the way she acts like a languishing lover rather than a spiritual being—but the comparison is with a comic male character, and the fun he makes is of her Gnostic authors— because she should not be languishing in misery because of a hopeless longing for the perfect Father at all. Instead, she should be happy, because the nature of the perfect God is to be found.[20]

Achamoth, the mother goddess, the detritus of Sophia's passion, would seem to be a particularly easy target for misogynist ridicule. But Irenaeus simply argues that she does not work as a logical entity, because everything that is supposed to make the creator God weak and unsatisfactory would also make her weak and unsatisfactory. He has no interest in arguing that female gods as such have no place in the cosmos. Instead, what interests Irenaeus is to argue that the same God who is creator of the world must also intend its salvation, and must also be the supreme being; and, in particular, that creation is not an unworthy act, but one that is entirely worthy of the most high God.[21]

Let us turn now to Eve, and the nature of woman as such.[22] Here, Irenaeus is so very keen to be positive about women that he gets himself into what might be seen as theological hot water, at least in some traditions. Eve, Irenaeus affirms, was disobedient, and consequently became the cause of death both for herself and for the whole human race. This is what the tradition has passed on, and Irenaeus therefore passes it on in his turn. But Irenaeus puts his own spin on it by using Mary as a foil for Eve, as the apostle Paul had done in the case of Adam and Christ. For as in Adam all die, even so in Christ shall all be made alive, Paul had argued (1 Cor. 15:22). Irenaeus picks up the structure and makes a parallel move of his own: as Eve, by her disobedience, became the cause of death for herself and for the whole human race, so Mary, in obeying, became for herself and for the whole human race the cause of salvation (*et sibi et universo generi humano causa facta est salutis*). Irenaeus's opponents, on the other hand, he argues, are wrong both to say that Joseph was the father of Jesus, and to say that he received nothing from the Virgin.[23] Mary represents the human race in its entirety in giving humanity to Jesus; all that is human in him comes from her. By the standards of ancient biology, even more than those of modern biology, this was an extraordinary claim. In these two regards, Irenaeus sets the groundwork for the highest of Orthodox and Roman Catholic Marian theology, and the highest possible theological anthropology of women.

Finally, let us look at what Irenaeus has to say about the role of women in the church. Let us return to the female disciples of Marcus the Gnostic teacher in the middle of their liturgy, first being called on by him to give thanks over the mixed cup and then to prophesy.[24] Pagels claims, erroneously, that "women were strictly forbidden [to prophesy] in the orthodox church"; the giving thanks she describes as "Worst of all, from Irenaeus's viewpoint."[25]

Irenaeus certainly called the woman who had given thanks "the deceived woman" (ἡ ἐξεπατημένη), but this is because, in his account, Marcus is in the middle of playing a magic trick on her: he has brought out a large cup, much bigger than the one she gave thanks over, empties hers into it, says a prayer, and it is miraculously filled from the smaller cup. Irenaeus says nothing at all about the desirability or otherwise of women giving thanks in orthodox settings. This silence is probably deliberate. Women giving thanks in private in houses which they owned may well have been a widespread practice in the early church, but as congregations became bigger and more like public assembles (albeit secret ones), the practice came to seem more anomalous. It is not unlikely that Irenaeus had seen this change happen in his own lifetime, and knew there was unhappiness about it. Having no clear scriptural precedent in its favor, he declined to express an opinion.

The case, however, is quite otherwise with prophecy. Irenaeus believes in the outpouring of the Holy Spirit, as prophesied in Joel and recalled by Peter in Acts 2:17-18: "And it shall come to pass that in the latter days I shall pour out my Spirit on all flesh; your sons and your daughters shall prophesy, your old shall dream dreams, and your young shall see visions. Yes, even on male and female slaves I shall pour out my Spirit" (Joel 3:28-29; cf *Haer.* III.11.9, "Donum Spiritus . . . quod in novissimis temporibus . . . effusum est in humanum genus"). But Irenaeus is conscious that others in the church (*alii*) do not, and therefore refuse to accept the Gospel of John with its promise to send the Paraclete, although he does not identify them. His argument is unequivocal: these people reject both the Gospel of John and at the same time the Holy Spirit.

However, he claims, they are also rejecting the apostle Paul, who in the Letter to the Corinthians spoke of prophetic charisms, and knows both men and women (*viros et mulieres*) prophesying in the church. By rejecting all these, Irenaeus argues, they commit the unforgivable sin, the sin against the Holy Spirit: "Per haec igitur omnia peccantes in Spiritum Dei in irremissibile peccatum."[26]

Perhaps I am putting undue strain on "haec omnia" here. But the logic of Irenaeus's argument is that rejecting women prophets is included among those things that represent the unforgivable sin against the Holy Spirit, because the whole story for Irenaeus is a package. It is the Holy Spirit that guarantees that the Old and New Testaments speak of the same God, and that the church is faithful to that God and to Christ. The Holy Spirit who spoke through the Old Testament prophets also spoke through John and Paul, and also spoke through women prophets known to Paul.[27] Thus he both insists that women prophets are found in tradition, and implies that more women prophets are therefore likely to arise in the future. To reject these things is to reject both Scripture and the Holy Spirit, Irenaeus argues. He has no greater sanction.

Let us return to the discussion of Marcus, for here we see a robust defense of what real prophecy is, a defense made by women.[28] These women, "some of the most faithful," it is worth noting in passing, who seem to have spent time in Marcus's orbit before turning against him, may be Irenaeus's source for some or all of the bootleg copies of the Gnostic scriptures he has gotten a hold of. They certainly offer a valuable glimpse into the lives and thoughts of the women who were attracted by or at least interested in Gnosticism.

The picture painted in *Haer.* I.13.3-4 is a revealing one. Marcus has obviously been holding some sort of assembly, which has clearly proved very popular. A lot of the well-born women of the area (again, by Irenaeus's account) have gone along. None of their friends or connections seems to have hindered them, or suggested there was any problem with attending such events. It was likely a very charismatic occasion, in the modern sense of the term. But these women have, despite the clear attractions of the assembly, smelled a rat, decided that this man is in it for himself, and shopped the operation to the bishop.

What they dislike about it is precisely the element of control. It is Marcus who orchestrates the events, calling forward individual women to prophesy, with the words "See, grace has descended on you: open your mouth and prophesy." But the women whose story Irenaeus gives are disgusted, breathing back out his supposed divine spirit at him and covering him with anathemas, separating themselves from his company. Their objection is that the gift of prophecy is not given to people by Marcus the magician but is sent by God from on high, and people who have it speak not on command but when and where God chooses. Whatever else they may or may not know about the faith, they know this for certain. Marcus's actions, to them, are blasphemous. Whatever about the Rule of Truth, it is their very strong understanding of the nature of the prophetic charism that, from Irenaeus's perspective, keeps them safe.

A trust in their sense of who God really is, and what sort of life they are being called to lead, is the basis of Irenaeus's pitch to the sort of women who might be attracted by Gnosticism. Although he is prepared to give space to feminine imagery where it can be found in the tradition, to insist on the true humanity of women and their centrality to salvation history, and to defend a space in the tradition for women prophets in the strongest language he has, Irenaeus's appeal to women is, ultimately, to treat them simply as full human beings, with all the theological richness that that implies for him. His message to them stands or falls on its own terms. Humanity is one, God is one, Christ is one, the church is one, salvation is one. God is not two, or three, or thirty, or 365. There is no aristocratic divine elite, a dinner party for thirty, refusing to get its hands dirty by interacting with creation, waiting for spirits to return to their true home or not as it may turn out. There is no Teflon-coated Christ who escapes all real suffering, or visits it on someone else. The Spirit is not a spirit in the hands of a few, reserved for the lucky ones who were born with the cosmological equivalent of a silver spoon in their mouths. There is the God of love, the Christ who suffered and died to save humankind, the Spirit poured out on all flesh, young and old, women and men, slave and free. There is not a world where no one takes responsibility, where those born into privilege save themselves and everyone else perishes. There is a God who created the world in love, who takes responsibility for what has been created, even when it goes wrong, and takes drastic action to restore it. There is a call to Christians to engage in return, take responsibility and live as created beings in the world, and face whatever suffering comes in the knowledge that Christ has suffered first and that the Holy Spirit is their advocate. That is what Irenaeus has to offer, and does offer, the intelligent women who are the target audience for the Gnostics. He can do little with the divine feminine, he cannot rewrite the story of Eve, though he can proclaim its reversal, and he is cautious in arguing for leading roles for women in a church which had inherited Paul's apparent prohibition on women speaking in public (for all Irenaeus is able to see that the roles held by women Paul knows and commends are important and various). But he does argue hard to protect a space for women prophets within the tradition, and to defend women's humanity. If theologians had followed him even to that extent for the last eighteen hundred years, the feminists of the 1970s and 1980s would not have had quite so much work to do.

CHAPTER FIFTEEN

Irenaeus and the Exegetical Roots of Trinitarian Theology

STEPHEN O. PRESLEY

In 1988 Michael Slusser published an important article entitled "The Exegetical Roots of Trinitarian Theology."[1] Slusser's thesis makes a significant contribution to the development of trinitarian theology in the early church. He calls attention to the dominance of analytical analysis in trinitarian discussions and reminds us that the very terms of the debate (*prosōpon, hypostasis, ousia,* and *physis*) are derived from the exegesis of scripture. Thus there is a genetic exegetical discussion underlying the analytical one and the analytical trinitarian debates should recognize their inherited exegesis. Slusser notes the earliest trinitarian term to gain currency in the theological exegesis of the early church fathers is "person" (*prosōpon*). The concept of *prosōpon* became particularly important in the interpretation of dialogical passages of scripture—such as Gen. 1:26 or Psalm 110:1—which became an exegetical practice that has now been technically labeled "prosopological exegesis." Concerning this manner of exegesis, Slusser concludes, "It was a method of literary and grammatical analysis of scripture that provided the early Christian thinkers with a way to talk about God in a trinitarian fashion."[2]

The concept of prosopological exegesis was identified first by Carl Andresen in his extensive article on the trinitarian concept of person in the early church published in 1961.[3] According to Andresen, the concept of "person" (*prosōpon*) in the Fathers was shaped by an exegetical practice he terms "prosopographic" (*prosopographische*) exegesis, which is the act of discerning the speaker(s) or *prosōpon* in a given passage of scripture. This kind of exegesis is highly intensive and the interpreter must attend to the literary and grammatical nature of the text. In this manner, particular individuals, pronouns, titles, or names were identified with a particular *prosōpon* of the Trinity. Following Andresen's work, Marie-Josèphe Rondeau published a detailed treatment on the patristic exegesis of the Psalms, which offer some of the premier examples of divine discourse.[4] Rondeau prefers the term "prosopological exegesis" given that it more technically describes the practice of identification of speakers in a given text.[5] Rondeau's work is thorough and lucid, and she finds a widespread early Christian literary analysis of the Psalms that sought to identify the proper interlocutors within the fabric of the textual dialogue. Furthermore, the early Fathers utilized this method in their theological analysis of the doctrine of the Trinity and the related concept of "person" (*prosōpon*).[6] Although they differ on certain points, it seems the general thesis of prosopological exegesis distilled by Andresen, Rondeau, and Slusser is sound, and one does not necessarily have to agree with this method to recognize that this is what is going on in Justin, Tertullian, Origen, and later Fathers.

It is observable, however, that in these treatments of early Christian prosopological exegesis Irenaeus receives minimal attention. Andresen, Rondeau, and Slusser each provide fine treatments of Justin and Tertullian. They all note that Justin has a detailed description of prosopological exegesis in *1 Apol.* 36 and, as Slusser observes, this method of exegesis is also essential to his "second God" argument in the *Dialogue*. Justin uses these dialogical scripture texts to demonstrate the existence of "another God besides the one who made all things."[7] Tertullian provides a similar analysis in *Adv. Prax.* 11 and supports his analysis with a discussion of several passages of scripture.[8]

It is obvious that Irenaeus is aware of this methodology. Both Rondeau and Slusser mention his use of prosopological exegesis in *Dem.* 49–50 and the identification of the interlocutors in Isa. 45:1 and Psalm 2:7.[9] Rondeau even suggests that Irenaeus is dependent upon Justin in this section. Furthermore, a recent article by Charles Kannengiesser reveals Irenaeus's exegetical preference for dialogical passages. According to Kannengiesser, Irenaeus frequently cites texts, in this case Genesis, "specifically for staging the scriptural 'deus locutor.'"[10] Kannengiesser infers that Irenaeus prefers these dialogical passages because they offer a means to explain his theological perspective. These very same dialogical passages are the focal texts of the early prosopological methodology.

Given the breadth with which this practice permeated early Christian exegesis, how can Irenaeus commit countless pages to argue through detailed exegesis of scripture texts, especially dialogical texts, and not more explicitly detail and utilize this method? I would like to suggest that the reason the bishop of Lyons is not more prominent in these discussions of prosopological exegesis is due principally to his polemical context and argumentation. Although he utilizes this method to a certain degree, Irenaeus is not nearly as enamored with it as others appear to be, because he recognizes that this is the very same method exploited by his Gnostic opponents. In the same manner as Justin, Irenaeus, and Tertullian, the Gnostics were discerning the speakers in a given passage and conforming the dramatic dialogical scenes to their theological framework. Irenaeus's explicit support for this method would only validate and enhance the Gnostic practice of discerning any number of speakers in scripture.

But it is to Irenaeus's credit that in the face of competing Gnostic exegesis, he recognizes that any prosopological methodology requires certain theological assumptions. Irenaeus must take a step back from the methodological discussions to defend the theological framework underlying the very procedure itself. For this reason, Irenaeus goes to great lengths to prove that "neither the prophets nor the apostles did ever name another God or call him Lord except the true and only God."[11] In other words, the only possible divine referent found in scripture is the one true God and, likewise, any divine allusion must refer to either Father or the Son. This naturally assumes a kind of theological framework or *regula fidei* by which the narratival accounts of scripture might be understood. Justin and Tertullian, it seems, have little concern for this dilemma and assume the only divine "persons" discernable in the text are the Father and the Son, who speak in and through the Spirit. But in the face of his Gnostic opponents, Irenaeus is not free to make this assumption. This keen recognition actually elevates Irenaeus's position and significance in these early discussions of prosopological exegesis and the trinitarian concept of "person."

Irenaeus on Gnostic Prosopological Exegesis

After completing his initial analysis of Valentinian cosmogony and cosmology in *Haer.* I.1-7, Irenaeus describes their manner of scriptural interpretation as an adaptation (*aptare*) of their own sayings to the sayings of the prophets, apostles and the Lord's words.[12] While there is an obvious complexity to their adaptation of scripture, at least according to Irenaeus, there is a clear sense in which an aspect of their method involves identification of divine titles and characters in scripture with various persons within the Valentianian cosmological and theological framework.[13] This practice yielded new meanings and new contexts for these narratival and dialogical passages when they were incorporated into the mythical thought patterns of Gnosticism. Irenaeus demonstrates an awareness of this interpretative framework in *Haer.* I.7.3 saying: "Moreover, they [Valentinians] divide the prophecies into various classes: one portion they hold was spoken by the Mother, another by the offspring, and still another by Demiurge. In the same manner, Jesus had his prophecies partly from Savior, partly from His Mother, partly from Demiurge, as we shall show as our work proceeds."[14]

Gnostic exegesis, in this case, Valentinian, included the practice of dividing up passages of scripture and identifying distinctive portions with different characters. Similar descriptions are found in *Haer.* I.24.2 and *Haer.* IV.35.1-4. In many cases, this also included the practice of inserting new events or dialogue into the accounts of scripture, thereby imaging new dramatic scenes within the contours of the scriptures. This description of isolation and identification of scriptural accounts with various Gnostic characters is clearly a type of Gnostic prosopological exegesis.

In addition to these descriptions of the Gnostic prosopological method, Irenaeus provides several specific examples that depend upon this method.[15] To begin with, there is the general use of scriptural titles for distinctive aeons within the Valentinian theological system. For example, the Ogdoad is composed of eight deities titled: Profundity, Thought, First-Beginning, Beginning, Grace, Silence, Mind, Only-Begotten, Truth, Word, Life, Man, and Church.[16] These titles are, for the most part, important terms found throughout the scriptures. The point Irenaeus makes is that these terms take on new symbolic meaning for the Gnostics; each term refers to their respective aeons. A similar example is found in *Haer.* I.3.1, where Irenaeus describes the Valentinian claim that any reference to "ages" in scripture, such as Ephesians 3:21, "To all generations of the age of ages," actually refers to the aeons of the Pleroma. We find a similar practice in *Haer.* I.8.5, where the individual terms of John 1:1-2 are identified with distinct aeons. After citing John 1:1-2, Irenaeus writes of the Valentinian interpretation saying, "First, he [John] distinguishes these three: God, Beginning, and Word. Then he [John] unites them in order to show the emission of each one singly, namely of Son and of Word, and the union of Son to Word, and both to the Father."[17] Irenaeus writes that the Marcosians interpret Genesis 1:1 in a similar fashion. The initial passage of Genesis sets fourth the Tetrad: God, the beginning, the heavens, and the earth.[18] We find similar descriptions of titles throughout his accounting of the various Gnostic systems in the first book of *Haer.*. The Gnostic revisionist framework tends toward the isolation of key terms and texts and identifies new Gnostic characters at work within these narratival and dialogical accounts.

In addition to the identification of aeons and isolated titles, there are several examples of the Gnostics incorporating the scriptural accounts into their mythical speculations. These commonly draw upon the narrative accounts of the Pentateuch, especially the creation accounts in Genesis. In *Haer.* I.5.3-6, it is the Demiurge and Achamoth involved in the creation of the world and humankind. There are several allusions to Genesis texts, all of which must be understood from the Gnostic perspective with these various aeons functioning as their referent. Thus, in *Haer.* I.5.4, it is the Demiurge who proclaims the words of Isa. 45:5-6/46:9, "I am God, beside me there is none other."[19] It is also important to note that the Gnostic reading of this text removes it from its context in Isaiah and inserts it into the narratival context of the creation accounts. In *Haer.* I.30.6, the same text is mentioned amid his summary of the Ophite tradition. Again, it is Jaldabaoth who proclaims the words of Isa. 45:5-6/46:9, but in this case, his Mother responds: "Do not lie, Jaldabaoth, for there is above you the Father of all things, who is the First-Man, and so is that Man who is in the Son of Man."[20] Jaldabaoth, however, is ignorant of his Mother and his various emanations are frightened by her voice. But Jaldabaoth distracts them by proclaiming the words of Gen. 1:26, "Come let us make man to the image."[21] Thus, this cohort of aeons together with Jaldabaoth assemble the first man. This assembling of texts demonstrates how, in the Gnostic framework, Isa. 45:5-6/46:9 is lifted out of its context and conformed to the creation account in Gen. 1:26. The passages are drawn together through their divine referents and create a new narrative, where the creation of humankind in Genesis 1–2 includes a multitude of divine persons. A similar account is found in Irenaeus's description of the cosmological system of Saturninus and Basilides. In this case, Gen. 1:26 is murmured among the cohort of 365 angels who actually carry out the formation of humankind.[22] These interchanges demonstrate the Gnostic revisionist tendency to utilize dialogical passages of scripture and incorporate them into their Gnostic cosmogony.[23] The Gnostic prosopological practice inserts new characters into the creation accounts and even creates new dialogue and events that revise the relationships of the divine characters in Genesis.

In a similar fashion, the Gnostics demonstrate a kind of christological prosopological exegesis, which involves the identification of the sayings and the deeds of Christ with two different speakers or agents. Slusser notes this particular kind of Gnostic exegesis.[24] For example, in *Haer.* I.7.4, it is the Savior who actually speaks the words of the centurion mentioned in the Gospel, "For I also am one having soldiers and servants under my authority; and whatsoever I command they do."[25] Irenaeus recognizes this exegetical practice in *Haer.* III.16.6, where he speaks of how the Gnostics separate the titles "Jesus Christ" and apply particular sayings and actions in the scriptures to these distinct persons.[26] Therefore, from Irenaeus's perspective a Gnostic exegete approaches the texts of scripture and discerns a host of persons functioning in and through the texts. This is not the only method Gnostic exegetes use, but it is an essential one. Like Justin, Irenaeus, Tertullian and others, these dialogical texts attract the Gnostic and through them they have means to convey their particular theological framework.

The Irenaean Response

Irenaeus responds to these descriptions of Gnostic prosopological exegesis in a number of places, but there is a concentrated effort in *Haer.* III.6.1-5. This chapter forms a pivotal turning point in the overall structure of Irenaeus's work as he moves from exposing the Gnostic systems in the first two books, to defending his own theological framework from the scriptures in the last three. The whole of *Haer.* 3.6.1-5 is aimed at proving that the Old Testament speaks of no other God besides the one true God and, in so doing, serves as a basic Irenaean lesson on the exegesis of scripture.

Beginning in *Haer.* III.6.1-2, Irenaeus manages to cite no less than eleven Old Testament passages, nearly all of which are dialogical texts. These texts form a network of scriptures bound together by the presence of multiple divine titles in each passage and divine discourse between the persons mentioned or implied in the passage. In this discussion, the distinctiveness of Irenaeus's approach becomes apparent. He begins this section saying: "Therefore neither the Lord, nor the Holy Spirit, nor the apostles would have ever named him God, who was not definitely and absolutely God, unless he were truly God; nor would they have named anyone in their own person (*ex sua persona*) Lord, except God the Father ruling over all things, and His Son who has received authority from His Father over all creation."[27] This opening statement and the subsequent network of scriptural texts contain all the prosopological markers. Irenaeus is speaking of the interpretation of divine titles and the identity of God. Even the language of "person" (*prosōpou, persona*) is found in the citation.[28] But in this statement, Irenaeus treads a slightly different path from that of his orthodox contemporaries. He follows two lines of argumentation: first, the scriptures would not attribute the title of "God" or "Lord" to someone other than the one true God and second, the scriptures would not have named anyone "in their own person" Lord except the Father and the Son. His former point argues that the very nature of the scriptures as derived from the Lord, Holy Spirit, or the Apostles would never have used the title of "Lord" in reference to any other God, except the one true God. His latter point is a qualification of the first in that the language of "Lord" or "God" in the scriptures can only refer to the one true God and, therefore, must refer to either the Father or the Son. According to Irenaeus, this implies that when an exegete arrives at the language of "God" or "Lord" in the text, the interpreter must acknowledge the only possible divine referents are the Father and the Son. This is not an assumption the Gnostics share and, in light of Gnostic prosopological exegesis, Irenaeus must provide the theological qualification to his prosopological methodology.

To demonstrate his points, Irenaeus utilizes his network of dialogical texts beginning with Psalm 110:1.[29] He cites this well-known passage and comments on it saying, "In this instance, it [scripture] reveals the Father speaking with the Son; He who gave him the inheritance of the nations and subjected all his enemies to him. Therefore, since the Father is truly Lord and the Son is truly Lord, the Holy Spirit has deservedly designated them with the title Lord."[30] Because, for Irenaeus, both the Father and Son are Lord, they have been designated as such in Psalm 110:1. The theological confession that the Father and Son are God, as expressed in his *regula fidei*, actually *precedes* the identifications of the individuals speaking in Psalm 110:1. The question, for Irenaeus, is not merely the identity of the speakers but the identity of the one who is "truly Lord." Distinct from the Gnostic tendencies mentioned earlier, the titles of "God" and "Lord" are used because the Father and Son are in reality "God" and "Lord."[31]

This discussion is followed closely by Gen. 19:24, another well-known christological passage that depicts the Lord's judgment of Sodom and Gomorrah. For Irenaeus, the one judging must be the Son, who previously spoke with Abraham and received power from the Father to judge the Sodomites. This combination of Psalm 110 and Gen. 19:24 is also found in *Dial.* 56.12-15, where Justin links these texts for the purpose of announcing the presence of two distinct persons functioning in the narrative. Justin's concern is the multiplicity of divine persons speaking in the text, while Irenaeus's concern is the more fundamental question of divine identity. This is most obvious in the context when, after citing Psalm 50:1, "God of gods, the Lord has spoken, and has called the earth," Irenaeus asks the most basic question, "Who is meant by God?" The rest of *Haer.* III.6.1 and 6.2 discusses the divine identities of other passages including Psalm 45:6, Psalm 82:1, Exod. 3, and Isa. 43:10 (LXX), all of which deal with dialogical accounts. It is only Psalm 82:1 that provides the interesting qualification where the term "gods" is used in reference to the faithful.[32]

But all this attention in *Haer.* III.6.1-2 to divine titles exposes a glaring problem for Irenaeus: scripture also uses the language of "god" in a negative sense for false gods and idols. How can the interpreter assume that there is only one true "God" when scripture itself refers to other "gods" and how would the interpreter know the difference between the use of similar divine titles? It is this problem he addresses in *Haer.* III.6.3,5, saying: "However, when scripture names those who are not gods, it does not in every sense, as I said beforehand, reveal them as gods, but with additional elements and indications through which they are revealed not to be gods at all." Having laid the theological groundwork for his first premise above, Irenaeus must now exclude its corollary. The only God identifiable in the text is the one true God and any other uses of the language of "god" that does not actually refer to a god at all. This point is especially important for his anti-Gnostic polemic. If multiple deities are discernable in the text, then the Gnostic prosopological method has more creditability. He cites several texts including Psalm 96:5, Psalm 81:9, and Jer. 10:11, where the gods "perish from the earth and are destroyed."[33] Their destruction, according to Irenaeus, exposes their false identification. They are in fact, not gods at all. He also invokes the story of Elijah on Mt. Carmel, who exposes that the prophets of Baal believed in a God that did not exists and Elijah invoking of the one true God incites Irenaeus to prayer in *Haer.* III.6.4. These texts convey, for Irenaeus, that the only "God" who properly can be called such is the one true God. This God, as he has argued, can only be identified as the Father or the Son.

Irenaeus continues citing a host of other texts including: Gal. 4:8-9, 2 Thess. 2:4, 1 Cor. 8:4, Deut. 5:8, Deut. 4:19, Exod. 7:7, and Heb. 3:5, all of which argue that there is no other God mentioned in scripture except for the one true God. This theme also dominates successive chapters of *Haer.* III.7-12. Similarly, this discussion of divine identity resurfaces in the opening of book IV. Bacq notes that the preface to book IV and *Haer.* IV.1 are dependent upon III.6.1ff.[34] The last lines of the preface to book IV remind one of *Haer.* III.6.1, "Therefore, since this is firm and steadfast, no other God and Lord is proclaimed by the Spirit, except the God who rules over all things with His Word and those who receive the Spirit of adoption." There is none other called God by the scriptures except the Father, the Son, and those who possess the adoption.[35] In other words, the language of "God" in scripture applies only to the Father, Son and the faithful. As we mentioned earlier, Irenaeus recognizes that the scriptures do term the faithful as "gods" in Psalm 82:1, 6-7 and elsewhere.[36] And Irenaeus reiterates himself in *Haer.* IV.1.1 where neither the prophets nor the apostles nor the Lord himself did name and identify any God who was not truly God. Once again, he distinguishes between those who are "god" in name only and the one who is truly God, and he states that it is an error of doctrine to confuse these.[37]

In conclusion, we have argued that prosopological exegesis is a significant method in early trinitarian discussion and the development of the trinitarian concept of "person." Although Irenaeus is not prominent in these discussions, it is not because he is unaware of this methodological practice. It is, on the contrary, the fact that his Gnostic opponents were utilizing this method in the revision of narratival and dialogical accounts in scripture. There is little doubt that he agrees with the interpretations of Justin, as he expresses in *Dem.* 49, but in the midst of Gnostic competition, Irenaeus realized the theological framework an exegete brings to the text naturally shapes the method of identifying speakers in a given text. The prosopological method did not preclude the Gnostic from discerning a multitude of deities within the fabric of the textual dialogues. Thus, Irenaeus revealed that the interpretation of divine titles and discourse in scripture largely depends upon, to borrow Irenaeus's question: "Who is meant by God?"[38] It is to Irenaeus's credit that he recognizes this issue calls for a framework or *regula fidei* that grounds the kind of prosopological exegesis carried out by Justin, Tertullian, and others. This analysis affords Irenaeus a key role in the early development of trinitarian theology and the understanding of the trinitarian concept of person.

CHAPTER SIXTEEN

The Image of God in Irenaeus, Marcellus, and Eustathius

Sophie Cartwright

The image of God is central to Irenaean theology and the extensive scholarship that explores it. Theological anthropology is deservedly important to this scholarship. God's image in Adam and Christ is fundamental to Irenaeus's anthropology both because Adam represents the human race and because Christ, as New Adam, is "the first-fruits of the resurrection of ἄνθρωπος."[1] He is the perfect human being—perfect ἄνθρωπος. Marcellus of Ancyra and Eustathius of Antioch have both, to varying degrees, been compared with Irenaeus, especially with reference to theological anthropology, and an "Asia Minor" school of thought.[2] The two fourth-century bishops are also linked in the context of the trinitarian controversies.[3] I will argue that both Marcellus and Eustathius are hugely indebted to Irenaeus in their understanding of God's image in Adam and Christ. Both later thinkers also depart from Irenaeus's conception, and from each other's, in important ways.

God's Image and Human Essence

Like Irenaeus, Marcellus and Eustathius both see God's image as fundamental to human essence as it is supposed to be, and that this is connected to the concept that Christ fulfills Adam. Also like Irenaeus, they understand "God's image" in extremely physical terms. However, the two later thinkers have a very different conception of the relationship between God and God's image. Marcellus emphasizes the distinction between the image and the thing that it is imaging while Irenaeus emphasizes the similarity. Although Eustathius sometimes applies "image" to the Son, whenever he applies it to Adam or Christ, he also emphasizes the distinction. Correspondingly, Marcellus and Eustathius both see humankind, made in God's image, as more distinct from God than Irenaeus does. This is part of a more autonomous conception of the human person. I will argue that the differences between these conceptions of God's image rely on divergent cosmological frameworks.

Marcellus and Eustathius see humanity and God as ontologically separate principally because God is ἀγένητος—"never having not been"—while humanity, like everything else, is γενητός—"having come to be."[4] Both are therefore concerned that the Son should not be seen as a "created thing."[5] This is a normative fourth-century categorization, novel in that period.[6] These categories are intrinsic: they define their subjects without reference to their relationship to anything else. Irenaeus thinks about the world in very different terms to fourth-century Christians. The state of *having been created by God* is fundamental in Irenaean anthropology: the primary distinction he makes is creator—creation—it is relational rather than intrinsic.

Marcellus, you will remember, broadly speaking, supported Nicaea, although he had an especially unified conception of the Godhead. With Eustathius, he insisted that there was only one hypostasis in God.[7] He controversially suggested that the incarnation would eventually end. I return to this doctrine later as it is significant to the current discussion. Marcellus's principal surviving work is *Against Asterius,* an anti-subordinationist writing from circa 330 of which only fragments remain.[8]

Eustathius, in opposing subordinationism, focused on *logos-sarx* Christology and himself developed a highly divisive Christology, within which he clearly articulated a concept of Christ's human soul. Eustathius's only work surviving in full is *De engastrimytho contra Origenem,* an exegetical treatise written after 311. There is also a substantial body of fragments, many from anti-subordinationist writings. José Declerck has recently established the Eustathian authorship of an epitome of *Contra Ariomanitas et de anima.*[9] Whilst most explicit references to image theology are outwith the epitome, it is invaluable here in elucidating Eustathius's use of a Pauline Adam-Christ framework that echoes Irenaeus.

The fragmentary nature of the sources renders it very difficult to establish the nuanced differences between Marcellus's and Eustathius's respective anthropologies, which are often remarkably similar. Nonetheless, comparison can, cautiously, be made. Notably, Eustathius articulates Christ's humanity more fully than Marcellus, and his concept of Christ as New Adam is consequently more robust.

Irenaeus

Drawing on the considerable existing scholarship, we must review several important elements of Irenaeus's understanding of God's image. Irenaeus uses the term *image of God* variously. Thinkers such as Eric Osborn and Denis Minns have discussed the nuances of Irenaeus's usage in detail.[10] Here I want only to observe, in line with Minns, that this diverse usage has a wider consistency. It is always central to Irenaeus's articulation of human essence. Sometimes God's image is what humanity progresses *from,* but even then it is the essence of humanity, the core that will remain in the new ἄνθρωπος. Irenaeus's conception of God's image is thus very concerned with the question: What is humankind supposed to be?

For Irenaeus, Christ is the image of God in that he reveals God. In Christ, the "invisible is made visible."[11] Christ also reveals Adam. As Ysabel de Andia observes, there is a "double visibilité" in the incarnation.[12] Often, when Irenaeus writes of Christ revealing Adam, what Christ reveals is that Adam is in God's image.[13] Thus, in revealing Adam, he reveals a connection between Adam and God.

For Irenaeus, Christ can simultaneously reveal both humanity and God because humanity was, in a sense, modelled on God. God, and more particularly the Son, is the archetype for Adam. God "made ἄνθρωπος in the image of God and the image of God is the Son, after whose image ἄνθρωπος was made."[14] There is a resemblance between humanity and God that the incarnation both displays and reinforces. Christ is perfect humanity because humanity was created with him in mind.

Whilst Adam often images specifically the Son, it is the eternal Son, rather than Incarnate Son, whom he images, and therefore the eternal Son who is archetype. Admittedly, Irenaeus is often vague about the distinction between the eternal Son, or Word, and Christ. Significantly, however, the incarnation clearly exhibited an *existing* similarity. For instance, Irenaeus writes that: "He appeared . . . that he might show the image [to be] like himself."[15] It is God qua God, not God made human, whom Adam resembles.

Minns contends that Irenaeus's most original interpretation of the "image of God" is that "a two-fold similarity between us and God is to be found in the human body."[16] He cites *Demonstration* 22: "He might show the image to be like himself." Flesh is emphatically part of God's image: Irenaeus refers to "that fleshly nature which was moulded according to the image of God."[17] Irenaeus often emphasizes the body in order to establish that the whole person is in God's image, contra "Gnostic" spiritualizing tendencies.[18] Nonetheless, this strategy signifies the belief, not only that people are properly physical but that human flesh is part of what resembles God.

The incarnation not only demonstrates a resemblance but also creates one. Christ "re-formed the human race."[19] Christ not only reveals Adam but also fulfills Adam; he is, in a sense, more Adam than Adam. Christ fulfills Adam by assimilating humankind to God: "the Word of God was made ἄνθρωπος, assimilating himself to ἄνθρωπος, and ἄνθρωπος to himself."[20] In becoming assimilated to God, humanity becomes what it is supposed to be. Christ is more Adam than Adam *because* he is also God and therefore unifies God and ἄνθρωπος.

So, Christ causes an existential change in humankind. This is reflected in Irenaeus's ontology of the human person. As Peter Foster has discussed in detail, the fullness of God's image is achieved by the addition of the Spirit to the human body and soul.[21] God's perfect image, or sometimes God's likeness, is body, soul, and spirit.[22] Whilst Irenaeus does not explain how these three components interact, he does have a coherent sense of how new humanity includes original humanity—body and soul, and improves on it—with the spirit. Irenaeus does not distinguish between human spirit and God's Spirit;[23] he therefore suggests that God's essence comprises part of God's perfect image.

Foster argues that Irenaeus risks reducing the autonomy of the human person by making God's spirit a necessary part of fulfilled humanity.[24] This may seem ironic, given Irenaeus's emphasis on human free will.[25] However, it is astute: in Irenaeus's scheme, by rejecting participation in God, one rejects life. Saved humanity has entirely relinquished the power of self-direction. God's image is intimately connected to God, but the trade-off is dependency on God.

Irenaeus's concept of shared essence between God and Adam coheres with his understanding of what an image is: an image has an ontological affinity with the thing it is imaging, so God's image necessarily has an ontological affinity with God. This is achieved because God, the one being imaged, is also the image-maker. Hence, expounding Gen. 1:26-27, Irenaeus explains that God took "from himself the substance of the creatures, and the pattern of things made."[26] God, the image-maker, pours himself into his image and the result is a mutual identity.

Irenaeus correspondingly defines creation by its relationship to its creator. This comes across strongly in his discussion of "Gnosticism." He basically argues that "Gnostic" cosmology is logically impossible because creatures are necessarily connected to their creator. Thus, he demands: "How . . . could either the angels, or the Creator of the world, have been ignorant of the supreme God, when . . . they were his creatures and were contained by him?"[27] A creature is defined by its relationship to its creator.

Importantly, as has often been noted, Irenaeus also emphasizes God's transcendence, but normally in the context of his creatures' total dependence on him.[28] This underscores the conception that the primary distinction between God and humanity is relational rather than intrinsic. It also suggests that a dependence on God inheres in shared identity with God.

I hope I have demonstrated that Irenaeus sees the term *image of God* as denoting a resemblance between God and Adam grounded in a progressive ontological affinity between God and humankind in which humanity shares part of God's being and is consequently dependent on God for its own being. Body and soul are both part of the subject of this affinity.

Marcellus

Marcellus shares many of Irenaeus's most distinctive claims about God's image: Christ is God's image because he reveals God. He "displays the whole of the Godhead bodily";[29] Christ is "the first new ἄνθρωπος,"[30] strongly echoing Irenaeus's "Second Adam."[31] Christ is also the blueprint for Adam. Again, God's image is corporeal. However, there are important differences. Here, I want to highlight Marcellus's divergent understanding of the relationship between an image and the thing it is imaging.

For Marcellus, Adam is a "statue" or ἀνδρία, for which God takes the pattern from himself.[32] This seems to echo Irenaeus's conception of resemblance between Adam and God. However, the statue metaphor has a particular sense of representing God in his absence, as statues represented the emperor in distant provinces.[33] Correspondingly, God takes the "pattern" from himself but not the "substance," as he does in Irenaeus's account. For Marcellus, the resemblance between God and Adam is not based in ontological affinity. Humanity, when perfect, reveals God in its own being, not, as in Irenaeus, as an outpouring of God, but as a living representation, an "ensouled statue" that God created to be distinct from himself.

Corresponding to this strong separation between God and ἄνθρωπος, the blueprint for Adam is clearly Christ Incarnate. Here's the salient passage: "[God said] . . . 'let us make a human being according to our own image and likeness,' well naming the human flesh 'image.' For he knew precisely that a little later it would be the image of his own word."[34]

Unlike in Irenaeus, God Incarnate, not God qua God, is Adam's archetype. Being modeled on Christ emphatically does not mean being modeled on God. In fact, Christ is the archetype for Adam in the sense that the incarnation was foreordained. This is possible in Marcellus because, unlike Irenaeus, he absolutely delineates between Incarnate Word and eternal Word: "Before the taking on of our body the Word was not in himself 'the image of the invisible God.'"[35] Marcellus has developed Irenaeus's sense that Adam is modeled on Christ so that it is indistinguishable from Adam being modeled on Perfect Adam. For Marcellus, Adam as he will be is an archetype for Adam as he starts out. Correspondingly, Christ *as human* is perfect Adam, not, as in Irenaeus, Christ *as human in union with God*. As in Irenaeus, Christ's humanity, and therefore all humanity, reveals God, but the humanity that is revealing God is more separate from him; it is as image that Christ makes God visible and as image that Christ is separate from God.

Marcellus's controversial assertion that the incarnation would end elucidates how he sees humanity as separate from God. Marcellus writes that the incarnation will end, following Christ's thousand-year reign, and the Word will return to the Father.[36] There is an ongoing dispute about the centrality of this doctrine in Marcellus's theology and whether he later retracted it.[37] These questions are interesting but beyond this paper's scope. Such an idiosyncratic doctrine is certainly very likely to have emerged for a reason, and therefore probably coheres with its exponent's wider theology. Significantly, it shows that if the incarnation were temporary, this would not remove anything from it that Marcellus sees as integral to its nature. I suggest that this is because, for Marcellus, while the incarnation is a real event, it is functional. After Christ's thousand-year reign, the incarnation will have achieved all it is supposed to achieve. God saves humanity by uniting with it, but humanity's union with God, which in Irenaeus is the ultimate end, is a means to an end in Marcellus; humanity is not ultimately meant to be in union with God.

In Marcellus, flesh is emphatically part of what delineates ἄνθρωπος from God. He sees in a flesh-Word contrast a parallel to his God-ἄνθρωπος contrast, using σάρξ and ἄνθρωπος (flesh and human) interchangeably to refer to Christ's humanity in contradistinction to his divinity.[38] This reflects a sense that humanity is, properly, corporeal. Marcellus initially seems to contradict himself in insisting that "the flesh profits nothing."[39] However, here he quotes John 6:63, and the way in which he quotes is revealing. This text could be applied to flesh generally but Marcellus applies it specifically to Christ's flesh in reference to the Word. Flesh profits nothing to the Word, because he is God: "not because of himself, but because of us he assumed human flesh."[40] Marcellus thus interprets a more readily anti-body passage so that it does not undermine flesh's value to humanity. Sara Parvis notes that Marcellus is sure that Christ's flesh will not be destroyed, and sees in his doctrine of the incarnation's impermanence "an attempt to value the flesh for its own sake, as God's good creation."[41] Marcellus sees no contradiction in the Word relinquishing the flesh and perfect humanity being fleshly because, unlike Irenaeus, he sees human destiny as starkly separate from God's destiny.

In juxtaposing fleshly ἄνθρωπος with the incorporeal God, Marcellus fails to practically articulate the fullness of humanity in the new ἄνθρωπος that is emotively so important to him. As Adam is an "ensouled statue," it is evident that Marcellus sees ἄνθρωπος, at least very broadly, in terms of a body and soul.[42] However, what survives of Marcellus's Christology is not cohesive with a clear belief that Christ assumed a soul. Both *logos-sarx* and *logos-anthropos* models have been suggested as the most plausible way of understanding his Christology.[43] Maurice Dowling is probably closest to the mark in suggesting that Marcellus is simply uninterested in Christ's human soul.[44] As Dowling hints, in focusing his God—ἄνθρωπος contrast on human flesh, Marcellus jeopardizes the sense that Christ encompasses Adam's humanity. The question of Christ's humanity does not arise in the same way in Irenaeus because he does not contrast God and ἄνθρωπος to the same extent.

Marcellus's conception of the distinction between God and ἄνθρωπος coheres with his understanding of what an image is. While Irenaeus emphasizes the similarity between an image and the thing it images, Marcellus emphasizes the difference. Marcellus insists that an image is not the thing imaged.[45] As Parvis notes, Marcellus's exegesis here is driven by his opponents. He accepts Asterius's argument that an image is different from the thing it images but says that this does not imply a distinction between God and his Word because the Incarnate Christ, and not the eternal Word, is image.[46] Nonetheless, the distinction is quite consistent in his extant fragments. He genuinely incorporated it into his theology. In Marcellan theology, referring to Christ as "God's image" does not denote his divinity.

Because Marcellus does not conceive of God's spirit as part of God's image, he avoids the loss of human autonomy in which Irenaeus's soteriology culminates, but humanity is correspondingly less intimate with God. As both thinkers have a strong sense of God's overwhelming power and glory, this sacrifice is logically required. Humanity may either be independent or indescribably intimate with God; Irenaeus and Marcellus share the implicit assumption that it cannot be both.

Eustathius

Eustathius's conception of God's image in Adam and Christ shares the principal themes common to Irenaeus and Marcellus: Christ fulfills Adam: he is "Last Adam," much like Irenaeus's "second Adam" and Marcellus's "first new ἄνθρωπος."[47] God's image in Adam and Christ is corporeal; God's image reveals God. Like Marcellus, Eustathius sees more disjunction between God and ἄνθρωπος than Irenaeus does. However, this disjunction plays out differently in Eustathius, with divergent anthropological consequences. In particular Eustathius's later, highly divisive Christology allows a fuller articulation of Christ's full humanity than is found in Marcellus.

For Eustathius, "God's image" describes both a relationship between the Father and the Son and a relationship between God, Christ, and Adam. The Son is the Father's image in the sense that "like having been begotten from like, the ones begotten appear as true images of their begetters."[48] Conversely, Christ is not "true image": "the human being whom . . . [the son] bore is the image of the son, as images are made from dissimilar colors by being painted on wax, some being wrought by hand deliberately and others coming to be in nature and likeness." Humanity is conformed to Christ's image.[49] Eustathius's anthropological definition of image shares much with Marcellus's: they both try to qualify the sense in which "God's image" implies resemblance between humanity and God, and both think that "God's image" in Adam and Christ denotes something totally other than God, which nonetheless represents God. Again, our image-status is dependent on Christ's.

Eustathius, like Marcellus and Irenaeus, thinks that Adam and Christ are images of God in that they reveal God. When Eustathius talks about God revealed in the incarnation, he believes that Christ reveals God because of the Word dwelling in him, but emphasizes the revelatory capacity of Christ's humanity within this context: we see the Word through Christ's humanity, and the whole Godhead through the Word: "the human being of Christ is a savior . . . a bringer of light to the human race. . . . [because] . . . we may behold the word and God through him, through the word we may behold the universally sovereign authority . . . through the one image looking at the dyad of father and son . . . in the dyad knowing the one godhead."[50] Paradoxically, the Word both is God and reveals God. This elucidates Eustathius's distinction between the Son as image and Christ as image: Christ reveals God by pointing to something that he himself is not; the Word Incarnate reveals God because he is God made manifest.[51] The revelatory nature of Christ's humanity is especially emphatic in this passage from *Contra Ariomanitas*, typically of Eustathius's later work, because it is not merely Christ *qua* human who is revealing image but ὁ ἄνθρωπος τοῦ Χριστοῦ —"the human being of Christ." This human being, however, reveals God because of the incarnation.

As in Marcellus, Adam nonetheless similarly (though not necessarily equally) reveals God. Adam's pre-ensouled body is "fashioned from [God] . . . prototypical ἄγαλμα of God . . . impressed copy of the divine image."[52] The statue (ἄγαλμα) metaphor echoes Marcellus particularly, with the same implication that Adam represents God in his absence. Eustathius's phraseology emphasizes affinity where Marcellus was careful to maintain difference.[53] Nonetheless, the underlying structure of the relationship between God and Adam is basically the same. Broadly speaking, Eustathius shares Marcellus's sense that Adam is a distinct representation of God.

As in Marcellus, humanity is a distinct representation of God, *and* God's image in being the image of Christ, in whom God is manifest. Eustathius may share Marcellus's view that Adam's image status anticipates the incarnation. However, there is no evidence for such synthesis, and it is equally likely that he simply holds these two ideas in tension. In any case, they hang together emotively in light of the strongly Irenaean sense that Christ is what Adam is supposed to be.

As in Irenaeus and Marcellus, Christ fulfills Adam's potential, and people fulfill their potential in becoming like Christ. Correspondingly, Eustathius draws heavily on Paul's distinction between "soul Adam" and "spiritual Adam," ψυχικὸν Adam and πνευματικὸν Christ—"Last Adam"—and thinks that saved people are likewise πνευματικὸν.[54] Again, in fulfilling Adam's potential, Christ is what we will become.

Eustathius's use of the Pauline πνευματικὸν motif to describe human perfection echoes Irenaeus in a way that Marcellus, apparently, does not: the difference between ultimate ἄνθρωπος and original ἄνθρωπος is the spirit. Eustathius's understanding of the term πνευματικὸν is hard to reconstruct. His principal concern in discussing it is that, applied to Christ, it does not imply *logos-sarx* Christology.[55] He establishes this partly by offering various scriptural contexts in which it is applied to people other than Christ, all of whom, presumably, had souls.[56] He therefore applies the term πνευματικὸν both to Christians in this life and to the resurrected just. It consistently denotes congruence with the spirit in moral decisions. This follows Irenaeus in seeing perfect ἄνθρωπος as reliant on God. It also echoes Irenaeus's sense that humans ultimately surrender their self-direction, though here there is more ambiguity than in Irenaeus. It differs very significantly in that there is no sense of a tripartite anthropology in which the spirit is a third component of human ontology.

Eustathius's view of the spirit's role in soteriology corresponds with his divisive Christology in that both are concerned to keep God's ontology separate from human ontology. God is more involved in Eustathius's perfect ἄνθρωπος than in Marcellus's, but Eustathius nonetheless agrees with Marcellus that God and humanity are totally other; where Marcellus frames the union of God and ἄνθρωπος in teleological terms and wonders whether it will last, Eustathius reduces the extent to which God and ἄνθρωπος are unified.

Eustathius's dyohypostatic Christology allows him to develop a fuller anthropology than Marcellus. Like Irenaeus and Marcellus, he sees flesh as central to God's image; this is strikingly evident in his description of Adam's pre-ensouled body as a statue of God. Further, like Marcellus, Eustathius insists that John 6:63 does not mean that the flesh is "useless."[57] However, unlike Marcellus, he places the human soul, with the body, in contradistinction to the Word: his God-ἄνθρωπος contrast does not run parallel to a contrast between corporeal and incorporeal realities.

Eustathius's practical emphasis on Christ's full humanity is in many ways a logical development from various themes in Irenaeus, set within Eustathius's very different metaphysical and christological frameworks: the idea that original ἄνθρωπος, body and soul, progresses to perfect ἄνθρωπος, body, soul and spirit, coheres best with the idea that Christ is new ἄνθρωπος if Christ has a human soul. Further, Eustathius's emphasis on Christ's soul shares with Irenaeus's emphasis on flesh a desire to defend the whole person. Nonetheless, Eustathius's articulation of Christ's human soul comes within a Christology that is far too divisive for Irenaeus. Eustathius explains the Adam-Christ connection better than Irenaeus or Marcellus, but only at the expense of the incarnation.

Irenaeus's Theological Anthropology

In Marcellus and Eustathius, we see that some of the most distinctive aspects of Irenaeus's theological anthropology left an abiding legacy into the fourth century. We also see significant divergences. Both later thinkers closely follow Irenaeus's understanding of the relationship between Adam and Christ, but have a different understanding of what the descriptor "God's image" says about the relationship between Christ and God. Consequently, a very similar conception of the relationship between Adam and Christ has significantly different implications for theological anthropology in Marcellus and Eustathius than in Irenaeus. Marcellus and Eustathius share a fundamental divergence from Irenaeus that shows the defining influence of fourth-century metaphysics: humanity is more distant from God, but its capacity, nevertheless, to reveal God, is all the more striking.

Marcellan anthropology, in particular, has sacrificed Irenaeus's sense of intimacy and interrelation between God and humankind, but it has gained in return the sense of human autonomy that Irenaeus lost. Marcellan humanity is self-sufficient; its integrity may even be more valuable than that of Irenaean humanity for precisely this reason. Eustathius's Christology suggests a greater chasm between God and humanity than Marcellus's does. Despite this chasm, Eustathius maintains a greater sense of saved humanity's reliance on God than Marcellus does. Whether, in this respect, he has the advantages of both Irenaeus and Marcellus, or the disadvantages of both, is a matter of perspective. Eustathius articulates Christ's humanity more coherently than either Irenaeus or Marcellus, which adds to his conception of New Adam, but at the expense of his incarnational theology.

These three thinkers share an important and distinctive nexus of ideas, key to which are a belief that Christ renews Adam and a belief that God's image is corporeal. Disparate metaphysical frameworks offered them different possibilities for understanding the human person. I hope that the comparison between them highlights some of the strengths and weaknesses of their distinctive and historically contingent worldviews for constructing a theological anthropology.

CHAPTER SEVENTEEN

Packaging Irenaeus

Adversus haereses *and Its Editors*

PAUL PARVIS

The Trappist monastery of Orval nestles in the midst of trees and green fields in southern Luxembourg, a mile or so from the French border. It is, of course, well known for beers, cheeses—and editions of Irenaeus. There Dom Adelin Rousseau, the editor of Irenaeus, died at the beginning of 2009, on 13 January, at the age of ninety-five.

His edition of *Adversus haereses*[1] is controversial, as well as magisterial, but it has been the fundamental resource for all serious work on the text for a generation now, and it shows no signs of relinquishing that role.

When we read Irenaeus—as when we read any ancient text—we are reading an artifact, a construction, something that is the product of the ingenuity and the industry and the bias of scribes and editors engaging with the text and with each other over a period of centuries. What I want to do in this chapter is to look at the process of editorial development that led up to Rousseau and to try to see how successive editors made Irenaeus their own and how, as they did so, Irenaeus came—for them—to interact with the problems and with the constraints of their own age.

No edition—indeed, no reading of a text—is ever value free, and surveying that process may, I hope, help us to become more aware of what *we* are doing when we pick up the text of Irenaeus. And it will, in any event, help us to appreciate the achievements and the idiosyncrasies of those whose labors over a period of nearly four centuries have brought the text of Irenaeus to us.

Erasmus

The *editio princeps* of *Adversus haereses* was prepared by Erasmus for the scholarly printer Froben in Basel in August 1526. There had been talk of an edition of Irenaeus for some time. As early as April 1522, Froben were hoping to get their hands on a manuscript of *Haer.* that Johannes Fabri was known to have had copied in Rome. Two years later, in October 1524, Archduke Ferdinand, the Emperor's younger brother, then a precocious 21, was expecting one to appear.[2]

But Erasmus, typically, cannot have spent very long preparing it. In May 1526, he was still trying to get his hands on Fabri's manuscript.[3] He duly succeeded, but Fabri exacted a price—he wanted the edition dedicated to his powerful friend Bernard von Cles, Prince-Bishop of Trent and one of the inner circle of advisors who were still pulling the strings of the Archduke.[4] Erasmus was obviously reluctant, but was encouraged by the prospect Fabri dangled before him of receiving "a most elegant and valuable gift" in return.[5] The Prince-Bishop was suitably grateful, and in due course sent a "little gift of money"—not, of course, "as a reward, but as an expression of our sincere affection for you."[6] The "little gift" was in fact *centum aureos*—a hundred gold Rhenish florins, which would, in 1526, have paid a master craftsman's wages for two years or— rather dearer to Erasmus's heart, one suspects—have purchased over 1850 liters of fine rhenish red wine.[7]

The dedicatory epistle[8] to von Cles serves as introduction and is dated 27 August 1526. Above all, Erasmus presents Irenaeus as a man of peace, who "fulfilled the promise of his name and became a stout defender of peace in the church."[9] In that he is, of course, picking up the word play developed by Eusebius in *HE* V.24.18, but there is more to it than that.

He speaks with feeling in that dedicatory epistle of "those . . . who trouble the world with their quarrels" (CWE xii, 290, 10–11), of "the present troubles in the church" (xii, 290, 15), of "the books that are now flying like weapons in both directions" (xii, 291, 18-19). The actions of "the peace-loving Irenaeus" in the Quartodeciman affair are contrasted with "our belligerent Ptolemies" who now "on the flimsiest of pretexts are quick to raise false charges of heresy and schism" (xii, 292, 66–68).

But Irenaeus brought to the task before him eloquence, learning, and a scriptural piety. Erasmus is not sure whether *Haer.* was written in Latin or in Greek; he is inclined to think Irenaeus wrote in Latin, but was actually more comfortable with Greek. But either way, "the flow of his language . . . is lucid, well-ordered, and logical" (xii, 291, 75–79); "he was familiar with all the liberal arts" (xii, 291, 83–84); and "fought against a multitude of heretics" "relying only on the help of scripture" (xii, 295, 118–19). With such a portrait it is little wonder that Erasmus proudly calls him "*Irenaeum meum*" (Allen, vi, 385, 20).

But the Lord "knows how to use what is good and turn what is wicked to his glory and the salvation of his church." So it was that in the past "the exertions of schismatics brought the faithful into a closer harmony, created, so to speak, a common battleline, and the ungodly teaching of heretics forced them to study the holy mysteries of Scripture" (CWE xii, 302, 228–30 and 302, 239–303, 241).

For Erasmus in 1526, that would be a consummation devoutly to be wished. For 1526 was not a good year for him. He had long been struggling to hold the middle ground—sympathetic to many of the Reformers' ideals and critical of the institution, but unwilling to break with the church or to compromise what he saw as the fundamentals of Catholic faith. It was a difficult position to maintain, and in 1526 he was being squeezed from both sides.

On the one side, he was under attack from hardline Catholics like Beda in Paris and Latomus in Leuven, who thought him unorthodox. In 1525, for example, Latomus published a series of works that attacked Erasmus, though not by name, while the Leuven Dominicans were not so squeamish from the pulpit. In May 1526, Beda—the syndic of the Faculty of Theology—had published a book of *Annotationes* cataloguing the errors of Erasmus. In August—the very month in which Irenaeus was published—intervention from Francis I, who was generally supportive of the humanist cause, forced the withdrawal of Beda's book from sale in Paris. But it was reissued that same month in Cologne. By the end of the next year, 1527, Beda's agitation would have borne fruit in the formal condemnation of Erasmus's works by the Faculty of Theology.[10]

On the other side, 1526 saw Erasmus's final and bitter break with Luther. Two years earlier, Erasmus had, in *De libero arbitrio* διατριβή *sive collatio*, rejected Luther's position on the bondage of the will. The Exocet from Luther, *De servo arbitrio*, was published at the end of 1525—on New Year's Eve, in fact. Erasmus, Luther declares, is a closet atheist; he harbors in his heart "a Lucian, or some other pig from Epicurus's sty who, having no belief in God himself, secretly ridicules all who have a belief and confess it."[11] Erasmus worked at frantic pace to get a reply (the first part of his *Hyperaspistes*) out, from Froben, in time for the Frankfurt book fair in March.

Even worse, the radicals were gaining ground in his beloved Basel. By 1525 he was engaged in an acrimonious quarrel with Oecolampadius and Pellican, who were misrepresenting his position on the Eucharist. By April 1529 he had moved to the safety of Freiburg im Bresgau.[12]

That is the climate in which Erasmus produced his edition of Irenaeus, the eloquent and learned man of peace.

The edition itself is something of an anticlimax. It offers Latin text only, with no Greek fragments—that is, of course, one reason why Erasmus could view with sympathy the idea that *Haer.* was written in Latin.[13] The reader is not given much help. Books II to V, though not the complex Book I, are each introduced by a short *argumentum* by Erasmus. The chapter divisions and titles of the manuscript tradition are provided for Books I to IV (V is undivided in the MSS). And there is an *index rerum* at the end. But there are no notes and only brief and rare marginalia. A few of the marginalia are catchwords; a number offer some Greek—the original of words transliterated in the Latin, the original of some Homeric tags, an occasional suggestion of the Greek phrase that might have been in Irenaeus's mind when he wrote his clumsy Latin. But these skimpy annotations become even rarer after about II.20.

And the hastily produced text is hardly faultless. One of Erasmus's successors, Massuet, noted with some annoyance in his own edition of 1710 that "his [Erasmus'] edition swarms with so many blunders, errors, and faulty and corrupt sentences that one often searches for Irenaeus in the very (work of) Irenaeus and it is difficult to follow his thought."[14] But it is the *editio princeps*, and of course it retains some critical value because of the possibility that some of his readings represent a lost manuscript rather than Erasmus's own conjectures.

Gallasius

The next edition that can be deemed major came nearly half a century later. It was by Gallasius—Nicolas des Gallars—and was published in 1570.

Gallasius was an influential member of the Company of Pastors at Geneva and a reasonably close associate of Calvin's. In the spring of 1560, Calvin had dispatched him to London to become the pastor of the French (Protestant) church in exile, housed in St. Anthony's chapel in Threadneedle Street. He survived some unpleasant internecine squabbling within the congregation, thanks in part to the support of Edmund Grindal, the Bishop of London, who had been designated superintendent of the exile communities.[15]

Grindal is one of those enigmatic figures of the Elizabethan settlement—charged with enforcing conformity but deeply in sympathy with the more radically Protestantizing movements in England and on the Continent. He is said to have told a Puritan group, "You see me wear a cope or a surplice in Paul's. I had rather minister without these things, but for order's sake and obedience to the prince."[16]

But Gallasius did not like the London climate and went back to Geneva in June 1563. By September he was minister in Orleans and Professor of Theology in the Reformed Academy there. That came to a dramatic end in 1568, when an outbreak of bloody sectarian violence forced him to flee. "I was so often in danger of my life," he says. "The fury of the populace was inflamed; they were demanding the slaughter of the ministers; and the gates of the city were being watched so closely that no one was able to leave." He did, however, manage to slip out by night, and a roundabout journey through the woods took him to the safety of the lands of the Duchess Renée de France. From there he made his way to Geneva.

Gallasius must have been rather crestfallen when he reported his adventures to the great Reformer Theodore Beza. Beza "asked me what I now had in hand. Then I replied that I was thinking only of easing and relaxing my mind from those cares by which it had long been vexed." But Beza gave the impeccably Calvinist admonition that he must redeem the time. "It is not your part to give way to indulgence and idleness. I know for sure that you cannot pass in leisure this free time which has been given you."

He had a plan. "You know, he said, how useful is the reading of the ancient doctors, which the many nonetheless neglect, both because of obscurity and also because of some impurity which those times—already on the slide (*labantia iam*)—brought to Christian doctrine." The solution was twofold. First, the works have to be divided into chapters, with key points prefixed in summary, so the reader can find his way. And, secondly, an "*admonitio seu censura*" should be appended in which the unsound bits can be pointed out and distorted exegesis of scripture set right.

We might, incidentally, remember that at the time of that rather strained interview, Beza had in his possession the great manuscript of the Gospels and Acts that still bears his name—Codex Bezae, the uncial D or 05. It was part of the spoils of the sack of the monastery of Saint Irenaeus at Lyons by a Huguenot mob in 1562, and it was to remain in Beza's possession until 1581, when he presented it to the University of Cambridge. What some lost in inter-communal violence, others gained.

In any event, Gallasius accepted the plan but thought that to tackle *all* those "volumes of the men of old" was a rather tall order, so he decided to work on just one, "the one who is reckoned the most ancient among the Latins"—Irenaeus.

Calvin himself—dead since 1564—would have approved. He had read Irenaeus by at least 1542, often cited him, and probably himself owned a copy of Erasmus's second edition of 1528.[17]

What we have just heard is Gallasius's rather brightly colored account of the genesis of the edition. It comes from the dedicatory epistle, signed "Geneva. 31 January 1569 (*Pridie Cal. Februarii.* M D LXIX)," and addressed to Edmund Grindal, Bishop of London.

The date cannot be right, and the place needs comment. The title page gives MDLXX and no place. But it announces that the edition was published "Apud Joannem le Preux et Joannem Paruum." Le Preux and Parvus were Parisian printers, who must have found shelter in Geneva. But 1570 must be right rather than 1569. Gallasius clearly worked as quickly and haphazardly as Erasmus had, but, even so, the last day of January 1569 simply does not give time for the various adventures and misadventures he recounted.

In January 1570 Grindal was still bishop of London, though later that year he was translated to York, where he busied himself energetically protestantizing the North, still infested with papistical practices; he was installed (in absentia) on 9 June but only left London in August.

Gallasius nails his editorial colors firmly to the mast. "They are mightily deceived who think that the description and refutation of those ancient heresies has nothing to do with our times." It is Anabaptists and antinomians who take most of the flak here, though there is a sideswipe at today's "fans and patrons of superstition (*superstitionum fautores et patroni*)" as well. "For what did Satan not try, now that the Gospel is being reborn, to divert or slow its course? But this pious bishop and other ancient doctors taught us by their own example what arms and weapons are to be used in resisting him. For they fight only by the teaching of Christ and the Apostles, against which they examine all dogmas, traditions, and rites." Finally, there is, once again, a play on the meaning of Irenaeus's name, but the tone is far different from that of Erasmus. Not only did you—Grindal—protect the peregrine churches in London from without, "But you made them immune within from fear, from dissent and division. You checked temerarious men and those desirous of novelty, you repressed the insolent and refractory, you tamed the proud, you protected the innocent, you settled quarrels and disputes, finally you showed yourself truly Irenaeus's and a champion of tranquility. . . . Therefore do I deservedly compare you to Irenaeus, whom in the same tasks you diligently imitated." Where Erasmus was sickened by the prospect of a church being torn in two, Gallasius was thinking of his own troubles in Threadneedle Street.

The editorial work was hardly thorough, though Gallasius has at least read his text carefully. While he proclaims, "Faults which occur I emended by comparing various copies and other passages of the author himself (*collatis exemplaribus et locis ipsius auctoris*)," it is clear that he consulted no new manuscripts. But he does help the reader—at least the right-minded reader—in a number of significant ways.

For one thing, he now knows that Irenaeus actually wrote in Greek and argues clearly for that conclusion. And Greek text now appears—he prints the long section of Book I quoted by Epiphanius.

And he heeds Beza's directions on chapters and summaries. He follows, as Erasmus did, the manuscript capitulation for Books I–IV, though he knows that it, like the titles that accompany it, cannot go back to Irenaeus himself. So he provides his own summaries at the head of each chapter as a guide to the reader. And he divides Book V into chapters, for the first time—thirty-six of them, each with its own summary.

All that, he says, involved reading and rereading the text often, but "I find it hardly surprising that those who are unable to swallow the tedium of examining this do not make much progress nor for long in the reading of this and similar authors—they don't eat the nut because they don't crack the shell."

And then there are the extensive—and pugnacious—notes to the text itself, most of which, according to the eighteenth-century editor Massuet, "contain nothing but meaningless and coarse declamations."[18] Indeed, "it seems that it was not so much Gallasius' plan to produce a more polished and more correct Irenaeus as to circumvent the thought of that most holy man with prolix notes drawn from Calvinist doctrine."[19]

The introduction to the Annotationes runs through various heresies. "Execrable were the Nicolaitans, who profaned marriage and permitted adultery. Their error is condemned in words by the Papacy, but in actual fact applauded." "The heresy of the Collyridians was once condemned; they worshipped and invoked Mary. But today not only Mary, but other saints as well are graced with divine honours, and those who say that they should not be invoked or worshipped are held to be heretics" (359).

The flavor of the annotations can be seen from his long note on the much controverted phrase "*potentiorem principalitatem*" ("pre-eminent authority"/"stronger rule"/"more powerful origin") used with reference to Rome and its bishops in his III.2, our III.3.2. "Great once was the authority of the Roman Church among other nations . . . But after it began to raise itself on high under the pretext of Roman imperium, to give orders to others, and to differ in mind from the Word of God . . . that authority was not only minished, but taken away. . . . From a chaste virgin it became an impudent whore."[20] Or, on *traditio* in III.4.2, "Of course, what the Apostles did not teach is not to be regarded as their tradition. But what they did teach and commanded all churches to observe is apparent from the Acts of the Apostles and their own letters. Therefore we are not to seek other things unless we wish to fall into error and to have Satan for our teacher."[21] But for all its faults, Gallasius's work did at least make the text of Irenaeus more accessible and launched a series of heavily annotated editions, each engaging with its predecessors in a conversation that would continue for nearly three hundred years.

Feuardent

Another of Gallasius's contributions was to provoke an impassioned reaction. Francis Feuardent, who was born in 1539 and died in 1610, was a Franciscan Friar, celebrated preacher on behalf of the Catholic League, and later Doctor and Professor of Theology in Paris, and a scholar of some standing. He produced a number of scriptural commentaries and a major edition of Nicholas of Lyra's *Gloss*, but his most important patristic work was Irenaeus. He produced two editions—one in Paris in 1575 and an expanded and rather more cumbersome revision in Cologne in 1596.

In the 1575 preface (to Cardinal Charles Bourbon),[22] he compares the *Gnostici* of Irenaeus's time to the *Hu-Gnostici*—the Huguenots—of his own time: "one egg is never found more like another than the latter are to the former" (+ (6 v)). It is, he thinks, by

divine providence that you can derive the word Hu-Gnostici by taking the first syllable
of the name of Ioannes Hussus.

It is a joke he obviously liked, for he repeats it often, both here and, twenty-one
years later, in the edition of 1596. Presumably, it had gone down well from the pulpit.

Feuardent was, indeed, something of a firebrand. The prefatory letter is signed
"Paris, on the ides of August, in the one thousand five hundred and seventy-fifth year
from the Virgin giving birth"—just under three years after the Saint Bartholomew's
Day massacre. It is ominous that in that political climate he can follow up a discussion of the trinitarian errors of Calvin and his followers with an impassioned plea:
"O Emperors! O kings! O men of power—you who await Christ our God and Lord as
judge—is it for no reason that you carry scepters and swords?" (++ (i r)).

A prefatory note informs the "pious reader" that the annotations include

> many things drawn from other martyrs and select Fathers which particularly
> pertain to the confirmation of the ecclesiastical faith, the forms and norms of
> doctrine, the rites of the sacraments, the mores of Christians, and the overthrow
> of heresies. . . . In addition to this, the heretics after their own fashion—espe-
> cially the men of Magdeburg [that is, the Centuriators] and a certain Nicolaus
> Gallasius, a preacher of the Calvinist pestilence at one time in Geneva, then
> in Orleans, afterward as they say in Basque country—industriously corrupted
> many passages from this writer, which it was worthwhile and fitting to restore
> and vindicate from their false interpretation. (+ ii (v))

His text itself, Feuardent says, presents "these books of the divine Irenaeus purged
by us, with much vigilance and labour, from innumerable faults with which they formerly abounded" (++ ii (v)). And it is indeed an improvement.

The 1575 edition has no Greek—the long Epiphanian citation from Book I is ban-
ished to an appendix and appears only in the translation of Billius (Jacques de Billy).
But for the Latin Feuardent has been able to bring onstream, for the first time, the late
fifteenth-century manuscript which became *Vossianus lat.* F. 33, which enabled him
to supply the last chapters of book V and fill in various holes in Erasmus's (and Gallasius's) text.

Feuardent's text itself is printed chapter by chapter—some of which are quite long—
each followed by annotations, many of which are also quite long. And often quite militant. He thinks, for example, that the *pseudoprophetae* of our IV. 33.6, his IV.61, are
Marcionites in particular, but include also the Valentinian Marcus. He then goes on,

> But the insolence and madness of all these is followed hook, line, and sinker (*ped-
> ibus et manibus*) by—among latter-day Gnostics—the Anabaptists, whose leader
> Munzer called himself and his adherents heavenly prophets—something which
> I think they learnt from Luther, who, as Calvin complains, was decked out by his
> people with the spoils of the greatest of the prophets, Elijah and John the Baptist.
> Beza isn't alone in making Calvin a distinguished prophet. See the force of an
> estranged mind! Indeed, even Calvin himself often boasts that such he is. (299)

Predictably, the reference just below, in our IV.33.7, his IV.62, to "those who work schism" (*qui schismata operantur*) sets him off again. There is a long and learned note, adorned with various patristic proofs—Clement of Rome (the *Apostolic Constitutions*, actually), Optatus, Augustine—to the effect that "the Fathers reckoned the crime of schism, by which various sects of the heresies rend the holy unity of the Church, to be so grave and horrifying that they believed no torments could sufficiently expiate it. That is what Irenaeus too openly indicates here." The note concludes with a plea: "Would that many of this age would pay closer attention to this!" (299).

The re-edition of twenty-one years later is reworked and appreciably fuller. There are now Greek fragments printed alongside the Latin—from Eusebius, Theodoret, and others, as well as from Epiphanius.

And the notes are reworked as well—but no more irenic. Thus the reference in our III.10.2 (Feuardent's III.11) to "Mary . . . prophesying on behalf of the Church" is now the trigger for a longish Marian note showing that "there is nothing unusual in the fact that in this passage Irenaeus attributes to the Blessed Mother of God at once the gift and the exercise of prophecy," for that gift is, after all, included in the fullness of grace with which she is endowed (260 B-C).

The note on modern false prophets at IV.33.6 (Anabaptists, Luther, Calvin) now ends with the comforting observation that "such wind-bag (*ventosi*) false prophets will not escape the strict judgement of God" (399A).

The fulmination at IV.33.7 on schism is now followed by a comment on "those who are outside the Church [*qui sunt extra ecclesiam*]"—"From this it is manifest that heretics and schismatics are not true members of the Catholic Church—that is, not sheep, but wolves; not shoots of the vine, but dry and lopped off twigs; not sons of the groom and the bride, but bastard and illegitimate offspring of the Devil, their father, and a heretical tart" (399 C-D).

Both Gallasius and Feuardent are militant, which is hardly surprising against the background of communal violence, amounting to virtual civil war, in the France in which or from the perspective of which they were writing. But both enriched the text. Both—especially Feuardent—brought much learning to bear on its elucidation and left behind a rich deposit of patristic parallels that was to be enthusiastically mined by their successors for centuries. And neither can be regarded as boring.

Grabe

Irenaeus slumbered through the seventeenth century, but the eighteenth was to see two great editions, one a reaction to the other.

In 1702 an Irenaeus was published in Oxford by John Ernest/Johann Ernst Grabe, who was born and educated in Königsberg, but had lived in England since 1697. It is dedicated to the Most Serene and Most Powerful King Frederick III of Prussia. (It was only in the previous year, 1701, that Frederick decided he would rather be a King than a mere Elector.)

Once again, the theme of Irenaeus as a man of peace is prominent; this time, with a play on the meaning of the name Frederick. Irenaeus's name "is indeed your name, since he who is called Irenaeus by the Greeks is called Frederick by Germans. . . . And you, Most Serene Frederick, in accordance with the augury of your name, attempt to join together the Christians in your lands, divided by controversy so gravely from each other, and to reconcile them in peace" (Dedicatio, 2–3).

Where one or the other is wrong, Lutherans should be prepared to learn from Calvinists and Calvinists from Lutherans.

> But where both have turned aside from ancient paths, following their own predecessors, but where those predecessors were wrongly carried away by a commendable zeal directed against the new traditions and huge abuses of the latter-day Roman Church and went on to scorn as well the old traditions of the Catholic Church and to reject the right use of certain sacred practices, slipping, as often happens, from one extreme to the other—there (in those circumstances) let both sides step back and return to the royal road—that is, the middle way and primitive form. And thus, truly Reformed, let them grow together into perfect union with the Christians of primitive times and mutual union among themselves.

"The writings of the most ancient Fathers" can teach us the doctrine and the ways of primitive Christianity, but "even Irenaeus by himself . . . speaks in his books so clearly that if these and certain other dissident parties should wish to accept him as an arbiter of peace and to hear him, every controversy would have an end and the whole Church would have peace" (Dedicatio, 4–5). And he concludes his dedication with an invocation of the wish of Erasmus, expressed "in the Dedication of the first edition of Irenaeus nearly two hundred years ago 'that some Irenaeuses might arise, who, in the spirit of the Gospel, would restore the world to concord.'"[23]

It was a heart-felt plea. Grabe's theological formation had been in the world of Lutheran "syncretism," with which his father, a Professor in Königsberg, was intimately involved. The "syncretists" were the heirs of Georg Calixtus, who saw the faith of the first five centuries and the supposed ubiquity and uniformity of ancient doctrine as the basis for the reconciliation and reunion of Lutherans, Calvinists, and Roman Catholics, and they were bitterly opposed by the pastors of Königsberg.

Grabe began to have doubts about the whole Lutheran system and to incline more and more toward Catholicism. In 1694 he was ordered to submit a written statement of his "Dubia" to the Consistory of Samland. This led to his arrest and a short imprisonment. He eventually fled to Breslau, with the intention of becoming a Catholic, but became persuaded that the only reasonable exegesis of the Apocalypse was that the whore of Babylon was indeed the church of Rome, which rather dissuaded him.

In the spring of 1697, he was received into the Anglican Church in Hamburg. From there he made his way to England and found shelter in the academic and ecclesiastical life of Oxford. There a great burst of creative energy saw his most brilliant patristic work done. The two volumes of his annotated anthology of second-century texts, the *Spicilegium*, appeared in 1698–1699; a distinguished edition of Justin's *First Apology* in 1700; and his Irenaeus in 1702.[24] The Anglican Church as a via media, resting securely on the foundation of the early Fathers—not the last time a High Churchman would work his way to that sort of position in Oxford.

In any event, we can see why peace in and between the churches mattered so much to him, both theologically and existentially, and how he had come to think that in the Anglican Church he had found a large and calm harbor. What was important was not the particularities of inter-confessional and intra-confessional doctrinal conflict, but the pattern disclosed by "the writings of the most ancient Fathers" that would show "what sort of doctrine, celebration of the sacred mysteries, ecclesiastical society, and, finally, discipline flourished among the Christ-faithful of primitive times."[25]

The edition shows a substantial improvement in the text, and Grabe is often happy in his conjectures—on a number of occasions confirmed by the discovery of the Armenian, first published in 1910 and first seriously utilized in Rousseau.[26] The printing is sumptuous, but the layout confusing—as Massuet was to complain: "the Greek fragments are indeed inserted opportunely in their own places, but so unfittingly arranged that the eyes of the reader are obliged to wander, as in a perpetual circuit, through the pages, often uncertain whither they ought to go."[27]

The notes are learned and extensive, but—hardly surprisingly—have much to say by implication at least about Grabe himself. In I.10.1, for example, Irenaeus says that at the end of the age the Lord will give life and eternal glory to those who have persevered in his love, "some from the beginning, but others from repentance." To the arch-Catholic Feuardent the former meant either newly baptized infants, who die before committing sin, or martyrs, for "by the privilege of martyrdom there is a direct passage to heaven without more laborious satisfaction either here or elsewhere, a thing not granted to others who sin after baptism."[28] Grabe replies tartly, "Note that eternal life *is given by grace* to the just and the penitent and that incorruption is *granted* to them. See the last verse of Rom. 6 and Apoc. 2:6"[29]—no room for purgatory or penitential machinery there.

Again, in the important discussion of the tradition of the apostles and the Roman church in III.3.1-2, Grabe tackles both Erasmus and Feuardent. "It is most apparent that Erasmus of Rotterdam was completely wrong when in that letter which is to this very day prefixed to these books he writes that Irenaeus himself fought against the mob of heretics with the help of the scriptures alone." On the contrary, from this passage as a whole, "it is plain and evident to all that Irenaeus overcame the Gnostics, not merely with the help of the scriptures, but also by the traditions and by the words and writings of the Fathers" (200).

Grabe there speaks unconsciously, as his contemporaries habitually did, of traditions in the plural, as if they were numerable items in a list, whereas Irenaeus always uses "tradition" in the singular, except when he is picking up the Gospel saying about the traditions of the (Jewish) elders (IV.12.1), which are a bad thing. Tradition is for Irenaeus an organic, indivisible whole, not a basket of discrete propositions.

Grabe is sure that the "ancient tradition," the *vetus traditio*, of III.4.2 is the Symbol—that is, the Apostles Creed—though he declines to enter into controversy over whether the Apostles had actually drafted it themselves.[30]

Massuet's verdict was harsh. "Imitating Gallasius, though it is for the Anglican Church, to which he had attached himself, that he is most zealous, he seems to have been more concerned to attach even an unwilling and resisting Irenaeus to the Anglican sect than to produce a more correct and better edited work."[31] Indeed, one of Grabe's significant achievements was precisely to provoke Massuet.

Massuet

Massuet's own edition of Irenaeus was published in Paris in 1710. He himself (1665–1716) was a Benedictine of the Congregation of St. Maur, who spent the last thirteen years of his life teaching at St. Germain des Prés.[32]

His Praefatio explains that it was both the success and the weaknesses of Grabe's edition that made the Maurists resolve to produce one of their own. He blames the Oxford printers for the fact that "that edition is so scarce overseas that it can be purchased only with the greatest difficulty and at quite a high price." The result was that booksellers in both Paris and Amsterdam were planning to reprint it.

In order to forestall that, "it seemed to men renowned for doctrine and piety that a new edition of Irenaeus was not only useful, but necessary—an edition which would both be more accurate and also one which Catholics could go through without tripping up. That labour they wished to be undertaken by one of our people"—that is, by one of the Maurists. "That burden was imposed on me. I baulked for a long time, but at last submitted" (vii).

The result was the most sumptuous of all the editions—it runs to 842 large folio pages, 211 quires in all. Layout and typography are magisterial. The medium is, as they say, the message. It is difficult to imagine that a concern with cost was the driving force behind the project.

The preface (v–xii) and the three long *Dissertationes* that follow—on Gnostics, on the life and works of Irenaeus, on his teaching (xiii–clxii)—are learned, elegant, weighty, and almost regal in tone. We have already seen some of the judgments he rendered on the work of his predecessors.

Massuet provides yet another set of chapter divisions, this time with subdivisions into sections. He explains that in subjoining his abundant annotations at the foot of the page, he has taken thought above all for "those who are moderately versed in these matters" and the need "to spare them tedium and labour," though he has tried to keep these notes as brief as the difficulty of the argument would allow. "Yet I did not go on to burden the margins with those notes that relate only to a display of erudition—in my case, small of course—or to dogmas and controversies of the faith, thinking—and having learned from my own experience—that nothing is more annoying to the reader than to be compelled to halt at almost every step by the interposition of some delay" (x).

And yet the work, though unimpassioned, is not dispassionate. It is certainly not neutral in tone. The beginning of the preface affirms that among the merits of Irenaeus is the fact that "certain principal dogmas of the Catholic faith, which we profess today, about the mysteries of the most holy Trinity and incarnation, about the sacraments, ecclesiastical hierarchy, the divine institution of bishops, the authority of tradition, the supreme dignity and primacy of Peter and his successors, and so on, are so eloquently explicated and confirmed that not only ancient heresies but those that emerged all the way from apostolic times to our own can be extirpated from the root and overturned from the foundation" (v).

On Irenaeus on the position of Rome: "But what seemed most efficacious and ineluctable to the holy Fathers for confuting all the heretics and schismatics of their own time ought to be no less efficacious for overthrowing the heretics of our time— Lutherans, Calvinists, and others, as many as seceded from the Roman Church" (cxv). On Irenaeus on the Eucharist: "So Irenaeus argues against the heretics, whether more recent heretics like it or not; if he does not do that, he does not do anything" (cxli). "The most illustrious Grabe did not refrain from very long annotations in order to twist and weaken the arguments. But he is wasting his words" (cxlvii). And he rounds off his introductory matter by saying in the very last paragraph of the final dissertation that "I would have wished it to be shorter, had it been possible. But it was made longer both by the complex difficulties of many passages . . . and by the importunities of the Protestants and especially the cavils of the recent editor of Irenaeus, which, lest they proceed to deafen our ears, it was worth the trouble to dissipate" (clxii).

The notes to the text often have a go at Grabe. He picks up Grabe's remark at I.10.1 that eternal life is a gift of grace. "The learned man is wasting his time," since the position he is attacking is not in fact Catholic doctrine, as he thinks it is. "If Grabe had wished to think about this carefully, he would have abstained from a useless note" (49).

At III.3.2, Grabe tries to "twist" the words about the Roman Church. Indeed, he is forced to "attribute quite absurd ideas to Irenaeus, which could not have entered the head of that most holy bishop unless he had become absolutely mad" (175). In the same passage, Grabe "tries to do violence to Irenaeus's words" about tradition from the apostles. Since he "was unable to deflect the weight of the apostolic tradition . . . he at least tries to confine it within narrower limits, lest it prove so pressing." And so Grabe takes it to mean the "symbol of the apostolic faith"—"as if the whole faith proclaimed to humankind were contained in the Apostles' Creed! As if the apostles had not handed down many other dogmas of the faith, which Protestants themselves profess along with us" (175).

Massuet's Irenaeus, like so many of the other Maurist editions, is a magnificent piece of work. But its tone and style, even its layout and typography, can only partially conceal what a polemical piece of work it is as well.

And it was destined to become something of a textus receptus. It is of course the edition reprinted in Migne's Patrologia (PG 7), and it reigned unchallenged for a century and a half.

Harvey

The year 1857 saw the appearance of W. Wigan Harvey's Cambridge edition. When we look at these two stout, sensibly bound octavos, it is difficult to resist the impression that they are, in their sound, commonsense values, truly English. Harvey, at least, would, I suspect, rather have liked that conceit.

He himself was a sound, commonsense member of the Anglican establishment— Eton; King's, Cambridge; Cambridge don and then, after his marriage, country vicar; a Tory and a magistrate. Ecclesiastically, he was High, but anti-Tractarian.

In 1841–1843 he had published a three-volume work entitled *Ecclesiae Anglicanae Vindex Catholicus*, which demonstrated the conformity of the Thirty-Nine Articles with the teaching of Christian antiquity. It consists of quite extensive extracts from patristic texts, arranged article by article—a procedure which on the one hand confirms the Articles and on the other casts a reassuringly comforting glow over the Fathers.

A Preface to Irenaeus looks briefly—very briefly—at manuscripts and editions. This is followed by "Preliminary Matter," consisting of a disquisition on "Sources and Phenomena of Gnosticism" and an account of "The Life and Writings of S. Irenaeus, Bishop of Lyons in Gaul."

The former fills 151 pages (I, i—cli), and, it must be said, takes a broad sweep, beginning with "the traditions of Paradise" (i)—"that glimpses of truth, of which man had an unclouded view in Paradise, were still retained in the earliest ages of the world, is very evident, so far as the Bible has revealed to us the religious history of the various families of the human race after the deluge"—and moving on to Melchizedek, Abraham (ii), and the Pharaoh of Joseph's Egypt (iii). We get to the Pre-Socratics by page xxxv, while Simon Magus comes on stage at page lxv.

"The Life and Writings" (I, cliii—clxxv) is rather more focused. The idiosyncrasies of the Latin version seem to be partially explained by the fact that it was a "Celt who made it"—a Celt "in every way inferior to the work that he undertook; independently of the barbarisms and solecisms with which his style abounds, he frequently is totally unable to catch his author's meaning" (I, clxiv).

The authenticity of the Pfaffian fragments is vigorously defended (I, clxxi—clxxii). Those four forged chunks of Irenaeus "discovered" by Chr. Matt. Pfaff in Turin and published by him in 1715 are useful to Harvey, above all, in defending the soundness of Irenaeus's teaching on the Eucharist, lest it be thought too Romanizing.

For it is there, and there alone, that Irenaeus is in some danger. The author of the *Vindex* explains that "with few exceptions, and those not at all dependent upon doctrinal discrepancies, the Articles of the Church of England might be illustrated singly from the statement of Irenaeus. . . . The subject of the Holy Eucharist alone has given rise to expressions that need a few words of explanation" (I, clxxiii).

"On the whole, the view of the eucharist put forth by Irenaeus agrees with the twenty-ninth article of our Church, scarcely perhaps with the latter portion of the twenty-eighth. In any case it should not be forgotten that an illustration may be very apt as helping the refutation of any particular heresy, and yet be far from edifying as an element of instruction. The teaching of the church to her children is excellently set forth" in one of the Pfaffian fragments (I, clxxiv—clxxv), which clearly shows the sacrifice to be spiritual and that it is through *reception* of the sacrament that we obtain remission of sins and eternal life.

Harvey was not, I think, overly plagued by self-doubt—an impression confirmed by the notes to his text. They are, on the whole, brief and businesslike and—an innovation in the editions—they are in the vernacular rather than in Latin, even the strictly textual ones. His churchmanship shows through in a note on the clause "And, among those who preside in the churches, neither will the one who is most able in word say other than these things"—a clause that occurs in our I.10.2, Harvey's I.3—for, yet again, an editor of Irenaeus renumbered the chapters. "At least here," Harvey tells us, "there is no reserve made in favor of any theory of development. If ever we find any trace of this dangerous delusion in Christian antiquity, it is uniformly the plea of heresy" (I, 94, n. 2).

The much controverted passage on Rome in III.3 gives Harvey the occasion to observe that "the holding of Apostolical tradition, *quod semper, quod ubique, quod ab omnibus*, is shown to be the true ground of catholic consent" (II, 9, n. 10). He is appealing there to the so-called Vincentian Canon, the dictum, emanating from Vincent of Lerins in the fifth century, that "that is to be believed which had been held always, everywhere, and by all." Except, of course, that that is not what Vincent says. His *Commonitorium* actually says everywhere, always, and by all (3.2), and it is clear from his whole discussion that that is the order in which his three tests are meant to be applied. But, revealingly, Harvey cites it in the order habitually used by Newman and others, an order which, consciously or unconsciously, privileges antiquity (*quod semper*) over ubiquity or Catholicity (*quod ubique*).

Harvey's shortcomings should not blind us to his merits. His approach to the text is conservative, but his judgment is often sound. The edition is convenient and user-friendly—apart from the idiosyncratic numbering of chapters. And he is able to bring to bear new Syriac and Armenian fragments.

His Irenaeus belongs to that twilight world of semi-critical texts, on the cusp of the fully critical era. In that it is not unlike, say, Field's editions of Chrysostom. And it is not out of place in such distinguished company.

Rousseau

And that brings us back to Adelin Rousseau. He had been a seminarian in Liège, joined the monastery in 1936, and stayed there for seventy-two years.

The ten chunky volumes of his edition are, together, more ample than even Massuet. It is the first to make systematic use of the Armenian, though it often, I think, over-privileges it at the expense of a perfectly sound Latin text. The "notes justificatives" are invariably learned and often illuminating. And repeatedly they manage to disengage from hoary controversies and move on to new ground. A classic instance would be his balanced and sane treatment of "*potentior principalitas*," the understanding of which had been bedevilled by Protestant—Catholic polemic since Gallasius.

There are, though, some places where a monastic piety might just peep through the learning. At IV.7.1, Irenaeus introduces a citation of the Magnificat with the words "But Mary too says . . . [*Sed et Maria ait . . .*]." Or at least that is what editors assumed he wrote. The text went uncommented upon until Harvey noted that two manuscripts ("the Clerm. and Voss. copies," that is, C [= *Berolinensis* lat. 43] and V [= *Vossianus* lat. F. 33]) "strangely read *Elizabeth*" (II, 163, n.4). Rousseau, however, knew that "Elizabeth" was also read by the Armenian. He, therefore, correctly drew the conclusion that that must be the original reading—and it is in fact a reading shared with some other Old Latin witnesses. But he could not actually bring himself to say that Irenaeus *meant* to attribute a canticle he sang in the monastic office day after day and year after year to anyone other than Our Lady. So he concludes that it is simply a slip—"an error or inadvertence"—on Irenaeus's part.[33]

The Stream of Tradition

If we survey the sweep of this editorial endeavor as a whole, we might note two features shared by almost all the tradition. The first is that the editions were engaged in a dialogue with each other, a conversation that lasted for over 300 years.

A simple example—who are the "false prophets," the *pseudoprophetae*, of IV.33.6? Feuardent thinks the Marcionites, but also Marcus the follower of Valentinus. Grabe thinks Montanists. Massuet asks why not both? We have seen other, more complex examples in the course of our discussion.

Even Harvey, in that twilight at the dawn of the fully critical era, is still in the game. He not infrequently cites the views of his predecessors—most commonly Grabe but also Feuardent—though he seldom takes the time to argue against them.

With Rousseau, it is not so. Though he frequently engages with modern secondary literature, he very seldom engages with his predecessors—indeed, virtually the only interest he evinces in the earlier editions is to discuss—thoroughly and usefully—their manuscript base. Editorial methods and editorial standards had changed.

The Trappist has broken off the conversation. Or, if you prefer, just as Orval itself was a new, twentieth-century foundation planted on a medieval site, so is Rousseau's edition a new construction built over an ancient tradition.

The second common element we can see is that each of our editors writes from a particular perspective with a particular purpose, and they look for different things. It could not, of course, be otherwise. There can be no text without context. An edition is a state of the text that exists in a particular place at a particular time.

Here again, it might seem at first blush as if Rousseau breaks the pattern. Over and over again he avoids obvious bias, as in his resolution of the misplaced dichotomies of much Catholic—Protestant polemic. Or perhaps it simply seems to us that he avoids obvious bias because we are on the same camber.

But it is worth remembering that the first two volumes—the text and notes to Book IV—appeared in 1965. They had received their *nil obstat* in March and were legally deposited in the fourth trimester. The fourth and last session of the Second Vatican Council occupied that same trimester. Change was in the air—change that radically affected the Church in France and monastic life throughout the world. There was a sense of old divisions being transcended, of windows opening. The air must have been like that Grabe breathed in the Oxford of 1700. He, too, felt that he could leave past controversies behind and that he was moving from a confined to a larger room.

Now, a generation later, we perhaps no longer feel that optimism, that realization of new possibilities of ecclesial life opening up before us. We live, I fear, in a world that is more cynical, more inclined to look for spin and rhetoric—in both the narrower and the wider meanings of the term. We look for rhetorical strategies and are wary of totalizing discourse. We are inclined to resort all too easily to "he would say that, wouldn't he?"

What sort of Irenaeus should we look for, in our own time, as editors, translators, readers? What sort of Irenaeus do we deserve?

Perhaps we should be more ready to make capital of our hermeneutic of rhetorical suspicion by exploring the shifts of register, the changes of tack and mood, that we find in *Haer.* as Irenaeus moves from purple passages of impassioned plea to close and careful argument and on to mordant wit and heavy sarcasm. There was a Baptist friend of the family who used to write in the margin of his sermon notes, "Weak point. Shout like hell." Does Irenaeus ever do that?

The text that emerges for us might be less of a piece. Its texture might be less homogeneous. We might see something more of an Irenaeus struggling like us and our contemporaries to try to make sense of an obdurate world. That is, of course, speculation. All we know is that there is no text without context, and our context is not quite what it was a generation ago.

CHAPTER EIGHTEEN

Tracing the Irenaean Legacy

Irenaeus M. C. Steenberg

Some legacies are easier to trace than others. Athanasius of Alexandria's role in promulgating the creed and language of Nicaea, however one might assess it, ensured that he was remembered, quoted, discussed, and debated for centuries to follow. Exploring his influence and legacy is a project supported by rich, extensive testimony. Elsewhere one finds similar stories. Basil of Caesarea, dying far younger than his kin could have anticipated, was heralded at once as a great teacher, the reflection on his writings becoming almost immediately an ecclesiastical project—and one that continued for centuries. After the death of Cyril of Alexandria in AD 444 (a repose that prompted some rather memorable funeral tributes[1]), an almost continuous reflection on his influence—assessed both positively and negatively—began, and would carry on over the coming decades and centuries. Appreciating his personal legacy too, if not always his personality or precise theological contribution, is a task which history facilitates by preserving a tremendous amount of evidence and testimony.

But when we come to Irenaeus, the story is somewhat different. He had been no less involved in the theological conflicts and controversies of his age than these. He had been no less a theologian of creative expression and robust articulation. He had been, his writings would lead us to believe, no less a "personality"—prone to rather aggressive fits of satire and mocking as much as he was ready to express the most tender emotions of forgiveness and repentance, even toward his enemies. He had composed a work unlike any other known at the time, bridging polemic and apologetic with positive doctrinal articulation, speaking in a voice that would earn him the reputation, in modern study, of the "first theologian" in the patristic heritage (as odd, and probably unhelpful, as that ascription really is). And yet there is no great or obvious Irenaean history in the decades and generations following his death. The man whose theological expression is today taken by many as a kind of landmark of the second century, who is described, rightly, as "one of the most important theologians in the period before the Council of Nicaea,"[2] is not remembered, not discussed, by his peers and successors—at least, not in theological terms (a critical distinction, on which more to follow). Irenaeus flourishes, but then, despite the fact that his works are translated and read, the name of Irenaeus as theologian seems to go rather quietly into the night.

Or does it?

In the modern day, Irenaeus's influence is at a peak. The fascination with the bishop of Lyons among scholars over the past century demonstrates a particularly modern appeal, and in and among the various themes and persons that mark out the second century, Irenaeus has today become a kind of figurehead. Of course, scholars have a penchant for digging up the long-lost and little-known and bringing them to center stage; but perhaps this interest has something to do with what Bernard Sesboüé, in his helpful and at times quite moving study published in 2000, called "la séduction d'Irénée."[3] He is, in the most positive sense of the term, a seducer: he draws one into his vision of the Church, of God, of redemption with a kind of potency and immediacy that has hardly diminished over the past 1,800 years. Or, to put it in the words of Sesboüé: "*Irénée de Lyon, qui fut une autorité pour l'Église ancienne et dont l'œuvre a été relue de siècle en siècle, se présente encore à nous comme un auteur 'séduisant' au sens noble de ce terme. Son texte est le témoignage de la jeunesse de la foi, thème qui lui est d'ailleurs cher. Il dit les choses avec une grande fraîcheur et un réalisme simple qui emportent la conviction.*"[4]

Perhaps this is a touch romantic, but it is grounded in reality. In the complex and often unclear array of voices and activities of the second century, scholars of the nineteenth and twentieth discovered in Irenaeus an apostolic disciple (through his connection to Polycarp), a peacemaker, a pastor, a kind of *defensor fidei* who nonetheless broke out of the pattern of focusing narrowly on any specific doctrinal question, to broach the whole vision of God, creation, man, and redemption that stands at the heart of Christian life. To characterize him in the words of the late Eric Osborn: "No one has presented a more unified account of God, the world and history than has Irenaeus."[5] One might challenge this assessment (though personally I would not); but one cannot deny something quite remarkable to his person, voice, and work.

Or, at least one shouldn't—but this will hardly stop the inevitable. Disparaging Irenaeus had become something of an academic pastime under Harnack and Loofs, and for a brief moment in the late-nineteenth and early-twentieth centuries it looked as if the Irenaean legacy had been reclaimed from history for the sole purpose of giving it a firm academic beating with the stick of a modern systematics and source-critical methodology.[6] But this has, thankfully, passed, and the theology of Irenaeus has gained a place in modern patristic study that it has perhaps never before quite had. Every aspect of his thought is undergoing renewed attention and flourish: his scriptural background; his anthropology; his cosmogony and cosmology; his witness to ecclesiology and apostolic succession; his anti-"Gnostic" testimony; his Mariology; his vision of history; and above all his vision of a recapitulative soteriology—and these are to name but a few. And this excellent work continues today.

But what was and is his legacy? Taking as rote the profound nature of his thought, the robust characteristics of his work, what can we say of the place his influence had in succeeding generations of Christian expression? This is an area of which we perhaps know less than we do of his thought proper, for Irenaeus's place in the limelight of history did not have the same lasting intensity and focus of an Athanasius, a Basil, or a Cyril. Comparatively speaking, we have far less material that bears witness to a direct Irenaean influence than we do for any of these; and when we examine this material as a whole, we find in it a curiously lopsided presentation of Irenaeus's work and significance. While a paucity of later testimony is hardly an uncommon situation in the patristic heritage, it does make the contours of Irenaeus's influence on later generations more difficult to trace out. It requires some digging to discover, some assembly to interpret, and—all the risks notwithstanding—some speculation to advance.

It is in this that I would like to engage, in the present paper; and I would like to do so under three broad headings. First, there is the question of the legacy Irenaeus himself inherited: the theological stream in which he stood as a pastor and theologian of the church. Understanding his influences and personal contexts is a necessary foundation for seeking out his heritage and influence. Second, I would like to examine that influence in its more or less immediate context, as well as slightly further afield in the patristic witness. Who read Irenaeus? Who knew of him, and who articulated the Christian vision of God in "Irenaean" terms? And then, third and finally, I would like to explore the question of an abiding Irenaean legacy in that context for which he so consciously felt himself a defender and supporter throughout his life: the ecclesiastical milieu of the worshipping church.

Past Networks, Inheriting a Legacy

A writer who bears authentic witness to Christian life and thought is always one who inherits a legacy rather than creates it—at least its substantive measure. This is itself part of the testimony of Irenaeus, who spends considerable time rebuking those who have fashioned a tradition and heritage of their own devising.[7] If we are to assess his legacy, we cannot then but start with his background. This is, however, an area that will not require too much space in our present study, as consideration of Irenaeus's theological ancestry and background has formed part of many of the investigations of his person over the past century and a half. What is necessary here is a brief reminder of the major contours.

First, Irenaeus was a disciple of Polycarp. This is a well-known, well-worn fact, yet one of essential significance in understanding Irenaeus's whole theological and ecclesiastical framework. His Johannine emphasis has a clear cornerstone here, as does his consideration of much of what scholars call the "Asiatic tradition" of eschatological thought (particularly with regard to his chiliastic comments in *Ref.* 5). But beyond this, the significance of Irenaeus's connection to Polycarp is that he learns the faith as a *traditio*, a thing "handed down," person to person, from the incarnate Christ to every generation of the faithful. He encounters the faith at the feet of his elder,[8] who had encountered it at the feet of his, who had encountered it at the feet of Christ. This experience grounds Irenaeus's lifelong insistence on theological creativity as a dangerous game, played primarily by heretics. Continuity is what demarcates true Christian expression.

This continuity, however, is chiefly of substance. Its *expression* Irenaeus is more than willing to embrace as a manifold, varying thing. So he treats of the fourfold expression of the one gospel as influenced by the differing backgrounds, characteristics and histories of the evangelists,[9] so he understands Paul's unique linguistic style and turns of phrase (which he acknowledges can be misleading to some readers),[10] and so, too, he understands the various means by which the truth can be examined and articulated by human reason and expression. Irenaeus's philosophical and cultural background comes to bear here, and is not insubstantial. Among the traditions with which he was aware, and with which he engages (Osborn follows Benoit and indicates 32 occasions in the *Ref.* on which Irenaeus explicitly cites the opinions of various philosophers, most of which occur in book II[11]), we can list the Middle Platonic, Stoic and Second Sophistic philosophies of the period; and he himself reveals his knowledge of writers such as Plato, Homer, Hesiod, and Pindar, as well as Aristophanes, Menander, and the pre-Socratics (particularly Xenophanes).[12] Whilst he tends not to engage directly with philosophical expression to anything near the degree of other writers of his era, this background is nonetheless an important part of his own formation and context, and Irenaeus certainly sees the best of "Pagan learning" as part of God's redemptive economy, useful to the Christian.[13]

Yet it is in interpersonal contacts, rather than systems or schools, that Irenaeus's real influences lie—and of these he had many. Once in Rome (having perhaps followed Polycarp there c. 155), and later in Gaul, Irenaeus became part of a network of significant ecclesiastical and theological figures that he in some sense expanded through his own background. His interactions with pope Victor betray a certain ecclesiastical significance, whatever his rank of presbyter may have meant in that age; and those same interactions also give evidence of ongoing links with the Asiatic traditions from which he had come. Beyond that dispute, Irenaeus acknowledges a wide array of influences. He more than one refers to respected elders and "certain men of ours" in his writings, one of which is Papias, another certainly Ignatius of Antioch[14]; and of the apostolic fathers such as Clement and the author of the *Shepherd of Hermas* he had a respect strong enough to consider their texts scriptural.[15] While it cannot be proved, his familiarity with the writings of Theophilus in Antioch seems fairly certain, given the similarities between portions of the *Ad Autolycum* and Irenaeus's comments in both the *Refutation* and *Demonstration*.[16] How precisely Irenaeus would have known Theophilus's works is a curious, and utterly speculative, question, especially given their overlapping chronologies.[17] Perhaps it can be attributed to Rome's significance in terms of intellectual and anti-Pagan Christian thought, attracting copies of relevant works from elsewhere, particularly amidst the flourish of apologetic activity that was only just calming in Irenaeus's day.

Somewhat more secure are the speculations we can put forward with regard to Justin's influence on Irenaeus. While he never mentions having met him, it seems entirely unlikely that Irenaeus would not have known Justin personally during his time in Rome. Justin was a significant figure, Irenaeus had a propensity for "sitting at the feet" of Christian teachers, and their dates put them in the city simultaneously for perhaps as many as ten or twelve years.[18] Justin's influence is certainly apparent in Irenaeus' writing.[19]

And then, of course, there is Valentinus. Irenaeus's great foe (at least rhetorically, pastorally) had once been an eminent member of the Christian community in Rome, having travelled there from Alexandria (perhaps c. 136) during the reign of pope Hyginus. Whether or not he and Irenaeus would ever have crossed paths—not impossible, given the lack of clear detail as to his whereabouts in the years leading up to his death in 160/1, though fairly improbable—is less important than the fact that Valentinus's influence emerged out of, and began to blossom in, the city and church that Irenaeus calls "the greatest and most ancient."[20] Though by the time he came to write the *Refutation* he had travelled to Gaul and succeeded Pothinus (†177) in Lyons, the text itself clearly betrays his experience of Roman Christianity and its perversions, and seems to have been written to a friend of that city or its environs (most probably a fellow presbyter-bishop there, together with those around him[21]).

In all, we find Irenaeus a participant in the broad Christian milieu of his age, an inheritor of what he viewed as the authentic apostolic preaching, and a recapitulator of the theological expression of his teachers and contemporaries. His own writings, for all their ingenuity of expression and uniqueness of voice, represent the vision of the church he sought to defend, in harmony with the voices of those others who aimed at the same ends. Characterizing the portrait of Irenaeus painted by Ziegler's 1871 study, Osborn summed up the bishop thus: "What we have in Irenaeus, according to Ziegler, is not so much his own system but rather the common doctrine of the ancient church. Irenaeus the bishop wishes to set out the main points of the universal church."[22]

Influencing Future Generations: Irenaeus in the Patristic Heritage

If Irenaeus thus wished to "set out the main points of the universal church," and, particularly, if he wished to do so in the face of attacks against that "common doctrine," then he aimed to be of influence. Taking up the materials he had been "traditioned" through his own youth and ministry, he aimed to provide his readers with tools by which to articulate and defend the apostolic preaching, as he himself says in the introduction to the *Refutation*.[23] So what, then, was the extent of this influence? Here we come to the second heading of our study: the influence of Irenaeus upon future generations in the patristic age.

Immediate Influence

Writing in the fourth century, the fact that Irenaeus's name means "peacemaker" was not lost on Eusebius, who made much of Irenaeus's role in calming the heated debates of the Quartodeciman controversy.[24] Much as he was willing to see the beauty of various expressions of the one gospel in the fourfold witness of the evangelists, so was Irenaeus willing to acknowledge a variety of expression of liturgical practice across the differing Eastern and Western traditions of the period. Peace, concord, and unity, Irenaeus firmly believed, are the authentic manifestations of the truth.[25] This role as peacemaker led Osborn to proclaim, "The name of Irenaeus as a peacemaker spread far and wide."[26] But we must ask: how far, really? How wide?

The earliest testimony to the Irenaean legacy comes in the Oxyrhynchus papyrus P.405, which is contemporary to Irenaeus himself and contains a portion of *Ref.* III.9.2, 3.[27] It should not surprise us terribly that Irenaeus's *Refutation* would make its way to Africa, and to Upper Egypt in particular, where the "Gnostic" problem was yet to reach its zenith. Still, the speed with which his works travelled overseas is notable. Irenaeus felt himself very much to be "out in the hinterlands," among the Celtic barbarians,[28] yet in his own lifetime his works traversed the Empire.[29]

They also traversed the Empire's linguistic divides. Irenaeus of course wrote in Greek, the native language of his Asiatic origins (and, we should recall from the testimony of, for example, Hippolytus, the language of some theological writing even in Rome[30]). Yet very quickly his *Refutation* was translated into Latin. Several scholars have tried to date the Latin version to sometime in the mid- to late-fourth century, on the evidence that Augustine was supposedly the first to refer to it.[31] This, however, ignores the evidence of Tertullian, who quotes from it in his *Adversus Valentinianos*, written sometime between c. 208–212.[32] We can more appropriately date the Latin translation to sometime in the first years of the third century, when, in the words of Unger, "Gnosticism" was "still a force to be reckoned with."[33] This puts Irenaeus's Greek original in Africa within his own lifetime, and a (presumably complete) Latin translation in the region within approximately ten to twenty years of his death[34]—a fairly significant achievement.

Irenaeus's contemporaries show that the spread of his works was accompanied by their employment in ecclesiastical considerations. Clement (c. 150–215) reads and makes use of his Greek edition in Alexandria,[35] as does Hippolytus (c. 170–236) in Rome.[36] The Roman connection needn't surprise us; the Alexandrian connection should at least encourage us. Irenaeus's articulation of the apostolic faith, framed in a manner aimed to thwart gnosticizing traditions, clearly found a ready home in African battles against such movements. Perhaps it was specifically because he managed to craft his polemic and apologetic in a manner that went beyond the disputes themselves, into the realm of a positive expression of doctrine, that his works were so widely and immediately received; though in both Clement and Hippolytus, Irenaeus was employed for exclusively heresiological ends.

So we have Irenaeus in Gaul, Italy, and Africa in what we might consider his more or less immediate timeframe. Was he also a voice in Roman Asia? Kraft and others have posited an ongoing Asia-Gaul link, given the importance of the city as a trading center; but this view has been challenged by others.[37] Nonetheless, Irenaeus's apparent familiarity with the works of Theophilus, together with his ongoing expression of Asiatic concerns and views, might suggest that there was some interaction between him and the eastern realms of the Empire, just as there was with the southern. But here we can only speculate, as least as regards these earliest days of his legacy.

Reflecting on the extent of Irenaeus's contemporary influence, Osborn was to note, "This shows the speed with which his ideas concerning concord between different traditions influenced the whole church."[38] We can rightly question this particular assessment. There is far less evidence to support a view of his reputation travelling because of these concord-inducing characteristics than there is of it travelling because it was an effective tool against the various sects and factions rampant across the Empire.[39] Still, it travelled, and to a degree that is significant in the period.

Influences Further Afield

Given that there existed copies of Irenaeus's *Refutation* in Greek and in Latin in various parts of the Empire within a few decades of his own lifetime, it will come as no surprise that the text is incorporated into a number of works by other patristic writers. We have already mentioned Tertullian, Clement, and Hippolytus, but these are hardly the extent of his legacy in the patristic corpus.

Greek Irenaeus was known to both Eusebius (c. 263–c. 339) and Epiphanius (c. 310/20–403), both of whom quote him extensively, particularly from books I and III of the *Refutation*. Both had their reasons for drawing Irenaeus into their repertoire, and both are fairly predictable. Eusebius's *Ecclesiastical History* not only attempted a narrative of the past but also dwelt on fostering the theme of unity and concord in the imperial church under Constantine. Irenaeus as "peacemaker" was a clear voice of support. The extensive quotations he provides are essential resources in our understanding of the bishop—including the only surviving texts of various Irenaean letters[40]—but also give us a helpful witness of how Irenaeus's reputation would be assessed by a later generation. For Eusebius, it was his martyric witness, his dedication to concord and unity in the face of division, that marked Irenaeus out as a voice of significance. Eusebius has nothing to say of any theological expression in Irenaeus. For Epiphanius, Irenaeus's attractiveness lay in his polemical acumen. The *Panarion* lifts whole sections from Irenaeus, particularly such as bear witness to "Gnostic" groups with which Epiphanius himself would have had no direct knowledge.

There is a possibility that Irenaeus was known to Cyril of Jerusalem (c. 313–386), based on a similarity of language in his *Catechetical Oration* 6.7, in which he refers to the unity of God who is "always like unto Himself"; but the supposed link to *Ref.* 2.13.3—one of Irenaeus's important re-presentations of Xenophanes—leaves out the heart of that passage. Cyril's wording could easily have come from elsewhere. A direct awareness of Irenaeus by Theodoret of Cyrrhus (c. 393–c. 457), posited by Grant and based on his wording in his *Commentary* on Psalm 129:2, is even harder to maintain.[41]

So, in the two centuries after his death, Irenaeus was remembered for that heresiological focus that had gained him reputation in his lifetime, as well as his activities as peacemaker and diplomat; but not, at least in the testimony of Eusebius and Epiphanius, for any specifically theological contributions.

Latin Irenaeus also found a wide readership. We have already had occasion to mention the quotations made by Augustine (354–430) from the translation, which are actually quite extensive.[42] What is more significant, however, is that in Augustine we have Irenaeus assessed and appropriated on theological terms—the first instance of such usage in our extant corpus.

So, for example, Augustine's *Against Julian* (written c. 421/2), in seeking to articulate a doctrine of "original sin" (as he calls it in I.7.32) and of redemption from the bondage of sin through Christ born of the Virgin, calls directly upon Irenaeus's *Refutation* IV.2.7 and V.19.1. The employment Augustine makes of Irenaeus is best seen by laying the two texts side by side:

Irenaeus, *Refutation* IV.2.7 (relevant extract):

Augustine, *Against Julian* I.3.5:

Consider, you who so often accuse us of Manichaeism, if you are alert, whom and what kind of men and what great defenders of the Catholic faith you dare insult with such a detestable charge. Indeed, I do not promise that I will gather the opinions of all on this matter, nor all the opinions of those whom I shall mention; it would take too long and I do not think it necessary. But I shall cite a very few, by which, however, our adversaries may be compelled to blush and to yield, if they have any fear of God or shame before men that can overcome that great evil of their obstinacy.

For the law never hindered them from believing in the Son of God; nay, but it even exhorted them so to do, saying that men can be saved in no other way from the old wound of the serpent than by believing in Him who, in the likeness of sinful flesh, is lifted up from the earth upon the tree of martyrdom, and draws all things to Himself, and vivifies the dead.

Irenaeus, Bishop of Lyons, lived not long after the time of the Apostles. He says: "Men cannot be saved in any other way from the ancient wound of the serpent except by believing in Him who according to the likeness of sinful flesh was lifted up from the earth on the tree of testimony and drew all things to Himself and gave life to the dead."

Irenaeus, *Refutation* V.19.1 (relevant extract):

And if the former did disobey God, yet the latter was persuaded to be obedient to God, in order that the Virgin Mary might become the advocate of the virgin Eve. And thus, as the human race fell into bondage to death by means of a virgin, so is it rescued by a virgin, virginal disobedience having been balanced in the opposite scale by virginal obedience. For in the same way the sin of the first created man [*protoplasti*] receives amendment by the correction of the First-begotten, and the coming of the serpent is conquered by the harmlessness of the dove, those bonds being unloosed by which we had been fast bound to death.

Again he says: "Just as the human race was bound to death by a virgin it is released through a virgin, the obedience of a virgin evenly counterbalancing the disobedience of a virgin. For the sin of the first-formed was wiped out by the chastisement of the First-born, the wisdom of the serpent was conquered by the simplicity of the dove, and we were released from the chains by which we were bound to death."
Do you understand the ancient man of God, and what he thinks about the ancient wound of the serpent, and about the likeness of sinful flesh through which the wound of the serpent is healed in the sinful flesh, and about the sin of the first-formed by which we had been bound?

Later in the same text, Augustine sums up his position against Julian with the following return to Irenaeus (as the first in a long litany of predecessors in the faith whom he considers substantiate his view): "Why do you boastfully say that you rejoice that this truth, which you consider error or wish to consider so, can find no supporter in such a great multitude? As if it were a slight proof that in this most sure and ancient foundation of the faith the very multitude scattered over the whole earth does not disagree. But, if you seek supporters for it among those who have produced something of literary value, and whose teaching is famous, then here is a memorable and venerable assembly and agreement of supporters. St Irenaeus says that the ancient wound of the Serpent is healed by the faith of Christ and the cross, and that we were bound by original sin as if by chains" (*Against Julian*, I.7.32).

In this—which is the most dramatic and important instance of Augustine employing Irenaeus—what stands out is that Irenaeus's writing is called upon, not to demonstrate or appropriate his polemical, heresiological arsenal (as has been the case in every other source we have mentioned), but in order to substantiate a theological position. Irenaeus is here a *theological voice*, in a way we have not encountered elsewhere. The same is true of Augustine's implicit reference to *Refutation* IV.33.10 in his *Catechizing of the Uninstructed* 3.6, where he imitates (rather closely) Irenaeus's language of typological Christology among the prophets; and to some extent also in his *On Christian Doctrine* II.40.60 (much touted as his earliest example of a familiarity with Latin Irenaeus, dating to c. 396–426), where he follows Irenaeus's *Refutation* IV.30.1 on the Hebrews carrying away the spoils of Egypt in the Exodus comprising a prophetic vision of the value to be found in Pagan philosophies.

Augustine seeks to employ Irenaeus to shore up his theological emphasis. It is worth noting that he speaks, in this context, of Irenaeus as an "ancient man of God," who he presumes stands as an authority for the traditional voice of Christian theology; and if he calls upon Irenaeus as such a representative of traditional theology, it is of further significance that he does so in order to support a particular reading of sin (i.e., "original sin," mentioned with particular reference to Irenaeus) that is, in Augustine's day, hardly traditional (and one which does not, in fact, wholly reflect Irenaeus's position). Irenaeus the traditional theologian is called in to support Augustine the creative theologian. This is an observation to which I would like to return below.

Augustine may be the most important reader of Latin Irenaeus, but he was not the only. C. A. Forbes has asserted that the language and imagery of Firmicus Maternus's (fourth century) *On the Error of Profane Religions* "argue for the probability that Firmicus knew the writings or at least the views of Irenaeus."[43] Jerome (c. 347–420), who is single-handedly responsible for our ascription of the title "martyr" to Irenaeus,[44] was familiar enough with his Latin text to refer to it as a work of "most learned and eloquent style"[45]—an interesting comment, given the Latin translator's slavish literality in rendering the Greek, his frequent inconsistencies, and in general a style characterized by Unger as "barbaric Latin."[46] Among Latin writers familiar with Irenaeus, we might also mention Gregory of Tours (sixth century), who similarly describes Irenaeus as a martyr but as part of a rather fanciful account of his having been sent to Lyons by Polycarp, converting the city and suffering great tortures before receiving his martyr's crown.[47] There is no evidence that Gregory actually knew Irenaeus's works; the passage in question seems to be drawn from a local Gallic passion account.

Assertions made of an Irenaean lineage present in Novatian (for example his language of God's eyes, ears, and so on, in *On the Trinity* 6), Hilary of Poitiers (in his commentary on Psalm 129:3), and Victricius of Rouen (*Praise of the Saints* 8) are debatable.[48] There is, however, an open question with respect to *On the Status of the Soul* I.21, by Claudianus Mamertus of Vienne (d. c. 473). This whole tract addresses the question of a corporeality of the soul, which Irenaeus treated at *Ref.* II.19.6 and II.33.4; though Mamertus speaks decidedly against it (claiming it to be un-apostolic), whereas Irenaeus had granted the soul a nonmaterial corporeality. It would hardly surprise us if an inhabitant of Irenaeus's own city, brother to the bishop of Vienne, was shown to know the works of Irenaeus; yet Mamertus seems to give more credible evidence of the ongoing fascination with the soul's nature in the era, than he does any specific awareness of Irenaeus's thought.

In the sixth century, amidst the flurry of translations of Christian texts into ecclesiastical Armenian, the *Refutation* and *Demonstration* are both translated into this language, from the Greek. We might speculate that the translation of the *Refutation* was complete, and that the extant manuscripts of books IV and V only are the result of losses through history (it could be argued that the Armenian translators would have found the earlier segments, dealing with various Italian and African heretical groups, less interesting than the later theological discussions and thus decided against translating them; but this could hardly account for the absence of the theologically significant book III). The translation of the *Demonstration*, the Greek of which had been known to (but not quoted by) Eusebius,[49] is our only extant version of that important tract.[50]

Irenaeus also finds his way into Syriac—never, so far as can be ascertained, through a complete or even partial translation of his works into that language, but through the inclusion of quotations and passages in various Syriac texts.[51]

So, in the centuries following his death, we find Irenaeus in Greek, Latin, Armenian, and Syriac, incorporated into the writings of a wide array of authors. The Latin translation has come down to us, as has the Armenian of the books mentioned; but one of the great mysteries in the legacy of Irenaeus is the loss of his Greek original. What came of it? Given this relatively wide spread of Irenaeus's readership in later generations, it is surprising that the original version should altogether disappear.

We can identify traces of the Greek version that at least give us a potential chronological limit to its existence as a more or less complete document. In the seventh century, a hundred or so years after the Greek text had been used as a foundation for the Armenian translation, John of Damascus (c. 676–749) has access to it when writing his *Sacra Parallela*, as well as the *Catenae*, in which it features.[52] Then, two centuries later, Photius (c. 810—c. 893) is known to have read a Greek copy, presumably in Baghdad, which he summarizes in the *Bibliotheca* as a complete, five-volume work.[53] This, though, is the last we hear of a Greek version. Unger, following other scholars, speculated that the copy known to Photius—perhaps the last, or at least the last known in public circles—was destroyed in the sack of Baghdad in 1258.[54] Perhaps.

The only thing of which we can be certain is that evidence of Irenaeus's major work in its original, for all the influence it clearly had across the Empire, was thereafter known only in fragments.[55]

Potential Further Influences

Thus far I have treated exclusively of direct Irenaean influence; that is, instances in which Irenaeus is directly mentioned, reflected upon, and his text quoted—and the above represents fairly well the full extent of that direct testimony. Is this, then, the extent of the Irenaean legacy?

There are compelling reasons to think that the answer is "no." Firstly, setting aside the instances of simple translation, I would like to return to the fact that the patristic references to Irenaeus mentioned above pay attention almost exclusively to his polemical and diplomatic significance, or to his testimony to the martyric witness of his day and locale. With the exception of Augustine, there is almost nothing in the extant witness that would count as a *theological* embrace of Irenaeus's legacy. That is, no extant quotation or reference in a patristic work that makes specific mention of Irenaeus does so in a manner that raises those theological topics by which we today would characterize him—recapitulation, trinity, soteriology, anthropology, etc. This is a significant observation. It would seem to suggest that, among his successors in the patristic era, the "Irenaean legacy" amounted chiefly to one of polemical and heresiological testimony, and hardly to a theological witness at all.

But this is precisely where the question of the Irenaean legacy becomes more interesting, for if the things that strike us as "Irenaean" today *were* in fact considered in the past, but without any ascription to Irenaeus, we can start to see more clearly how Irenaeus is giving voice to wider tradition, and not simply his own unique expression.

There are passages in Athanasius, for example, that sound as if they could have been uttered directly from the lips of Irenaeus. This is particularly true of his *De incarnatione Verbi*, written in the early days of his episcopacy, before his ongoing involvement in the post-Nicene controversies caused him to adopt a more technical vocabulary.[56] Here he speaks in a voice that has not been significantly shaped by the anti-Arian disputes, and that voice sounds surprisingly "Irenaean."[57] Still, for all such similarities, Athanasius does not claim his expressions to have an Irenaean origin (nor does he mention Irenaeus's text, even though it existed in Alexandria at the time). This ought to prompt us to ask just what is "Irenaean" about the "Irenaean theology" we so often explore. We might today characterize a recapitulative soteriology, a lack of "fall" language and concept of maturing humanity, and the like, as "Irenaean" themes, but Athanasius can discuss each of these without tying them to the bishop of Lyons.

This is equally true elsewhere. Gregory of Nyssa, Gregory of Nazianzus, Maximus the Confessor—all betray signs of "Irenaean" expression but do not link it to Irenaeus.[58] It is interesting (and, as I will demonstrate in a moment, telling) that among those who specifically identify Irenaeus in their writings, elements of "Irenaean theology" are rarely if at all mentioned; while among those in whom we identify strong elements of such theological vision, it is Irenaeus himself who is not mentioned.

An Ecclesiastical Legacy

This strange observation brings me to my final heading: the question of an ecclesiasti-cal dimension to the Irenaean legacy. Apart from the doctrinal, dogmatic, heresio-logical, and other theological contexts of the patristic age, is there any sense in which Irenaeus contributes to the ecclesiastical heritage of Christianity? Here I would suggest that the answer is a strong "yes" precisely because the answer to the question of a direct *theological* influence in the patristic era is a "no." Irenaeus's legacy is borne out in the ecclesiastical context of which he was such an ardent defender, precisely because Ire-naeus was successful in doing just what he set out to do: articulate the apostolic faith in a manner that preserves its authenticity and makes it newly immediate to each genera-tion, without introducing the kind of "creative" innovations he so laments in others.

When we examine the textual evidence of Irenaeus's influence on immediate and future patristic writers, as we have done above, the lopsidedness of their testimony becomes overwhelmingly clear. What is relayed and re-presented in their testimony is Irenaeus the polemicist, Irenaeus the diplomat, Irenaeus the "philosopher." Not Ire-naeus the theologian. And the most sensible interpretation of the almost complete lack of any theological reflection on Irenaeus by future generations is that he was perceived as articulating and advancing a theological vision that was *not* unique, *not* unexpected, *not* "nameable" as stemming particularly from him. Irenaeus's theology was simply the church's theology; and though in the second century we are speaking of an era before there existed any universally agreed-upon mode of articulating, of expressing, that theological vision (and so Irenaeus may speak in language, in images, that are not known to or embraced by others), the lack of theological attention paid to Irenaeus's works demonstrates that what readers experienced, when they read his works, was a theology they already knew. This is reinforced by the rather different testimony of Augustine, who *does* make theological use of Irenaeus, but does so precisely to support a doctrinal position that *challenged* traditional expressions—that represented some-thing new, something different.

It is possible, of course, to interpret the contemporary and later treatment of Ire-naeus in another way: as evidence that his theological views were perceived as unhelp-ful, incomplete, problematic. Irenaean scholarship of the last century was certainly not without those who attempted just this. But here the evidence is too strong against. Recent studies of Irenaeus—including the ongoing work evidenced in the scholars and studies represented in this volume—have simply given us too much evidence of Ire-naeus's theological acumen to allow such a reading, and have similarly shown that much of the criticism levelled against Irenaeus in this regard stems from anachronistic readings of later Nicene developments back into the early generations of the church, in the light of which many (if not most) pre-Nicene figures are found wanting.

Perhaps the greatest testimony to the Irenaean legacy comes in the fact that the theological vision by which we characterize him today *does* carry on in the church, even if the vicissitudes of history are such that other forms of expression became so dominant, at least in certain areas, that what struck his contemporaries simply as "Christian theology" strike us today as "Irenaean theology." The church has never been without those who expressed a vision of incarnational soteriology that is wholly in accord with Irenaeus's writings; a maturational anthropology that echoes his own; an emphasis on the creative work of the Holy Spirit that he expressed long before the Council of Constantinople; a vision of sin and redemption perceived in developmental terms, and the like. If in some senses these themes strike readers today as unique, the fact that to Irenaeus's contemporary readers, together with the patristic traditions that carried on reading and quoting and copying him for centuries, they did not, gives the Irenaean legacy significance even today.

It is somehow quite fitting that Irenaeus's theological significance comes through the silent dimensions of his legacy. He was quoted wide and far, but the abiding influence of the bishop of Lyons lies in the powerful theological vision that his contemporaries felt no need to attach to him. It was Christ's gospel. Irenaeus had effectively shaken off the dust of various perversions; but the message that was left was Christ's, not his. And this, we can be sure, is exactly as Irenaeus would have wished it. To conclude with his own words on the unchanging gospel: "No great ruler among the Churches, however highly gifted he may be in point of eloquence, teaches doctrines different from [those of the apostles]—for no one is greater than the Master; nor, on the other hand, will he who is deficient in power of expression inflict any injury on the tradition. One who is able to discourse on it at great length does not add anything to it; nor does one who can say but little, diminish it: for the faith is ever one and the same."[59]

Abbreviations

AJP	*American Journal of Philology*
ANRW	*Aufstieg und Niedergang der römischen Welt*
ASE	*Abhandlungen zur Socialethik*
ATR	*Anglican Theological Review*
BETL	Bibliotheca ephemeridum theologicarum lovaniensium
CCSG	Corpus Christianorum Series Graeca
CPh	*Classical Philology*
CQ	*Classical Quarterly*
CSCO	Corpus Scriptorum Christianorum Orientalium
CSEL	Corpus Scriptorum Ecclesiasticorum Latinorum
Dem.	*Demonstratio*
GCS	Griechische christliche Schriftsteller
Haer.	*Adversus haereses*
HE	*Historia Ecclesiastica*
HTR	*Harvard Theological Review*
JAC	*Jahrbuch für Antike und Christentum*
JEH	*Journal of Ecclesiastical History*
JJS	*Journal of Jewish Studies*
JSNT	*Journal for the Study of the New Testament*
JTS	*Journal of Theological Studies*
LDAB	Leuven Database of Ancient Books
MEFRA	*Mélanges de l'École française de Rome: antiquité*

NHMS	Nag Hammadi and Manichaean Studies
NTM	New Testament Monographs
NTS	*New Testament Studies*
NTTS	New Testament Tools and Studies
ODNB	*Oxford Dictionary of National Biography*
PCPhS	*Proceedings of the Cambridge Philological Society*
PG	Patrologia Graeca, ed. J. P. Migne
P.Oxy.	Oxyrhynchus papyrus
QL	*Questions liturgiques*
REA	*Revue des études Augustiniennes*
RecSR / RSR	*Recherches de science religieuse*
Ref.	*Refutatio*
RPh	*Revue de philologie*
SC	Sources chrétiennes
SNT	Studien zum Neuen Testament
SNTSMS	Society for New Testament Studies Monograph Series
Stud Theol	*Studia Theologica*
TDNT	*Theological Dictionary of the New Testament*, ed. Gerhard Kittel et *al.*, trans. Geoffrey W. Bromiley
TS	*Theological Studies*
TU	Texte und Untersuchungen
TWNT	*Theologisches Wörterbuch zum Neuen Testament*, ed. Gerhard Kittel et al.
Van Haelst	Joseph van Haelst, *Catalogue des papyrus littéraires juifs et chrétiens.* Paris: Sorbonne, 1976
VC / VChr	*Vigiliae Christianae*
WBC	Word Biblical Commentary
WUNT	Wissenschaftliche Untersuchungen zum Neuen Testament
ZNW	*Zeitschrift für die neutestamentliche Wissenschaft*

Notes

The Writings of Irenaeus

1. Published by Grenfell and Hunt in *The Oxyrhynchus Papyri*, vol. 3 (1903), 10–11, and again in vol. 4 (1904), 264–65. Discussed by Louis Doutreleau in *Contra les hérésies, Livre IV*, vol. 1 (SCh 210), 126–31, and by Charles E. Hill, "Irenaeus, the Scribes, and the Scriptures: Papyrological and Theological Observations from P.Oxy. 405" in this volume.

2. Discussed by Rousseau in *Contra les hérésies, Livre V*, vol. 1 (SCh 152), 119–57, with a reconstruction of the text at 355–77.

1. Who Was Irenaeus: An Introduction to the Man and His Work

1. There is an excellent general account of Irenaeus in Denis Minns, *Irenaeus, An Introduction* (London: T&T Clark, 2010)—an expanded and updated version of Minns, *Irenaeus*, Outstanding Christian Thinkers (London: Chapman, 1994).

2. For the various editions Eusebius produced and their date, see Timothy D. Barnes, *Constantine and Eusebius* (Cambridge: Harvard University Press, 1981), 128.

3. There has been an enormous amount of discussion of the exact date, with 155, 156, or 167 often being canvassed. But 157 now appears to have been conclusively established: Timothy D. Barnes, *Early Christian Hagiography and Roman History* (Tübingen: Mohr Siebeck, 2010), 367–78. For a very vivid and plausible reconstruction of the events surrounding the martyrdom, see Sara Parvis, "The Martyrdom of Polycarp," in *The Writings of the Apostolic Fathers*, ed. Paul Foster (London: T&T Clark, 2007), 126–46.

4. Whether Polycarp is to be identified with the anonymous "elder" whose teaching Irenaeus reports in *Haer.* IV is debated in this volume by Sebastian Moll, "The Man with No Name: Who Is the Elder in Irenaeus's *Adversus haereses* IV?" and Charles E. Hill, "The Man Who Needed No Introduction: A Response to Sebastian Moll."

5. That mistake seems to me to be made in, for example, Elaine Pagels, *The Gnostic Gospels* (Harmondsworth: Penguin, 1982), where we have a rather romantic picture of the healthy diversity of quasi-egalitarian Gnostic groups squashed by the power of jack-booted bishops and hierarchical authority.

6. Clearly in place by the time of Leo the Great in the fifth century.

7. Irenaeus is cited here from the ten-volume edition by Adelin Rousseau in the Sources chrétiennes series. For details of this edition and available translations, see "The Writings of Irenaeus."

8. The relevance and importance of the "successions" in the schools was developed in the seminal work by Alain Le Boulluec, *La notion d'hérésie dans la littérature grecque IIe-IIIe siècles*, 2 vols. (Paris: Études Augustiniennes, 1985) and is explored by Allen Brent in his contribution to this volume, "How Irenaeus Has Misled the Archaeologists."

9. On so-called "Asia Minor theology"—a notion developed above all by the great historian of dogma Theodor Zahn—see, for example, Zahn's classic *Marcellus von Ancyra: Ein Beitrag zur Geschichte der Theologie* (Gotha: Friedrich Andreas Perthes, 1867).

10. Jared Secord's contribution to this volume, "The Cultural Geography of a Greek Christian: Irenaeus from Smyrna to Lyons" has an illuminating discussion of what Irenaeus might have meant by this and demonstrates conclusively Irenaeus's continuing Eastern perspective.

11. It has been very plausibly argued that on his way west Irenaeus in all probability spent some time in Rome and there heard Justin Martyr (who was executed about 165): Michael Slusser, "How Much Did Irenaeus Learn from Justin?" *Studia Patristica* XL (2006), 515–20.

12. The conventional date is 177, but that simply follows Eusebius's reconstruction of events and, while it cannot be very far out, is not a hard date. See Barnes, *Early Christian Hagiography*, 61–63, and, for the whole incident, *Les martyrs de Lyons* (Paris: du Cerf, 1978).

13. That is, the Roman province of Asia, centered around the great city of Ephesus on the Asia Minor coast—the same province that Irenaeus himself was from.

14. For a recent and concise presentation, with a useful, annotated bibliography, see Christoph Markschies, *Gnosis, An Introduction*, trans. John Bowden (London: T&T Clark, 2003). There is an excellent anthology of Gnostic texts—from Nag Hammadi and patristic sources, including Irenaeus—in Bentley Leyton, *The Gnostic Scriptures* (Garden City: Doubleday, 1987). For a complete translation of the fourteen codices that comprise the Nag Hammadi find, see James M. Robinson, ed., *The Nag Hammadi Library in English*, 3rd ed. (San Francisco: Harper & Row, 1988).

15. For a brief but very helpful discussion of the problem, see Mary Ann Donovan, *One Right Reading? A Guide to Irenaeus* (Collegeville: Liturgical, 1997). There is a careful and detailed look at one vitally important gnostic text, the *Apocryphon of John*, and the corresponding account in Irenaeus in Alastair Logan, *Gnostic Truth and Christian Heresy* (Edinburgh: T&T Clark, 1996).

16. That there is a key to "the various gnostic systems" is itself a highly contentious claim. What groups should be included under the umbrella term and, indeed, whether such an umbrella term has any utility or meaning at all are keenly debated issues. For a careful, deconstructionist view, see Michael Allen Williams, *Rethinking "Gnosticism": An Argument for Dismantling a Dubious Category* (Princeton: Princeton University Press, 1996).

17. It is older than Augustine, who quotes it at *Contra Julianum* I.3.5, written in 421.

18. The Armenian of IV and V was first published in 1910 and first systematically exploited by Rousseau. For publication data, see The Writings of Irenaeus in the front of this volume.

19. Near the end of the text (*Dem*. 99), Irenaeus denounces the "heretics" as "wicked men and blasphemers against their Creator and Father, as we have shown in the 'Exposure and overthrowal of knowledge falsely so called'" (translation from *St. Irenaeus, Proof of the Apostolic Preaching*, trans. Joseph P. Smith, Ancient Christian Writers 16 [Westminster: Newman, 1952], 108).

20. There is a valuable discussion of categorizations of age in antiquity in Charles E. Hill, "The Man Who Needed No Introduction: A Response to Sebastian Moll" in this volume.

21. For the origins of the legend in Jewish tradition, see the *Letter of Aristeas* in *The Old Testament Pseudepigrapha*, ed. James H. Charlesworth, 2 vols. (London: Darton, Longman & Todd, 1983–1985), ii:12–34.

22. Including Hebrews, the formative role of which in the thought of Irenaeus is discussed by D. Jeffrey Bingham in his paper "Irenaeus and Hebrews" in this volume.

23. For a brief discussion of Irenaeus's "canon," see, for example, Bruce M. Metzger, *The Canon of the New Testament* (Oxford: Clarendon, 1987), 153–56. Metzger reckons that 1,075 quotations from the books of our New Testament (154) appear in the text of Irenaeus.

24. For Irenaeus's knowledge of other Gospels, see Paul Foster, "Irenaeus and the Noncanonical Gospels," in this volume.

25. "Saving plan" is here *oikonomia*—"economy, disposition, arrangement." It refers to the whole mode of God's dealings with the created order and above all to the divine game plan of salvation.

26. It may be noted that the second of these affirmations speaks of God, Son, and Spirit, while the former speaks only of the "one God" and of "Christ Jesus, the Son of God." Both twofold (binitarian) and threefold (trinitarian) forms are found elsewhere in Irenaeus as well. In this collection, Alistair Stewart, "'The Rule of Truth . . . which He Received through Baptism' (*Haer*. I.9.4): Catechesis, Ritual, and Exegesis in Irenaeus's Gaul," proposes a liturgical explanation for this curious phenomenon.

27. On Irenaeus's views on the last things, see Minns, *Irenaeus*, 140–47, and Brian E. Daley, *The Hope of the Early Church, A Handbook of Patristic Eschatology* (Peabody: Hendrickson, 2003), 28–32.

28. The importance of the body in Irenaeus's theology is discussed by Sophie Cartwright, "The Image of God in Irenaeus, Marcellus, and Eustathius" in this volume.

29. Eusebius says that Irenaeus also wrote "to very many other rulers of the churches" on the matter (V.24.18). That may well be true: Eusebius obviously had access to a substantial dossier of documents on the controversy, though his tendency to generalize— to assume that if he knows of one martyr or one orthodox writer of a given period or one work of a given author, there must have been many—can never be ignored.

30. In *HE* V.7.1-6, Eusebius collected and cited three passages from *Haer*. to show that charismatic gifts remained in the church in the time of Irenaeus.

2. The Cultural Geography of a Greek Christian: Irenaeus from Smyrna to Lyons

* This paper has benefited from the comments and suggestions of the participants at the Edinburgh conference, and several of my colleagues and professors at the University of Michigan. Particular thanks go to David Potter for reading and commenting on a draft of the paper, and to Ray Van Dam for his assistance and comments at all stages of this project.

1. The phenomenon is studied by Noy in considerable detail: David Noy, *Foreigners at Rome: Citizens and Strangers* (London: Duckworth, 2000).

2. For example, Jean-Claude Decourt and Gérard Lucas, *Lyon dans les textes Grecs et Latins* (Lyon: FU Maison de l'Orient Méditerranéen, 1993), 70. "Il nous a paru difficile d'exclure totalement Irénée de ce recueil. Pourtant ce qui frappe, dans cette œuvre, c'est l'absence presque totale du mentions, non seulement de la ville où il résidait, mais plus généralement du pays dont il a dû longtemps être le seul évêque. Il nous a ainsi fallu chercher pour découvrir un passage où il fût fait au moins allusion sinon à Lyon, du moins aux Gaules."

3. Jean Colin, *L'empire des Antonins et les martyrs gaulois de 177* (Bonn: Rudolf Habelt, 1964).

4. Ewen Bowie, "The Geography of the Second Sophistic: Cultural Variations," in *Paideia: The World of the Second Sophistic*, ed. Barbara E. Borg (Berlin: de Gruyter, 2004), 68. Smyrna belongs in a similar category to such cities as Athens, Ephesus, Pergamum, and Rome.

5. André Benoit, *Saint Irénée: Introduction a l'étude de sa théologie* (Paris: Presses Universitaires de France, 1960), 50, 58–59.

6. As suggested by Robert M. Grant, "Irenaeus and Hellenistic Culture," *HTR* 42, no. 1 (1949): 50.

7. See Grant, "Irenaeus and Hellenistic Culture," 43–47; William R. Schoedel, "Philosophy and Rhetoric in the *Adversus haereses* of Irenaeus," *VChr* 13, no. 1 (1959): 23–24.

8. One example is Irenaeus's reference to the common belief that hens could be impregnated by the blowing of the wind (*Haer.* II.12.4). Others who express this opinion include Plutarch, Athenaeus, and Aelian. References to these and others in Conway Zirkle, "Animals Impregnated by the Wind," *Isis* 25, no. 1 (1936): 95–130. Similarly, Irenaeus suggests that the images a woman saw during intercourse had an impact on the shape and appearance of the child conceived (*Haer.* II.19.5-6). Justification for this belief could have been found in the doxographical collection of pseudo-Plutarch (Hermann Diels, *Doxographi Graeci*, 2nd ed. [Berlin: de Gruyter, 1929], 423, col. a, lines 17-21), a collection containing much material with which Irenaeus was familiar. Further references to the theme are collected by M. D. Reeve, "Conceptions," *PCPhS* 35 (1989): 81–112.

9. See Mark Humphries, "A New Created World: Classical Geographical Texts and Christian Contexts in Late Antiquity," in *Texts and Culture in Late Antiquity: Inheritance, Authority, and Change*, ed. J. H. D. Scoufield (Swansea: Classical Press of Wales, 2007), 43–44, with reference to Strabo I.2.28.

10. Irenaeus, *Haer.*, III.11.8, ed. Adelin Rousseau and Louis Doutreleau, *Contre les Hérésies, Livre III*, 2 vols. (Paris: du Cerf, 1974): Ἐπεὶ γὰρ τέσσαρα κλίματα τοῦ κόσμου ἐν ᾧ ἐσμὲν καὶ τέσσαρα καθολικὰ πνεύματα, κατέσπαρται δὲ ἡ ἐκκλησία ἐπὶ πάσης τῆς γῆς, στῦλος δὲ καὶ στήριγμα ἐκκλησίας τὸ εὐαγγέλιον καὶ Πνεῦμα ζωῆς, εἰκότως τέσσαρας ἔχειν αὐτὴν στύλους πανταχόθεν πνέοντας τὴν ἀφθαρσίαν καὶ ἀναζωπυροῦντας τοὺς ἀνθρώπους. As this passage shows, the number four has much significance for Irenaeus, and he elsewhere defends the idea that the earth has four regions (κλίματα) against the heretical suggestion that it has twelve. See *Haer.* I.17.1.

11. See James M. Scott, *Geography in Early Judaism and Christianity: The Book of Jubilees* (Cambridge: Cambridge University Press, 2002), 55–56, with references to Luke 24:46-47 and Acts 1:8.

12. The phrase "a medio auferuntur" corresponds roughly to the next passage quoted from *Haer.* IV.4.1: "de medio ablata est," a phrase whose Greek original is ἐκ μέσου ἐγένετο. For the definition of the phrase ἐκ μέσου as "away," see LSJ, sv. μέσος III.c.

13. Irenaeus, *Haer.* IV.4.1, ed. Rousseau et al., *Contre les Hérésies, Livre IV*, 2 vols. (Paris: du Cerf, 1965): "Quemadmodum autem haec [sc. sarmenta vineae] non propter se principaliter facta sunt, sed propter crescentem in eis fructum, quo maturo facto et ablato, derelinquuntur a medio auferuntur quae iam non sunt utilia ad fructificationem: sic et Hierosolyma."

14. Ibid. Εἰς ὅλην οὖν τὴν οἰκουμένην τοῦ καρποῦ αὐτοῦ διασπαρέντος εἰκότως ἐγκατελείφθη καὶ ἐκ μέσου ἐγένετο τὰ ποτὲ μὲν καρποφορήσαντα καλῶς—ἐξ αὐτῶν γὰρ τὸ κατὰ σάρκα ὁ Χριστὸς ἐκαρποφορήθη καὶ οἱ ἀπόστολοι—νῦν δὲ μηκέτι εὔθετα ὑπάρχοντα πρὸς καρποφορίαν.

15. Ibid., IV.21.3. "Peregre nascebatur duodecimtribus genus Israel, quoniam et Christus peregre incipiebat duodecastylum firmamentum Ecclesiae generare." This is part of a larger comparison between Christ and Jacob, in this case relating the birth of Jacob's twelve sons in Mesopotamia to Christ's selection of the apostles.

16. Ibid., I.26.2, ed. Rousseau, *Contre les Hérésies, Livre I*, 2 vols. (Paris: du Cerf, 1979): "Et Hierosolymam adorent, quasi domus sit Dei."

17. Ibid., III.12.9.

18. Ibid.

19. Rome: ibid., III.1.1, III.3.2. Ephesus: III.3.4. Smyrna: III.3.4.

20. Ibid., V.34.3, ed. Rousseau, Doutreleau, and Charles Mercier, *Contre les Hérésies, Livre V*, 2 vols (Paris: du Cerf, 1969): "Quoniam autem repromissiones non solum prophetis et patribus, sed Ecclesiis ex gentibus coadunatis annuntiabuntur, quas et insulas nuncupat Spiritus, eo quod in medio turbulae sint constitutae et tempestatem blasphemiorum sufferant et salutaris portus periclitantibus exsistant et refugium sunt eorum qui [veritatem] ament." Cf. Theophilus of Antioch, *Ad Autolycum*, II.14.

21. Irenaeus, *Haer.* I.10.2: τοῦτο τὸ κήρυγμα παρειληφυῖα, καὶ ταύτην τὴν πίστιν, ὡς προέφαμεν, ἡ Ἐκκλησία, καίπερ ἐν ὅλῳ τῷ κόσμῳ διεσπαρμένη, ἐπιμελῶς φυλάσσει, ὡς ἕνα οἶκον οἰκοῦσα . . . καὶ οὔτε αἱ ἐν Γερμανίαις ἱδρυμέναι ἐκκλησίαι ἄλλως πεπιστεύκασιν, ἢ ἄλλως παραδιδόασιν, οὔτε ἐν ταῖς Ἰβηρίαις, οὔτε ἐν Κελτοῖς, οὔτε κατὰ τὰς ἀνατολάς, οὔτε ἐν Αἰγύπτῳ, οὔτε ἐν Λιβύῃ, οὔτε αἱ κατὰ μέσα τοῦ κόσμου ἱδρυμέναι· ἀλλ᾽ ὥσπερ ὁ ἥλιος, τὸ κτίσμα τοῦ Θεοῦ, ἐν ὅλῳ τῷ κόσμῳ εἷς καὶ ὁ αὐτός, οὕτω καὶ τὸ κήρυγμα τῆς ἀληθείας πανταχῇ φαίνει, καὶ φωτίζει πάντας ἀνθρώπους τοὺς βουλομένους εἰς ἐπίγνωσιν ἀληθείας ἐλθεῖν.

22. Menander Rhetor, ed. and trans. D.A. Russell and N.G. Wilson (Oxford: Clarendon, 1981), 344: θέσιν τοίνυν χώρας δοκιμάζομέν τε καὶ κρίνομεν ὅπως κεῖται πρὸς γῆν ἢ <πρὸς> θάλατταν ἢ πρὸς οὐρανόν . . . πρὸς δὲ οὐρανόν, εἰ ἐν δυσμαῖς, ἢ ἐν ἀνατολαῖς, ἢ ἐν μεσημβρίᾳ, ἢ ἐν ἄρκτῳ, ἢ ἐν τῷ μέσῳ τούτων.

23. See Robert M. Grant, *Greek Apologists of the Second Century* (Philadelphia: Westminster, 1988), 186, for the suggestion that Irenaeus knew books one and two of Theophilus's *Ad Autolycum*, rather than a lost work written against Marcion.

24. Theophilus of Antioch, *Ad Autolycum*, II.32, trans. Robert M. Grant (Oxford: Clarendon, 1970).

25. As C. P. Jones ("A Syrian in Lyon," *AJP* 99.3 [1978]: 340) observes, the label Κελτοῖς "is the usual literary term for the Gauls, being both more classical and also more easily manipulated in verse than Γαλάται." On Iberia, Jürgen Deininger (review of Colin, *L'empire des Antonins et les martyrs gaulois de 177*, *Gnomon* 37 [1965]: 290) comments, "Die Pluralform [sc. ἐν ταῖς Ἰβηρίαις] kann nur die drei spanischen Provinzen (Tarraconensis, Baetica, Lusitania) meinen." And Mason Hammond (review of Colin, *AJP* 87.4 [1966]: 493) argues that ἐν Γερμανίαις refers to the German provinces, even without the inclusion of the definite article.

26. Some examples in Galen, especially in *De Compositione Medicamentorum secundum Locos*, for example, "From Iberia or Hispania, or however else someone might want to call it [ἀπὸ τῆς Ἰβηρίας ἢ Ἰσπανίας, ἢ ὅπως ἄν τις ὀνομάζειν ἐθέλοι]" (Kühn 12.388). Cf. Athenaeus, *Deipnosophistae*, VIII.1: "Iberia, which now the Romans call Spain [τῆς Ἰβηρίας, ἣν νῦν Ῥωμαῖοι Σπανίαν ὀνομάζουσι]"; Ptolemy, *Geographia*, II.4.1: "Hispania, which is Iberia, according to the Greeks [Τῆς Ἰσπανίας, κατὰ δὲ Ἕλληνας Ἰβηρίας]."

27. For example, Cassius Dio, LIV.25.1. "Augustus managed all the affairs in the Gallic, Germanic, and Iberian provinces." ὁ δ᾽ οὖν Αὔγουστος ἐπειδὴ πάντα τά τε ἐν ταῖς Γαλατίαις καὶ τὰ ἐν ταῖς Γερμανίαις ταῖς τ᾽ Ἰβηρίαις . . . διῳκήσατο.

28. Biographical details for Philostratus are now summarized in Ewen Bowie, "Philostratus: The Life of a Sophist," in *Philostratus*, ed. Ewen Bowie and Jas' Elsner (Cambridge: Cambridge University Press, 2009), 19–32.

29. Philostratus, *Vitae Sophistarum*, 489; 591.

30. Ibid., 576.

31. Irenaeus, *Haer.* I. praef. 3. This passage will be quoted in full below.

32. Ibid., I.13.6. "In our regions of the Rhone." καὶ ἐν τοῖς καθ᾽ ἡμᾶς κλίμασι τῆς Ῥοδανουσίας.

33. For example, Strabo IV.1.14 on Massilia and Narbo as famous cities.

34. For example, Philostratus, *Vitae Sophistarum*, 489, where the city of Arles is located with reference to the Rhone.

35. For example, Oppian, *Halieutica*, III.544: Μασσαλίην, ἱερὴν πόλιν; III.626: Φωκαίης τε παλαίφατοι ἐνναετῆρες.

36. Ibid., III.544.

37. For example, Philostratus, *Vitae Sophistarum*, 512.

38. More discussion of this point below.

39. Strabo IV.1.2.

40. Ptolemy, *Tetrabiblos*, 2.3.17. περὶ τὸ μέσον ἐσχηματισμένα τῆς ὅλης οἰκουμένης.

41. The list is given in four parts: 2.3.17; 29; 37; 46.

42. Cf. Ursula Maiburg, "'Und bis an die Grenzen der Erde . . .' Die Ausbreitung des Christentums in den Landerlisten und deren Verwendung in Antike und Christentum," *JAC* 26 (1983): 47, n.62: "Mit der 'Mitte der Welt' sind wohl Italien und Griechenland gemeint." And compare Robert M. Grant, "Early Christian Geography," *VChr* 46.2 (1992): 108, who suggests that Irenaeus "presumably viewed Rome as in the middle."

43. Aelius Aristides 44.3; Dio Chrysostom 32.47.7; Galen, *In Hippocratis aphorismos commentarii* (Kühn 17b.598).

44. Irenaeus, *Haer.* IV.30.3. "Sed et mundus pacem habet per eos [sc. Romanos] ut nos sine timore in viis ambulemus et navigemus quocumque voluerimus." Cf. Lionel Casson, *Travel in the Ancient World* (Baltimore: Johns Hopkins University Press, 1994), 122: "The first two centuries of the Christian Era were halcyon days for a traveler. . . . He could sail through any waters without fear of pirates, thanks to the emperor's patrol squadrons. A planned network of good roads gave him access to all major centers, and the through routes were policed well enough for him to ride them with relatively little fear of bandits."

45. Consider, for instance, the fragment of Irenaeus's lost treatise *On the Ogdoad* (Eusebius, *HE* V.20.2-3) where he encourages future copyists of his work to transcribe it carefully!

46. Irenaeus, *Haer.* I. praef.3. Rome seems the likeliest choice given both Irenaeus's previous links with the city, and the fragments of his correspondence directed to its bishop (e.g., Harvey's [1857] Syriac Fragment 28). Rome was also the nearest major Christian center, and a place from which further copies of the work could be sent to other communities. See Harry Y. Gamble, *Books and Readers in the Early Church: A History of Early Christian Texts* (New Haven: Yale University Press, 1995), 137, for discussion.

47. Compare what is said in the letter concerning the martyrdom of Lyons about Alexander, a martyr and doctor originally from Phrygia (Eusebius, *HE* V.1.49): "he had resided in the Gallic provinces for many years (πολλοῖς ἔτεσιν ἐν ταῖς Γαλλίαις διατρίψας)." The similarity in phrasing is striking, but one must note that the author of this letter uses the more Roman phrase ἐν ταῖς Γαλλίαις instead of Irenaeus's preferred ἐν Κελτοῖς. This discrepancy in geographical terminology makes it less likely, I would suggest, that Irenaeus was the author of the letter (as Pierre Nautin, *Lettres et écrivains chrétiens des IIe et IIIe siècles* [Paris: du Cerf, 1961], 54–61, argues), which also uses the Roman terminology τῆς Γαλλίας in its address (V.1.3). For the argument that this address is genuine, and not a later addition to the text, see G. W. Bowersock, *Martyrdom and Rome* (Cambridge: Cambridge University Press, 1995), 85–98.

48. Irenaeus, *Haer.* I. praef.3. Οὐκ ἐπιζητήσεις δὲ παρ᾽ ἡμῶν τῶν ἐν Κελτοῖς διατριβόντων, καὶ περὶ βάρβαρον διάλεκτον τὸ πλεῖστον ἀσχολουμένων, λόγων τέχνην, ἣν οὐκ ἐμάθομεν, οὔτε δύναμιν συγγραφέως, ἣν οὐκ ἠσκήσαμεν, οὔτε καλλωπισμὸν λέξεων, οὔτε πιθανότητα, ἣν οὐκ οἴδαμεν.

49. Ibid., I.10.2 of the diverse languages of the world; III.21.2 on Greek and Hebrew in the context of the production of the Septuagint; III.1.1 on Hebrew.

50. Ibid., V.30.3. "None of the idols which are adored publicly among the Greeks and barbarians have this name [sc. Titan, a possible name for the Antichrist]." "Neque eorum quae publice adorantur idolorum apud Graecos et barbaros habet vocabulum hoc."

51. Ibid., III.4.2.

52. The classic example of this phenomenon is provided by Strabo XIV.2.28, now discussed by Eran Almagor, "What Is a Barbarian? The Barbarians in the Ethnological and Cultural Taxonomies of Strabo," in *Strabo's Cultural Geography: The Making of a Kolossourgia*, ed. Daniela Dueck, Hugh Lindsay, and Sarah Pothecary (Cambridge: Cambridge University Press, 2005), 42–55.

53. References to Christians as a "third race" collected and discussed by Arthur J. Droge, *Homer or Moses? Early Christian Interpretations of the History of Culture* (Tübingen: Mohr Siebeck, 1989), 196–97.

54. Cf. Fergus Millar, "Culture grecque et culture latine dans le haut-empire: la loi et la foi," in *Les Martyrs de Lyon (177): Colloque international du Centre national de la recherche scientifique, Lyon, 20–23 septembre 1977* (Paris: CNRS, 1978), 193. "Il est possible que l'on ait raison de croire . . . qu'Irénée parlait de la langue celtique; mais ne peut-on suggérer qu'un écrivain grec, comme Irénée, quand il parlait du dialecte barbare du milieu occidental où il vivait et travaillait, voulait dire tout simplement le latin?"

55. Strabo, for instance, implicitly includes the Romans with other barbarian races (βάρβαρα ἔθνη) in a transitional comment signaling that he is moving from the western parts of Europe to Greece (VIII.1.1). He also comments that the regions of southern Italy that were once Greek have been, with few exceptions, "completely barbarized (ἐκβεβαρβαρῶσθαι)" (VI.1.2). This passage is discussed by G. W. Bowersock, "Les Grecs 'barbarisés,'" *Ktema* 17 (1992): 249–57. Polybius also calls the Romans barbarians, once implicitly in his own voice (XII.4b.2-3), and three times in reported speeches (V.104.1-11; IX.32.3–39.7; XI.4.1—6.8).

These passages are discussed by Craige Champion, "Romans as *Barbaroi*: Three Polybian Speeches and the Politics of Cultural Indeterminacy," *CPh* 95.4 (2000): 425–44, who is more eager to believe that Polybius calls the Romans barbarians than Andrew Erskine, "Polybios and Barbarian Rome," *Mediterraneo Antico* 3 (2000), 165–82, who comes to slightly different conclusions. Plutarch's *Pyrrhus* also contains explicit references to the Romans as barbarians, all in reported speech (16.7 and 16.13 are the most telling). This work is now discussed by Judith Mossman, "*Taxis ou Barbaros*: Greek and Roman in Plutarch's *Pyrrhus*," *CQ* 55.2 (2005): 502–4. My thanks to David Potter for drawing my attention to this reference.

56. The evidence is discussed by Michel Dubuisson, "Le latin est-il une langue barbare?" *Ktema* 9 (1984): 55–68.

57. Plutarch describes the circumstances of his time in Italy in *Demosthenes*, 2.

58. Useful discussion with examples in Susan Mattern, *Galen and the Rhetoric of Healing* (Baltimore: Johns Hopkins University Press, 2008), esp. 50–52.

59. Some examples are collected, for instance, by Noy, *Foreigners at Rome*, 228–30. Cf. Ramsay MacMullen, "The Unromanized in Rome," in *Diasporas in Antiquity*, ed. Shaye J.D. Cohen and Ernest S. Frerichs, Brown Judaic Studies 288 (Atlanta: Scholars, 1993), 47–64.

60. A summary in Peter Lampe, *From Paul to Valentinus: Christians at Rome in the First Two Centuries*, trans. Michael Steinhauser, ed. Marshall D. Johnson (Minneapolis: Fortress Press, 2003), 143–46, with references to earlier scholarship.

61. The evidence is presented in detail by Noy, *Foreigners at Rome*, 172–74.

62. Cf. the status of Greek as an "in-group" language for Jews in Italy well into the late antique period. See David Noy, "Writing in Tongues: The Use of Greek, Latin, and Hebrew in Jewish Inscriptions from Roman Italy," *JJS* 48 (1997): 300–11, and Margaret Williams, "The Jews of Early Byzantine Venusia: The Family of Faustinus I, the Father," *JJS* 50 (1999): 38–52, for detailed studies.

63. Gustave Bardy, *La question des langues dans l'église ancienne* (Paris: Beauchesne, 1948), 81–115, provides a detailed review of the evidence relating to language among Christians at Rome. He comments (156), with only slight hyperbole, that "au début du IIIᵉ siècle, tout le monde à Rome parle grec."

64. Irenaeus's connections with Justin are now explored by Michael Slusser, "How Much Did Irenaeus Learn from Justin?" *Studia Patristica* XL (2006): 515–20.

65. For Greek orators at Lyons, see Suetonius, *Caligula*, 20. A Greek actor at Lyons is attested by Cassius Dio LXXVIII.21.2, who scoffs that his success there owed more to the rusticity of the audience! Cf. Pliny the Younger, *Ep.* IX.11, who expresses his surprise that his writings were being sold in Lyons. He apparently had not realized that the city possessed any booksellers!

66. A survey of the epitaphs from Lyons is provided by A. Audin and Y. Burnand, "Chronologie des épitaphes romaines de Lyon," *REA* 61 (1959): 320–52. Burnand, "La datation des épitaphes romaines de Lyon: remarques complémentaires," in *Inscriptions Latines de Gaule Lyonnaise*, ed. F. Bérard and Y. Le Bohec (Paris: Collection Centre d'Etudes romaines et gallo-romaines n.s. 10, 1992), 21–27, updates and revises slightly the original study.

67. Greek inscriptions from Gaul are collected in an appendix to *IG* 14. A more inclusive and up-to-date survey of Greek epigraphy from Gaul is provided by F. Biville, "Les hellénismes dans les inscriptions latines paiennes de la Gaule (1er–4ème s. ap. J.-C.)," in *La langue des inscriptions de la Gaule. Actes de la Table-ronde tenue au C.E.R.G.R. les 6 et 7 Octobre 1988* (Lyon: Centre d'études romaines et gallo-romaines, 1989), 29–40.

68. For example, *CIL* 13.1854 = *IG* 14.2526.

69. For example, *CIL* 13.2004 = *IG* 14.2529.

70. Jean-Claude Decourt, "χαῖρε καὶ ὑγίαινε: à propos de quelques inscriptions lyonnaises," *RPh* 67 (1993): 245.

71. Cf. J. N. Adams, *Bilingualism and the Latin Language* (Cambridge: Cambridge University Press, 2003), 364, n.129.

72. Discussion in Noy, *Foreigners at Rome*, 172.

73. On these "Gallo-Latin" inscriptions, see Greg Woolf, *Becoming Roman: The Origins of Provincial Civilization in Gaul* (Cambridge: Cambridge University Press, 1998), 94–96.

74. See ibid., 78, 96, for Gaul in general. For Lyons, see Audin and Burnand, 326.

75. Woolf, 103, discusses the change. Statistics are provided by Jean-Jacques Hatt, *La tombe gallo-romaine* (Paris: Presses universitaires de France, 1951), 23–42 with comments by Marcel Le Glay, "Remarques sur l'onomastique gallo-romaine," in *L'Onomastique Latine*, ed. Noël Duval (Paris: CNRS, 1977), 269–77.

76. Cf. Woolf, 103, 203.

77. Three examples are *CIL* 13.2002, 2004, and 2005.

78. *CIL* 13.2448 = *IG* 14.2532.

79. He also likely spoke Aramaic. Cf. Adams, 688.

80. See the example discussed by Jones, with further references cited there.

81. Cf. Josef Herman, "La langue latine dans la Gaule romaine," *ANRW* 2.29.2 (1983): 1051: "Cette situation déjà complexe était rendue plus complexe encore par la présence d'individus et de groupes dont la langue d'origine n'était ni le latin ni le gaulois, soit parce qu'ils appartenaient à des ethnies minoritaires, soit parce qu'ils venaient de provinces ou de régions de langue non latine (Orientaux divers, soldats de troupes auxiliaires, esclaves importés). Pour eux—et avec eux—le seul moyende communication utilisable devait normalement être le latin."

82. Woolf, 103; 38.

83. Attalus of Pergamum: Eusebius, *HE* V.1.17; Alexander of Phrygia: Eusebius, *HE* V.1.49.

84. Ibid., V.1.52.

85. Ibid., V.1.20.

86. G. W. Bowersock, "Les églises de Lyon et de Vienne: relations avec l'Asie," in *Les Martyrs de Lyon (177): Colloque international du Centre national de la recherche scientifique, Lyon, 20–23 septembre 1977* (Paris: CNRS, 1978), 249–55, provides a sensible discussion of the martyrs' names. He suggests that the name Blandina may possibly be Celtic in origin. But cf. Garth Thomas, "La condition sociale de l'église de Lyon en 177," in *Les Martyrs de Lyon (177)*, 99, for other possibilities concerning the name Blandina.

87. Eusebius, *HE* V.1.5. Such a comment recalls the circumstances of Justin's school at Rome, located in a public and visible place "above the bath of Myrtinus (ἐπάνω . . . τοῦ Μυρτίνου βαλανείου)." *Acta Justini et Septem Sodalium*, 3.3 (recension a). See now Harlow Gregory Snyder, "'Above the Bath of Myrtinus': Justin Martyr's 'School' in the City of Rome," *HTR* 100, no. 3 (2007): 335–62, for a discussion of the location of Justin's school.

88. Bardy, 75.

89. Eusebius, *HE* V.20.2-3.

90. References in *Haer.* I. praef. 2; I.31.2; IV. praef. 2.

91. This is made particularly clear by his letter addressed to Victor: Harvey (1857), Syriac Fragment 28.

92. Examples from Eusebius include V.20.1, V.20.4-8, V.24.11-17, V.24.18.

93. Irenaeus, *Haer.* I.25.5.

94. Ibid., III.7.1-2.

95. Ibid., V.30.1-3.

96. T. D. Barnes, "Pre-Decian *Acta Martyrum*," *JTS* n.s. 19, no. 2 (1968): 510–14, surveyed the possible dates of the martyrdom and concluded that 156 was most likely, but has now put forward a very strong argument for 157 (*Early Christian Hagriography and Roman History* [Tübingen: Mohr Siebeck, 2010], 367–78). The significance of this date for the biography of Irenaeus is based on the statement in the Moscow manuscript of the *Martyrdom of Polycarp* (22.2) that Irenaeus was in Rome when Polycarp was martyred.

97. Strabo IV.1.5. Other examples of Greek doctors in Gaul are cited by A. Trevor Hodge, *Ancient Greek France* (London: Duckworth, 1998), 136–37. And compare the practice at Rome, where Greek doctors and teachers were also encouraged to come to the city. See Noy, *Foreigners at Rome*, 47.

98. Eusebius, *HE* V.1.49. Another Greek doctor from Lyons is credited with an antidote to scorpion venom by Galen, *De Antidosis* (Kühn 14.177).

99. Ibid., V.1.29.

100. Later local tradition as reported by Gregory of Tours held that (*Historiae* I.29) "The most blessed Irenaeus . . . in a short period of time turned the entire city [of Lyons] to Christianity, especially by his preaching." "Beatissimus vero Hireneus . . . in modici temporis spatio praedicatione sua maxime in integrum civitatem reddidit christianam." The claim that Irenaeus converted the entire city is certainly an exaggeration, but it does raise interesting possibilities about his preaching in the city in Latin.

101. This painfully literal Latin translation is perhaps the same version Tertullian used in his *Adversus Valentinianos* early in the third century. (Argument and details in Adhémar D'Alès, "La date de la version latine de saint Irénée," *RecSR* 6 [1916]: 133–37.) The language of the translation is such that it would be useful as a crib for a reader struggling with the original Greek, and is perhaps indicative of an early date of production in a community that was still making a transition from Greek to Latin. But a definitive solution to the date of the

Latin translation is still lacking. My thanks to Matthew Steenberg for his comments and suggestions in this area. Another interesting and related possibility is provided by the suggestion that the citations from scripture in the letter concerning the martyrdom at Lyons show some indications of having been freely translated from a Latin version *back* into Greek. See J. Armitage Robinson, *The Passion of S. Perpetua*, Texts and Studies 1.2 (Piscataway: Gorgias, 2004 [1891]), 97–100. Cf., 116–17; Bowersock, "Les églises de Lyon et de Vienne: relations avec l'Asie," 252.

102. The language of the Gallic churches in the third century seems to have been predominantly Latin, and the one named bishop of Lyons known to us from this period has a Latin name. This is a certain Faustinus of Lyons who appears in the correspondence of Cyprian. See Bardy, 118.

103. Interesting examples are provided by Arrian's *Periplus Ponti Euxini*, where he notes the bad Greek of an inscription carved by barbarians (1.2), and the names of places corrupted by barbarians (21.2). But he also refers without pause or complaint about the reports *in Latin* that he has submitted and will submit to Hadrian (6.2; 10.1). Arrian had good reason to speak and to write in Latin, and he is able to reconcile this easily with his Hellenic and classical outlook.

104. Irenaeus cites 1 Clement at *Haer.* III.3.3, and he may even have regarded it as scripture. Rousseau's arguments (*Contre les Hérésies, Livre IV*, 1:248–50) concerning the scriptural status for Irenaeus of 1 Clement and the *Shepherd of Hermas* are not convincing, especially for the latter of the two texts. I see no reason to disagree with Eusebius (*HE* V.8.7, referring to *Haer.* IV.20.2) that Irenaeus regarded the *Shepherd of Hermas* as scripture.

105. 1 Clement 5.6-7. κῆρυξ γενόμενος ἔν τε τῇ ἀνατολῇ καὶ ἐν τῇ δύσει, τὸ γενναῖον τῆς πίστεως αὐτοῦ κλέος ἔλαβεν· δικαιοσύνην διδάξας ὅλον τὸν κόσμον καὶ ἐπὶ τὸ τέρμα τῆς δύσεως ἐλθὼν.

106. Theodoret, *Eranistes*, 95.18-19. καὶ Εἰρηναῖον, ὃς τῆς Πολυκάρπου διδασκαλίας ἀπήλαυσεν, Γαλατῶν δὲ τῶν ἑσπερίων ἐγεγόνει φωστήρ.

3. How Irenaeus Has Misled the Archaeologists

1. Ps. Hippolytus, *Elenchos* IX.12.14.

2. Eusebius, *HE* V.24.11-13.

3. V. Fiocchi Nicolai and J. Gyon, "Relire Styger: Les origins de l'Area I du cimetière de Calliste et la crypte des papes," in V. Fiocchi Nicolai and J. Guyon, *Origine delle catacombe romane* (Sussidi allo studio delle antichità Cristiana 18; Pontificia Istituto di archaeologia cristiana: Roma, 2006), 127.

4. Hegesippus, apud Eusebius, *HE* IV.22.3.

5. N. Hyldahl, "Hegesipps Hypomnemata," in *Stud. Theol.* XIV (1960): 100–3, cf. A. Brent, *Hippolytus and the Roman Church in the Third Century: Communities in Tension before the Emergence of a Monarch-Bishop*, Supplements to Vigiliae Christianae 31 (Leiden: Brill, 1995), 448–49.

6. Hegesippus, apud Eusebius, *HE* IV.22.3.

7. *Didasc.* 9.25; *Ap. Const.* II.26.30-31.

8. Eusebius, *Dem. Ev.* VIII.2.62; A. Ehrhardt, *The Apostolic Tradition in the First Two Centuries of the Church* (London: Lutterworth, 1953), 42.

9. 1 Chron. 6:10; Neh. 12:10; Josephus, *Ant.* XI–XII. See also Ehrhardt (1953), 48–61.

10. W. Telfer, *The Office of a Bishop* (London: Darton, Longman and Todd, 1962), 74–77.

11. Brent (1995), 478–81.

12. Irenaeus, *Adv. Haer.* IV.8.3 (50–73), cf. Telfer (1962), 115.

13. Irenaeus, *Adv. Haer.* IV.8.3 (62–63), commenting on Matt. 12:3-5.

14. Irenaeus, *Adv. Haer.* IV.17.5-6 (146–56) and 18.1 (1–5).

15. Eusebius-Hieronymus, *Cronicon* CCXX.VIIII (= Helm, p. 194.17–18); Eusebius, *HE* IV.4.

16. Hegesippus, apud Eusebius, *HE* IV.22.3.

17. Irenaeus, *Adv. Haer.* III.3.1.

18. Irenaeus, *Adv. Haer.* III.3.3 (32-35).

19. Clement, *Cor., inscr.*: ἡ ἐκκλησία τοῦ θεοῦ ἡ παροικοῦσα Ῥώμην τῇ ἐκκλησίᾳ τοῦ θεοῦ τῇ παροικούσῃ Κόρινθον.

20. Dionysius of Corinth, apud Eusbius, *HE* IV.23.11; Irenaeus, *Adversus haereses*. III.3.3 (32–44); (cf. Eusebius, *HE* III.38.1-4; V.6).

21. Eusebius, *HE* II.25.8: (ἐπίσκοπος); III.4.10: ἀρχαίων τις, ἕτερος Διονύσιος, τῆς Κορινθίων παροικίας ποιμήν . . .; IV.21 (ἐπίσκοπος); 23.1 (τὸν τῆς ἐπισκοπῆς ἐγκεχείριστο θρόνον).

22. Polycarp, *Philippians, praef.*, Πολύκαρπος καὶ οἱ σύν αὐτῷ πρεσβύτεροι, cf. A. Brent, *Ignatius of Antioch: A Martyr Bishop and the Origin of Episcopacy* (London: Continuum, 2007), 12–13, 149–50.

23. Clement, *Cor.* 44.5.

24. Ibid., *Cor.* 44.1.

25. Dionysius of Corinth, apud Eusebius, *HE* IV.23.11.

26. I came to this conclusion in my article, A. Brent, "Pseudonymity and Charisma in the Ministry of the Early Church," *Augustinianum*, 27.3 (1987): 347–76. In the following year, I was pleased to observe corroboration in P. Lampe, *Die stadtrömischen Christen in den ersten beiden Jahrhunderten* (Wissenschaftliche Untersuchungen zum neuen Testament 2.18; Tübingen, Mohr Siebeck, 1987/1989), 339.

27. Hegesippus, apud Eusebius, *HE* IV.22.2.

28. Ibid., IV.22.1.

29. Diogenes Laertius, *Lives*. See A. Brent, "Diogenes Laertius and the Apostolic Succession," *JEH* 44, no. 3 (1993): 372–75.

30. See my account of this phenomenon in A. Brent, *Ignatius of Antioch and the Second Sophistic: A Study of an Early Christian Transformation of Pagan Culture*, Studien und Texte zu Antike und Christentum 36 (Tübingen: Mohr Siebeck, 2006).

31. Irenaeus, *Adv. Haer.* III.2.2 (17–22).

32. Diogenes Laertius, *Lives* IV.1.

33. Ibid., V.52–53.

34. Ibid., V.62.

35. Diogenes Laertius, *Lives* V.65: τοῦτον διεδέξατο Λύκον, cf. previously (of Theophrastus's successor) V.58: διεδέξατο δ᾽ αὐτοῦ τὴν σχολὴν Στράτων.

36. Diogenes Laertius, *Lives* V.70.

37. Brent (1995), 402–6.

38. Lampe (1987/1989) 313, 316; cf. Brent (1995), 407–9.

39. Justin Martyr, *1 Apol.* 66.3; *Acts of Justin* 3.2: G. A. Bisbee, *Pre-Decian Acts of Martyrs and Commentarii*, Harvard Dissertations in Religion 22 (Philadelphia: Fortress Press, 1988); Lampe (1987/1989), 233–45; Brent (1995), 400 ff.

40. Justin Martyr, *Dial.* 8.1.

41. "Elder/presbyter"—"bishop"—"president." Lampe (1987/1989), 324–25, 331–32; Brent (1995), 414–15, 420–21.

42. Irenaeus, *Adv. Haer.* I.11.1 (1197–1199), and Brent (1995), 420–27.

43. *Elenchos* IX.12.26.

44. Ibid., IX.12.20-21.

45. Irenaeus, *Adv. Haer.* IV.6.2 (27–29); V.26.12 (76–79), cf. Eusebius, *HE* IV.18.9. See also J. Armitage Robinson, "On a Quotation from Justin Martyr in Irenaeus," *JTS* 31, no. 4 (1930): 374–78.

46. See above, footnote 11 and associated text.

47. Eusebius, *HE* IV.23.9-10.

48. Eusebius, *HE* V.4.2.

49. 1 Tim. 4:14.

50. 1 Cor. 5:4-5.

51. Rom. 16:23.

52. Clement, *Cor.* 44.3. See also B. E. Bowe, *A Church in Crisis: Ecclesiology and Paraenesis in Clement of Rome*, Harvard Dissertations in Religion 23 (Minneapolis: Fortress Press, 1988), and A. Brent, *A Political History of Early Christianity* (New York: Continuum, 2009), 176–78.

53. *Ap. Trad.* 2. I translate here from the Verona Latin Palimpsest, noting that the variation in S(AE) is indicative of some tampering in the textual transmission.

54. E. C. Ratcliff, "'Apostolic Tradition': Questions Concerning the Appointment of the Bishop," in *Liturgical Studies*, edited by A. H. Couratin and D. H. Tripp (London: SPCK, 1976), 156–60. See also Brent (1995), 468–71; P. Bradshaw et al., *The Apostolic Tradition: Translation and Commentary*, Hermeneia (Minneapolis: Fortress Press, 2002), 1–17; and A. Stewart-Sykes, *Hippolytus, on the Apostolic Tradition, an English Translation with Introduction and Commentary* (Crestwood: St. Vladimir's Seminary Press, 2001), 50.

55. Eusebius, *HE* V.23-24.

56. See above, footnote 2.

57. Irenaeus, *Adv. Haer.* IV.17.4 (139–45).

58. P. Styger, "L'origine del cimitero di S. Callisto sull' Appia," *Rendiconti Pontificia Accademia di Archeologia* 4 (1925–1926): 91–153; Fiocchi Nicolai and Gyon (2006), 121–75.

59. P. Testini, *Le catacombe e gli antichi cimiteri cristiani in Roma* (Bologna, 1966), 128–35; Ph. Pergola and P. M. Barbini, *Le catacombe cristiane di Roma. Storia e topografia* (Rome, 1997); V. Fiocchi Nicolai, F. Bisconti, and D. Mazzoleni, *Le catacombe cristiane di Roma. Origini, sviluppo, apparati decorative, documentazione epigrafica* (Regensburg, 1998), 16–17.

60. Fiocchi Nicolai and Gyon (2006), 121–75.

61. Ibid., 127: "Si l'on désirait augmenter la capacité du cimetière, les piles régulières de *loculi* qui comptaient les parois des galeries a et b empêchaient l'ouverture de corridors transversaux; dès lors, la solution ne pouvait passer que par un approfondissement. La chose est advenue alors que le réseau initial arrivait à saturation, quelques rares places restant seules disponibles à l'extrémité de a et b (cfr. tav. 1); au sein de l'area, la pratique des inhumations collectives rencontrait donc une réelle faveur et cela explique que l'approfondissement a été mise à profit pour donner au cimetière une toute autre ampleur que précédemment."

62. Ibid., 131: "Le deuxième approfondissement a procédé des mêmes causes que le premier et il a suivi la même logique, portant à achèvement, ou presque, le plan en forme de gril ébauché précédemment, grâce au percement de trois galléries transversales, H et F et G déjà signalées (fig. 4); ainsi, par petites touches, les *fossores* ouvraient là aux cimetières souterrains les voies de l'avenir."

63. Ibid., 159.

64. *Acta S. Callisti Papae Martyris Romae* 8, in Migne, *P.L.* 10, col. 120.

65. Cassius Dio LXXX.20.2; Herodian V.9.8; *Scriptores Historiae Augusti*, Elagabalus 17.1-3, cf. A. Brent, *The Imperial Cult and the Development of Church Order: Concepts and Images of Authority in Paganism and Early Christianity before the Age of Cyprian*, Supplements to Vigiliae Christianae 45 (Leiden: Brill, 1999), 310–28.

66. *Liber Pontificalis* I.18.

67. E. Rébillard, *Religion et sépulture, l'Église, les vivants et les morts dans l'Antiquité tardive*, Civilisations et Sociétés (Paris: Éditions de l'École des hautes Études en sciences sociales, 2003), 16: "Le mot koimeterion, au singulier ou même au pluriel, ne désigne pas un lieu de sépulture mais la ou les tombes de martyrs, et par extension le lieu de culte qu'elles sont devenues." See also, "'Koimeterion' et 'coemeterium'. Tombe sainte et nécropole," in *MEFRA* 105 (1993): 975–1001; "L'Église de Rome et le developpement des catacombs: à propos de l'origine des cimetières chrétiens," *MEFRA* 109 (1997): 741–63; "Chrétiens et Formes de sepulture collective à Rome aux IIe et IIIe siècles," in Fiocchi Nicolai and Guyon (2006), 41–47.

68. Rébillard (2003), 12. See also ibid., 14, on the examples of Tertullian, *De anima* 5.17; the Hippolytan *Commentary on Daniel*; and Origen, *Homilies on Jeremiah* IV.3.16.

69. Chronographer of 354, *Episcopi Romani*, entry for Pontianus, cf. *Depositio Martyrum*, iv id. Aug.

70. Chronographer of 354, *Episcopi Romani*, entry for Fabius (sic).

71. E. Josi, "Cimitero alla sinistra della via Tiburtina al viale Regina Margherita," *Rivista Archeologia Cristiana* 10 (1933): 187–233, and *Rivista Archeologia Cristiana* 11 (1934): 233–58. Cf. R. Giordani, "Novatiano betissimo martyri Gaudentius diaconus fecit. Contributo all'identificazione del martire Novaziano della catacomba anonima sulla via Tiburtina," *Rivista Archeologia Cristiana* 68 (1992): 233–58.

72. M. Borgolte, *Petrusnachfolge und Kaiserimitation. Die Grablegen der Päpste, ihre Genese und Traditionsbildung*, Veröffentlichungen des Max-Planck-Instituts für Geschichte 95 (Göttingen: Vandenhoeck and Ruprecht, 1989), 33–36.

4. The Parable of the Two Sons (Matt. 21:28-32) in Irenaeus and Codex Bezae

1. *Novum Testamentum Sancti Irenaei Episcopi Ludgunensis*—edited from the MSS with introductions apparatus notes and appendices by the late W. Sanday and C. H. Turner, assisted by many other scholars and especially by A. Souter (Oxford: Clarendon, 1923), cxii.

2. *The New Testament in the Original Greek,* the text revised by B. F. Westcott and F. J. A. Hort (Cambridge and London: Macmillan, 1882), 160 (§ 220).

3. *Novum Testamentum Sancti Irenaei*, cxxxix.

4. K. Aland and B. Aland, *The Text of the New Testament. An Introduction to the Critical Editions and to the Theory and Practice of Modern Textual Criticism*, 2nd ed., revised and enlarged (Grand Rapids: Eerdmans, 1989), 55.

5. C. B. Amphoux, "Le texte," in D. C. Parker and C. B. Amphoux, eds., *Codex Bezae. Studies from the Lunel Colloquium, June 1994* (Leiden: Brill, 1996), 341. Unfortunately, I have not been able to see Amphoux's "Les contextes de la Parabole des deux fils (Matt. 21:28-32)," *Langues orientales anciennes, philologie et linguistique*, 3 (1991): 215–48.

6. Second edition (Stuttgart: Deutsche Bibelgesellschaft, 1994), 45.

7. Cf. Westcott and Hort, *The New Testament in the Original Greek*, vol. 2, Appendix, 16; M. J. Lagrange, *Évangile selon saint Matthieu*, 3rd ed. (Paris: Leciffre, Gabalda, 1927), 409–10; Metzger, *Textual Commentary*, 45f; E. Riggenbach, "Zur Exegese und Textkritik zweier Gleichnisse Jesu," *Aus Schrift und Geschichte, Festschrift A. Schlatter* (Stuttgart: Calwer, 1922), 17–34; J. Schmid, "Das textgeschichtliche Problem der Parabel von den zwei Söhnen. Mt 21:28-32," in N. Adler, ed., *Vom Wort des Lebens: Festschrift für Max Meinertz zur Vollendung des 70. Lebensjahres 19 Dezember 1950* (Münster: Aschendorff, 1951), 75, 83.

8. J. Schmid, "Das textgeschichtliche Problem"; A. Orbe, *Parábolas Evangélicas en san Ireneo*, 2 vols. (Madrid: Catolica, 1972), 2:102.

9. P. Bacq, *De l'ancienne à la nouvelle Alliance selon S. Irénée. Unité du Livre IV de l'Adversus haereses* (Paris: Lethielleux, 1978), 251 n.3.

10. Cf. Bacq, *De l'ancienne à la nouvelle Alliance*, 30, 235ff; A. Rousseau, *Contre les hérésies, Livre IV* (Paris: du Cerf, 1965), 1:343.

11. Cf. *Haer.* IV.14.2; III.11.8; 23.5, and P. Siniscalco, "La parabola del figlio prodigo (Lc 15:11-22) in Ireneo," *Studi e materiali di storia delle religioni* 38 (1967): 538, 541, 545–50.

12. Orbe, *Parábolas Evangélicas*, 1:282f.

13. Riggenbach proposed that it was, in fact, the mistaken assumption of a correspondence between the two sons and the two groups that had given rise to the reversal of the order of the two sons in Matt. 21:29-30 ("Zur Exegese und Textkritik zweier Gleichnisse Jesu," 29–30).

14. J. Ramsey Michaels, "The Parable of the Regretful Son," *HTR* 61 (1968): 15–26, proposes that in its original form the parable told not of a son who repented and went into the vineyard, but of a son who "went away regretful."

15. *Parábolas Evangélicas*, 2:103.

16. E. Riggenbach, "Zur Exegese und Textkritik zweier Gleichnisse Jesu," 31–32.

17. "Jesús echaba en cara a los judíos, no que no hicieran (ni hubieran de hacer) penitencia, sino que no la hicieran saludable, *para creer en El*. Ireneo señala lo mismo. El pueblo judío hizo luego penitencia, mas no para terminar creyendo en Jesús; *una penitencia sin fe*, un llanto sobre las proprias calamidades, de nada les servía," *Parábolas Evangélicas*, 2:103.

18. J. Schmid, "Das tetxtgeschichtliche Problem," 78 n.17.

19. "Parable of the Regretful Son," 25.

20. Bacq, *De l'ancienne à la nouvelle Alliance*, 241.

21. Cf. Bacq, *De l'ancienne à la nouvelle Alliance*, 243.

22. M. W. Holmes, "Codex Bezae as a Recension of the Gospels," in D. C. Parker and C. B. Amphoux, eds., *Codex Bezae. Studies from the Lunel Colloquium, June 1994*, 151–52. Cf. B. Ehrman's essay in the same collection: "The Text of the Gospels at the end of the Second Century," 95–122.

5. Irenaeus and Hebrews

1. Photius, *Cod.232* (Migne, PG 103.1103).

2. Eusebius, *Hist. eccl.* V.26; trans. G. A. Williams, rev. ed. A. Louth, *Eusebius, The History of the Church from Christ to Constantine* (New York: Penguin, 1989), 174.

3. Luke Timothy Johnson, *Hebrews: A Commentary* (Louisville: Westminster John Knox, 2006), 3. Cf. B. F. Westcott, *The Epistle to the Hebrews* (Grand Rapids: Eerdmans, 1984), lxii–lxiii.

4. *An Introduction to the New Testament* (New York: MacMillan, 1900), 33n.2.

5. Eusebius, *Hist. Eccl.* III.38.1-3; trans. H. J. Lawlor and J. E. L. Oulton, Eusebius, *Ecclesiastical History*, vol. 1, *Translation* (London: SPCK, 1927), 98.

6. D. A. Hagner, *The Use of the Old and New Testaments in Clement of Rome* (Leiden: Brill, 1973), 179.

7. Hagner, *The Use of the Old and New Testaments in Clement of Rome*, 194–95.

8. "1 Clement and the Writings That Later Formed the New Testament," in *The Reception of the New Testament in the Apostolic Fathers*, ed. A. Gregory and C. Tuckett (Oxford: Oxford University, 2007), 152. He references P. Ellingworth, "Hebrews and *1 Clement*: Literary Dependence or Common Tradition?" *Biblische Zeitschrift*, ns. 23 (1979): 262–69.

9. Gerd Theissen, *Untersuchungen zum Hebräerbrief*, SNT 2 (Gütersloh: Gerd Mohn, 1969), 33–38. I am grateful to James Thompson for this reference.

10. "Heb. 1:1-14, *1 Clem.* 36:1-6 and the High Priest," *Journal of Biblical Literature* 97 (1978): 437–40.

11. *The Epistle to the Hebrews* (Philadelphia: Fortress Press, 1989), 6–7.

12. *Hebrews as Pseudepigraphon: The History and Significance of the Pauline Attribution of Hebrews*, WUNT 235 (Tübingen: Mohr Siebeck, 2009), 29–30.

13. Westcott, *The Epistle to the Hebrews*, lxii.

14. J. Verheyden, "The Shepherd of Hermas and the Writings That Later Formed the New Testament." In Gregory and Tuckett, eds., *The Reception of the New Testament in the Apostolic Fathers*, 293–329.

15. Verheyden, "The Shepherd of Hermas and the Writings That Later Formed the New Testament," 329.

16. R. E. Brown and J. P. Meier, *Antioch and Rome* (Mahwah: Paulist, 2004), 147. Particularly, the issues of difference concern the Levitical cult (Clement) and forgiveness after baptism (*Hermas*).

17. Brown and Meier, *Antioch and Rome*, 147.

18. Ibid., 148.

19. Ibid.

20. Ibid., 204.

21. Westcott, *The Epistle to the Hebrews*, lxv.

22. A. Camerlynck, *Saint Irénée et le canon du Noveau Testament* (Louvain: Istas, 1896), 36; *Sancti Irenaei Episcopi Lugdunensis Libros quinque adversus haereses*, 2 vols., ed. W. W. Harvey (Cambridge: Academic, 1857), 2:522.

23. A. Camerlynck, *Saint Irénée et le canon du Noveau Testament*, 36–37.

24. Harvey, *Sancti Irenaei*, 1:clxvii–clxviii.

25. A. Camerlynck, *Saint Irénée et le canon du Noveau Testament*, 36.

26. J. Hoh, *Die Lehre des hl. Irenäus über das Neue Testament* (Münster: Aschendorffschen, 1919), 198.

27. F. R. M Hitchcock, *Irenaeus of Lugdunum: A Study of His Teaching* (Cambridge: Cambridge University Press, 1914), 230.

28. C. H. Turner, "Appendix II: De Epistula ad Hebraeos," in *Novum Testamentum Sancti Irenaei Episcopi Lugdunensis*, ed. W. Sanday, C. H. Turner, and A. Souter (Oxford: Clarendon, 1923), 226–27.

29. A. Benoit, *Saint Irénée: introduction a l'étude de sa théologie* (Paris: Universitaires de France, 1960), 143.

30. Ibid., 144.

31. *Hebrews as Pseudepigraphon*, 30–31.

32. *New Testament Apocrypha*, vol. 1, *Gospels and Related Writings*, rev. ed., W. Schneemelcher, trans. R. McL. Wilson (Louisville: Westminster John Knox, 1991), 26.

33. N. Brox, "Irenaeus and the Bible," in C. Kannengiesser, *Handbook of Patristic Exegesis* (Leiden: Brill, 2006), 484.

34. Brox, "Irenaeus and the Bible," 484.

35. R. M. Grant, *A Historical Introduction to the New Testament* (New York: Harper and Row, 1963), 31.

36. R. M. Grant, *Irenaeus of Lyons* (New York: Routledge, 1997), 1; R. M. Grant, *Heresy and Criticism* (Louisville: Westminster John Knox, 1993), 92.

37. Luke Timothy Johnson, *Hebrews*, 4.

38. *Marcion and His Influence* (London: SPCK, 1948).

39. *Irenaeus of Lugdunum*, 230. See Jerome, *Adv. Jov.* 2.3; *Ep. 41 ad Marcellam* 3; Tertullian, *De pudic.* 20.1-2; Pacian, *Ep. Symp.* 1.2 and Germanus, *Syn. Haer.* 5 on Hebrews 6:4-6 and rigorist views concerning repentance and penance in Montanism and Novationism. Cf. W. Tabbernee, *Fake Prophecy and Polluted Sacraments: Ecclesiastical and Imperial Reactions to Montanism* (Leiden: Brill, 2007), 364–66; C. Trevett, *Montanism: Gender, Authority and the New Prophecy* (Cambridge: University Press, 1996), 117, 131. F. E. Vokes, "Penitential Discipline in Montanism," *Studia Patristica* 14 (1976): 62–76; W. Tabbernee, "To Pardon or Not to Pardon? North African Montanism and the Forgiveness of Sins," *Studia Patristica* 35 (2001): 375-86; Z. Garcia, "El Perdón de los pecados en la primitiva iglesia: Tertuliano y polemica catholico-montanista," *Razón y Fe* 23 (1909): 360–67; P. C. De Labriolle, *La Crise Montaniste* (Paris: Leroux, 1913), 404–57.

40. On Hebrews as a work of Christian prophecy attractive to Montanists and therefore as a text minimized or rejected by Montanism's opponents, see Trevett, *Montanism*, 131, and H. Lietzmann, *Kleine Schriften*, vol. 2, TU 68 (Berlin: Akademie, 1958), 81–84.

41. The following indices were consulted: *Biblia Patristica: Index des citations et allusions bibliques dans la littérature patristique*, vol. 1, *Des origins à Clement d'Alexandrie et Tertullien*, Centre d'Analyse et

de Documentation Patristique, ed. J. Allenbach et al. (Paris: Éditions du Centre National de la Recherche Scientifique, 1975), 520–25; the website, *BiblIndex: Index of Biblical Quotations and Allusions in Early Christian Literature*; and the index in the SC critical edition (I have used the cumulative index in the single volume French translation of the SC volumes of *Haer*. (*Irénée de Lyons Contre les hérésies*, trans. A. Rousseau [Paris: Cerf, 1984], 705). Combined, they list the following references for Hebrews in Irenaeus: Heb. 1:3; 1:8-9; 1:13; 2:8; 2:10; 3:5; 3:14; 5:9; 5:14; 8:5; 9:11-14; 9:23; 10:1; 10:26; 10:38; 11:1; 11:4; 11:5; 11:8-10; 11:13; 11:19; 13:12 (Heb. 1:3 *Haer.*—II.30.9 [SC294: 318.224]; Heb. 1:8-9—III.6.1 [SC211: 66.19]; Heb. 1:13—II.28.7 [SC294: 286.189]; Heb. 2:8—I.29.2/ IV.33.13 [SC264: 360.27/100.2: 840.306]; Heb. 2:10—III.12.13 [SC211: 234.445]; Heb. 3:5—II.2.5/III.6.5/IV.15.2 [SC294: 40.81/211: 80.122/100.2: 554.47]; Heb. 3:5-6—IV.30.4 [SC100.2: 784.119-20]; Heb. 3:14—III.1.2 [SC211: 24.31]; Heb. 5:9—III.22.4 [SC211: 440.68]; Heb. 5:14—IV.38.2 [SC100.2: 950.43]; Heb. 6:5—III.7.1 [SC211: 82.18-19]; Heb. 8:5—*Dem*. 9/ *Haer*. IV.11.4/ IV.14.3/ IV.19.1/ V.35.2 [SC62: 46.5/ SC100.2: 508.86/ 548.79/ 614.3/ SC153: 450.106]; Heb. 9:11-14—IV.8.2 [SC100.2: 470.42]; Heb. 9:23—IV.11.4 [SC100.2: 508.86]; Heb. 10:1—IV.11.4 [SC100.2: 508.86]; Heb. 10:26—IV.27.2 [SC100.2: 742.112]; Heb. 10:38—*Dem*. 35 [SC62: 88.2]; Heb. 11:1—*Dem*. 3 [SC62: 32.1]; Heb. 11:4—*Haer*. III.23.4 [SC211: 454.88]; Heb. 11:5—IV.16.2/V.5.1 [SC100.2: 562.36; 564.31/ SC153: 62.8]; Heb. 11:8-10—IV.5.3 [SC100.2: 432.61]; Heb. 11:13—IV.25.1 [SC100.2: 704.7]; Heb. 11:19—V.3.2 [SC153: 44.32]; Heb. 13:12—III.5.3 [SC211: 62.77]).

42. *Haer*. II.30.9; Trans. *Against Heresies, Books 1–5 and Fragments*, trans. A. Roberts and W. H. Rambaut, in *The Ante-Nicene Fathers* (ANF), vol. 1, *The Apostolic Fathers with Justin Martyr*, rev. ed. (Edinburgh: T&T Clark; reprint Peabody: Hendrickson, 1994), 406; hereafter ANF 1. Critical edition used was *Irénée de Lyons: Contre les hérésies, Livres 1–5*, ed. trans. and annotated A. Rousseau, L. Doutreleau, B. Hemmerdinger, and C. Mercier, SC 263, 264 [Livre 1], 293, 294 [Livre 2], 210, 211 [Livre 3], 100.1, 100.2 [Livre 4], 152, 153 [Livre 5] (Paris: Cerf, 1979 [Livre 1], 1982 [Livre 2], 1974, 2002 [Livre 3], 1965 [Livre 4], 1969 [Livre 5]).

43. *Haer*. II.30.9, SC 294: 318.224. I believe this is a partial quotation or citation of Hebrews 1:3. However, I think that all the other references to Hebrews mentioned in this paper are best classified as "allusions," not "quotations" or even "echoes." Such terms have been the topic of much discussion in New Testament studies (e.g., R. B. Hays, *Echoes of Scripture in the Letters of Paul* [New Haven: Yale, 1989], 19–32; R. B. Hays, *The Conversion of the Imagination: Paul as Interpreter of Israel's Scripture* [Grand Rapids: Eerdmans, 2005], 163-89; S. E. Porter, "Further Comments on the Use of the Old Testament in the New Testament," in *The Intertextuality of the Epistles: Explorations of Theory and Practice*, ed. T. L. Brodie, D. R. MacDonald, and S. E. Porter, NTM 16 [Sheffield: Sheffield Phoenix, 2007], 98–110; S. E. Porter, "Allusions and Echoes," in *As It is Written: Studying Paul's Use of Scripture*, ed. S. E. Porter and C. D. Stanley [Atlanta: SBL, 2008], 29–40; C. D. Stanley, *Paul and the Language of Scripture: Citation Technique in the Pauline Epistles and Contemporary Literature*, SNTSMS 74 [Cambridge: Cambridge University, 1992]). I have adopted the definitions of Porter: allusion indirectly invokes a specific "external person, place, or literary work" to bring it into the contemporary text or material; echo indirectly invokes language that is thematically associated with a "more general notion or concept" into the contemporary text (Porter, "Allusions and Echoes," 33, 39–40).

44. *Haer*. II.30.9 (SC 294: 318.219).

45. *Haer*. II.30 (SC 294: 305.54-306.55). And Heb. 1:3 in *Haer*. IV.25.1 (SC100.2: 706.10) might inspire him again. When alluding to Ephesians 2:20, he speaks of Christ, the chief-cornerstone, "sustaining all things" (*omnia sustinens*; πάντα βαστάζων). Heb. 1:3 has φέρων τε τὰ πάντα. Cf. A. Orbe, *Teología de San Ireneo: Commentario al Libro V del "Adversus haereses,"* 3 vols. (Madrid: Biblioteca de Autores Cristianos, 1985, 1987, 1988), 3:334–35.

46. *Haer*. II.30.9 (SC 294: 318. 224-320.225).

47. *Haer*. II.30.9 (SC 295: 320.238-39).

48. *Haer*. II.30.9 (SC 294: 320.248).

49. I am grateful to Fr. Roch Kereszty for bringing this to my attention.

50. *Haer*. I.22.1 (SC 264: 308.2-3).

51. *Haer*. I.8.1—9.5.

52. Camerlynck, *Saint Irénée et le canon du Noveau Testament*, 36. Cf. T. Zahn, *Geschichte des Neustestamentlichen Kanons* (Erlangen/Leipzig: A. Deichert, 1888–92), 1:298, n.2.

53. He does, further down in III.6.2, employ Isa. 43:10 with "Lord God" and "Son."

54. Cf. Turner, "Appendix II: De Epistula ad Hebraeos," 226, who draws these prophetic texts to our eyes seeming to prefer an Old Testament origin for Irenaeus's words due to his statement regarding the Spirit's (not

the Lord's or the apostles') testimony concerning Moses. However, Irenaeus could simply be recognizing the prophetic origin of the words and their setting in Hebrews.

55. D. A. Hagner, *The Use of the Old and New Testaments in Clement of Rome* (Leiden: Brill, 1973), 191.

56. *Haer.* III.22.2-3.

57. *Haer.* III.22.4; trans. Roberts and Rambout, ANF 1:258.

58. Ibid., 1:758.

59. *Haer.* V.19.1; trans. Roberts and Rambout, ANF 1:919.

60. Ibid., 1:919.

61. *Haer.* III.23.1; trans. Roberts and Rambout, ANF 1:759.

62. B. de Margerie, "Mary Coredemptrix in the Light of Patristics," in *Mary Coredemptrix, Mediatrix, Advocate, Theological Foundations: Towards a Papal Definition?*, ed. M. I. Miravalle (Santa Barbara: Queenship, 1995), 8. See further on the theme in Irenaeus M. C. Steenberg, "The Role of Mary as Co-Recapitulator in Saint Irenaeus of Lyons," *Vigiliae Christianae* 58 (2004): 117–37.

63. De Margerie, "Mary Coredemptrix in the Light of Patristics," 8.

64. Ibid., 9.

65. *Haer.* IV.38.1; trans. Roberts and Rambout, ANF 1:874, slightly altered.

66. Ibid., 1:874.

67. *Haer.* IV.38.1; trans Roberts and Rambout, ANF 1:874.

68. *Haer.* IV.38.2 (SC 100.2: 950–51); trans. Roberts and Rambout, ANF 1:875, slightly altered.

69. SC 100.1: 281–82.

70. *Haer.* IV.11.4; trans. Roberts and Rambout, ANF 1:793.

71. *Haer.* IV.11.4 (SC 100.2: 508–9).

72. The language in quotation marks comes from *Haer.* IV.11.3, the paragraph preceding the one in which he alludes to Hebrews 8:5, and *Haer.* IV.11.4. Trans. Roberts and Rambout, ANF 1:792.

73. See, e.g., J. Daniélou, *Gospel Message and Hellenistic Culture*, trans. J. A. Baker (Philadelphia: Westminster, 1973), 285–86.

74. *Haer.* IV.14.3 (SC 100.2: 546–47).

75. *Haer.* IV.19.1 (SC 100.2: 616–17).

76. Ibid., (SC 100.2: 616–17).

77. *Haer.* III.23.4 (SC211: 454.88).

78. *Haer.* IV.16.2 (SC100.2: 562.35-38); V.5.1 (SC153: 62.8–9).

79. *Teología de San Ireneo*, 1:233

80. See the citation from Eusebius, *Hist. Eccl.* V.26 given at the beginning of this paper. This, then, might answer, at least in part, Hoh's question concerning why Eusebius mentions both Hebrews and Wisdom in the same remark. He had wondered if it concerned Eusebius's curiosity over why Irenaeus would cite from two disputed books or Eusebius's surprise that Irenaeus had so greatly employed these two books together (*Die Lehre des hl. Irenäus über das Neue Testament*, 46). Cf. Orbe (*Teología de San Ireneo*, 1: 233), who sees in *Haer.* V.5.1 a connection between the Eusebius statement and Irenaeus's exegesis. M. C. Steenberg believes the "little book," spoken of by Eusebius, was "*on* the Epistle to the Hebrews and the Wisdom of Solomon [emphasis mine]" (*Irenaeus on Creation: The Cosmic-Christ and the Saga of Creation* [Leiden: Brill, 2008], 19, n. 60). Irenaeus apparently cites Wisdom (6:19) literally only at the very end of *Haer.* IV.38.3 (SC100.2: 956.83–84). However, the editors of SC note the following accommodated citations or allusions in Wis. 1:7 (*Haer.* III.11.8; IV.20.6; V.2.3; V.18.3); Wis. 1:14 (I.22.1; II.10.2); Wis. 2:24 (IV. pref.4; IV.40.3; V.25.4); Wis. 4:10 (IV.16.2; V.5.1); Wis. 7:5 (II.34.2); Wis. 10:4 (I.30.10); Wis. 11:20 (IV.4.2); Wis. 14:21 (III.5.3).

81. C. Spicq notes that Irenaeus already seemed to have recognized the similarities and he references the Eusebius remark as evidence (*L'Épitre aux Hébreux*, 2 vols. [Paris: Gabalda, 1952], 1:42). Maybe he even joined the just, dead man of Wisdom 4:16 to the just, dead Cain of Hebrews 11:4. It is not difficult to see Irenaeus composing a small book demonstrating the unity of the testimony of these two books to prove the unity of redemption and revelation, of anticipation and fulfillment, of the old and the new.

82. The recognition of some level of similarity, particularly in language and thought, between the two texts has caused remarkable theses. For example, E. H. Plumptre argued that they had a common author, Apollos, who penned Wisdom while a Jew and Hebrews after conversion to Christianity ("The Writings of Apollos," *The Expositor* n.s. 1 (1885): 329–48; 409–35); cf. E. H. Plumptre, *Ecclesiastes* (Cambridge: University Press, 1890), 68–70. Plumptre concluded his essay with the argument that his thesis concerning Apollos explains

Irenaeus's grouping of Hebrews with Wisdom; they were from the same author ("The Writings of Apollos," 435). L. Noack (*Der Ursprung des Christentums* [Leipzig: Fleischer, 1857], 222) had earlier argued for Apollos, but thought he wrote Wisdom as a Christian convert (e.g., Wis. 2:20 is a key sign). See also for an argument of the literary influence of Wisdom upon Hebrews: H. von Soden, *Hand Commentar zum Neuen Testament*, vol. 3.2, *Hebraerbrief, Briefe des Petrus, Jakobus, Judas* (Leipzig: Mohr Siebeck, 1899). Parallels recognized between the two books include: Heb. 1:1/Wis. 7:22; Heb. 1:3/Wis. 7:26, 1:21; Heb. 1:6/Wis. 1:7; Heb. 2:5/Wis. 1:7; Heb. 2:10/Wis. 4:13; Heb. 2:14/Wis. 2:24; Heb. 2:15/Wis. 12:2; Heb. 3:3-4/Wis. 13:4; Heb. 3:4/Wis. 9:2; Heb. 3:5/Wis. 17:21; Heb. 3:6/Wis. 16:6, 19:1; Heb. 3:12/Wis. 3:10, 14:25; Heb. 3:14/Wis. 16:21; Heb. 4:6/Wis. 14:6; Heb. 4:9/Wis. 4:7, 18:22; Heb. 4:12-13/Wis. 1:6, 7:22-24; Heb. 5:9/Wis. 4:13; Heb. 5:12/Wis. 13:6l; Heb. 5:13/Wis. 13:18; Heb. 6:1; Wis. 6:15; Heb. 6:6/Wis. 6:9, 18, 7:27; Heb. 6:20/Wis. 12:8; Heb. 7:16/Wis. 1:3, 5:23, 7:25, 12:15, 17; Heb. 7:26/Wis. 3:13, 4:2; Heb. 8:2, 9, 11/Wis. 9:8; Heb. 8:8/Wis. 11:14; Heb. 8:1/Wis. 18:24; Heb. 9:2-6/Wis. 13:4; Heb. 10:1/Wis. 9:25; Heb. 10:19/Wis. 5:1; Heb. 10:36/Wis. 13:6; Heb. 11:1/Wis. 16:21; Heb. 11:5/Wis. 4:10; Heb. 12:6-11/Wis. 3:5; Heb. 12:10/Wis. 18:7; Heb. 12:17/Wis. 12:10; Heb. 12:28/Wis. 4:10; Heb. 13:7/Wis. 2:17; Heb. 13:20/Wis. 13:21, 16:13; Heb. 13:21/Wis. 4:10, 9:10. Cf. Plumptre, "The Writings of Apollos," 332–34; A. Nairne, *The Epistle to the Hebrews* (Cambridge: University Press, 1922), cx–cxii; Spicq, *L'Épitre aux Hébreux*, 1:42; *The Book of Wisdom with Introduction and Notes*, ed. A. T. S. Goodrick (London: Rivingtons, 1913), 8. Note also the similarities between Sir. 24:1-29, Wis. 10:1-21, and Heb. 11 (cf. P. Enns, "Wisdom of Solomon and Biblical Interpretation in the Second Temple Period," in J. I. Packer and Sven K. Soderlund, eds., *The Way of Wisdom: Essays in Honor of Bruce K. Waltke* (Grand Rapids: Zondervan, 2000), 223, 225n.17. P. Ellingworth notes Wis. 7:27 as a text the author of Hebrews certainly employed in writing Heb. 3:4 (in addition to Heb. 1:3/Wis. 7:26) and points to the commonality between Heb. 4:12 and Wis. 7:22—8:11 (esp. 7:23, 24) (*The Epistle to the Hebrews: A Commentary on the Greek Text* [Grand Rapids: Eerdmans, 1993], 205, 261. F. F. Bruce thinks that Heb. 2:14 indicates that the author belonged to the circle out of which Wisdom (he has in mind here: Wis. 1:13, 14 and 2:23, 24) earlier arose (*The Epistle to the Hebrews* [Grand Rapids: Eerdmans, 1990], 85–86). The interest in these parallels, evident in earlier works, does not seem to have continued in the more recent studies on Hebrews.

83. *Haer.* IV.5.3; IV.25.1 (SC100.2: 432.62; 704.7); V.32.1 (SC153: 396.8-9 [Heb. 6:12; 11:39]); V.32.2 (SC153: 400.33[Heb. 11:13], 42 [Heb. 11:8-9]). Cf Orbe, *Teología de San Ireneo*, 3: 356 [Heb. 6:12; 11:39], 367 [Heb. 11:13], 372 [Heb. 11:8-9]; Roberts and Rambaut, ANF 1: 561, n.6. The SC retroversion has κομίζω rather than ἀπολαμβάνω as in Heb. 11:39. Despite the difference, Orbe still says that "It is very probable that Irenaeus was inspired by Heb. 11:39" (Orbe, *Teología de San Ireneo*, 3: 356). Orbe also draws our attention to Heb. 4:1; 6:12; and 10:36 as also parallel texts to the concepts developed in *Haer.* V.32.1-2 (Orbe, *Teología de San Ireneo*, 3: 356).

84. *Haer.* V.3.2 (SC153: 44.32). Orbe believes Eph 1:19-20 or Rom 8:11 probably influence Irenaeus here rather than Heb. 11:19, apparently because, as he notes, Irenaeus doesn't consider Hebrews to be from Paul's hand and the current chapter, in his mind, is controlled by that apostle's witness (*Teología de San Ireneo*, 1: 180). However, the tone of Irenaeus's discussion pleads for the Hebrew text. He is responding to those who do not have faith in the resurrection and who reject it (cf. V.2.2 and V.3.2). This makes Abraham's faith in the face of circumstances a perfect testimony to these false teachers.

85. *Haer.* III.1.2 (SC211: 24.31).

86. *Haer.* III. pref. (SC211: 20.26-37).

87. *Haer.* III.pref. (SC211: 20.28-30).

88. *Haer.* III.5.3 (SC211: 62.76-77).

89. J. Vansina, *Oral Tradition as History* (Madison: University of Wisconsin, 1985), 147. Emphasis added.

90. Ibid., 190.

91. Ibid.

92. W. A.Graham, *Beyond the Written Word: Oral Aspects of Scripture in the History of Religions* (Cambridge: Cambridge University, 1987), 112.

93. I am grateful to Fr. Denis Farkasfalvy for bringing this insight on Tertullian to my attention.

94. The critical edition of *Adversus Marcionem* consulted was *Contre Marcion*, ed., trans., and annot. R. Braun, Sources chrétiennes 368 (book 2) and 399 (book 3) (Paris: Cerf, 1991, 1994). See *Adv. Marc.* II.9.7 (SC 368: 68.51); III.14.3, 7 (SC 399: 132.16-18; 134.42-43). E. Evans seems to concur on the allusion to Heb. 1:14 (*Tertullian Adversus Marcionem Books 1-3* [Oxford: Clarendon, 1972], 112, n.9.a). Braun also see possible allusions to Heb. 1:7 and 10:39 (*Adv. Marc.* II.8.2; II.18.1) , but these seem to be citations of the Old Testament

passages of Ps. 103:4 and Deut. 32:35 (SC 368: 62.14-15; 112.8-9) that Hebrews also cites. *Biblia Patristica*, 1:520–25 and the website index, *BiblIndex: Index of Biblical Quotations and Allusions in Early Christian Literature*, http://www.biblindex.mom.fr/index.php?option=com_content&view=article&id=6&Itemid=8&lang =en list the following references to Hebrews within *Adv. Marc.*: Heb. 1:2; 1:13-14; 2:9; 4:12; 4:15; 5:5-9; 7:17; 8:8-12; 10:30 (V.4.2; II.9.7; IV.21.12; III.14.3,7; V.14.1; V.9.9; V.11.4; IV.14.12). The critical edition of *Adv. Val.* consulted was *Contre les Valentiniens*, ed., trans., and annot. J.-C. Fredouille, Sources chrétiennes 280 (Paris: Cerf, 1980). For Tertullian's defense of Paul's epistles without Hebrews, see *Adv. Marc.* V.1-21.

95. On Tertullian and Hebrews, see J. F. Jansen, "Tertullian and the New Testament," *Second Century* 2 (1982): 192–93.

6. Irenaeus's Contribution to Early Christian Interpretation of the Song of Songs

1. This theme is explored at length in Elizabeth A. Clark, *Reading Renunciation: Asceticism and Scripture in Early Christianity* (Princeton: Princeton University Press, 1999).

2. There is, additionally, a lengthy Armenian fragment of chapters 24 and 25 and several Greek fragments from a paraphrase of Hippolytus's exegetical works. For a brief introduction and Latin translation, see Georges Garitte, *Traités d'Hippolyte sur David et Goliath, sur le Cantique des cantiques et sur l'Antéchrist: version géorgienne*, CSCO 263 (Louvain, 1965), esp. i–iv.

3. The evidence for an early work (or works) on the Song comes from a letter of Jerome and the *Philocalia* of Basil of Caesarea and Gregory of Nyssa. There is, however, a slight discrepancy as to whether Origen composed one or two "tomes": contrast Jerome's *"scripsit . . . in Canticum Canticorum libros X et alios tomos II, quos super scripsit in adulescenti"* (*ep.* 33.4; CSEL 54: 257) with the claim in the *Philocalia*, ἐκ τοῦ εἰς τὸ Ἄσμα μικροῦ τόμου ὃν ἐν τῇ νεότητι ἔγραψεν (7.1; SC 302: 326). The *Commentary*, so Eusebius tells us, is in ten books, with the first five written in Athens, and the remaining five completed upon his return to Caesarea (*HE* VI.32.1-2). This would place its composition around the years 245–247. Regarding the *Homilies*, Jerome had access to two alone, and there is no other mention of them in Antiquity that would indicate how many Origen delivered. It is traditionally estimated that they were delivered in the years following 245, on the basis of Eusebius's remark that Origen did not allow his διαλέξεις to be taken down by stenographers until he was older than sixty years of age (*HE* VI.36.1). J. Christopher King, *Origen on the Song of Songs as the Spirit of Scripture: The Bridegroom's Perfect Marriage Song* (Oxford: OUP, 2005), 10–11, in my view, successfully refutes the equation of διαλέξεις with homilies, and argues persuasively for placing his preaching on the Song several years before the composition of the *Commentary*, to the years 241–242.

4. *Hom. in Cant.* 1.1; *Comm. In Cant.* praef.

5. His commentary is now lost, but Jerome makes mention of it in *De viris illustribus* 74 (PL 23:683B-C): "These are his writings: Commentaries on Genesis, Exodus, Leviticus, Isaiah, Ezekiel, Habakuk, Ecclesiastes, Song of Songs, and the Apocalypse of John, a work against all heresies, and many others."

6. Gregory of Nyssa, *In Cancticum Canticorum*, in W. Jaeger, ed., *Gregorii Nysseni Opera* 6 (Leiden: Brill, 1986); Nilus of Ancyra, *Commentarius in Canticum Canticorum*, in M.-G. Guérard, ed., *Nil d'Ancyre. Commentaire sur le Cantique des Cantiques* (SC 403; Paris: Cerf, 1994); Theodoret of Cyrrhus, *Explanatio in Canticum Canticorum*, in *Opera Omnia* (PG 81: 27–214); Gregory of Elvira, *Tractatus de Epithalamio*, in E. Schulz-Flügel (ed.), *Gregorius Eliberritanus: Epithalamium sive Explanatio in Canticis Canticorum* (Freiburg: Herder, 1994); Apponius, *In Canticum Canticorum Expositio*, in B. de Vregille and L. Neyrand (ed.), *Commentaire sur le Cantique des Cantiques*, SC 420 (Paris: Cerf, 1997).

7. Looking back over the complex and contested history of Song interpretation, William Phipps, "The Plight of the Song of Songs," *JAAR* 42/1 (1974): 82, remarks, "It is one of the pranks of history that a poem so obviously about hungry passion has caused so much perplexity and has provoked such a plethora of bizarre interpretations." He laments that the obvious, plain meaning of the Song has been so thoroughly obscured by centuries of misguided interpreters, beginning with Origen, whose fear of the erotic forced them to "convert" this "passionate paean . . . into what was thought to be harmless mysticism" (87). In the same vein, Harold Rowley, "The Interpretation of the Song of Songs," in *The Servant of the Lord and Other Essays on the Old Testament* (London: Lutterworth, 1952), 232, remarks, "The view I adopt finds in it nothing but what it appears to be lovers' songs, expressing their delight in one another. . . . All other views find in the Song what they bring to it." Indeed, even scholars working self-consciously from a "post-modern" perspective have been influenced by this rhetoric of repression, most notably New Testament scholar Stephen Moore (Stephen D. Moore, "The Song of Songs in the History of Sexuality," *Church History* 69, no. 2 [2000]) in his recent queer reading of

the Christian history of Song interpretation. He playfully argues that male exegetes tried to avoid the Song's sexuality but unwittingly embraced it, only not as an erotic encounter between a woman and a man, but rather, because they took upon themselves the role of Bride, as one between two men.

8. *HE* VI.8.

9. Moore, "History of Sexuality," 332.

10. King, *Marriage Song*, 89–133.

11. King, *Marriage Song*, 51–56, lucidly demonstrates that Origen's "carefully constructed terminology points to a real distinction between *gramma*—the fixity, structure, and form of the written text—and *sôma*—the fixed and limited understanding found in, and in a sense imputed to, the *gramma* by the materialistic *habitus* that is our mind's second nature" (55). The Song thus has a "literal" sense, but the spiritual meaning is immediately and entirely transparent to it.

12. King, *Marriage Song*, 126.

13. King spends but three pages linking Origen's Song exegesis to trajectories in first- and second-century Christian thought (1–3).

14. *Allegorical Readers and Cultural Revision in Ancient Alexandria* (Los Angeles: University of California Press, 1992), 7–8, is worth quoting at length: "Consequently, although the 'literal sense' has often been thought of as an inherent quality of a literary text that gives it a specific and invariant character . . . the phrase is simply an honorific title given to a kind of meaning that is culturally expected and automatically recognized by readers. It is the 'normal,' 'commonsensical' meaning, the product of a conventional, customary reading. The 'literal sense' thus stems from a community's generally unself-conscious decision to adopt and promote a certain kind of meaning, rather than from its recognition of a text's inherent and self-evident sense."

15. For the Apostolic Fathers, I follow the Greek text of Michael Holmes, *Apostolic Fathers: Greek Texts and English Translations of their Writings* (Grand Rapids: Baker, 1992). Translations are my own.

16. *2 Clem.* 14.2 (Holmes, 120).

17. *2 Clem.* 14.3 (Holmes, 120).

18. Paul Parvis, "*2 Clement* and the Christian Homily," in *The Writings of the Apostolic Fathers*, ed. Paul Foster (London: T&T Clark, 2007), 39.

19. *Herm.* 1.2 (Holmes, 336).

20. *Herm.* 1.8 (Holmes, 344).

21. I follow the Greek text of Philippe Bobichon, *Justin Martyr: Dialogue avec Trypho, Vol. 1* (Fribourg: Academic, 2003). Translations are my own.

22. *Dial.* 126.1 (Bobichon, 522).

23. *Dial.* 63.4 (Bobichon, 354).

24. *Haer.* I.7.1 (SC 264: 100).

25. *Haer.* I.8.4 (SC 264: 128).

26. *Haer.* V.9.1 (SC 153: 106).

27. *Haer.* V.9.2. (SC 153: 110).

28. *Haer.* V.9.4 (SC 153: 116).

29. *Haer.* IV.20.12 (SC 100[2]: 668-70).

30. *Haer.* IV.20.12 (SC 100[2]: 670).

31. *Haer.* IV.20.12 (SC 100[2]: 670). Cf. 1 Cor. 7:14.

32. *Haer.* IV.20.12 (SC 100[2]: 670). Cf. Rom. 11:17.

33. *Haer.* 4.20.12 (SC 100[2]: 670).

34. *Dem.* 94 (SC 406: 209). Translations are based upon the Latin retroversion provided by A. Rousseau.

35. *Dem.* 94 (SC 406: 210).

36. *Dem.* 94 (SC 406: 210).

37. Origen, *Hom. In Cant.* 1.2 (SC 37: 63): "For how long will my spouse send kisses to me through Moses, will he send kisses through the prophets? I wish to touch his mouth—would that he come, would that he descend."

38. *Comm. In Cant.* 2.1.4 (SC 375: 262): "*quae paternae eruditionis non habeat claritatem.*"

39. *Comm. In Cant.* 2.1.21 (SC 375: 272).

40. *Comm. In Cant.* 2.1.22 (SC 375: 272).

41. *Comm. In Cant.* 2.1.23 (SC 375: 272).

7. The Man with No Name: Who Is the Elder in Irenaeus's *Adversus haereses IV?*

1. Charles Hill, *From the Lost Teaching of Polycarp*, WUNT 186 (Tübingen: Mohr Siebeck, 2006).

2. Ibid., 15.

3. ANF 1:568.

4. For the following, cf. Norbert Brox, *Offenbarung, Gnosis und gnostischer Mythos bei Irenäus von Lyon* (Salzburg: Anton Pustet, 1966), 146–48. Brox is strikingly missing from Hill's index of authors.

5. *Haer.* III.34.

6. Cf. Paul Foster, Review "Charles Hill, *From the Lost Teaching of Polycarp*," WUNT 186, Tübingen: Mohr Siebeck, 2006, *Expository Times* 118 (2006): 78–79.

7. Hill, *Lost Teaching*, 13.

8. Polycarp's *Second Letter to the Philippians* has also often been considered to contain anti-Marcionite teaching; however, there is no specifically anti-Marcionite element to be found in the text (cf. Sebastian Moll, *The Arch-Heretic Marcion* [Tübingen: Mohr Siebeck, 2010]).

9. Cf. Adolf von Harnack, *Chronologie der altchristlichen Literatur bis Eusebius I* (Leipzig: Hinrichs, 1897), 338, n.2; Friedrich Loofs, *Theophilus von Antiochien Adversus Marcionem und die anderen theologischen Quellen bei Irenaeus*, TU 46/2 (Leipzig: Hinrichs, 1930), 101–13; Gerhard May, "Marcion in Contemporary Views: Results and Open Questions," *Second Century* 6 (1987/88): 129–51, at 133 (= *Gesammelte Aufsätze*, 17).

10. Antonio Orbe ("Ecclesia, sal terrae según san Ireneo," *RSR* 60 [1972]: 220, n.8) tried to show that certain aspects of the elder's argumentation make it very unlikely that it was directed against Marcion, but his reasons for this view are most questionable. The first two may suffice to demonstrate this. Orbe claims that in an anti-Marcionite text one would not find frequent references to the Old Testament and to the Gospel of Matthew as both documents are of no value to an "auténtico discípulo de Marción"; but the whole point of this argument is to defend the Old Testament against Marcion's attacks. How is anyone supposed to do that without referring to it? Has Orbe not considered Tertullian's work against Marcion, in which the Carthaginian also constantly refers to the Old Testament in order to refute his opponent? To say nothing about the fact that it is not true that the Old Testament would not have any value to Marcion. This is true for Matthew's Gospel, but I am unable to see why a Christian opponent of Marcion's should not use it in an argument against him. Orbe's second point is that the allegorical exegesis would not be used against Marcion since he refused to accept it; but this is exactly the reason why! To point out the allegorical meaning of scriptural passages is one of the most common ways to refute the arch-heretic; cf. for example Origen, *De princ.* II.5.2: "But they [the Marcionites] see these things in this way, because they have not understood to hear anything beyond the letter."

11. Cf. *Hom. Ies.* XII.3.

12. For the problem of the Latin *in diminutione*, see Adelin Rousseau, *Irénée de Lyon: Contre les hérésies, Livre IV* (Paris: Cerf, 1965), 1: 264.

13. *Indocti et audaces adhuc etiam et impudentes inveniuntur omnes qui, propter transgressionem eorum qui olim fuerunt et propter plurimorum indictoaudientiam, alterum quidem aiunt illorum fuisse Deum, et hunc esse mundi Fabricatorem et esse in diminutione, alterum vero a Christo traditum Patrem, et hunc esse qui sit ab unoquoque eorum mente conceptus* (my translation).

14. Cf. *Haer.* I.5.1-2.

15. Cf. *Haer.* I.6.1.

16. *Adv. Marc.* II.14.4.

17. *Adv. Marc.* II.20.

18. Hill has correctly perceived these two different kinds of arguments in the elder's teaching, calling the reproaches against certain Old Testament individuals "the argument from God's friends" and the reproaches against the Old Testament God "the argument from God's enemies" (Hill, *Lost Teaching*, 33). He did, however, mistakenly assume that they were both directed against Marcion.

19. *Haer.* IV.28.1.

20. Rousseau, *Contre les hérésies, Livre IV*, 1: 265. I am generally a little skeptical as far as the reconstruction of the originally Greek text of *Adversus haereses* by the *Sources chrétiennes* edition is concerned; however, the Latin *contrario opponentes* is so close to Tertullian's wording *contrariae oppositiones* (*Adv. Marc.* I.19.4) that I believe it is justified to assume the above mentioned allusion.

21. There is a discrepancy between *Haer.* IV.27.1, where the Latin translation speaks of an elder who heard from those who had seen the apostles, and IV.32.1, where the elder is described as *discipulus apostolorum*. For a long time there was a scholarly consensus that the first notion was more precise and that the second was to be understood in a looser sense, until in 1904 a sixth-century Armenian translation was found in which IV.27.1 also described the elder as an immediate disciple of the apostles (cf. Hill, *Lost Teaching*, 9). The *Sources chrétiennes* (1965) have adapted to the Armenian translation of the passage, whereas the *Fontes Christiani* version by N. Brox (Freiburg: Herder, 1995) prefers the Latin version.

22. Cf. Brox, *Offenbarung*, 147, n.104.

23. For a collection of passages see ibid., 152.

24. Hill, *Lost Teaching*, 23–24.

25. In my presentation of this paper at the Edinburgh conference, I compared this situation to a game of *Clue* (or *Cluedo*). At the beginning of each game, the murderer is randomly picked from a selection of six persons. The players do not know who it is, but (and that is the big difference compared to the historian trying to identify an anonymous source) they know it must be one out of the six.

8. The Man Who Needed No Introduction: A Response to Sebastian Moll

1. I cannot say I am yet convinced by the proposal. This element may not occur in other writers, but all of them are later than the testimony of Irenaeus's elder, who was involved with a very early form of Marcion's teaching, perhaps even an unpublished form that circulated in Asia Minor before Marcion moved to Rome. In any event, I have argued that this element of the polemic against the God of the Old Testament did predate Marcion (see Charles E. Hill, *From the Lost Teaching of Polycarp*, WUNT 186 [Tübingen: Mohr Siebeck, 2006], 29–30, 39, 67).

2. See Hill, *Lost Teaching*, 29–30, 39, 67, cf. 88.

3. The lines quoted by Moll from *Haer.* IV.27.4, cited to show that there was some element of polemic against Valentinianism in the presbyter's teaching, actually do not come from one of the quotations of the presbyter but are Irenaeus's own words. I would have some quibbles with Moll's translation, which seems to overplay the possible traces of Valentinianism. But if any reference to Valentinianism does exist there, it probably came from Irenaeus and not from the presbyter, as there appears to be nothing in the material attributed to him that is specifically aimed at Valentinianism. But even if there were, this would not defeat the proposal. For elsewhere Irenaeus says that Polycarp encountered some followers of both Marcion and Valentinus during his sojourn in Rome in the time of Anicetus, and persuaded them to return to the church (*Haer.* III.3.4). This most likely indicates that, at least according to Irenaeus, Polycarp did know something about Valentinianism.

4. This is one element I believe can help us determine the relative sequence of the *Letter to Florinus* and *Haer.* IV.27-32. Irenaeus refers to Florinus as serving "in the royal court" and then in the *Haer.* IV refers to Christians who are "in the royal court." These are the only two times we know of when Irenaeus uses the phrase. In the latter instance, he seems to playing on the irony of certain Christians who complain about the supposed immorality of God spoiling the Egyptians while at the same time these Christians, who inhabit the royal court, live off of what belongs to Caesar. The comment only functions this way, however, if it was written after the letter to Florinus.

5. On the text-critical issues, see Hill, *Lost Teaching*, 8–11.

6. The passages mentioned by Norbert Brox, *Offenbarung, Gnosis und gnostischer Mythos bei Irenäus von Lyon* (Salzburg: Anton Pustet, 1966), 152, are II.22.5; V.5.1; V.33.3; V.36.2; *Flor.* (Eusebius, *HE* V.20.4); *Proof* 3).

7. In addition, there are two places where he speaks in a more general way about preceding elders, *Flor.* (Eusebius, *HE* V.20.4), and *Proof* 3, in each of which the group could have included Polycarp.

8. See, e.g., C. K. Barrett, *The Gospel according to St. John: An Introduction with Commentary and Notes on the Greek* Text (London: SPCK, 1965), 88, "On his own showing Irenaeus was young and Polycarp very old when Irenaeus heard some of Polycarp's sermons; and while one may admit the truth of Irenaeus's views on youthful memory as regards vividness, they may well be questioned as regards accuracy"; Raymond E. Brown, *The Gospel according to John (I–XII)*, Anchor Bible (Garden City: Doubleday, 1966), xc, "the fact that Irenaeus would have been very young at the time he claims to have known Polycarp makes confusion at least a possibility"; George R. Beasely-Murray, *John*, WBC 36 (Dallas: Word, 1987), lxviii, "There is no reason to doubt his veracity in recounting to Florinus his memories of Polycarp, but there is ground for questioning his understanding as a boy of Polycarp's references to 'John.'"

9. It is hard to miss the cynicism when it is said that Irenaeus "boasts that he had sat at the feet of the famous bishop Polycarp of Smyrna (ca. A.D. 100–167), even though he was still a child at the time"; "Irenaeus . . . acquainted,

as he claims, with the great bishop while still a child . . ." (Helmut Koester, *Introduction to the New* Testament, vol. 2 *History and Literature of Early Christianity* [Berlin: de Gruyter, 1982, 2000], 10; 309).

10. Septuagint: παιδάριον μικρὸν.

11. In chapter 104, Philo seems to acquiesce to the ten-age scheme of Solon, but elsewhere employs both a seven-age scheme (*On the Cherubim* 2.114; *On Joseph* 127, but with varying terminology) and a five-age scheme (*On the Eternity of the World* 60). In this latter scheme, the stage of παῖς is succeeded by that of μειράκιον.

12. See Valdis Leinieks, *The City of Dionysos: A Study of Euripides' Bakchai*, Beiträge zur Altertumskunde 88 (Stuttgart: Teubner, 1996), 199–200. Leinieks summarizes, "Although the words used and the exact age limits vary, it is clear that a scheme of four age-classes is implicit in the vocabulary of fifth-century [B.C.E.] Greek. The words most frequently used for these four age-classes are: παῖδες 'boys,' νεανίσκοι 'youths,' ἄνδρες 'men,' and γέροντες 'old men'" (*City*, 201). Leinieks identifies also a three-class scheme (παῖδες, ἄλκιμοι νεανίαι [strong young men], *old men*) used by Plutarch, with some flexibility in terminology, in Sophocles, Pindar, and Plato, which essentially collapsed the two middle ages of the four-class scheme into one (*City*, 204).

13. Thomas Wiedemann, *Adults and Children in the Roman* Empire (New Haven: Yale University Press, 1989), 119.

14. Ibid., 119.

15. Leinieks, *City*, 201. See also Mark Golden, *Children and Childhood in Classical Athens* (Baltimore: Johns Hopkins University Press, 1990), 4, who says that παῖδες were "boys before their admission to their deme at the age of seventeen or eighteen, girls before their marriage" (cf. 15).

16. Wiedemann, *Adults and Children*, 114.

17. Beryl Rawson, *Children and Childhood in Roman Italy* (Oxford: Oxford University Press, 2003), 142.

18. Mary Harlow and Ray Laurence, *Growing Up and Growing Old in Ancient Rome: A Life Course Approach* (New York: Routledge, 2002), 67.

19. Harlow and Laurence, *Growing Up*, 68. See also Wiedemann, *Adults and Children*, 116, "What marriage did for a girl, the adult toga did for a boy: it turned them into adults with an individual personality." It was at this important juncture in a boy's life that his name was recorded in the list of citizens in the *tabularium*, the state record office located in the temple of Saturn (Wiedemann, *Adults and Children*, 116). Such ceremonies took place in the provinces as well. Cicero had his nephew, about sixteen years of age, undergo the ceremony at Laodicea in 50 C.E. (*Att.* 6.1.12).

20. Diodorus Siculus, *Library of History* 1.54.5, says that the fellow warriors of Sesoösis "had striven after a reputation for valour from their youth (ἐκ παίδων)." Diodorus also speaks of hereditary warriors who "inasmuch as they become zealous students of warfare from their boyhood up (ἐκ παίδων) . . . turn out to be invincible by reason of their daring and skill" (1.73.90). Aeschines, *Speeches* 1.80, says members of the Lacedaemonian council of elders were "men of sobriety from boyhood (ἐκ παίδων) to old age." In each case, the subjects only began the activity in question while boys; the activity did not cease when they ceased to be boys.

21. Gen. 37:2 LXX uses the word νεόν for Joseph at seventeen. The same word is used for Moses' assistant, the young man Joshua son of Nun in Ex. 33:11.

22. Anthony A. Barrett, *Caligula: The Corruption of Power* (New Haven: Yale University Press, 1989), 75.

23. Erasmus, followed by later editors, at II.24.4 inverted *puer* and *parvulus*. As there appears to be no manuscript support for this change of the order, it is most likely a slip.

24. So Rousseau and Doutreleau, SC 293, 286.

25. *Quia autem xxx annorum aetas prima indolis est iuuenis et extenditur usque ad quadragesimum annum, omnis quilibet confitebitur; a quadragesimo autem et quinquagesimo anno declinat iam in aetatem seniorem.* The French translation of Rousseau and Doutreleau is "Car, tout le monde en conviendra, l'âge de trente ans est celui d'un homme encore jeune, et cette jeunesse s'étend jusqu'à la quarantième année: ce n'est qu'à partir de la quarantième, voire de la cinquantième année qu'on descend vers la vieillesse."

26. This is apparently how Eusebius understood the expression, for, referring to this passage he says, "we have learned that he [Irenaeus] had been a hearer of Polycarp at the age of a youth (κατὰ τὴν νέαν . . . ἡλικίαν)"; this would most naturally indicate a young man and not a παῖς. Compare what Leinieks, *City*, 205, says about a νεανίας in fourth-century Athens: "It is reasonable to infer . . . that the upper age limit of a νεανίας was the same as the upper age limit of an ἀνήρ, that is the age of the end of active military service, or fifty. A νεανίας was then someone between the ages of eighteen and fifty."

27. *Lives of the Sophists*, 523, from W. C. Wright, *Philostratus and Eunapius. The Lives of the Sophists*, LCL (Cambridge: Harvard University Press, 1968).

28. See Hill, *Lost Teaching*, 57–65.

29. Ulric Neisser and Lisa K. Libby, "Remembering Life Experiences," in Endel Tulving and Fergus I. M. Craik, eds., *The Oxford Handbook of Memory* (Oxford: Oxford University Press, 2000), 317. They are citing the title and conclusion of the work of D. C. Rubin et al., "Things Learned Early in Adulthood are Remembered Best," *Memory and Cognition* 26 (1998): 3–19. In this study, "early in adulthood" means from about age ten to thirty.

30. Rubin et al., "Things Learned," 7. They cite a 1991 study by W. R. Mackavey, J. E. Malley, and A. J. Stewart, "Remembering Autobiographically Consequential Experiences: Content Analysis of Psychologists' Accounts of their Lives," *Psychology and Aging* 6 (1991): 50–59, that found that "even for these carefully composed, well-contemplated intellectual autobiographies, events and experiences from early adulthood, and especially from the college years, were mentioned most often" (8). In the words of the authors, "The greatest concentration of memories for our subjects did not occur during the recent time of their lives, but rather some fifty or so years earlier" ("Remembering," 57).

31. Rubin, *et al.*, "Things Learned," 16.

32. Ibid.

33. For example, Asher Koriat, "Control Processes in Remembering," in Tulving and Craik, *The Oxford Handbook of Memory*, 338, "as far as intentional retrieval is concerned, it would seem that practice retrieving an item from memory is what makes retrieval of that item more automatic."

34. It does not appear to me that Irenaeus stayed up nights looking for opportunities to throw Polycarp's name around in order to bolster his arguments or adorn his own reputation. In the entire five books of *Against Heresies*, he mentions Polycarp by name in only two places. One is the section III.3.4 and the other is a passing reference in V.33.4 where he merely says that Papias was "a companion of Polycarp." He does not mention Polycarp at all in his *Proof of the Apostolic Preaching*, though he does speak there of the importance of following the elders. He mentions Polycarp, of course, in his letter to Florinus, but both he and Florinus had known the man; and he mentions Polycarp in his letter to Victor on the paschal controversy, when he informs Victor of what happened when one of his predecessors in Rome was visited by Polycarp and the two bishops disagreed on paschal observance. In this letter, at least in the fragment we have, Irenaeus does not mention that he personally knew Polycarp (doubtless Victor knew that already). There are several instances in which Irenaeus cites an older Christian teacher (I.praef.2; I.13.3; I.15.6; III.17.4; IV.41.2; V.17.4), one or more of which might be a reference to Polycarp (see Hill, *Lost Teaching*, 68–71). But while his respect for this teacher, or these teachers, is clear, in none of these places does Irenaeus give the teacher a name. It is as if Irenaeus thought name dropping would somehow be unbecoming. And Irenaeus's practice is not so different from that of other students who had revered Christian teachers in the second century. Clement of Alexandria speaks of Pantaenus as a renowned teacher, but we have next to nothing that he passed in his master's name (in what survives; the lost *Hypotyposeis* may have been different). The same may be said of Tatian and his teacher Justin.

35. The back-referencing continues with even greater specificity in the next paragraph, IV.32.2, where he reminds the reader of the apostles' teaching of one God revealed in both testaments, "as I have proved in the third book from the very teaching of the apostles."

9. Irenaeus and the Noncanonical Gospels

1. The edition of the *Adversus haereses* that is used as the basis for the discussion in this paper is Irénée de Lyon, *Contre les Hérésies*, édition critique par A. Rousseau, L. Doutreleau (B. Hemmerdinger, C. Mercier), Sources chrétiennes 100 (2 vols.), 152, 153, 210, 211, 263, 264, 293, 294 (Paris: Cerf, 1965–1982). However, the English translations used throughout are based on that by J. Keble in the *Library of Fathers* (1872), and by A. Roberts and W. H. Rambaut in the *Ante-Nicene Fathers* (Edinburgh, 1868–1869, reprint Grand Rapids: Eerdmans: 1979).

2. The existence of the text of the *Gospel of Judas* was announced to the scholarly world previously at the Eighth Congress of the International Association for Coptic Studies in Paris on July 1, 2004.

3. See R. Kasser, M. Meyer, and G. Wurst, eds., "The Gospel of Judas," with additional commentary by Bart Ehrman, *National Geographic* (May 2006): 78–95 (Washington, DC: National Geographic, 2006); H. Krosney, *The Lost Gospel: The Quest for the Gospel of Judas Iscariot* (Washington, DC: National Geographic, 2006).

4. The Coptic text is available in two critical editions of Codex Tchacos: J. Brankaer and H.-G. Bethge, eds., *Codex Tchacos: Texte und Analysen*, Texte und Untersuchungen zur Geschichte der altchristlichen Literatur 161 (Berlin: de Gruyter, 2007); and R. Kasser, G. Wurst, M. Meyer, and F. Gaudard, eds., *The Gospel of Judas*

together with the Letter of Peter to Philip, James, and a Book of Allogenes from Codex Tchacos: Critical Edition (Washington, DC: National Geographic, 2007).

5. A. D. DeConick, *The Thirteenth Apostle: What the Gospel of Judas Really Says* (London: T&T Clark, 2007).

6. R. Kasser, M. Meyer, and G. Wurst, eds., *The Gospel of Judas*, 130–31.

7. DeConick, *The Thirteenth Apostle*, 125.

8. For an assessment of these options see the brief comments in P. Foster, *The Apocryphal Gospels—A Very Short Introduction* (Oxford: Oxford University Press, 2009), 122–23.

9. DeConick, *The Thirteenth Apostle*, 174.

10. This formulation is chosen not simply to reflect the fact that in antiquity no two manuscripts of the same text were identical; that is self-evident. The word "version" is more deliberately chosen and used in line with New Testament textual criticism to denote the fact that whereas the version of the text found in Codex Tchacos was written in Coptic, the version known to Irenaeus may have been written in a different language, most plausibly Greek.

11. If this document is identical with the text that is given this name in the Nag Hammadi corpus, it is interesting to note a debate in the secondary literature concerning the authorship of this text as either being due to a disciple or a group of followers as Irenaeus suggests, or whether it was largely composed by Valentinus himself—which would then mean that Irenaeus may have been incorrect, or even that the two texts are not identical. Attridge and MacRae note that "On the basis of literary and conceptual affinities between this text and the exiguous fragments of Valentinus, some scholars have suggested that the Gnostic teacher was himself the author. That remains a distinct possibility, although it cannot be definitely established." H.W. Attridge and George W. MacRae, "The Gospel of Truth (I,3 and XII,2)," in James M. Robinson, ed., *The Nag Hammadi Library in English*, rev. ed. (Leiden: Brill, 1996), 38. Among those who have identified Valentinus as the author, see H. C. Puech and G. Quispel, "Les écrits gnostiques du Codex Jung," *VC* 8 (1954): 22–38. However, many subsequent commentators have challenged this identification. See C. Markschies, *Valentinus Gnosticus? Untersuchungen zur valentinianischen Gnosis mit einem Kommentar zu den Fragmenten Valentins*, WUNT 65 (Tübingen: Mohr Siebeck, 1992), 339–65.

12. E. Thomassen, *The Spiritual Seed: The Church of the "Valentinians,"* NHMS 60 (Leiden: Brill, 2006), 147.

13. Attridge and MacRae, "The Gospel of Truth (I,3 and XII,2)," 38.

14. Ibid.

15. Thomassen, *The Spiritual Seed*, 147.

16. Pearson notes that in this text the "Decad (ten aeons) is projected from Word and Life, the Duodecad (twelve aeons) from Man and Church." Birger A. Pearson, *Ancient Gnosticism: Tradition and Literature* (Minneapolis: Fortress Press, 2007), 183.

17. C. Schmidt, ed., *The Books of Jeu and the Untitled Text in the Bruce Codex*, trans. V. MacDermot (Leiden: Brill, 1978).

18. On the use of number symbolism in Jewish and early Christian texts, see Reinharts Staats, "Ogdoas als ein Symbol für die Auferstehung," *VC* 26 (1972): 29–52; Francois Bovon, "Names and Numbers in Early Christianity," *NTS* 47 (2001): 267–88.

19. The *Infancy Gospel of Thomas* occurs in at least four major different recensions. This problematizes making unqualified statements about "the text" of the *Infancy Gospel of Thomas*. For a recent overview of the issues surrounding these recensions, see T. Chartrand-Burke, "The Greek Manuscript Tradition of the *Infancy Gospel of Thomas*," *Apocrypha* 14 (2004): 129–51; and T. Chartrand-Burke, "The *Infancy Gospel of Thomas*," in Paul Foster, ed., *The Non-Canonical Gospels* (London: T&T Clark, 2008), 126–38.

20. For a full discussion of these four recensions, see T. Chartrand-Burke, "The *Infancy Gospel of Thomas*: The Text, Its Origins, and Its Transmission," unpublished PhD dissertation (Graduate Department of Religion, University of Toronto, 2001). Although the dissertation has not been published, it is available at: www.collectionscanada.gc.ca/obj/s4/f2/dsk3/ftp05/NQ63782.pdf.

21. For an extended discussion of these issues, see Andrew Gregory, "Hindrance or Help: Does the Modern Category of 'Jewish-Christian Gospel' Distort Our Understanding of the Texts to Which It Refers?" *JSNT* 28 (2006): 387–413; and Andrew Gregory, "Jewish-Christian Gospels," in Paul Foster, ed., *The Non-Canonical Gospels* (London: T&T Clark, 2008), 54–67.

22. P. Vielhauer and G. Strecker, "Jewish-Christian Gospels," in W. Schneemelcher, ed., *New Testament Apocrypha*, vol. 1, *Gospels and Related Writings*, rev. ed. (Edinburgh: T&T Clark, 1991), 136.

23. Pearson, *Ancient Gnosticism*, 61.

24. C. Schmidt, *Philoktesia: Paul Kleinert zum 70. Geburtstag dargebracht* (Berlin, 1907), 315–36. It is well-known that Schmidt's edition of the Berlin Codex was destroyed due to a burst water pipe at the printing house in 1912. It was not until the publication of Till's edition in 1955 that the text of the Berlin Codex was widely available. W. C. Till, *Die gnostischen Schriften des koptischen Papyrus Berolinensis 8502* (Berlin, 1955).

25. Pearson, *Ancient Gnosticism*, 63.

26. The translation used here is that of Frederik Wisse, "The Apocryphon of John (II,*1*, III,*1*, IV, *1*, and BG 8502, 2)," in James M. Robinson, ed., *The Nag Hammadi Library in English*, rev. ed. (Leiden: Brill, 1996), 104–23.

27. Such apophatic statements may have connections with the Neo-Pythagoreanism philosophy that came to prominence in the first and second centuries.

28. On this central element of the cosmology of the *Apocryphon*, see M. Waldstein, "The Primal Triad in the *Apocryphon of John*," in J. D. Turner and A. McGuire, eds., *The Nag Hammadi Library after Fifty Years: Proceedings of the 1995 Society of Biblical Literature Commemoration* (Leiden: Brill, 1997), 154–87.

29. As Waldstein states, "In the emergence of Barbelo, the Father acts within himself. Barbelo, by contrast, gazes into the light of another, the Father. The Father's light shines actively into her and forms her knowledge so her offspring comes forth 'from the Father' (*Ap. John* 15.14) and can be called his 'son'" (*Ap. John* 15.16). Waldstein, "The Primal Triad in the *Apocryphon of John*," 171.

30. Waldstein, "The Primal Triad in the *Apocryphon of John*," 160.

31. DeConick provides an excellent diagrammatic representation of the way the divine triad was conceptualized in Sethian thought, where the aeons together with the triad form the Sethian pleroma. See DeConick, *The Thirteenth Apostle*, 36.

32. Pearson does not directly suggest that Irenaeus used a shorter form of the *Apocryphon* but he does suggest that a shorter pre-Christian form did exist at one stage. He states,

"When we remove the apocalyptic framework at the beginning and the end, together with the dialogue feature involving ten questions put to Christ by his interlocutor John, we are left with material in which nothing identifiably Christian remains, except for some easily removed glosses. The first part, containing the revelation discourse, may have originally been a separate unit. It is precisely this material that is parallel to Irenaeus's paraphrase of a text used by the Gnostics" (*Against Heresies* 1.29). Pearson, *Ancient Gnosticism*, 63. Despite this assessment, it is debatable whether these "glosses" are so easily removed from the revelation discourse.

33. R. M. Grant, *Irenaeus of Lyons* (Abingdon: Routledge, 1997), 19.

34. On issues surrounding the *Diatessaron* including its dating, see P. Foster, "Tatian," *Expository Times* 120 (2008): 105–18. It is striking that although Irenaeus refers to Tatian (unfavorably) on two occasions (*Haer.* I.28.1; III.23.8), he does not mention the *Diatessaron*. Whether anything can be concluded from this—Irenaeus's ignorance of this work, or that he did not deem it heretical—is mere speculation.

35. Both Klauck and Gregory, in their respective treatments of the *Gospel of the Ebionites*, take the statements in Epiphanius's *Panarion* as the principal source of evidence and draw nothing from the writings of Irenaeus. Hans-Josef Klauck, *Apocryphal Gospels: An Introduction*, trans. Brian McNeil (London: T&T Clark, 2002), 51–54; Andrew Gregory, "Jewish-Christian Gospels," 61–66.

10. Irenaeus, the Scribes, and the Scriptures: Papyrological and Theological Observations from P.Oxy. 3.405

1. See C. E. Hill, *From the Lost Teaching of Polycarp. Identifying Irenaeus' Apostolic Presbyter and the Author of Ad Diognetum* (Tübingen: Mohr Siebeck, 2006), 73–77.

2. This sentence is not present in the Greek preserved by Eusebius (*HE* V.8.5) but occurs in both the Latin and the Armenian, and is judged by Birdsall to be genuine; J. N. Birdsall, "Irenaeus and the Number of the Beast. Revelation 13,18," in A. Denaux, ed., *New Testament Textual Criticism and Exegesis. Festschrift J. Delobel*, BETL 161 (Leuven: Peeters, 2002), 352.

3. The Latin *probatissimus* might be translated "most approved," but here the Greek σπουδαίοις does survive. LSJ, σπουδαῖος, II.2 "*good* of its kind, *excellent . . . the most elaborate, costliest.*"

4. E. G. Turner, *Greek Papyri. An Introduction* (Oxford: Oxford University Press, 1968, 1980), 110, tells us that the Alexandrian scholars had categories of "the better" and "old copies" for their Homeric manuscripts, though "we do not know what significance to attach to these divisions."

5. Among many studies that illustrate this phenomenon, see John Whittaker, "The Value of Indirect Tradition in the Establishment of Greek Philosophical Texts or the Art of Misquotation," in John N. Grant, ed., *Editing Greek and Latin Texts: Papers Given at the Twenty-Third Annual Conference on Editorial Problems, University of Toronto 6–7 November 1987* (New York: AMS, 1989), 63–95; Christopher D. Stanley, *Paul and the Language of Scripture: Citation Technique in the Pauline Epistles and Contemporary Literature* (Cambridge: Cambridge University Press, 1992); Sabrina Inowlocki, "'Neither Adding nor Omitting Anything': Josephus' Promise not to Modify the Scriptures in Greek and Latin Context," *Journal of Jewish Studies* 56/1 (2005): 48–65; idem, *Eusebius and the Jewish Authors: His Citation Technique in an Apologetic Context* (Leiden: Brill, 2006).

6. A. Souter, "The New Testament Text of Irenaeus," in W. Sanday and C. H. Turner, eds., *Nouum Testamentum Sancti Irenaei Episcopi Lugdunensis* (Oxford: Oxford University Press, 1923), cxii.

7. Kurt Aland and Barbara Aland, *The Text of the New Testament: An Introduction to the Critical Editions and to the Theory and Practice of Modern Textual Criticism*, 2nd ed., trans. Erroll F. Rhodes (Grand Rapids: Eerdmans, 1995), 55.

8. The translation of Robert M. Grant, *Irenaeus of Lyons* (New York: Routledge, 1997), 161. Rousseau's translates "conservation." See A. Rousseau, B. Hemmerdinger, C. Mercier, and L. Doutreleau, *Irénée de Lyon: Contre les Hérésies Livre iv*, 2 vols., SC 100, t. I (Paris, 1965). The SC text is *quae pervenit usque ad nos custoditio sine fictione Scripturarum, plenissima tractatio neque additamentum neque ablationem recipiens, et lectio sine falsatione, et secundum Scripturas expositio legitma et diligens et sine periculo et sine blasphemia . . .* Rousseau's retroversion of *custoditio* is diath/rhsiv.

9. B. P. Grenfell and A. S. Hunt, *The Oxyrhynchus Papyri*, Part 3 (London: Egypt Exploration Society, 1903), 10.

10. C. H. Roberts, *Manuscript, Society and Belief in Early Christian Egypt*, The Schweich Lectures of the British Academy 1977 (London, 1979), 23.

11. Ibid., 23, it "certainly comes from the later part of the [second] century." It is a "scholarly" text: "One of the criteria Turner employs for identifying the 'scholarly' texts is the presence of critical signs and other scribal practices" (23–24), and P.Oxy. 405 has them, as we shall see.

12. Ibid., 53. Of course, we really do not know when it reached Oxyrhynchus. Roberts elsewhere suggests that the MS may have been produced in a scriptorium either in Alexandria—perhaps in relation to the school founded by Pantaenus—or in Oxyrhynchus itself (24).

13. Peter R. Rodgers, "Irenaeus and the Text of Matthew 3.16-17," in J. Harold Ellens, ed., *Text and Community: Essays in Memory of Bruce M. Metzger*, vol. 1 (Sheffield: Phoenix, 2007), 51.

14. Grenfell and Hunt apparently judged that these were in the original hand of the scribe. Having examined the papyrus myself (8 August 2008), with the help of the icam iris video enlarger in the conservation department at the Cambridge University Library, I can confirm that this is the case. The *diplai* exhibit the same color and density of ink, the same quality of line as the written text, and they correspond to the scribe's use of space-filling *diplai* in the text at column i, lines 10 and 14.

15. Kathleen McNamee, *Sigla and Select Marginalia in Greek Literary Papyri*, Papyrologica Bruxellensia 26 (Brussels: Fondation Égyptologique Reine Élisabeth, 1992), 9 n.2.

16. Ibid., 15–16; E. G. Turner, *Greek Papyri: An Introduction* (Oxford: Oxford University Press, 1968, 1980), 117. An example of this may be seen in the same Oxyrhynchus Papyri volume that contains the editio princeps of the Irenaeus fragment, in P.Oxy. 445, a fragment of the sixth book of the Iliad from the late second or early third century, thus exactly contemporary with the Irenaeus fragment (*Oxyrhynchus Papyri* 3: 84). The scribe of this copy of the Iliad used *diplai* in the left margin to mark lines for which there existed a corresponding critical scholion. Some of these scholia are written in this manuscript, others are not. Other examples may be seen in Plates I and II in L. D. Reynolds and N. G. Wilson, *Scribes and Scholars: A Guide to the Transmission of Greek and Latin Literature*, second ed. (Oxford: Oxford University Press, 1974). Diogenes Laertius, writing of the copying of Plato's works, says "that the *diple* (>) calls attention to doctrines and opinions characteristic of Plato" (*Lives and Opinions of Eminent Philosophers* III.66). C. D. Yonge, *The Lives and Opinions of Eminent Philosophers* (London: Henry G. Bonn, 1953). Origen adapted two of the Aristarchian signs for his Hexapla, the obelisk to mark passages of the Septuagint not found in the Hebrew, and the asterisk to mark the parts in Hebrew or other Greek versions but not found in the LXX (McNamee, *Sigla*, 12, n.18). See S. P. Brock, "Origen's Aims as a Textual Critic of the Old Testament," *Studia Patristica* X (1970): 215–18.

17. McNamee, *Sigla*, 7.

18. It may be noted that the fourth-century Coptic manuscript given the title Tripartite Tractate was so named by modern scholars because "the text has already been divided into three different parts by means of diples (>>>>>)" (Ismo Dunderberg, "The School of Valentinus," in Antti Marjanen and Petri Luomanen, eds., *A Companion to Second-Century Christian "Heretics,"* Supplements to Vigiliae Christianae 76 (Leiden: Brill, 2005), 86).

19. Noting that 405 contains "a quotation from St. Matthew iii. 16-7 describing the Baptism, which is indicated by wedge-shaped signs in the margin similar to those employed for filling up short lines, e.g. in Fr. (a) ll. 9 and 13," Bernard P. Grenfell, Arthur S. Hunt, *The Oxyrhynchus Papyri*, Part III (London: Egypt Exploration Fund, 1903), 10. Here Grenfell and Hunt draw attention to another use of the *diple*, at least in Christian manuscripts, as fillers in short lines. They astutely perceived that lines 10 and 14 (9 and 13 in the original publication) of P.Oxy. 405 end with *diplai*, the very ends of which remain intact and discernable. Clearer examples of the diple as line-filler are found, for example, in P.Oxy. 1 (Bodleian MS. Gr. Th. E7 (P)), a fragment corresponding to sayings 26-29, 30 and 77 of the Gospel of Thomas, which uses a single diple at the end of lines 3, 9, 17, 18 of the verso. A photo of the latter may be seen in Larry Hurtado, *The Earliest Christian Artifacts: Manuscripts and Christian Origins* (Grand Rapids: Eerdmans, 2006), 239, plate 7. Another example may be seen in the photo of Codex Boernerianus (G^p, 9th c.) in Aland and Aland, *The Text of the New Testament*, 111, at the end of Romans.

20. McNamee, *Sigla*, 7. The full quote is "If we leave aside the signs normally used to mark new sections in an ancient text . . . and also the decorative space-fillers at the ends of lines, there are roughly three hundred Greek literary papyri from Egypt in which sigla appear in the margin or between the lines."

21. Three are from the third, one from the fifth, one from fifth-sixth, one from sixth-seventh, and one from the seventh. McNamee is cataloguing texts found in Egypt. Across the Mediterranean in Herculaneum, she says, "The practice of scribes . . . diverges . . . in their very common use of the diple where we are used to seeing paragraphi" and "in the presence of the double penstroke (//) to mark a citation . . . " (*Sigla*, 24–25).

22. Such as P.Oxy. 406 (van Haelst 1152; LDAB 3500), a third-century papyrus codex fragment of a theological text suggested to belong to Origen,

23. Cornelia Eva Römer, "7.64. Gemeinderbrief, Predict oder Homilie über den Menschen im Angesicht des Jüngsten Gerichts," in *P. Michigan Koenen* (= *P. Mich. xviii*): *Michigan Texts Published in Honor of Ludwig Koenen*, ed. Cornelia E. Römer and Traianos Gagos, (Amsterdam: Gieben, 1996), 35–43.

24. My thanks to Malcom Choat, who informed me of this manuscript.

25. The original edition by the discoverer (P. Scheil's in *Mémoires publiés par les membres de la Mission Archéologique francaise au Caire* 9.2 [Paris, 1893], v) dates it to the sixth century, but "little was then known about the dating of Greek Papyrus MSS," as Roberts says (C. H. Roberts, *Buried Books in Antiquity*, Arundell Esdaile Memorial Lecture 1962 [The Library Association], 1963), 12). Subsequent scholars, including A. S. Hunt, Roberts, Turner, and Hurtado, date it to the third century.

26. *Quis Rerum Divinarum Heres Sit* and *De Sacrificiis Abelis et Caini*.

27. Roberts, *Buried Books*, 13. See also Larry Hurtado, *The Earliest Christian Artifacts: Manuscripts and Christian Origins* (Grand Rapids: Eerdmans, 2006), 167. See Erik G. Turner, *The Typology of the Early Codex* (Philadelphia: University of Pennsylvania Press, 1977), 113 and the photograph of this document, plate 2. Roberts, *Buried Books*, 12, says the text of the MS has marked affinities with other copies of Philo's work produced in Caesarea.

28. Scheil, iv. Scheil says that at least two scribes produced the volumes.

29. Possibly another text of Philo, P.Oxy. 1356, folio 10, a fragment of an unidentified work. Grenfell and Hunt, *The Oxyrhynchus Papryi*, Part XI (London: Egypt Exploration Fund, 1915), 18, say, "A similar sign is employed in 405 to mark a quotation, and possibly this is the meaning of the sign here." But as only a single word of the corresponding line survives, it is impossible to be sure if this is the significance of the mark, or to know what, if anything, Philo might have been quoting. Against the possibility that it is a mark of quotation is that, in another fragment of this codex, preserving a portion of *De Ebrietate*, there is a short quotation of Gen. 27:30 that is not marked; see Grenfell and Hunt, *The Oxyrhynchus Papryi*, Part IX (London: Egypt Exploration Fund, 1912), 22.

30. The kurzgefasste Liste has it as "III/IV (?)," http://intf.uni-muenster.de/vmr/NTVMR/ListeHandschriften.php.

31. Unfortunately this MS, transcribed by von Soden in 1902 and Gregory in 1903 at the Archäologischen Museum der Geistlichen Akademie in Kiev, is now lost. See Kurt Aland, *Studien zur Überlieferung des Neuen Testaments und seines Textes* (Berlin: de Gruyter, 1967), 137–40. It contains the nomina sacra for Jesus (IC) and Spirit (ΠΝC, ΠΝI).

32. Plate and description in M. B. Parkes, *Pause and Effect: An Introduction to the History of Punctuation in the West* (Berkeley/Los Angeles: University of California Press, 1993), 168, 169.

33. The editor says that these marks are in a brownish ink, paler than that of the columns, and suggests they might have been added sometime after the text was completed. Jean Scherer, *Entretien d'Origène avec Héraclide et les évêqes ses collues sur le père, le fils, et l'âme* (Cairo: Imprimerie de l'institut francais d'archéologie orientale, 1949), 11.

34. As reported by V. Gardthausen, *Griechische Palaeographie*, 2nd. ed., vol 2, Die Schrift, *Unterschriften und Chronologie im Altertum und in byzantinischen Mittelalter* (Leipzig: Veit & Comp., 1913), 406. I have not seen any facsimile of this work, portions of which are in London, Paris, Vienna, and Dublin, but according to Wevers and Kraft at http://ccat.sas.upenn.edu/gopher/text/religion/biblical/lxxvar/1Pentateuch/02Exod-Wevers-Intro.html, it contains many citations from Exodus.

35. Roberts, *Manuscript, Society, and Belief*, 23, mentioned almost in passing seeing "quotation signs" in P[4,64,67], but Skeat, who noted Roberts's remark, said he could find none (T. C. Skeat, "The Oldest Manuscript of the Four Gospels?" *NTS* 43 [1997]: 2, 7). Nor could I. The text of P[75] is damaged at most points at which its text of Luke or John cites the Old Testament, but the margin is clearly visible, for instance, at Luke 7:27, where there are no marginal markings noting the citation of Ex. 23:20/Mal. 3:1. One may see from the page containing John 1:21-30 in P[66] that at 1:23, where John the Baptist cites Isaiah 40:3, there is no *diple* in the margin. See the photo on plate 43 in W. J. Elliott and D. C. Parker, eds., *The New Testament in Greek IV: The Gospel according to St. John*, vol. 1, *The Papyri*, NTTS 30 (Leiden/New York/Köln: Brill, 1995). By contrast, this is marked in Vaticanus (see below). Kenyon notes that in P[45], "A filling-mark (>) occurs rarely at the end of a line" (Frederick G. Kenyon, *The Chester Beatty Biblical Papyri: Descriptions and Texts of Twelve Manuscripts on Papyrus of the Greek Bible*, three fascicles, fascicle II, *The Gospels and Acts* [London: Oxford University Press, 1933], ix). But there is no sign of this mark used in the left margin for quotations. Nor have I observed the practice as of yet in P[46], P[13] (P.Oxy. 657; inv. 1532 verso), or any other New Testament manuscript predating the fourth century.

36. This is stated also by Wileand Wilker on his website devoted to Codex Vaticanus, at http://www-user.uni-bremen.de/~wie/Vaticanus/umlauts.html.

37. Image available at http://www.bible-researcher.com/vaticanus1.html.

38. This is confirmed by a look at the facsimile edition at, for instance, Matthew 2:6, citing Micah 5:1, 3, where portions of the original ink show through in the letters next to the diplai and may be compared with the ink of the diplai. See also the photograph of the column containing John 1:23 at http://www.bible-researcher.com/vaticanus8.jpg.

39. H. J. M. Milne and T. C. Skeat, *Scribes and Correctors of the Codex Sinaiticus*, including contributions by Douglas Cockerell (London: British Museum, 1938), 37; see also 45. Dirk Jongkind, *Scribal Habits of Codex Sinaiticus*, Texts and Studies, third series, vol. 5 (Piscataway: Gorgias, 2007), 47, n.54, states that he is not convinced that these corrections (called the B corrections) are by scribe A or D, citing the fact "that the kai-ligature of the B corrections . . . is different from both scribe A and scribe D. See e.g. folio 73.3 (NT 3), line 2.12, and 4.19 in the outer margin." Tischendorf, he notes, thought that these "corrections" came from a slightly later hand not from the original scriptorium.

40. Codex Sinaiticus q. 74, f. 1v. Col. 1 lines 1–6. British Library Board Add. 4413.

41. In Acts 1:20 they are accompanied by an indentation in the text. There is no marking of the source in the margin as in Matthew 2:6.

42. See F. G. Kenyon, *The Codex Alexandrinus (Royal MS. 1 D v–viii) in Reduced Photographic Facsimile* (London: British Museum, 1909). Kenyon's only comment on the diplai is, "Quotations are indicated by arrow-head marks in the margin, opposite all the lines of the passage in question" (9).

43. Mark 10:5-9, where Jesus quotes Genesis 1:27 and 5:2, where the scribe misses the first couple of lines and continues his markings after the quotation to the end of Jesus' pronouncement, dotted diple; Mark, 11:9-10, where Psalm 118:25 is cited, obelized, dotted diple (. >–); Mark 11:17, where Isaiah 56:7 is cited (simple *diple*); Mark 12:10-11, citing Psalm 118:22-23 (dotted diple); Mark 12:36, citing Psalm 110:1 (dotted *diple*).

44. Codex Alexandrinus 39a, col. 1, lines 17–24. Center for the Study of New Testament Manuscripts.

45. Codex Alexandrinus 17a, col. 1, lines 7–16. Center for the Study of New Testament Manuscripts.

46. Citing Isaiah 40:3-5 at 3:4-6; Isaiah 61:1-2; 58:6 at 4:18-19; Deuteronomy 6:5 at 10:27.

47. It is notable that, for whatever reason, the same thing may be said concerning the epistles credited to Clement in the Constantinopolitan document dated A.D. 1056. 1 Clement has diplai, at least for longer quotations of scripture, but 2 Clement has none, though it quotes scripture as well. See the photographs in J. B. Lightfoot, *The Apostolic Fathers*. Part 1, S. *Clement of Rome*, 2nd ed., 2 vols. (London: Macmillan, 1890, repr. Grand Rapids: Baker, 1981), 425–74.

48. According to Kenyon, one scribe (scribe III) did Matthew and Mark, another (scribe IV) did Luke through 1 Corinthians 10:7, then scribe III takes over again, writing to the end of the epistles. Another scribe (scribe V) does the Apocalypse, and scribe II, who did much of the Old Testament, executes the Clementines (Kenyon, *Alexandrinus*, 9–10).

49. Codex Alexandrinus 82a (56a), col. 2, lines 34–41. Center for the Study of New Testament Manuscripts.

50. For instance, the quotation of Malachi 3:1 in Matthew 11:10 in Codex Bezae contains no marginal markings, as may be seen in the photograph at: www.bible-researcher.com/codex-d1big.html. Images of W may be examined online at csntm.org.

51. During his presentation "Citation Markers, Corrections, and Some Preliminary Observations on Trends in the Textual Tradition of Both Testaments" at the Society of Biblical Literature, November 23, 2009.

52. The Sangallensis MS may now be viewed online at http://www.e-codices.unifr.ch/en/csg/0048. The attempt by the scribe is surely to be complete but one may notice the accidental omission of a marginal diple at Matthew 2:6, the quotation of Micah 5:1-3. Sometimes the diplai are filled in with colored ink, as are so many of the letters of this manuscript, sometimes they are not. Examples of both on the same page may be seen at http://www.e-codices.unifr.ch/en/csg/0048/28/medium.

53. Monastery of St. Gall in Switzerland. The text of Mark in Sangallensis is said by Metzger/Ehrman to be Alexandrian, but in the other Gospels Byzantine; Bruce M. Metzger and Bart D. Ehrman, *The Text of the New Testament: Its Transmission, Corruption, and Restoration*, 4th ed. (Oxford: Oxford University Press, 2005), 83. An almost contemporary (third quarter of ninth century) Latin Gospel MS., Sang. 50, does not use marginal *diplai*.

54. For a *diple* in Boernerianus, see Rom. 1:17 (at www.Biblical-data.org) citing Hab. 2:4, and note the word Hambakuk beside the diple. And see plate 28 containing 1 Cor. 2:9—3:3 in Bruce M. Metzger, *Manuscripts of the Greek Bible: An Introduction to Greek Palaeography* (Oxford: Oxford University Press, 1981), 104. Boernerianus also contains diplai at the end of short lines, like P.Oxy. 405.

55. See, for example, minuscule 2813 (13th c.) at John 12:38-40 (available at csntm.org). But a check of several other codices online at the Center for the Study of New Testament Manuscripts website shows, for instance, no marginal diplai marking quotations in 676, a thirteenth-century minuscule containing the Gospels, Acts, Paul, and Catholic Epistles, nor in 2444, a thirteenth-century Gospels minuscule. But 2813, a thirteenth-century parchment manuscript containing Luke and John, does use them. Web address is http://www.csntm.org/Manuscripts.aspx. Another example is Bodleian Library MS. Auct. D. 2. 16, a Latin Gospels codex from the late ninth or early tenth century (accessible at http://image.ox.ac.uk/show?collection=bodleian&manuscript=msauctd216), which does not have diplai.

56. Codex Sangallensis (page 23, lines 1–9). Stiftsbibliothek St. Gallen.

57. LDAB 2460; van Haelst, 672.

58. See Fritz Uebel, "Der Jenaer Irenäuspapyrus: Ergebnisse einer Rekonstruktion und Neuausgabe des Textes," *Eirene* 3 (1964): 51–109, plates between pages 64–65. This text does use the nomina sacra abbreviations.

59. http://papyri-leipzig.dl.uni-leipzig.de/servlets/MCRIViewServlet/IAwJPapyri_derivate_00500270/PJen-Irenaeus1-9R300.jpg?mode=generateLayout&XSL.MCR.Module-iview.move=draged.

60. My thanks to Larry Hurtado for this observation.

61. See the plate of Cod. C fol. 197a as frontispiece of W. Sanday and C. H. Turner, eds., *Novum Testamentum Sancti Irenaei Episcopi Lugdunensis* (Oxford: Oxford University Press, 1923).

62. Codex Claromontanus (Phillips 1669, formerly Berolinensis lat. 43), fol. 197a. Staatsbibliothek zu Berlin.

63. The relevant page from the Codex Sangallensis 231, copied about 880–890, may be viewed at www.e-codices.unifr.ch/en/csg/0231/36/medium. The relevant page from Codex Sangallensis 237, copied sometimes after 800 but not as carefully, may be viewed at http://www.e-codices.unifr.ch/en/csg/0237/20/medium.

64. The text of Cod. Sang. 231 is, diple hanc scriptores nostri apponunt in libris ecclesiasticorum virorum adseparanda vel demonstranda testimonia sanctarum scripturarum. The translation is that of Stephen A. Barney, W. J. Lewis, J. A. Beach, Oliver Berghof, *The Etymologies of Isidore of Seville* (Cambridge: Cambridge University

Press, 2006). Isidore goes on to specify different modifications of the diple (with one or two dots, with obelisk, reverse *diple*, and so on) that serve other critical functions in literary texts.

65. Page 1, col. B (1.5 Yonge).

66. On page 18, col. B (24.116 Yonge), he quotes the proverb "the beginning is half of the whole" and on page 31, col. B (39.189 Yonge) he quotes a line from the poet, "with thee I'll end, with thee I will begin," with no diplai, though by this time the scribe seems to have stopped marking even Scriptural quotations.

67. Vaticanus does not mark Luke 11:49 with diplai, where Jesus says, "the Wisdom of God said, 'I will send them prophets and apostles, some of whom they will kill and persecute.'" Presumably this is because there is no specific Old Testament passage that corresponds very closely to Jesus' quotation (and cf. Matt. 23:34).

68. "For in him we live and move and have our being." It is possible, of course, that this was not perceived as a quotation.

69. ἡμᾶς is also read in P⁷⁴ (7th c.), 049, 326, 614, 1646c, 1837, 2344 (the last of these has ἡμᾶς σοφῶν instead of ἡμᾶς ποιητῶν).

70. The scribe does not mark the quotation "the Lord rebuke you" in Jude 9.

71. Despite its advocacy by Tertullian, and its occasional favorable citation by other Fathers, *1 Enoch* is absent from all the fourth- and fifth-century canon lists, nor is it contained in any of the great uncial codices, including Codex Vaticanus itself.

72. It may be of interest to note that diplai are present for the marking of both Deuteronomy 25:4 and Luke 10:7 in 1 Timothy 5:18.

73. For example, *Haer.* II.27.2 (the Gospels); III.1.1; III.16.2. See D. Jeffrey Bingham, *Irenaeus's Use of Matthew's Gospel in* Adversus haereses, Traditio Exegetica Graeca 7 (Louvain: Peeters, 1998).

74. The origins of the practice of abbreviating the *nomina sacra* are still under discussion. One aspect of that discussion concerns the suggestion that the abbreviations were invented to save time or space. We may be sure that at least the "diplai sacra" were not adopted as a time-saving measure.

75. P.Mich. 764 (mentioned above), however, is roughly contemporary and so possibly is older. It too contains a *nomen sacrum*. Paris Bib. Nat. P.Gr. 1120 (Philo), is the next oldest.

76. *Rectissime scientes quia Scripturae quidem perfectae sunt, quippe a Verbo Dei et Spiritu eius dictae* (A. Rousseau and L. Doutreleau, *Irénée de Lyon: Contre les Hérésies Livre ii*, vol. 2, SC 294 [Paris: Cerf, 1982]).

77. Larry Hurtado, *The Earliest Christian Artifacts: Manuscripts and Christian Origins* (Grand Rapids/ Cambridge: Eerdmans, 2006), 58.

78. Metzger and Ehrman, *Text*, 67.

79. Souter, "The New Testament Text of Irenaeus," cxii.

11. The Heart of Irenaeus's Theology

1. See my paper from the 2003 International Conference on Patristic Studies at Oxford: "How Much Did Irenaeus Learn from Justin?" *Studia Patristica* XL, ed. Edward J. Yarnold, Maurice F. Wiles, and Paul Parvis (Leuven: Peeters, 2006), 515–20.

2. Joseph Caillot, "La grâce de l'union selon saint Irénée," in *Penser la foi*, ed. Joseph Doré and Christoph Theobald (Paris: du Cerf, 1993), 391–412.

3. Yoshifumi Torisu, *Gott und Welt. Eine Untersuchung zur Gotteslehre des Irenäus von Lyon*, Studia Instituti Missiologici Societatis Verbi Divini Sankt Augustin 52 (Nettetal: Steyler, 1991). The passage is on p. 15: "God is actually unknowable, but according to Irenaeus God has revealed himself in history to all, through his own hands, i.e., through the Son and the Holy Spirit, and he leads humanity to himself through the economy of salvation" (my translation).

4. Irenaeus, *haer.* I.6.2; III.2.1-2.

5. *haer.* III.15.2. The translation, here and elsewhere in this article, is my own.

6. For an exhaustive study of the background of these terms, see Harald A. T. Reiche, "A History of the Concepts θεοπρεπές and ἱεροπρεπές," unpublished Ph.D. thesis, Harvard University, 1955.

7. See the brief discussion in Robert M. Grant, *After the New Testament* (Philadelphia: Fortress Press, 1967), 104–5; idem, *Jesus after the Gospels* (Louisville: Westminster John Knox, 1990), 96–99.

8. The citations in Irenaeus are in *haer.* I.12.2; II.13.3 and 8; II.28.4; and IV.11.2.

9. Grant, *After the New Testament*, 105.

10. He has already referred to this axiom in *haer.* I.15.5, cited it in I.22.1, and appealed to it again in II.4.2. It may be implied in *haer.* IV.6.2, where Irenaeus is quoting from Justin Martyr. For an excellent analysis of where this axiom comes from and how Irenaeus's use of it goes beyond that of his predecessors, see William

R. Schoedel, "'Topological' Theology and Some Monistic Tendencies in Gnosticism," in *Essays on the Nag Hammadi Texts in Honour of Alexander Böhlig*, ed. Martin Krause, Nag Hammadi Studies 3 (Leiden: E.J. Brill, 1972), 101–2, and William R. Schoedel, "Enclosing, Not Enclosed: The Early Christian Doctrine of God," in *Early Christian Literature and the Classical Intellectual Tradition: In honorem Robert M. Grant*, ed. William R. Schoedel and Robert L. Wilken (Paris: Beauchesne, 1979), 75–86.

11. Rowan A. Greer, "The Dog and the Mushrooms: Irenaeus's View of the Valentinians Assessed," in *The Rediscovery of Gnosticism*, I: *The School of Valentinus*, ed. Bentley Layton, Studies in the History of Religions 41 (Leiden: Brill, 1980), 156.

12. Schoedel, "Enclosing, Not Enclosed," 80: "Irenaeus' Gnostic opponents were not unaffected by such arguments. Some, we learn from Irenaeus, were prepared to grant that God contains all; and they went on to argue that talk of things within and without the Fulness have only to do with knowledge of God or lack of it."

13. The Latin *a nullo caperetur* renders the Greek ἀχώρητον, the same term used in Hermas, *mand.* I. On the controverted text of this passage in *haer.* I.1.1, see the note in St. Irenaeus of Lyons, *Against the Heresies* I, translated and annotated by Dominic J. Unger, with further revisions by John J. Dillon, Ancient Christian Writers 55 (New York: Paulist, 1992), 133, note 4. I see no reason for A. Rousseau's note in Irénée de Lyon, *Contre les hérésies, Livre I*, vol. 1, ed. Adelin Rousseau and Louis Doutreleau, Sources chrétiennes 263 (Paris: du Cerf, 1979), 172, that fails to recognize in the Latin a good translation of the Greek and instead treats it as an intruded gloss.

14. Μόνον χωροῦντα τὸ μέγεθος τοῦ Πατρός. In Latin, *solum capientem magnitudinem Patris*.

15. Irenaeus notes that the Valentinians use familiar words in proposing their doctrines: *haer.* III.14.1, *lingua quidem unum Christum Iesum confitentes, divisi vero sententia* (cp. Chalcedon *gnōrizomenon*!); *haer.* IV.33.3, *Linguas itaque horum videlicet solas in unitatem cessisse, sententiam vero eorum et sensum, quae profunda sunt scrutari decidentem ab unitate, incidere in multiforme Dei iudicium*.

16. Richard A, Norris, *God and World in Early Christian Theology* (London: Adam and Charles Black, 1966), 69–70 (italics in the original).

17. Bruno Reynders, *Lexique comparée du texte grec et des versions latine, arménienne et syriaque de l'Adversus haereses de saint Irénée*, Corpus Scriptorum Christianorum Orientalium Subsidia 6 (Louvain: Imprimerie orientaliste L. Durbecq, 1954).

18. See SC 293: 244–45, note to SC 294: 117, note 2.

19. Rousseau sees here a reference to Eph. 3.19 (SC 294, ad loc.), but that seems quite speculative to me.

20. According to Rousseau et al., the words *et continet* found in the Latin have no parallel in the Armenian, and the French translation omits them without comment; see Irénée de Lyon, *Contre les hérésies, Livre IV*, vol. 2, ed. Adelin Rousseau et al., Sources chrétiennes 100 (Paris: du Cerf, 1965), 624–25. The earlier use of *mensurari* and the later mention that creation is contained by God still give solid assurance that *The Shepherd's* depiction of God in Mandate 1 is an integral part of the context for this passage.

21. According to Rousseau's edition, SC 100, vol.2, the Armenian uses the cognate of φιλανθροπίαν.

22. The famous passage, often quoted and written about, is *Gloria Dei vivens homo; vita autem hominis visio Dei*.

12. Irenaeus and the Knowledge of God as Father: Text and Context

1. Irenaeus's use of the word *Father* for God is not a topic that has been taken up in the scholarly literature. His understanding of the idea of adoption as sons has, as we shall see below, but it has not been brought into conjunction with his references to God as Father.

2. See the article by Gottlob Schrenk and Gottfried Quell on πατήρ, πατρῷος, πατρία, α)πάτωρ, πατρικός, *TWNT* 5 (1954), 946–1024 (English version in *TDNT* 5 [1967], 945–1022). References are to *TDNT*.

3. Joachim Jeremias, *Abba: Studien zur neutestamentlichen Theologie und Zeitgeschichte* (Göttingen: Vandenhoeck & Ruprecht, 1966); selected articles trans. by John Bowen and others in *The Prayers of Jesus* (London: SCM, 1967). References are to *The Prayers of Jesus*.

4. Schrenk, *TDNT* 5: 955.

5. Jeremias, *The Prayers of Jesus*, 29ff.; Schrenk, *TDNT* 5: 982ff.

6. For an examination of Justin's use of the word "Father" for God, see Peter Widdicombe, "Justin Martyr and the Fatherhood of God," *Laval Théologique et Philosophique* 54 (1998): 109–26.

7. Whereas none of Justin's do. C. E. Hill, "Was John's Gospel among Justin's *Apostolic Memoirs*?" in *Justin Martyr and His Worlds*, ed. Sara Parvis and Paul Foster (Minneapolis: Fortress Press, 2007), 89, argues that

the Gospel of John is to be included in the *Memoirs* known to Justin, but whatever Justin's knowledge of the Gospel, it left no discernible mark on his description of God as Father.

8. *Tim.* 29e in *Haer.* III.25.5 (SC 211: 486).

9. For an analysis of the conception of divine fatherhood in the writings of Origen and Athanasius, see Peter Widdicombe, *The Fatherhood of God from Origen to Athanasius*, rev. ed. (Oxford: Clarendon, 2000).

10. SC 294: 114–16.

11. SC 100: 640–44. Greek citations are from the fragments collected in the SC edition of *Haer.*

12. SC 294: 362.

13. Origen discusses the issue of names and God in *Contra Celsum* VII.42-5 and elsewhere. In *Commentary on John* XIX.5, he appears to regard "Father" as one of the names for God. In *De decretis* 22 and *de Synodis* 34-5, Athanasius maintains that the name "Father" signifies God's essence itself.

14. *1 Apol.* 61.10-11.

15. *Haer.* III.17.1 (SC 211: 328–30); *Dem.* 3. The translation of *Dem.* used in this study is that of John Behr, *On the Apostolic Preaching* (Crestwood: St. Vladimir's Seminary Press, 1997).

16. In *Dial.* 4.1, in the course of describing the Platonic understanding of how human beings come to a knowledge of God, Justin alludes to a collage of the Platonic texts commonly referred to by Middle Platonists in their discussions of divine ineffability.

17. In *dial.* 5.5-6.

18. One of three ways to approach a conception of God set out by Alcinous in *Didaskalikos* 10.5-6.

19. *Autol.* I.3-4.

20. SC 294: 60.

21. He had charged his opponents with this misinterpretation earlier, in I.20.3, but did not give a reply there. Here, Irenaeus introduces the discussion in IV.6.1 by explaining that Christ made the statement to reprove the Jews, who thought that they had the knowledge of God while nevertheless rejecting the Word through whom he is known. The question of the nature of the Jewish knowledge of God will arise again below.

22. SC 100: 436-8. See the discussion by Rousseau in SC 100: 207-8, and, with reference to the occurrence of the verse in *Haer.* I.20.2, in SC 263: 266. Justin Martyr also knew the verse with the verb in the aorist rather than in the present (*1 Apol.* 63.3), but does not comment on it. Irenaeus appears to have been unconcerned about the order in which the words *Father* and *Son* appear in the verse, as he himself used both orders (cf. *Haer.* II.6.1; IV.6.3; IV.6.7).

23. *Haer.* IV.6.1 (SC 100: 438).

24. *Haer.* IV.6.6 (SC 100: 448). One might have thought that Irenaeus would have appealed to the occurrence of references to God as Father in the Old Testament to help make his point. He certainly knew texts in which God is described as Father—he quotes Malachi 2:10, for instance, in *Haer.* III. 20.2. That he does not may simply reflect that fatherhood usage is not something about which he has a deliberative sense. Origen, on the other hand, makes the references to God as Father in the Old Testament a matter of discussion. Despite his concern to refute Marcionism, Origen downplays the significance of the references in the Old Testament in favor of his contention that the incarnation brought about an intimacy in the addressing of God as Father not seen in the Old Testament. God, according to Origen, is not addressed as "Father" in prayer in the Old Testament (*ComJn* XIX.26-8; *Prayer* 20.1, 22.1).

25. *Haer.* IV.6.2 (SC 100: 438).

26. *Haer.* IV.6.6 (SC 100: 448).

27. *Dem.* 8.

28. SC 211: 478–80.

29. SC 153: 220–22.

30. SC 100: 534–36.

31. SC 100: 570–74.

32. SC 211: 370–74.

33. *ComJn* I.29.201-2.

34. *ComJn* XX.17.135-9.

35. A point he makes on a number of occasions. See *ComJn* XIX.5.26-28; *Prayer* 22.1; *Hom. in Lc.*, frg. 73.

36. For instance, in *Haer.* II.9.1 (SC 294: 82); V.17.1 (SC 153: 222). Irenaeus did not make prayer a topic of discussion in his writings, whereas, of course, Origen did.

37. SC 211: 364–66.

38. SC 211: 370–74.

39. *Contra* John Behr, *Asceticism and Anthropology in Irenaeus and Clement* (Oxford: Oxford University Press, 2000), 70, who cites the passage as evidence that Irenaeus thought that God incorporates those who are adopted into the *sonship* of the Son.

40. SC 211: 66–68.

41. Denis Minns, *Irenaeus* (London: Geoffrey Chapman, 1994), 110–12; followed by John Behr, *Asceticism and Anthropology*, 69–70.

42. In *Haer.* III.19.2, referring to the discussion in III.6.1, he asserts that he "demonstrated from the Scriptures that no one among the sons of Adam is called God or named Lord in an absolute sense" (SC 211: 374–76).

43. SC 100: 984–92. The text of *Haer.* IV.41.2 is uncertain. See Rousseau's discussion of it, SC 100: 283-5. Rousseau and Behr favor the Armenian translation, Minns the Latin. Rousseau's discussion has been relied on for this study.

44. *Haer.* III.20.2 (SC 211: 390).

45. SC 100: 638–40.

46. SC 153: 92–96.

47. *ComJn* I.16.91. Origen ends the discussion in section 91 with an allusion to John 17:21, a verse Irenaeus never cites. This perfect sonship will be realized, says Origen, "when we become one as the Son and the Father are one."

48. In *Haer.* III.11.6 (SC 211: 154–56), for instance, he quotes the verse in conjunction with allusions to Matthew 11:27.

13. "The Rule of Truth . . . which He Received through Baptism" (*Haer.* I.9.4): Catechesis, Ritual, and Exegesis in Irenaeus's Gaul

1. Such is the manner in which H.J. Carpenter, "Creeds and baptismal rites in the first four centuries," *JTS* 44 (1943): 7 interprets this passage.

2. *Haer.* I.10.1.

3. Carpenter, "Creeds and baptismal rites."

4. It is also found in Socrates, *HE* I.8.35 and Theodoret, *HE* I.12.1 and is critically edited as document 21 in Hans-Georg Opitz, ed., *Athanasius Werke* III.1, *Urkunde zur Geschichte des arianischen Streites 318–328* (Berlin and Leipzig: de Gruyter, 1935), 42–47.

5. *Traditio Apostolica* 21.14. This is taken as possibly the earliest extant creed that is roughly contemporary with Irenaeus. For a recent defense of the dating of this creed to the time of Irenaeus, see my "The Baptismal Creed in *Traditio apostolica*: Original or Expanded?" *QL* 90 (2009): 199–213.

6. P. Smulders, "Some Riddles in the Apostles' Creed," *Bijdragen* 32 (1971): 350–66.

7. L.H. Westra, *The Apostles Creed: Origin, History and Some Early Commentaries* (Turnhout: Brepols, 2002), 38–39.

8. E.g., *Haer.* III.1.2, III.4.2.

9. Cf. J. N. D. Kelly, *Early Christian Creeds* (London: Longmans, 1950), 76–82.

10. *Contra Noetum* 1.7: "We too know a single God. We know Christ. We know that the Son suffered as indeed he suffered, died as indeed he died, rising up on the third day and is at the right hand of the Father and is coming to judge living and dead."

11. S.G. Hall, "The Christology of Melito: A Misrepresentation Exposed," in E.A. Livingstone (ed.), *Studia Patristica* XIII = TU 116 (Berlin: Akademie, 1975), 154–68.

12. Polycarp, *Phil.*1.2: "He (Christ) persevered to the point of death on account of our sins. God raised him up, releasing the labour pains of Hades."

13. See the scholarly orthodoxy on the date of the *traditio* represented by Johnson (apparently unaware of the evidence of Eusebius): "The first references we have to the *traditio* and *redditio symboli* are at the earliest, mid-to-late fourth century." M. E. Johnson, "The Problem of Creedal Formulae in *Traditio apostolica* 21.12-18," *Ecclesia orans* 22 (2005): 174. Here we are talking, however, of verbally fixed creeds that are rehearsed on a separate occasion from the baptism itself. Carpenter, "Creeds and Baptismal Rites," 11, after a careful examination of the evidence, suggests the middle of the third century as the time in which the practice of the *traditio* originated.

14. Acts 8:37.

15. On this homily, see my "The Pseudo-Hippolytean Homily on the Theophany (CPG 1917): A Neglected Witness to Early Syrian Baptismal Rituals," *Studia Liturgica* 39 (2009), 23–39.

16. So Chrysostom in the Stavronikita catechetical homilies 2.20-21, in Antoine Wenger, ed., *Huit catéchèses baptismales*, SC 50bis (Paris: du Cerf, 1970), 145: "I renounce you, Satan, your pomp, your worship, and your works. And I pledge myself to you (συντάσσομαὶ σοι), Christ." *Apostolic Constitutions* VII.41.3: "I pledge myself to Christ" (συντάσσομαι τῷ Χριστῷ). This statement is made after the *apotaxis*.

17. "The Christological Form of the Earliest Syntaxis: The Evidence of Pliny," *Studia liturgica* 4.1 (2011): 1–8) with reference to Pliny *Ep.*X.96.7.

18. Kelly, *Early Christian Creeds*, 79.

19. Ibid.

20. J. Haussleiter, *Zur Vorgeschichte des apostolischen Glaubensbenntnisse* (Munich: Beck, 1893).

21. Paul F. Bradshaw, "The Profession of Faith in Early Christian Baptism," *Ecclesia orans* 23 (2006): 337–38.

22. Classically by Carpenter, "Creeds and Baptismal Rites," followed by Kelly, *Early Christian Creeds*, 30–52.

23. Bradshaw, "Profession of Faith".

24. H. Lietzmann "Die Anfänge des Glaubensbekenntnisses," in *Kleine Schriften* III, TU 74 (Berlin: Akademie, 1962), 167 (originally published in 1921). Lietzmann was following on from an observation by Karl Holl, "Zur Auslegung des 2. Artikels des sog. apostolischen Glaubensbekenntnisses," in *Gesammelte Aufsätze zur Kirchengeschichte* II (Tübingen: Mohr-Siebeck, 1928), 116–22 (originally published in 1919). Holl's work was also taken up by A. von Harnack, "Zur Abhandlung des Hrn. Holl: 'zur Auslegung des 2. Artikels des sog. apostolischen Glaubensbekenntnisses,'" in *Kleine Schriften zur alten Kirche: Berliner Akademieschriften 1908–1930* (repr. Leipzig: Zentralantiquariat der deutschen demokratischen Republik, 1980), 562–66.

25. Lietzmann, "Die Anfänge des Glaubensbekenntnisses," 169.

26. This is the implication of my argument in "The Baptismal Creed in *Traditio apostolica*: Original or Expanded?" though it is not spelled out. In that article, it is suggested that there was no original short form of the christological sequence which had become expanded (as suggested by, among others, Wolfram Kinzig, "'Natum et passum etc.' Zur Geschichte der Tauffragen in der lateinischen Kirche bis zu Luther," in Kinzig, Christoph Markschies, and Markus Vinzent, *Tauffragen und Bekenntnis: Studien zur sogenannten 'Traditio Apostolica,' zu den 'Interrogationes de fide' und zum 'Römischen Glaubensbekenntnis'* (Berlin: de Gruyter, 1999), 75–183, and Johnson, "The Problem of Creedal Formulae."

27. *Cat. myst.* 1.4-11.

28. *Cat. myst.* 2.4.

29. So L. Mitchell, "The Baptismal Rite in Chrysostom," *ATR* 43 (1961): 401; Juliette Day, *The Baptismal Liturgy of Jerusalem: Fourth and Fifth-century Evidence from Palestine, Syria, and Egypt* (Aldershot: Ashgate, 2007), 60. Cf., however, Bradshaw "Profession of Faith," 142.

30. *Hom.*40 *in I Cor.* 379B Montfaucon.

31. T. M. Finn, *The Liturgy of Baptism in the Baptismal Instructions of St John Chrystostom* (Washington, DC: Catholic University of America, 1967), 150–51; Wenger, *Huit catéchèses baptismales*, 95–96.

32. A problem pointed out by Bradshaw, "Profession of Faith," 138.

33. *Baptismal Instruction* (Papadopoulos-Kerameus) 11.14.

34. Mitchell, "Baptismal Rite in Chrysostom," 401, suggests that the formula is "new" and has replaced the "older" interrogation. This assumes, of course, that the interrogation had ever had a place in these rituals, as Mitchell presupposes.

35. Finn, *Liturgy of Baptism*, 150–51; Wenger, *Huit catéchèses baptismales*, 95–96.

36. See the apparently declarative statements to which Proclus alludes at *Hom.* 27.56 and the statement at 27.44 that "the words of the confession have been thoroughly taught to you."

37. *Dem.* 3.

38. *Dem.* 7.

39. Kelly, *Early Christian Creeds*, 77.

40. Ibid., 78.

41. David N. Power, *Irenaeus of Lyons on Baptism and Eucharist*, Alcuin Club and the Group for Renewal of Worship Joint Liturgical Studies 18 (Bramcote: Grove, 1991), 2.

42. Power, *Irenaeus*, 25.

43. Willy Rordorf, "An Aspect of the Judeo-Christian Ethic: The Two Ways," in J. A. Draper, ed., *The Didache in Modern Research* (Leiden: Brill, 1996), 158.

44. Lietzmann, "Anfänge," 171. The text may be found at F. C. Conybeare, *Rituale Armenorum* (Oxford: Clarendon, 1905), 92.

45. H. von Campenhausen, "Das Bekenntnis Eusebs von Caesarea," in *Urchristliches und altkirchliches: Vorträge und Aufsätze* (Tübingen: Mohr-Siebeck, 1979), 278–99.

46. Here working on the assumption, as argued above, that this is original in the Palestinian rite and that the interrogatory creed found in Jerusalem is an importation.

47. Trinitarian statements at the *syntaxis* are found in Cyril of Jerusalem, *Cat. myst.* 1.9; Theodore of Mopsuestia, *Hom. cat.* 13.13; and implied by the narratives of the *Historia Johannis* (Syriac, 44; English, 40; Syriac, 59; English, 54, in the page numbers of the edition by W. Wright, *Apocryphal Acts of the Apostles* [London, 1871; repr. Piscataway: Gorgias, 2005]).

48. *Haer.* I.9.3.

14. Irenaeus, Women, and Tradition

1. Elaine Pagels, *The Gnostic Gospels* (New York: Random, 1979).

2. See, for example, Karen L. King, ed, *Images of the Feminine in Gnosticism*, Studies in Antiquity and Christianity 4 (Philadelphia: Fortress Press, 1988).

3. Jonathan Cahana, "Androgyne or Undrogyne? Queering the Gnostic Myth," *Studia Patristica*, forthcoming. Cahana points to passages such as the *Apocryphon of John* 5.5-6, "She became a womb for the entirety, for she was prior to all, the mother-father, the first human, the holy spirit, the thrice male, the three powers; the thrice-androgynous name," in support of his claim that Gnostics meant to challenge ancient assumptions about gender to the core.

4. Michael Allen Williams, *Rethinking "Gnosticism": An Argument for Dismantling a Dubious Category* (Princeton: Princeton University Press, 1996), 108.

5. Ibid., chapter 3.

6. Williams argues that "Gnosticism" should be dismantled in favor of the more restricted category of "biblical demiurgical" myths and writings. This proposed terminology has the advantage for Irenaeus scholars of concentrating on exactly the aspects of these writings that Irenaeus himself most disliked and objected to. Its disadvantage is that it also makes Irenaeus's move of preferring a respectable, agreed, and authoritative scholarly narrative over the joys of free-spinning myth-making, thus offering to rob these writings of much of their romance in the popular imagination. (The much-loved category of "Celtic Christianity" faces a similar problem when confronted with cold, sober historical reality.) As I think the emotional appeal Irenaeus is both making and countering depends on presenting his opponents as one coherent, distinctive, and at least superficially attractive package, I will continue to use the term *Gnostic* in this paper, with all its baggage.

7. I am here taking Irenaeus's description of the teaching of "those around Ptolemy" given in *AH* I.1-9 as representative of the core of the doctrine he is opposing, as he does (*AH* Book I Pref. 2). However, on the assumption that all the Gnostic texts to which Irenaeus refers come from his contacts in Valentinian circles, even those which are not themselves originally Valentianian, I will also draw on the exegetical and theological moves made in other Gnostic traditions he discusses, particularly the narratives of I.29-30.

8. I.5.4; see also I.29.4, I.30.6.

9. I.30.7-9. Ialdabaoth punishes Adam and Eve by expelling them to Earth, but Prounikos takes pity on them and returns to them what made them divine (which she had previously removed from them to protect it from their punishment). The power struggle between the Demiurge and his mother does not appear in Ptolemy's version of the myth, in which the Demiurge rejoices when he finally hears the truth about the realms above him from the Savior (I.7.4).

10. I.13.2-3.

11. In Ptolemy's system; in other systems, the highest God may be both male and female, half of an equal male/female pair, or neither, though never simply female (I.11.5).

12. I.2.2 in Ptolemy's system; there are a number of different but related versions of this myth cited by Irenaeus.

13. I.13.5-7. Williams, *Rethinking "Gnosticism,"* 174–78, doubts the truth of Irenaeus's charges, although he concentrates on the ritual side of them. Accusations against teachers of seducing women are common enough in ancient polemic to raise doubts about their veracity, but on the other hand the account Irenaeus gives of Marcus's actions is quite circumstantial, and fits well with a certain psychological profile (Marcus's

teaching and liturgies, at least as Irenaeus describes them, and in contrast to those of other Gnostics, are very self-focused). Whether Irenaeus has specific evidence against any of Marcus's male associates, who he claims have caused marital ravages on the banks of the Rhone, is another question. They may be a group of libertines casually breaking hearts and marriages, or they may simply be an attractive target for bored local women.

14. See II.30.9, III.24.2, IV.7.4 (the famous "hands of God" passage), IV.20.1-4.

15. E.g., III.24.2.

16. III.24.1.

17. II.12.2.

18. II.12.3.

19. II.18.1.

20. II.18.5-6.

21. II.30.1-9.

22. Mary Ann Donovan (*One Right Reading? A Guide to Irenaeus* [Collegeville: Liturgical, 1997] 88, 157) gives a helpful account of Irenaeus's teaching on Mary and Eve (as on much else). She also quotes from an interesting unpublished paper of Rebecca Lyman's on this topic, given in 1988. The Mary and Eve passages are found at *Haer.* III.22.4 and V.19.1.

23. III.21.10—22.3.

24. I.13.2-3.

25. Pagels, *Gnostic Gospels*, 59–60. Having no Irenaean quotation to give to back up her claim regarding his views on women and the Eucharist, she cites the views of the layman and Montanist Tertullian from a different part of the Empire a generation later instead.

26. "Through all these things, therefore, they are sinning against the Spirit of God with an unpardonable sin." III.11.9.

27. The Montanists, including the women prophets Priscilla and Maximilla, are likely to be lurking in the background of this passage.

28. I.13.4.

15. Irenaeus and the Exegetical Roots of Trinitarian Theology

1. Slusser, "The Exegetical Roots of Trinitarian Theology," *TS* 49 (1988): 465.

2. Ibid., 475.

3. Carl Andresen, "Zur Entstehung und Geschichte des trinitarischen Personbegriffes," *ZNW* 52 (1961): 1–39.

4. Marie-Josèphe Rondeau, *Les commentateurs patristiques du Psautier (IIIe–Ve siècles) 1: Les travaux des Pères grecs et latins sur le Psautier. Recherches et bilan; 2: Exégèse prosopologique et théologie* (Rome: Pont. Institutum Studiorum Orientalium, 1982, 1985).

5. Rondeau, *Les commentateurs*, 1: 19. Rondeau and Slusser agree that "prosopological exegesis" more clearly explains this early Christian method of exegesis, because this term implies the identification of speakers in a text. On the other hand, Andresen's term, "prosopographic exegesis," suggests a listing or catalog of speaker(s) in a text. See Slusser, "Exegetical Roots," 462–63.

6. Rondeau, *Les commentateurs*, 2: 13–14.

7. Slusser, "The Exegetical Roots," 466–68. Cf. *Dial.* 50.1.

8. Justin describes this prosopological method in *1 Apol.* 36 saying: "Sometimes He [the Logos] declares things that are to come to pass, in the manner of one who foretells the future, sometimes he speaks as from the person of God the Lord and Father of all; sometimes as from the person of Christ; sometimes as from the person of the people answering the Lord or His Father." *St. Justin Martyr: The First and Second Apologies*, trans. Leslie W. Barnard, Ancient Christian Writers (New York: Paulist, 1997). In *1 Apol.* 37–49, Justin follows the description of this method with examples of prosopological exegesis. Likewise, Tertullian also describes his prosopological method in *Adv. Prax.* 11: "So in these [passages], few though they be, yet the distinctiveness of the Trinity is clearly expounded: for there is the Spirit himself who makes the statement, the Father to whom he makes it, and the Son of whom he makes it. So also the rest, which are statements made sometimes by the Father concerning the Son or to the Son, sometimes by the Son concerning the Father or to the Father, sometimes by the Spirit, establish each several Person as being himself and none other." *Adversus Praxean Liber: Tertullian's Treatise against Praxeas*, trans. Ernest Evans (London: SPCK, 1948), 144–45. There is a sense in which Tertullian's last statement may hint as Irenaeus's concerns.

9. Rondeau, *Les commentateurs*, 2: 29. Slusser appears to concur with this connection as well. Slusser, "The Exegetical Roots," 464. The passage of *Dem.* 49 reads: "Since David says, 'The Lord says to me,' it is necessary to affirm that it is not David nor any other one of the prophets, who speaks from himself—for it is not man who utters prophecies—but that the Spirit of God, conforming Himself to the person (*prosopon*) concerned, spoke in the prophets, producing words sometimes from Christ and at other times from the Father." Unless otherwise noted, translations of the *Demonstration* are drawn from John Behr, *On the Apostolic Preaching* (Crestwood: St. Vladimir's Seminary Press, 1997).

10. Charles Kannengiesser, "The 'Speaking God' and Irenaeus's Interpretative Pattern: The Reception of Genesis," *ASE* 15/2 (1998): 344. Kannengiesser writes: "Chapter 3 is the most often quoted chapter of Genesis in Irenaeus. . . . Thus the detailed quotation of Genesis 3 in *Haer.* III and V reveals the same inclination in Irenaeus's predispositions to stage the 'speaking' God, the 'deus locutor' of the biblical narrative. He catches thereby one of the most dramatic elements in that narrative, and assimilates it to his own theological discourse" ("The 'Speaking God,'" 342).

11. *Haer.* III.8.1.

12. *Haer.* I.8.1.

13. For a recent discussion of this practice, see Gerard P. Luttikhuizen, *Gnostic Revisions of Genesis Stories and Early Jesus Traditions* (Leiden: Brill, 2006). Luttikhuizen borrows from the work of Jauss and describes how "[T]he response of Gnostics to scripture and early Christian texts was greatly determined by the relationship of these texts to their own favored traditions. The intertextual tension between the scripture texts and their Gnostic interpretations betrays that on essential points the thought structure of the interpreters differed from what they found in the texts" (*Gnostic Revisions*, 5).

14. Unless otherwise noted, translations from *Haer.* I are adapted from D. J. Unger and J. J. Dillon, *St. Irenaeus of Lyons Against the Heresies*, Ancient Christian Writers (New York: Newman, 1992). As we will discuss later, Slusser notes this passage and briefly discusses a type of christological Gnostic exegesis, but clearly Irenaeus's point is not reserved to christological discussions. The "prophecies" must include the Old Testament, and his point emphasizes the variety of Gnostic deities that are discernable in the scriptures.

15. *Haer.* IV.35.4.

16. *Haer.* IV.1.1.

17. *Haer.* IV.8.5.

18. *Haer.* IV.18.1.

19. *Haer.* IV.5.4.

20. *Haer.* IV.30.6.

21. *Haer.* IV.30.6.

22. *Haer.* IV.24.1.

23. See similar use of Isa. 45:5-6: *Haer.* I.29.4.

24. Slusser, "The Exegetical Roots," 470. Slusser writes: "Neither Origen nor Justin, however, engages in dividing up the sayings and deeds of Christ and assigning them to two speakers or agents as some other writers of their time did. The first to do that were the Gnostics, particularly those concerned to distinguish the Christ from above and the Jesus from below." Slusser goes on to discuss how Tertullian had a similar practice that identified particular passages with the divinity or the humanity of Christ, respectively. Cf. *Adv. Prax.* 27 and 30.

25. *Haer.* I.7.4.

26. *Haer.* III.16.6.

27. *Haer.* III.6.1.

28. The key prosopological formula "as from a person" (*hos apo prosopou*) is found throughout the early Fathers from Justin onward. Slusser, "The Exegetical Roots," 463–64. Andresen, "Zur Entstehung," 12–14. Rondeau, *Les commentateurs*, 2: 8.

29. His mentions of scripture include: Psalm 110:1, Gen. 19:24, Psalm 45:6, Psalm 82:1, Psalm 50:1, Psalm 50:3, Isa. 65:1, Psalm 82:6, Exod. 3:14, Exod. 3:8, and Isa. 43:10. He also cites Rom. 8:15.

30. *Haer.* III.6.1.

31. Irenaeus does discuss the theological implications of the interactions of the Father and the Son, in Psalm 110:1. This is the Father addressing the Son. Irenaeus argues, therefore, that the Father gives and the Son receives and the Father subjects and the Son is the one to whom all things are subjected. But the

framing of this trinitarian relationship and the interaction of the Father and the Son is only a consequence of his first premise.

32. The dual use of divine titles is found in Psalm 82:1, "God stood in the congregation of the gods, He judges among the gods." But with Psalm 82:1, the pronoun "he" refers to the Father, while "God" refers to the Son, who has gathered the "gods," that is the faithful, to himself.

33. *Haer.* III.6.3.

34. Philippe Bacq, *De l'ancienne à la nouvelle alliance selon S. Irénée: Unite du Livre IV de l'Adversus haereses* (Paris: Éditions Lethielleux, 1978), 38 n.2.

35. *Haer.* IV. praef.4. In book IV, Irenaeus reveals a further qualification to this method. He emphasizes the words of the Lord as a witness to the identity of the true God. But, Irenaeus claims in *Haer.* IV.2.3, the words of Moses are the words of Christ and cites John 5:46-47. Commenting upon *Haer.* IV.2.1-2, Antonio Orbe suggests that Irenaeus is dealing with a concept of inspiration. Bacq, however, is right to correct Orbe on this point by noting that Irenaeus's concern is with "identify" in the saying of Moses and the prophets. Bacq, *De l'ancienne*, 52.

36. Cf. *Haer.* IV.38.4.

37. *Haer.* IV.1.2. Cf. Bacq, *De l'ancienne*, 47.

38. *Haer.* III.6.1.

16. The Image of God in Irenaeus, Marcellus, and Eustathius

1. *Against Heresies* III.19.3. Translations of Irenaeus are my own.

2. Cf. Friedrich Loofs, *Paulus von Samosata*, TU 44.5 (Leipzig: Hinrichs, 1924), 309.

3. Cf. Kelley McCarthy Spoerl, "Two Early Nicenes: Eustathius of Antioch and Marcellus of Ancyra," in Peter W. Martens, ed., *In the Shadow of the Incarnation: Essays on Jesus Christ in the Early Church in Honor of Brian E. Daley, S.J.* (Notre Dame: University of Notre Dame Press, 2008), 121–48.

4. Cf. R. P. C. Hanson, *The Search for the Christian Doctrine of God* (Edinburgh: T&T Clark, 1988), 202–6.

5. Marcellus fragment K40; Eustathius fragment D107. For Marcellus, the numbering referred to throughout is that of E. Klostermann, ed., *Eusebius Werke*, iv, *Gegen Marcell, Über die kirchliche Theologie, Die Fragmente Marcells*, 2nd ed., G. C. Hansen, GCS (Berlin: Akademie, 1972). I have generally followed Sara Parvis's forthcoming translation. References to the fragments of Eustathius follow José H. De Clerck, ed., *Eustathii Antiocheni, patris Nicaeni, opera quae supersunt omnia*, CCSG 51 (Turnhout: Brepols; Leuven: Leuven University Press, 2002). Translations of Eustathius are my own, under the supervision of Paul Parvis.

6. Cf. Sara Parvis, *Marcellus of Ancyra and the Lost Years of the Arian Controversy* (Oxford: Oxford University Press, 2006), 54; Rowan Williams, *Arius, Heresy and Tradition*, rev. ed. (London: SCM, 2001), 81–98; Rebecca Lyman, *Christology and Cosmology: Models of Divine Activity in Origen, Eusebius, and Athanasius* (Oxford: Clarendon, 1993), 15–17.

7. Cf. Marcellus fragment K61; Eustathius fragment D88.

8. Cf. Joseph T. Lienhard, *Contra Marcellum: Marcellus of Ancyra and Fourth-Century Theology* (Washington, DC: Catholic University of America Press, 1999), 47; Parvis, 118–23.

9. De Clerck contains a comprehensive discussion of Eustathius's sources, XXVIII–CCCCLXII.

10. Cf. Denis Minns, *Irenaeus* (London: Chapman, 1994), 59–62, and Eric Osborn, *Irenaeus of Lyons* (Cambridge: Cambridge University Press, 2001), 211–16.

11. *Haer.* III.16.6.

12. Y. de Andia, *Homo Vivens* (Paris: Études Augustiniennes, 1986), 69.

13. Cf. *Haer.* V.16.2.

14. *Demonstration of the Apostolic Preaching* 22. I have used J. Armitage Robinson's translation from the Armenian (London: SPCK, 1920). What Robinson renders as "man" I have retroverted to ἄνθρωπος.

15. *Demonstration* 22.

16. Minns, 60.

17. *Haer.* V.6.1.

18. Cf. *Haer.* V.6.1.

19. *Haer.* IV.24.1.

20. *Haer.* V.16.2.

21. Peter Foster, "God and the World in Saint Irenaeus" (unpublished PhD Thesis, University of Edinburgh, 1985), 310–20.

22. *Haer.* V.6.1.

23. Cf. Foster, 316.

24. Ibid., 320.

25. Cf. *Haer.* IV.4.3.

26. *Haer.* IV.20.1.

27. *Haer.* II.6.1.

28. Cf. *Haer.* II.34.4.

29. K16.

30. K6.

31. *Haer.* III.21.10.

32. K58.

33. Cf. Peter Stewart, *Statues in Roman Society: Representation and Response* (Oxford: Oxford University Press, 2003), 170.

34. K95.

35. K92.

36. K119, K120.

37. For a useful summary, cf. Alexandra Riebe, "Marcellus of Ancyra in Modern Research" (unpublished MA thesis, University of Durham, 1992), 31–37.

38. Cf. K74.

39. K117; K118.

40. K119.

41. Parvis, 37.

42. K58; see above.

43. Cf. Lienhard, 58–61, and Spoerl, 130–36 respectively.

44. M.J. Dowling, "Marcellus of Ancyra: Problems of Christology and the Doctrine of the Trinity" (unpublished PhD thesis, University of Belfast, 1987), 245.

45. K96.

46. Parvis, 36.

47. D44. See 1 Corinthians 15:45-46.

48. D68.

49. D68. The distinction between the two kinds of images echoes Origen's *On First Principles*, I.2.6.

50. D21.

51. A Latin fragment of Eustathius's *On Psalm 92* (D95) says, conversely, that the Word "bears the same *imaginem* as the begetter, being an *imago divinae substantiae*." This suggests more distinction between the Son and the Father. So much division in the Godhead jars with Eustathius's anti-subordinationist polemic. Sara Parvis's suggestion, that the Latin renders the Greek phrase χαρακτήρ τῆς ἀποστάσεως τὸν θεόν, "imprint of God's being," after Hebrews 1:3, is persuasive: Parvis, 58–59.

52. D61.

53. Eustathius's use of ἄγαλμα where Marcellus uses ajndria may signify also a greater sense of affinity in Eustathius, but Marcellus's ἀνδριάς is bound up with an extended metaphor about statue building, so its significance is hard to ascertain.

54. D44.

55. Eustathius often calls the divine in Christ "spirit." Cf. D76.

56. D44–50.

57. D20.

17. Packaging Irenaeus: *Adversus haereses* and Its Editors

1. The editions considered in this paper are: Erasmus (Basel: Froben, 1526, 1528, 1534); Gallasius ([Geneva]: Apud Ioannem le Preux & Ioannem Paruum, 1570; Feuardent (Paris: Apud Sebastianum Niuellium via Iacobaea sub Ciconiis, 1575; Cologne: Officina Birckmanniana, 1596); Grabe (Oxford: E Theatro Sheldoniano, 1702); Massuet (Paris: Typis Joannis Baptistae Coignard, 1710); Harvey (2 vols.; Cambridge: Typis academicis, 1857); Rousseau (10 vols.; Paris: du Cerf, 1965–82).

Fuller bibliographical data are in the bibliography and in the Writings of Irenaeus section.

2. See José Ruysschaert, "Le manuscrit 'Romae descriptum' de l'édition érasmienne d'Irénée de Lyon," in *Scrinium Erasmianum* I, 269–76, cited in Alexander Dalzell and Charles G. Nauert Jr., *The Correspondence of*

Erasmus, Letters 1658 to 1801, January 1526–March 1527, Collected Works of Erasmus xii (Toronto: University of Toronto Press, 2003), 214, note 1.

3. Ep. 1715, Johannes Fabri to Erasmus, 16 May 1526.

4. Fabri says, "You would perhaps have preferred, dear Erasmus, to dedicate your Irenaeus to someone else" (Ep. 1739; CWE xii, 306), while Erasmus himself explains that "Johannes Fabri, who supplied a manuscript, would not hear of my dedicating it to anyone but the bishop of Trent" (Ep. 1754, Erasmus to Jacobus Piso, 9 Sept. 1526; CWE xii, 365—this is admittedly a piece of special pleading since he is trying to explain away the fact that he has not dedicated something major to Stanislaus Thurzo, the bishop of Olomouc). Translations of Erasmus' letters are here taken from CWE. All translations from the prefaces and annotations of various editions of Irenaeus are my own.

5. Ep. 1739, Johannes Fabri to Erasmus, 28 August 1526; tr. from CWE xii, 306.

6. Ep. 1793, Bernard von Cles to Erasmus, 20 March 1527; tr. from CWE xii, 490.

7. For the *centum aureos*, see Ep. 1771, Johannes Fabri to Erasmus, 20 December 1526. For the price equivalents, see the elaborate tables compiled by John H. Monroe for CWE xii, especially 661.

8. Ep. 1737: critical edition in P. S. and H. M. Allen, eds., *Opus Epistolarum Des. Erasmi Roterdami*, vol. vi, *1525–1527* (Oxford: Clarendon, 1926), 384–91; trans. in CWE xii, 289–305.

9. CWE xii, 290, lines 5–6.

10. On all this, see CWE xii, xiv–xvii.

11. CWE xii, introduction to Ep. 1667 (= xii, 36-41) and introduction to Ep. 1688 (= xii, 135).

12. See CWE xii, xii-xiii for Erasmus's troubles with the Basel radicals and with Luther.

13. Erasmus of course knew Eusebius's *HE* with its fragments of Irenaeus, but in 1526 only Rufinus's Latin version was in print, having appeared as early as an anonymous edition of 1473. A Greek edition had to wait until 1544.

14. Massuet, "Praefatio," v–vi.

15. See Andrew Spicer, "Gallars, Nicolas des (c.1520–1581)," *ODNB*, and, for Gallasius's London period, Patrick Collinson, *Archbishop Grindal, 1519–1583* (London: Jonathan Cape, 1979), 130–34.

16. Quoted in Patrick Collinson, "Grindal, Edmund (1516x20–1583)," *ODNB*.

17. See Anthony N. S. Lane, *John Calvin, Student of the Church Fathers* (Edinburgh: T&T Clark, 1999), esp. 76–77.

18. Massuet, "Praefatio," x.

19. Ibid., vi.

20. On III.3 in Gallasius' numbering = pp. 379–80.

21. On his III.4 = p. 282.

22. Feuardent (1575), + iii (r)— ++ iii (v).

23. Dedicatio, p. 5, evoking Erasmus, Ep. 1738 (Allen, vi, 390, lines 262–63; CWE xii, 304, lines 270–71); it is a paraphrase, not a direct quote.

24. On Grabe's career and theological development, see Günther Thomann, "John Ernest Grabe (1666–1711): Lutheran Syncretist and Anglican Patristic Scholar," *JEH* 43 (1992), 414–27, and Thomann, "Grabe, John Ernest (1666–1711)," *ODNB*.

25. Dedicatio, 4.

26. An example is Grabe's reading of *sigilla* at IV.6.7 in place of the *singula* that prevails in the Latin tradition; see Rousseau's note in *Contre les hérésies, Livre IV*, 2: 210.

27. Massuet, "Praefatio," vii.

28. (1575), 22–23; (1596), 53.

29. On his I.2, 45.

30. The comment occurs in Grabe's notes to the phrase "from the Apostles" in his I.2 (our I.10.1) = 45.

31. "Praefatio," vi.

32. See J. Carreyre, "Massuet, René," *Dictionnaire de théologie catholique* 10 (1928), 279–80.

33. Rousseau, *Contre les hérésies, Livre IV*, 1: 211–12.

18. Tracing the Irenaean Legacy

* In memoriam: Eric Osborn (1922–2007).

1. There is, for example, *Ep.* 180 of Theodoret of Cyrrhus, which rejoices over the news of Cyril's death but expresses the fear that "though his departure delighted the living, it perhaps saddened the dead" and so advises that "the guild of undertakers be ordered to put a very large and very heavy stone on his tomb" lest the dead send him back (PG 83: 1490C—1491A; critical edition in ACO IV.1, ed. Johannes Straub [Berlin:

de Gruyter, 1971], 135.10—136.15). The letter may, however, not be genuine. It is transmitted only in Latin, in the Acts of the Fifth Council of 553, and in the manuscript tradition—which is not good—is addressed to John of Antioch, who was dead by 444, the year of Cyril's death, and had been replaced as bishop of Antioch by Domnus.

2. From M. Simonopetritis, *The Synaxarion: The Lives of the Saints of the Orthodox Church*, vol. 6: July-August (Ormylia: Indiktos, 2008), 579 n. 14.

3. B. Sesboüé, *Tout récapituler dans le Christ: Christologie et sotériologie d'Irénée de Lyon*, Jésus et Jésus-Christ 80 (Paris: Desclée, 2000), section heading on page 29.

4. Ibid., 29, 30: "Irenaeus of Lyons, who was an authority for the ancient Church and whose work has been read from century to century, presents himself ever as a 'seductive' author, in the noble sense of that term. His text represents the teaching of the youthfulness of the faith, a theme that is ever dear. He says things with a great freshness and simple realism that carries conviction."

5. E. Osborn, *Irenaeus of Lyons* (Cambridge: Cambridge University Press, 2001), 9.

6. See A.v. Harnack, *Philotesia zu Paul Kleinert zum LXX-Geburtstage dargebracht* (Berlin, 1907), 1–38; W. Bousset, *Jüdische-christlicher Schulbetreib in Alexandria und Rom: Literarische Untersuchungen zu Philo und Clemens von Alexandria, Justin und Irenaus* (Göttingen: Vandenhoeck und Ruprecht, 1915); F. Loofs, *Theophilus von Antiochien: Adversus Marcionem und die anderen theologischen Quellen bei Irenäus* (Leipzig: Hinrichs, 1930). For a compendium of their views, together with an analysis of the shift in appreciation for Irenaeus, see K. M. Tortorelli, "Some Notes on the Interpretation of St. Irenaeus in the Works of Hans Urs von Balthasar," *Studia Patristica* XXIII (1989), 284; and M. A. Donovan, *One Right Reading? A Guide to Irenaeus* (Collegeville: Liturgical, 1997), 10, 11.

7. E.g. *Refutation* III.4.3: "Before Valentinus, of course, the Valentinians did not exist; and before Marcion, there were no Marcionites. And the rest of the evil-minded heretics whom we mentioned above did not exist at all before the originators and inventors of their perverse systems." (Irenaeus's own title for the work so often known as *Against the Heresies* was *Refutation and Overthrow of the Knowledge Falsely So Called*, and so it will be cited here as *Ref.*)

8. See his *Letter to Florinus*, preserved in Eusebius of Caesarea, *Ecclesiastical History* V.20.4-8.

9. See *Ref.* III.1.1, 2; and more broadly the whole address of the fourfold Gospel that consumes Irenaeus's attention in the first half of book III.

10. See *Ref.* III.7.1, 2.

11. See Osborn, *Irenaeus*, 8; cf. A. Benoît, *Saint Irénée, introduction à l'étude de sa théologie* (Études d'histoire et de philosophie religieuses, 52; Paris: Presses universitaires de France, 1960), 73.

12. Cf. Sesboüé, *Tout récapituler*, 17; Osborn, *Irenaeus*, 3. The latter refers in a note to the further speculations on Irenaeus's philosophical and rhetorical training of P. Nautin, *Lettres et écrivains chrétiens des IIe et IIIe siècles* (Paris: Cerf, 1961), 33–104, which we would also commend; though the assertion that Irenaeus went to Rome to study rhetoric seems fairly groundless, and would contradict his own testimony at *Ref.* I.Praef. R. M. Grant, *Irenaeus of Lyons*, The Early Church Fathers (London: Routledge, 1997), 44, 45, rightly draws attention to the significance of Xenophanes to Irenaeus's writing.

13. Cf., e.g., *Ref.* IV.30.1.

14. Irenaeus refers by name to Papias at *Ref.* V.33.4; cf. Papias, *Fragments* IV in U. H. J. Körtner and M. Leutzsch, *Papiasfragmente: Hirt des Hermas*, Schriften des Urchristentums, Dritter Teil (Darmstadt: Wissenschaftliche, 1998), 54–55. It is clear that Papias is of influence on Irenaeus throughout much of *Ref.* V in particular. The "certain man of ours" at V.28.4 is Ignatius, from his *Letter to the Romans* 4, though the Antiochene bishop is not named by Irenaeus.

15. This particularly with respect to *Hermas*, which I have argued elsewhere Irenaeus viewed as a scriptural text, despite the propensity of some scholars to interpret his use of *graphe* in reference to it as simply meaning "a writing." See my article, M. C. Steenberg, "Scripture, *Graphe*, and the Status of Hermas in Irenaeus," *St. Vladimir's Theological Quarterly* 53.1 (2009): 29–66.

16. Particularly with regard to Theophilus's treatment of the Tree of Knowledge and the narrative of Adam and Eve in *Ad Autol.* 2.25; cf. *Demonstration* (*Dem.*), 14–16.

17. For more on the relationship of Theophilus to Irenaeus, see R. M. Grant, "The problem of Theophilus," in *Christian Beginnings: Apocalypse to History* (London: Variorum Reprints, 1950/1983), 179–96; and Loofs, *Theophilus*, 44–80.

18. This on the speculation that Irenaeus traveled from Asia Minor to Rome sometime soon after Polycarp in 155/6, and that Justin was martyred during the prefecture of Junius Rusticus (162–168); cf. A. Birley, *Marcus*

Aurelius, A Biography (New York: Routledge, 2000), 152. We do not know precisely when Irenaeus moved from Rome to Gaul; the earliest specific testimony of his presence there is his conveyance of a letter from the confessors of Lyons to Pope Eleutherius c. 177. In any case, it is doubtful that he would have left for Gaul prior to the supposed dating of Justin's martyrdom.

19. See *Ref.* IV.6.2, the famous passage where Irenaeus considers Justin by name, quoting him as a forebear in articulating a recapitulative soteriology; cf. Eusebius, *Ecclesiastical History* IV.18.9. On the difficulties involved in this passage, see M.C. Steenberg, *Irenaeus on Creation: The Cosmic Christ and the Saga of Redemption*, Supplements to Vigiliae Christianae 91 (Leiden: Brill, 2008), 17, 18; Grant, *Irenaeus*, 39. There are many other passages where Irenaeus is clearly influenced by Justin, giving evidence also that he knew Justin's now-lost *Against All Heresies*.

20. *Ref.* III.3.2. For an assertion that there was indeed an overlap between Irenaeus and Valentinus in Rome, see W.C. van Unnik, *Newly Discovered Gnostic Writings: A Preliminary Survey of the Nag Hammadi Find*, Studies in Biblical Theology 30 (London: SCM, 1960), 62.

21. Irenaeus' admonitions to his reader-recipient in *Ref.* I.Praef. seem clearly addressed to someone of clerical office and episcopal responsibility. See the useful comments to this end in D. Unger and J. Dillon, *St. Irenaeus of Lyons, Against the Heresies, Book 1*, Ancient Christian Writers 55 (New York: Paulist, 1992), 4–6.

22. Osborn, *Irenaeus*, 9; after H. Ziegler, *Irenäus der Bischof von Lyon* (Berlin: Georg Reimer, 1871).

23. Cf. *Ref.* I.Praef.2, 3.

24. See Eusebius, *Ecclesiastical History* V.24.11-14.

25. Cf. *Ref.* I.10.1, 2; *Dem.* 1, 3.

26. Osborn, *Irenaeus*, 6.

27. There are also portions of *Ref.* V.3.2—V.13.3 in the fourth-century "Irenäus-Papyrus" fragments in the Jena Collection (P.Jen.Inv. Irenaeus Frgs.). It is a great boon to Irenaean studies that these fragments are now available in good-resolution on-line versions, thanks to Prof. Dr. R. Thiel at the Institut für Altertumswissenschaften in Jena.

28. Cf. *Ref.* I.Praef.3.

29. We should not take the presence of Irenaeus in Africa in his lifetime as evidence that the *Refutation* was written to the Christian community there; there is simply too much evidence of its Italian focus. See Unger and Dillon, *Against Heresies*, 5, 6.

30. To repeat Unger's reminder: "Hippolytus wrote in Greek at Rome for the Romans" (ibid., 5).

31. A view that was first put forward by H. Dodwell, *Dissertationes in Irenaeum* (Oxford: E Theatro Sheldoniano, 1689), 400, 401; see also B. Altaner, *Augustinus und Irenäus*, TU 83 (Darmstadt: Wissenschaftliche, 1967), 172. Further details on the history of this view are found in Irenaeus, *Against the Heresies* I, trans. Unger and Dillon, 122–23, n.75.

32. This was strongly asserted by Unger and Dillon, *Against Heresies*, 14; cf. F. J. A. Hort, "Did Tertullian Use the Latin Irenaeus?" in *Novum Testamentum Sancti Irenaei Episcopi Lugdunensis*, ed. W. Sanday and C. H. Turner (Oxford: Clarendon, 1923), xliv. Unger reminds us, too, of the (indefensible, as he shows) claim put forward by Feuardent, that Tertullian himself translated Irenaeus into Latin (cf. PG 1.1340c, D); as well as the (equally indefensible) claim of Dodwell, *Dissertationes in Irenaeum*, 397–400, that the Latin translator had used Tertullian.

33. Unger and Dillon, *Against Heresies*, 14, 15. See Unger's listing of scholars who have supported this earlier dating (121, n.74). These include Grabe, Massuet, Sanday, D'Alès, Hitchcock, Sagnard, and Camelot.

34. There is significant testimony to the Latin version in the nine manuscripts that survive. For a brief survey, see Unger and Dillon, *Against Heresies*, 12–15.

35. See Clement of Alexandria, *Instructor* III.21 (cf. *Ref.* IV.16.4, 5); *Miscellanies* IV.13 (cf. *Ref.* I.5). At *Miscellanies* I.21, Clement contradicts Irenaeus on the interpretation of the "year of the Lord" in Isaiah 61:2 indicating a one-year duration to Christ's public preaching (cf. *Ref.* II.22.5), though it is unclear whether he had Irenaeus's reading in mind when doing so.

36. See Hippolytus, *Refutation of All Heresies* VI.37, 50. The tradition of Hippolytus being Irenaeus' disciple, recounted by Photius (*Bibliotheca* 121), we can consider spurious.

37. Cf. Osborn, *Irenaeus*, 7. For details on various positions argued as to an Asia Minor-Gaul connection, see *Les martyrs de Lyon (177)* (Paris: Colloques Internationaux du Centre National de la Recherche Scientifique, 1978).

38. Osborn, *Irenaeus*, 6, 7.

39. It is noteworthy that the praise of Irenaeus as peacemaker, as bringer of unity, comes from Eusebius, who, following the Nicene debates and his support of Constantine, was himself wont to identify voices of unity from history.

40. In his *Ecclesiastical History* (V.20.1), Eusebius lists Irenaeus's letters as: *On Schism*, written to Blastus in Rome; *On the Sole Sovereignty* or *That God Is Not the Author of Evils*, written to Florinus (much of which is quoted in V.20.4-8); and *On the Ogdoad*, also to Florinus (a brief extract is provided at V.20.2). To this may also be added the "Letter from the Churches in Gaul," which style indicates is almost certainly by Irenaeus; and a letter to Pope Victor, quoted at V.24.11-17. In V.26, Eusebius mentions a treatise called *Concerning Knowledge*, written against the Greeks, as well as an unnamed "little book on the Epistle to the Hebrews and the Wisdom of Solomon."

41. See Grant, *Irenaeus*, 44, together with note 17 on p. 193.

42. Augustine quotes *Ref.* IV.2.7 and V.19.1 in *C.Iul.* I.3.5; and when he sums up in I.7.32, he mentions Irenaeus by name. This text dates to 422. Augustine may also have used Irenaeus's *Ref.* I.23.1 in his *Haer.* 1; and *Ref.* IV.33.10 in his *Catech. Rud.* 3.6. It is more certain that he used *Ref.* IV.30.1 in his *Doctr. Christ.* II.40.60, written chiefly in 396–397.

The influence of Irenaeus on Augustine, and the latter's use of Irenaeus's writings, was studied in 1949 by B. Altaner, "Augustinus und Irenäus: Eine quellenkritische Untersuchung," *Theological Quarterly* 129 (1949): 162–72; and this was followed by a great many others.

43. C. A. Forbes, from his commentary notes on his translation, published as C. A. Forbes, *The Error of Pagan Religions*, Ancient Christian Writers 37 (New York: Newman, 1970), 213, n. 470. See Unger's notes in Unger and Dillon, *Against Heresies*, 123, n.75 for a consolidation of the passages from the *Ref.* that Forbes sees as influencing Firmicus.

44. This ascription first appears in his *Commentary on Isaiah*, ch. 64, written c. 410. It is, interestingly, not found in his *De viris illustribus*. See J. van der Straeten, 'Saint-Irénée fut-il martyre?' in *Les martyres de Lyons (177)* (Paris: CNRS, 1978), 145–52; cf. Osborn, 2.

45. Jerome, *Epi.* 75.3.

46. Cf. Unger and Dillon, *Against Heresies*, 14.

47. Gregory of Tours, *History of the Franks* I.29.

48. For all, see Grant, *Irenaeus*, 193, n.17.

49. *Ecclesiastical History* V.26.

50. The Armenian of the *Dem.* was discovered by K. Ter-Mekerttschian in 1904, and published as K. Ter-Mekerttschian and E. Ter-Minassiantz, *Des heiligen Irenäus Schrift zum Erweise der apostolischen Verkündigung*, TU 35.2 (Leipzig: Hinrichs, 1907[10]). The best English translation is that of J. Behr, *On the Apostolic Preaching—Translation and Introduction* (New York: St. Vladimir's Seminary Press, 1997).

51. For example, by Severus and Timothy Aelurus; cf. Unger and Dillon, *Against Heresies*, 123, n.78.

52. Nearly forty fragments of *Ref.* are transmitted in the manuscripts of the *Sacra Parallela*; see Karl Holl, ed., *Fragmente vornicänischer Kirchenväter aus den Sacra Parallela*, TU 20.2 (Leipzig: Hinrichs, 1899), no. 137 (58)–174 (83). The manuscript tradition is, however, very complex, and what part of the surviving texts is to be assigned to John himself is unclear; see Andrew Louth, *St John Damascene, Tradition and Originality in Byzantine Theology* (Oxford: Oxford University Press, 2002), 24–25.

53. Cf. Photius, *Bibliotheca* cod. 120.

54. This view, summarized in Unger and Dillon, *Against Heresies*, 12, is discussed in Sources chrétiennes 100: 15; as well as by L. Doutreleau, "Saint Irénée de Lyon," in the *Dictionnaire de spiritualité* (Paris, 1932–), VII.2 (1934).

55. For a close examination of the fragmentary evidence of the Greek version of *Ref.*, see SC 263: 61–100; 293: 83–100; 210: 49–132; 100: 51–87; 152: 64–157.

56. See M.C. Steenberg, *Of God and Man: Theology as Anthropology from Irenaeaus to Athanasius* (New York: Continuum, 2009), 161, 162.

57. See, e.g., the most self-evident "Irenaean" parallels at *De incarnatione Verbi*, 3, 4, 5, 54.

58. As to whether or not any of these would have known Irenaeus's writings directly, one can only speculate. Certainly the two Gregories would have had ready access to the *Refutation*; and the fact that the Greek version of the same was accessible to both John of Damascus and Photius suggests that it would not have been impossible for Maximus to have access to it also.

59. *Ref.* I.10.2.

Bibliography

See also 'The Writings of Irenaeus' on pages xi–xiii.

Adams, J. N. *Bilingualism and the Latin Language*. Cambridge: Cambridge University Press, 2003.

Aland, Kurt. *Studien zur Überlieferung des Neuen Testaments und seines Textes*. Berlin: de Gruyter, 1967.

——— and Barbara Aland. *The Text of the New Testament: An Introduction to the Critical Editions and to the Theory and Practice of Modern Textual Criticism*. 2nd ed. Translated by Erroll F. Rhodes. Grand Rapids: Eerdmans, 1995.

Allen, P. S., and H. M., eds. *Opus Epistolarum Des. Erasmi Roterdami*, vol. 6, *1525–1527*. Oxford: Clarendon, 1926.

Almagor, Eran. "What Is a Barbarian? The Barbarians in the Ethnological and Cultural Taxonomies of Strabo." In *Strabo's Cultural Geography: The Making of a Kolossourgia*, ed. Daniela Dueck, Hugh Lindsay, and Sarah Pothecary, 42–55. Cambridge: Cambridge University Press, 2005.

Altaner, Berthold. "Augustinus und Irenäus: Eine quellenkritische Untersuchung." *Theological Quarterly* 129 (1949): 162–72 (reprinted in Altaner. *Kleine patristische Schriften*. TU 83. Darmstadt: Wissenschaftliche, 1967).

Amphoux, C. B. "Le texte." In D. C. Parker and C.-B. Amphoux, eds., *Codex Bezae: Studies from the Lunel Colloquium, June 1994*, 337–54. Leiden: Brill, 1996.

———. "Les contextes de la Parabole des deux fils (Mt. 21:28-32)." *Langues orientales anciennes, philologie et linguistique* 3 (1991): 215–48.

Andresen, Carl. "Zur Entstehung und Geschichte des trinitarischen Personbegriffes." *ZNW* 52 (1961): 1–39.

Apponius. *Commentaire sur le Cantique des Cantiques*. B. de Vregille and L. Neyrand, eds. SC 420. Paris: du Cerf, 1997.

Aristeas, Letter of. In James H. Charlesworth, ed., *The Old Testament Pseudepigrapha*, 2 vols. Translated by R. J. H. Schutt. 2:12–34. London: Darton, Longman and Todd, 1985.

Armitage Robinson, J. "On a Quotation from Justin Martyr in Irenaeus." *JTS* 31, no. 4 (1930): 374–78.

Attridge, H. W. *The Epistle to the Hebrews*. Philadelphia: Fortress Press, 1989.

——— and George W. MacRae. "The Gospel of Truth (I,3 and XII,2)." In *The Nag Hammadi Library in English*, rev. ed., edited by James M. Robinson. Leiden: Brill, 1996.

Audin, A., and Y. Burnand. "Chronologie des épitaphes romaines de Lyon." *REA* 61 (1959): 320–52.

Bacon, B. W. *An Introduction to the New Testament*. New York: MacMillan, 1900.

Bacq, Philippe. *De l'ancienne à la nouvelle alliance selon S. Irénée: Unité du Livre IV de l'Adversus haereses*. Paris: Éditions Lethielleux, 1978.

Bardy, Gustave. *La question des langues dans l'église ancienne*. Paris: Beauchesne, 1948.

Barnes, Timothy D. *Constantine and Eusebius.* Cambridge: Harvard University Press, 1981.

―――. *Early Christian Hagiography and Roman History.* Tübingen: Mohr Siebeck, 2010.

―――."Pre-Decian *Acta Martyrum.*" *JTS* 19, no. 2 (1968): 509–31.

Barrett, Anthony A. *Caligula: The Corruption of Power.* New Haven: Yale University Press, 1989.

Barrett, C. K. *The Gospel according to St. John: An Introduction with Commentary and Notes on the Greek Text.* London: SPCK, 1965.

Beasely-Murray, George R. *John.* WBC 36. Dallas: Word, 1987.

Behr, John. *Asceticism and Anthropology in Irenaeus and Clement.* Oxford: Oxford University Press, 2000.

Benoit, André. *Saint Irénée: Introduction a l'étude de sa théologie.* Paris: Presses Universitaires de France, 1960.

Biblia Patristica: Index des citations et allusions bibliques dans la literature patristique, vol. 1, *Des origins à Clement d'Alexandrie et Tertullien.* Edited by J. Allenbach et al. Paris: Éditions du Centre National de la Recherche Scientifique, 1975.

Bingham, D. Jeffrey. *Irenaeus' Use of Matthew's Gospel in* Adversus haereses. Traditio Exegetica Graeca 7. Louvain: Peeters, 1998.

Birdsall, J. N. "Irenaeus and the Number of the Beast. Revelation 13,18." In A. Denaux, ed., *New Testament Textual Criticism and Exegesis. Festschrift J. Delobel,* 349–59. BETL 161. Leuven: Peeters, 2002.

Birley, A. *Marcus Aurelius, A Biography.* New York: Routledge, 2000.

Bisbee, G. A. *Pre-Decian Acts of Martyrs and Commentarii.* Harvard Dissertations in Religion 22. Philadelphia: Fortress Press, 1988.

Biville, F. "Les hellénismes dans les inscriptions latines paiennes de la Gaule (1er–4ème s. ap. J.-C.)." In *La langue des inscriptions de la Gaule: Actes de la Table-ronde tenue au C.E.R.G.R. les 6 et 7 Octobre 1988,* 29–40. Lyon: Centre d'études romaines et gallo-romaines, 1989.

Blackman, E. C. *Marcion and His Influence.* London: SPCK, 1948.

Borgolte, M. *Petrusnachfolge und Kaiserimitation: Die Grablegen der Päpste, ihre Genese und Traditionsbildung.* Veröffentlichungen des Max-Planck-Instituts für Geschichte 95. Göttingen: Vandenhoeck and Ruprecht, 1989.

Bousset, W. *Jüdische-christlicher Schulbetreib in Alexandria und Rom: Literarische Untersuchungen zu Philo und Clemens von Alexandria, Justin und Irenäus.* Göttingen: Vandenhoeck und Ruprecht, 1915.

Bovon, Francois. "Names and Numbers in Early Christianity." *NTS* 47 (2001): 267–88.

Bowe, B. E. *A Church in Crisis: Ecclesiology and Paraenesis in Clement of Rome.* Harvard Dissertations in Religion 23. Minneapolis: Fortress Press, 1988.

Bowersock, G. W. "Les églises de Lyon et de Vienne: relations avec l'Asie." In *Les Martyrs de Lyon (177): Colloque international du Centre national de la recherche scientifique, Lyon, 20–23 septembre 1977,* 249–55.

―――. "Les Grecs 'barbarisés.'" *Ktema* 17 (1992): 249–57.

―――. *Martyrdom and Rome.* Cambridge: Cambridge University Press, 1995.

Bowie, Ewen. "Philostratus: The Life of a Sophist." In *Philostratus,* edited by Ewen Bowie and Jas' Elsner, 19–32. Cambridge: Cambridge University Press, 2009.

―――. "The Geography of the Second Sophistic: Cultural Variations." In *Paideia: The World of the Second Sophistic,* edited by Barbara E. Borg, 65–83. Berlin: de Gruyter, 2004.

Bradshaw, Paul F. "The Profession of Faith in Early Christian Baptism." *Ecclesia orans* 23 (2006): 337–55.

――― et al. *The Apostolic Tradition, Translation and Commentary.* Hermeneia. Minneapolis: Fortress Press, 2002.

Brankaer, J., and H.-G. Bethge, eds. *Codex Tchacos: Texte und Analysen.* TU 161. Berlin: de Gruyter, 2007.

Brent, A. *A Political History of Early Christianity.* London and New York: Continuum, 2009.

———. "Diogenes Laertius and the Apostolic Succession." *JEH* 44.3 (1993): 372–75.

———. *Hippolytus and the Roman Church in the Third Century: Communities in Tension before the Emergence of a Monarch-Bishop.* Supplements to Vigiliae Christianae 31. Leiden: Brill, 1995.

———. *Ignatius of Antioch: A Martyr Bishop and the Origin of Episcopacy.* London: Continuum, 2007.

———. *Ignatius of Antioch and the Second Sophistic: A Study of an Early Christian Transformation of Pagan Culture.* Studien und Texte zu Antike und Christentum 36. Tübingen: Mohr Siebeck, 2006.

———. *The Imperial Cult and the Development of Church Order: Concepts and Images of Authority in Paganism and Early Christianity before the Age of Cyprian.* Supplements to Vigiliae Christianae 45. Leiden: Brill, 1999.

———. "Pseudonymity and Charisma in the Ministry of the Early Church." *Augustinianum* 27.3 (1987): 347–76.

Brock, S. P. "Origen's Aims as a Textual Critic of the Old Testament." *Studia Patristica* X (1970): 215–18.

Brown, Raymond E. *The Gospel according to John (I-XII).* Anchor Bible. Garden City: Doubleday, 1966.

———, and J. P. Meier. *Antioch and Rome.* Mahwah: Paulist, 2004.

Brox, Norbert. "Irenaeus and the Bible." In *Handbook of Patristic Exegesis*, vol. 1, edited by C. Kannengiesser, 483–506. Leiden: Brill, 2004.

———. *Offenbarung, Gnosis und gnostischer Mythos bei Irenäus von Lyon.* Salzburg: Anton Pustet, 1966.

Bruce, F. F. *The Epistle to the Hebrews.* Grand Rapids: Eerdmans, 1990.

Burnand, Y. "La datation des épitaphes romaines de Lyon: remarques complémentaires." In *Inscriptions Latines de Gaule Lyonnaise*, edited by F. Bérard and Y. Le Bohec, 21–27. Paris: Collection Centre d'Etudes romaines et gallo-romaines n.s. 10, 1992.

Cahana, Jonathan. "Androgyne or Undrogyne? Queering the Gnostic Myth." *Studia Patristica*, forthcoming.

Caillot, Joseph. "La grâce de l'union selon saint Irénée." In *Penser la foi*, ed. Joseph Doré and Christoph Theobald, 391–412. Paris: du Cerf, 1993.

Camerlynck, A. *Saint Irénée et le canon du Noveau Testament.* Louvain: Istas, 1896.

Carpenter, H. J. "Creeds and Baptismal Rites in the First Four Centuries." *JTS* 44 (1943): 1–11.

Casson, Lionel. *Travel in the Ancient World.* Baltimore: Johns Hopkins University Press, 1994.

Champion, Craige. "Romans as *Barbaroi*: Three Polybian Speeches and the Politics of Cultural Indeterminacy." *CPh* 95.4 (2000): 425–44.

Chartrand-Burke, T. "The Greek Manuscript Tradition of the *Infancy Gospel of Thomas*." *Apocrypha* 14 (2004): 129–51.

———. "The *Infancy Gospel of Thomas*." In *The Non-Canonical Gospels*, edited by Paul Foster, 126–38. London: T&T Clark, 2008.

———. "The Infancy Gospel of Thomas: The Text, Its Origins, and Its Transmission." Unpublished PhD dissertation, Graduate Department of Religion, University of Toronto, 2001.

Clark, Elizabeth A. *Reading Renunciation: Asceticism and Scripture in Early Christianity.* Princeton: Princeton University Press, 1999.

Cockerill, G. L. "Hebrews 1:1-14, *1 Clem.* 36:1-6, and the High Priest." *Journal of Biblical Literature* 97 (1978): 437–40.

Colin, Jean. *L'empire des Antonins et les martyrs gaulois de 177.* Bonn: Rudolf Habelt, 1964.

Collinson, Patrick. *Archbishop Grindal, 1519–1583.* London: Jonathan Cape, 1979.

———. "Grindal, Edmund (1516x20–1583)." *Oxford Dictionary of National Biography*, electronic version.

Conybeare, F. C. *Rituale Armenorum.* Oxford: Clarendon, 1905.

Daley, Brian E. *The Hope of the Early Church: A Handbook of Patristic Eschatology.* Peabody: Hendrickson, 2003.

D'Alès, Adhémar. "La date de la version latine de saint Irénée." *RecSR* 6 (1916): 133–37.

Dalzell, Alexander, and Charles G. Nauert Jr. *The Correspondence of Erasmus, Letters 1658 to 1801, January 1526–March 1527*. Collected Works of Erasmus xii. Toronto: University of Toronto Press, 2003.

Daniélou, J. *Gospel Message and Hellenistic Culture*. Translated by J. A. Baker. Philadelphia: Westminster, 1973.

Dawson, David. *Allegorical Readers and Cultural Revision in Ancient Alexandria*. Los Angeles: University of California Press, 1992.

Day, Juliette. *The Baptismal Liturgy of Jerusalem: Fourth and Fifth-Century Evidence from Palestine, Syria and Egypt*. Aldershot: Ashgate, 2007.

De Andia, Y. *Homo Vivens*. Paris: Études Augustiniennes, 1986.

DeConick, A. D. *The Thirteenth Apostle: What the Gospel of Judas Really Says*. London: T&T Clark, 2007.

Decourt, Jean-Claude. "χαῖρε καὶ ὑγίαινε: à propos de quelques inscriptions lyonnaises." *RPh* 67 (1993): 237–50.

———, and Gérard Lucas. *Lyon dans les textes Grecs et Latins*. Lyon: Maison de l'Orient Méditerranée, 1993.

Deininger, Jürgen. Review of Colin, *L'empire des Antonins et les martyrs gaulois de 177*. *Gnomon* 37 (1965): 289–92.

De Labriolle, P. C. *La Crise Montaniste*. Paris: E. Leroux, 1913.

De Margerie, B. "Mary Coredemptrix in the Light of Patristics." In *Mary Coredemptrix, Mediatrix, Advocate, Theological Foundations: Toward a Papal Definition?*, edited by M. I. Miravalle. Santa Barbara: Queenship, 1995.

Dodwell, H. *Dissertationes in Irenaeum*. Oxford: Sheldoniano, 1689.

Donovan, Mary Ann. *One Right Reading? A Guide to Irenaeus*. Collegeville: Liturgical, 1997.

Doutreleau, L. "Saint Irénée de Lyon: I. Vie, II. Oeuvres." *Dictionnaire de spiritualité* VII.2 (1934): 1923–38.

Dowling, M. J. "Marcellus of Ancyra: Problems of Christology and the Doctrine of the Trinity." Unpublished PhD thesis, University of Belfast, 1987.

Doxographi Graeci. Edited by Hermann Diels. 2nd ed. Berlin: de Gruyter, 1929.

Droge, Arthur J. *Homer or Moses? Early Christian Interpretations of the History of Culture*. Tübingen: Mohr Siebeck, 1989.

Dubuisson, Michel. "Le latin est-il une langue barbare?" *Ktema* 9 (1984): 55–68.

Dunderberg, Ismo. "The School of Valentinus." In Antti Marjanen and Petri Luomanen, eds., *A Companion to Second-Century Christian "Heretics,"* 64–99. Supplements to Vigiliae Christianae 76. Leiden: Brill, 2005.

Ehrhardt, A. *The Apostolic Tradition in the First Two Centuries of the Church*. London: Lutterworth, 1953.

Ehrman, B. D. "The Text of the Gospels at the End of the Second Century." In *Codex Bezae. Studies from the Lunel Colloquium, June 1994*, edited by D. C. Parker and C. B. Amphoux, 95–122.

Ellingworth, P. *The Epistle to the Hebrews: A Commentary on the Greek Text*. Grand Rapids: Eerdmans, 1993.

———. "Hebrews and *1 Clement*: Literary Dependence or Common Tradition?" *Biblische Zeitschrift* 23 (1979): 262–69.

Elliott, W. J., and D. C. Parker, eds. *The New Testament in Greek IV: The Gospel according to Saint John*, vol. 1, *The Papyri*. NTTS 30. Leiden: Brill, 1995.

Enns, P. "Wisdom of Solomon and Biblical Interpretation in the Second Temple Period." In *The Way of Wisdom: Essays in Honor of Bruce K. Waltke*, edited by J. I. Packer and Sven K. Soderlund. Grand Rapids: Zondervan, 2000.

Erskine, Andrew. "Polybios and Barbarian Rome." *Mediterraneo Antico* 3 (2000): 165–82.

Eusebius of Caesarea. *Werke, IV, Gegen Marcell, Über die kirchliche Theologie, Die Fragmente Marcells*. Edited by E. Klostermann. 2nd ed. G.C. Hansen. GCS. Berlin: Akademie 1972.

Eustathius of Antioch. *Eustathii Antiocheni, patris Nicaeni, opera quae supersunt omnia*. Ed. José H. De Clerck. CCSG 51. Turnhout: Brepols; Leuven: Leuven University Press, 2002.

Finn, T. M. *The Liturgy of Baptism in the Baptismal Instructions of St John Chrystostom.* Washington, DC: Catholic University of America, 1967.

Fiocchi Nicolai, V., F. Bisconti, and D. Mazzoleni. *Le catacombe cristiane di Roma. Origini, sviluppo, apparati decorative, documentazione epigrafica.* Regensburg: Schnell and Steiner, 1998.

Fiocchi Nicolai, V., and J. Gyon. "Relire Styger: Les origins de l'Area I du cimetière de Calliste et la crypte des papes." In *Origine delle catacombe Romane,* edited by V. Fiocchi Nicolai and J. Guyon, Sussidi allo studio delle antichità Cristiana 18. Rome: Pontificia Istituto di archaeologia cristiana, 2006.

Foster, Paul. Review of Charles Hill. *From the Lost Teaching of Polycarp.* WUNT 186. Tübingen: Mohr Siebeck, 2006. *Expository Times* 118 (2006): 78–79.

———. "Tatian." *Expository Times* 120 (2008): 105–18.

———. *The Apocryphal Gospels: A Very Short Introduction.* Oxford: Oxford University Press, 2009.

Foster, Peter. "God and the World in Saint Irenaeus." Unpublished PhD Thesis, University of Edinburgh, 1985.

Gamble, Harry Y. *Books and Readers in the Early Church: A History of Early Christian Texts.* New Haven: Yale University Press, 1995.

Garcia, Z. "El Perdón de los pecados en la primitiva eglesia: Tertulliano y polemica catholico-montanista." *Razón y Fe* 23 (1909): 360–67.

Gardthausen, V. *Griechische Palaeographie,* vol. 2, *Die Schrift, Unterschriften und Chronologie im Altertum und in byzantinischen Mittelalter.* 2nd ed. Leipzig: Veit, 1913.

Giordani, R. "Novatiano betissimo martyri Gaudentius diaconus fecit. Contributo all'identificazione del martire Novaziano della catacomba anonima sulla via Tiburtina." *Rivista Archeologia Cristiana* 68 (1992): 233–58.

Golden, Mark. *Children and Childhood in Classical Athens.* Baltimore: Johns Hopkins University Press, 1990.

Goodrick, A. T. S. *The Book of Wisdom with Introduction and Notes.* London: Rivingtons, 1913.

Graham, W. A. *Beyond the Written Word: Oral Aspects of Scripture in the History of Religions.* Cambridge: Cambridge University Press, 1987.

Grant, Robert M. *A Historical Introduction to the New Testament.* New York: Harper and Row, 1963.

———. *After the New Testament.* Philadelphia: Fortress Press, 1967.

———. "Early Christian Geography." *VChr* 46.2 (1992): 105–11.

———. *Greek Apologists of the Second Century.* Philadelphia: Westminster, 1988.

———. *Heresy and Criticism.* Louisville: Westminster John Knox, 1993.

———. "Irenaeus and Hellenistic Culture." *HTR* 42.1 (1949): 41–51.

———. *Irenaeus of Lyons.* The Early Church Fathers. New York: Routledge, 1997.

———. *Jesus after the Gospels.* Louisville: Westminster John Knox, 1990.

———. "The Problem of Theophilus." In *Christian Beginnings: Apocalypse to History,* edited by Robert McQueen Grant, 179–96. London: Variorum, 1983.

Greer, Rowan A. "The Dog and the Mushrooms: Irenaeus's View of the Valentinians Assessed." In *The Rediscovery of Gnosticism,* vol. 1, *The School of Valentinus,* edited by Bentley Layton, 146–75. Studies in the History of Religions 41. Leiden: Brill, 1980.

Gregory of Elvira. *Epithalamium sive Explanatio in Canticis Canticorum.* Edited by E. Schulz-Flügel. Freiburg: Herder, 1994.

Gregory of Nyssa. *In Cancticum Canticorum.* Edited by W. Jaeger. In *Gregorii Nysseni Opera* 6. Leiden: Brill, 1986.

Gregory, Andrew F. "1 Clement and the Writings That Later Formed the New Testament." In *The Reception of the New Testament in the Apostolic Fathers,* edited by A. Gregory and C. Tuckett, 129–57. Oxford: Oxford University Press, 2007.

———. "Hindrance or Help: Does the Modern Category of 'Jewish-Christian Gospel' Distort Our Understanding of the Texts to Which It Refers?" *JSNT* 28 (2006): 387–413.

———. "Jewish-Christian Gospels." In *The Non-Canonical Gospels*, edited by Paul Foster, 54–67. London: T&T Clark, 2008.

Grenfell, Bernard P., and Arthur S. Hunt. *The Oxyrhynchus Papyri*, Part III. London: Egypt Exploration Fund, 1903.

———. *The Oxyrhynchus Papyri*, Part IX. London: Egypt Exploration Fund, 1912.

———. *The Oxyrhynchus Papyri*, Part XI. London: Egypt Exploration Fund, 1915.

Hagner, D. A. *The Use of the Old and New Testaments in Clement of Rome*. Leiden: Brill, 1973.

Hall, S. G. "The Christology of Melito: A Misrepresentation Exposed." *Studia Patristica* XIII (= TU 116): 154–68.

Hammond, Mason. Review of Colin, *L'empire des Antonins et les martyrs gaulois de 177*. *AJP* 87.4 (1966): 491–94.

Hanson, R. P. C. *The Search for the Christian Doctrine of God*. Edinburgh: T&T Clark, 1988.

Harlow, Mary, and Ray Laurence. *Growing Up and Growing Old in Ancient Rome: A Life Course Approach*. London and New York: Routledge, 2002.

Hatt, Jean-Jacques. *La tombe gallo-romaine*. Paris: Presses universitaires de France, 1951.

Haussleiter, J. *Zur Vorgeschichte des apostolischen Glaubensbenntnisse*. Munich: Beck, 1893.

Hays, R. B. *Echoes of Scripture in the Letters of Paul*. New Haven: Yale University Press, 1989.

———. *The Conversion of the Imagination: Paul as Interpreter of Israel's Scripture*. Grand Rapids: Eerdmans, 2005.

Herman, Josef. "La langue latine dans la Gaule romaine." *ANRW* 2.29.2 (1983): 1045–60.

Hill, Charles E. *From the Lost Teaching of Polycarp*. WUNT 186. Tübingen: Mohr Siebeck, 2006.

———. "Was John's Gospel among Justin's *Apostolic Memoirs*?" In *Justin Martyr and His Worlds*, edited by Sara Parvis and Paul Foster, 88–94. Minneapolis: Fortress Press, 2007.

Hippolytus. *Traités d'Hippolyte sur David et Goliath, sur le Cantique des cantiques et sur l'Antéchrist: Version géorgienne*. Edited by Georges Garitte. CSCO 263. Louvain: Secr. du Corpus SCO, 1965.

Hitchcock, F. R. M. *Irenaeus of Lugdunum: A Study of His Teaching*. Cambridge: Cambridge University Press, 1914.

Hodge, A. Trevor. *Ancient Greek France*. London: Duckworth, 1998.

Hoh, J. *Die Lehre des hl. Irenäus über das Neue Testament*. Münster: Aschendorffschen, 1919.

Holl, Karl, ed. *Fragmente vornicänischer Kirchenväter aus den Sacra Parallela*. TU 20.2. Leipzig: Hinrichs, 1899.

———. "Zur Auslegung des 2. Artikels des sog. apostolischen Glaubensbekenntnisses." In *Gesammelte Aufsätze zur Kirchengeschichte*, vol. 2, 116–22. Tübingen: Mohr-Siebeck, 1928.

Holmes, M. W. "Codex Bezae as a Recension of the Gospels." In *Codex Bezae: Studies from the Lunel Colloquium, June 1994*, edited by D. C. Parker and C. B. Amphoux, 123–60.

Hort, F. J. A. "Did Tertullian Use the Latin Irenaeus?" In *Novum Testamentum Sancti Irenaei Episcopi Lugdunensis*, edited by W. Sanday, C. H. Turner, and A. Souter.

Humphries, Mark. "A New Created World: Classical Geographical Texts and Christian Contexts in Late Antiquity." In *Texts and Culture in Late Antiquity: Inheritance, Authority, and Change*, edited by J. H. D. Scoufield, 32–67. Swansea: Classical Press of Wales, 2007.

Hurtado, Larry. *The Earliest Christian Artifacts. Manuscripts and Christian Origins*. Grand Rapids: Eerdmans, 2006.

Hyldahl, N. "Hegesipps Hypomnemata." *Stud Theol* XIV (1960): 100–3.

Inowlocki, Sabrina. *Eusebius and the Jewish Authors: His Citation Technique in an Apologetic Context*. Leiden: Brill, 2006.

———. "'Neither Adding nor Omitting Anything': Josephus' Promise Not to Modify the Scriptures in Greek and Latin Context." *Journal of Jewish Studies* 56, no. 1 (2005): 48–65.

Irenaeus of Lyon. *Against Heresies, Books 1–5 and Fragments*. Translated by A. Roberts and W. H. Rambaut. The Ante-Nicene Fathers, vol. 1, *The Apostolic Fathers with Justin Martyr*. Grand Rapids: Eerdmans, 1987.

———. *Against the Heresies* I. Translated and annotated by Dominic J. Unger, revised John J. Dillon. Ancient Christian Writers 55. New York: Paulist, 1992.

———. *Contre les hérésies*. Translated by A. Rousseau. Paris: du Cerf, 1984.

———. *Contre les heresies, Livres 1–5*. Edited and translated by A. Rousseau, L. Doutreleau, B. Hemmerdinger, and C. Mercier. Sources chrétiennes 263, 264 (Livre 1); 293, 294 (Livre 2); 210, 211 (Livre 3); 100.1, 100.2 (Livre 4); 152, 153 (Livre 5). Paris: du Cerf, 1965–82.

———. *Demonstration of the Apostolic Preaching*. Translated by J. Armitage Robinson. London: SPCK, 1920.

———. *Libros quinque adversus haereses*. Edited by W. W. Harvey. 2 vols. Cambridge: Academic Press, 1857.

———. *On the Apostolic Preaching*. Translated by John Behr. Crestwood: St. Vladimir's Seminary Press, 1997.

———. *Proof of the Apostolic Preaching*. Translated by Joseph P. Smith. Ancient Christian Writers 16. Westminster: Newman Press, 1952.

Jansen, J. F. "Tertullian and the New Testament." *Second Century* 2 (1982): 192–93.

Jeremias, Joachim. *Abba: Studien zur neutestamentlichen Theologie und Zeitgeschichte*. Göttingen: Vandenhoeck and Ruprecht, 1966.

———. *The Prayers of Jesus*. Translated by John Bowden et al. London: SCM, 1967.

John Chrysostom. *Huit catéchèses baptismales*. Edited by Antoine Wenger. SC 50bis. Paris: du Cerf, 1970.

Johnson, Luke Timothy. *Hebrews: A Commentary*. Louisville: Westminster John Knox, 2006.

Johnson, M. E. "The Problem of Creedal Formulae in *Traditio apostolica* 21.12-18." *Ecclesia orans* 22 (2005): 159–75.

Jones, C. P. "A Syrian in Lyon." *AJP* 99.3 (1978): 336–53.

Jongkind, Dirk. *Scribal Habits of Codex Sinaiticus*. Texts and Studies, 3rd series 5. Piscataway: Gorgias, 2007.

Josi, E. "Cimitero alla sinistra della via Tiburtina al viale Regina Margherita." *Rivista Archeologia Cristiana* 10 (1933): 187–233, and 11 (1934): 233–58.

Kannengiesser, Charles. "The 'Speaking God' and Irenaeus's Interpretative Pattern: The Reception of Genesis." *ASE* 15, no. 2 (1998): 337–52.

Kasser, R., M. Meyer, and G. Wurst, eds. *The Gospel of Judas*, with additional commentary by Bart D. Ehrman. Washington, DC: National Geographic, 2006.

———, G. Wurst, M. Meyer, and F. Gaudard, eds. *The Gospel of Judas Together with the Letter of Peter to Philip, James, and a Book of Allogenes from Codex Tchacos: Critical Edition*. Washington, DC: National Geographic, 2007.

Kelly, J. N. D. *Early Christian Creeds*. London: Longmans, 1950.

Kenyon, Frederick G. *The Chester Beatty Biblical Papyri. Descriptions and Texts of Twelve Manuscripts on Papyrus of the Greek Bible*, fascicle II, *The Gospels and Acts*. London: Oxford University Press, 1933.

———. *The Codex Alexandrinus (Royal ms. 1 D v-viii) in Reduced Photographic Facsimile*. London: British Museum, 1909.

King, J. Christopher. *Origen on the Song of Songs as the Spirit of Scripture: The Bridegroom's Perfect Marriage Song*. Oxford: Oxford University Press, 2005.

King, Karen L., ed. *Images of the Feminine in Gnosticism*. Studies in Antiquity and Christianity 4. Philadelphia: Fortress Press, 1988.

Kinzig, Wolfram. "'Natum et passum etc.' Zur Geschichte der Tauffragen in der lateinischen Kirche bis zu Luther." In *Tauffragen und Bekenntnis: Studien zur sogenannten "Traditio Apostolica," zu den "Interrogationes de fide" und zum "Römischen Glaubensbekenntnis,"* edited by Christoph Markschies Kinzig and Markus Vinzent, 75–183. Berlin: de Gruyter, 1999.

Klauck, Hans-Josef. *Apocryphal Gospels: An Introduction.* Translated by Brian McNeil. London: T&T Clark, 2002.

Körtner, U. H. J., and M. Leutzsch, *Papiasfragmente: Hirt des Hermas.* Darmstadt: Wissenschaftliche Buchgesellschaft, 1998.

Koester, Helmut. *Introduction to the New Testament,* vol. 2, *History and Literature of Early Christianity.* New York and Berlin: de Gruyter, 1982. 2nd ed. 2000.

Koriat, Asher. "Control Processes in Remembering." In *The Oxford Handbook of Memory,* edited by Endel Tulving and Fergus I. M. Craik, 333–46. Oxford: Oxford University Press, 2000.

Krosney, H. *The Lost Gospel: The Quest for the Gospel of Judas Iscariot.* Washington: National Geographic, 2006.

Lagrange, M. J. *Évangile selon saint Matthieu.* 3rd ed. Paris: Leciffre, Gabalda, 1927.

Lampe, Peter, *Die stadtrömischen Christen in den ersten beiden Jahrhunderten.* Wissenschaftliche Untersuchungen zum neuen Testament 2.18. Tübingen: Mohr Siebeck, 1987/1989. Translated as *From Paul to Valentinus: Christians at Rome in the First Two Centuries.* Translated by Michael Steinhauser. Edited by Marshall D. Johnson. Minneapolis: Fortress Press, 2003.

Lane, Anthony N. S. *John Calvin, Student of the Church Fathers.* Edinburgh: T&T Clark, 1999.

Layton, Bentley. *The Gnostic Scriptures.* Garden City: Doubleday, 1987.

Le Boulluec, Alain. *La notion d'hérésie dans la littérature grecque IIe–IIIe siècles.* 2 vols. Paris: Études Augustiniennes, 1985.

Le Glay, Marcel. "Remarques sur l'onomastique gallo-romaine." In *L'Onomastique Latine,* edited by Noël Duval, 269–77. Paris: CNRS, 1977.

Leinieks, Valdis. *The City of Dionysos: A Study of Euripides' Bakchai.* Beiträge zur Altertumskunde 88. Stuttgart: Teubner, 1996.

Les Martyrs de Lyon (177): Colloque international du Centre national de la recherche scientifique, Lyon, 20–23 septembre 1977. Paris: CNRS, 1978.

Lienhard, Joseph T. *Contra Marcellum: Marcellus of Ancyra and Fourth-Century Theology.* Washington: Catholic University of America Press, 1999.

Lietzmann, H. *Kleine Schriften.* 3 vols. TU 67, 68, 74. Berlin: Akademie, 1958–62.

Lightfoot, J. B. *The Apostolic Fathers,* part 1, *S. Clement of Rome.* 2nd ed. 2 vols. London: Macmillan, 1890.

Logan, Alastair. *Gnostic Truth and Christian Heresy.* Edinburgh: T&T Clark, 1996.

Loofs, Friedrich. *Paulus von Samosata.* TU 44.5. Leipzig: J. C. Hinrichs, 1924.

———. *Theophilus von Antiochien Adversus Marcionem und die anderen theologischen Quellen bei Irenaeus.* TU 46,2. Leipzig: J. C. Hinrichs, 1930.

Louth, Andrew. *St John Damascene, Tradition and Originality in Byzantine Theology.* Oxford: Oxford University Press, 2002.

Luttikhuizen, Gerard P. *Gnostic Revisions of Genesis Stories and Early Jesus Traditions.* Leiden: Brill, 2006.

Lyman, J. Rebecca. *Christology and Cosmology: Models of Divine Activity in Origen, Eusebius, and Athanasius.* Oxford: Clarendon, 1993.

Mackavey, W. R., J. E. Malley, and A. J. Stewart. "Remembering Autobiographically Consequential Experiences: Content Analysis of Psychologists' Accounts of Their Lives." *Psychology and Aging* 6 (1991): 50–59.

MacMullen, Ramsay. "The Unromanized in Rome." In *Diasporas in Antiquity,* edited by Shaye J. D. Cohen and Ernest S. Frerichs, 47–64. Brown Judaic Studies 288. Atlanta: Scholars, 1993.

Maiburg, Ursula. "'Und bis an die Grenzen der Erde': Die Ausbreitung des Christentums in den Landerlisten und deren Verwendung in Antike und Christentum." *JAC* 26 (1983) 38–53.

Markschies, Christoph. *Gnosis, An Introduction*. Translated by John Bowden. London: T&T Clark, 2003.

———. *Valentinus Gnosticus? Untersuchungen zur valentinianischen Gnosis mit einem Kommentar zu den Fragmenten Valentins*. WUNT 65. Tübingen: Mohr Siebeck, 1992.

Mattern, Susan. *Galen and the Rhetoric of Healing*. Baltimore: Johns Hopkins University Press, 2008.

May, Gerhard. "Marcion in Contemporary Views: Results and Open Questions." *Second Century* 6 (1987/88): 129–51.

McNamee, Kathleen. *Sigla and Select Marginalia in Greek Literary Papyri*. Papyrologica Bruxellensia 26. Brussels: Fondation Égyptologique Reine Élisabeth, 1992.

Metzger, Bruce M. *A Textual Commentary on the Greek New Testament: A Companion Volume to the United Bible Societies' Greek New Testament*. 3rd ed. London: United Bible Societies, 1971.

———. *Manuscripts of the Greek Bible: An Introduction to Greek Palaeography*. Oxford: Oxford University Press, 1981.

———. *The Canon of the New Testament*. Oxford: Clarendon, 1987.

———, and Bart D. Ehrman. *The Text of the New Testament: Its Transmission, Corruption, and Restoration*. 4th ed. Oxford: Oxford University Press, 2005.

Michaels, J. Ramsey. "The Parable of the Regretful Son." *HTR* 61 (1968): 15–26.

Millar, Fergus. "Culture grecque et culture latine dans le haut-empire: la loi et la foi." In *Les Martyrs de Lyon (177): Colloque international du Centre national de la recherche scientifique, Lyon, 20–23 septembre 1977*, 187–93.

Milne, H. J. M., and T. C. Skeat. *Scribes and Correctors of the Codex Sinaiticus*, including contributions by Douglas Cockerell. London: British Museum, 1938.

Minns, Denis. *Irenaeus*. Outstanding Christian Thinkers. London: Geoffrey Chapman, 1994.

———. *Irenaeus: An Introduction*. London: T&T Clark, 2010.

Mitchell, L. "The Baptismal Rite in Chrysostom." *ATR* 43 (1961): 397–403.

Moll, Sebastian. *The Arch-Heretic Marcion*. Tübingen: Mohr Siebeck, 2010.

Moore, Stephen D. "The Song of Songs in the History of Sexuality." *Church History* 69, no. 2 (2000): 328–49.

Mossman, Judith. "*Taxis ou Barbaros*: Greek and Roman in Plutarch's *Pyrrhus*." *CQ* 55.2 (2005): 498–517.

Nairne, A. *The Epistle to the Hebrews*. Cambridge: Cambridge University Press, 1922.

Nautin, Pierre. *Lettres et écrivains chrétiens des IIe et IIIe siècles*. Paris: du Cerf, 1961.

Neisser, Ulric, and Lisa K. Libby. "Remembering Life Experiences." In *The Oxford Handbook of Memory*, edited by Endel Tulving and Fergus I. M. Craik, 315–32. Oxford: Oxford University Press, 2000.

Nilus of Ancyra. *Commentarius in Canticum Canticorum*. In *Nil d'Ancyre: Commentaire sur le Cantique des Cantiques*. Edited by M. G. Guérard. SC 403 Paris: du Cerf, 1994.

Noack, L. *Der Ursprung des Christentums*. Leipzig: Fleischer, 1857.

Norris, Richard A. *God and World in Early Christian Theology*. London: Adam and Charles Black, 1966.

Noy, David. *Foreigners at Rome: Citizens and Strangers*. London: Duckworth, 2000.

———. "Writing in Tongues: The Use of Greek, Latin, and Hebrew in Jewish Inscriptions from Roman Italy." *JJS* 48 (1997): 300–11.

Orbe, Antonio. "Ecclesia, sal terrae según san Ireneo." *RSR* 60 (1972): 219–40.

———. *Parábolas Evangélicas en san Ireneo*. 2 vols. Madrid: Catolica, 1972.

———. *Teología de San Ireneo: Commentario al Libro V del "Adversus haereses."* 3 vols. Madrid: Biblioteca de Autores Cristianos, 1985, 1987, 1988.

Osborn, Eric. *Irenaeus of Lyons*. Cambridge: Cambridge University Press, 2001.

Pagels, Elaine. *The Gnostic Gospels*. New York: Random, 1979; Harmondsworth: Penguin, 1982.

Parkes, M. B. *Pause and Effect: An Introduction to the History of Punctuation in the West*. Berkeley: University of California Press, 1993.

Parvis, Paul. "2 Clement and the Christian Homily." In *The Writings of the Apostolic Fathers*, edited by Paul Foster, 32–41. London: T&T Clark, 2007.

Parvis, Sara. *Marcellus of Ancyra and the Lost Years of the Arian Controversy 325–345*. Oxford Early Christian Studies. Oxford: Oxford University Press, 2006.

———. "The Martyrdom of Polycarp." In *The Writings of the Apostolic Fathers*, edited by Paul Foster, 126–46. London: T&T Clark, 2007.

Pearson, Birger A. *Ancient Gnosticism: Tradition and Literature*. Minneapolis: Fortress Press, 2007.

Pergola, Ph., and P. M. Barbini. *Le catacombe cristiane di Roma. Storia e topografia*. Rome: Carocci, 1997.

Phipps, William. "The Plight of the Song of Songs." *Journal of the American Academy of Religion* 42, no. 1 (1974): 82–100.

Plumptre, E. H. *Ecclesiastes*. Cambridge: Cambridge University Press, 1890.

———. "The Writings of Apollos." *The Expositor* n.s. 1 (1885): 329–48, 409–35.

Porter, S. E. "Allusions and Echoes." In *As It Is Written: Studying Paul's Use of Scripture*, edited by S. E. Porter and C. D. Stanley, 29–40. Atlanta: Society of Biblical Literature, 2008.

———. "Further Comments on the Use of the Old Testament in the New Testament." In *The Intertextuality of the Epistles: Explorations of Theory and Practice*, edited by T. L. Brodie, D. R. MacDonald, and S. E. Porter, 98–110. NTM 16. Sheffield: Sheffield Phoenix, 2007.

Power, David N. *Irenaeus of Lyons on Baptism and Eucharist*. Alcuin Club and the Group for Renewal of Worship Joint Liturgical Studies 18. Bramcote: Grove, 1991.

Puech, H. C., and G. Quispel. "Les écrits gnostiques du Codex Jung." *VC* 8 (1954): 1–54.

Ratcliff, E. C. "'Apostolic Tradition': Questions Concerning the Appointment of the Bishop." In *Liturgical Studies*, edited by A. H. Couratin and D. H. Tripp, 156–60. London: SPCK, 1976.

Rawson, Beryl. *Children and Childhood in Roman Italy*. Oxford: Oxford University Press, 2003.

Rébillard, E. "Chrétiens et formes de sépulture collective à Rome aux IIe et IIIe siècles." In *Origine delle catacombe romane*, edited by Fiocchi Nicolai and Guyon, 41–47.

———. "'Koimeterion' et 'coemeterium': Tombe sainte et nécropole." *MEFRA* 105 (1993): 975–1001.

———. "L'Église de Rome et le development des catacombs à propos de l'origine des cimetières chrétiens." *MEFRA* 109 (1997): 741–63.

———. *Religion et sépulture, l'Église, les vivants et les morts dans l'Antiquité tardive*. Civilisations et Sociétés. Paris: Éditions de l'École des hautes Études en sciences sociales, 2003.

Reeve, M. D. "Conceptions." *PCPhS* 35 (1989): 81–112.

Reiche, Harald A. T. "A History of the Concepts θεοπρεπές and ἱεροπρεπές." Unpublished Ph.D. thesis, Harvard University, 1955.

Reynders, Bruno. *Lexique comparée du texte grec et des versions latine, arménienne et syriaque de l'Adversus haereses de saint Irénée*. Corpus Scriptorum Christianorum Orientalium Subsidia 6. Louvain: Imprimerie orientaliste L. Durbecq, 1954.

Reynolds, L. D., and N. G. Wilson. *Scribes and Scholars: A Guide to the Transmission of Greek and Latin Literature*. 2nd ed. Oxford: Oxford University Press, 1974.

Riebe, Alexandra. "Marcellus of Ancyra in Modern Research." Unpublished MA thesis, University of Durham, 1992.

Riggenbach, E. "Zur Exegese und Textkritik zweier Gleichnisse Jesu." In *Aus Schrift und Geschichte: Theologische Abhandlungen*, 17–34. Stuttgart: Calwer, 1922.

Roberts, C. H. *Buried Books in Antiquity*. Arundell Esdaile Memorial Lecture 1962. London: Library Association, 1963.

———. *Manuscript, Society, and Belief in Early Christian Egypt*. Schweich Lectures of the British Academy 1977. London: Oxford University Press, 1979.

Robinson, J. Armitage. *The Passion of S. Perpetua*. Texts and Studies 1.2. Piscataway: Gorgias, 2004 (1891).

Robinson, James M., ed. *The Nag Hammadi Library in English*. 3rd ed. San Francisco: Harper and Row, 1988.

Rodgers, Peter R. "Irenaeus and the Text of Matthew 3.16-17." In *Text and Community: Essays in Memory of Bruce M. Metzger*, vol. 1, edited by J. Harold Ellens, 51–55. Sheffield: Phoenix, 2007.

Römer, Cornelia Eva. "7.64. Gemeinderbrief, Predict oder Homilie über den Menschen im Angesicht des Jüngsten Gerichts." In *P. Michigan Koenen (= P. Mich. xviii): Michigan Texts Published in Honor of Ludwig Koenen*, edited by Cornelia E. Römer and Traianos Gagos, 35–43. Amsterdam: Gieben, 1996.

Rondeau, Marie-Josèph. *Les commentateurs patristiques du Psautier (IIIe–Ve siècles)*, vol. 1, *Les travaux des Pères grecs et latins sur le Psautier. Recherches et bilan*; vol. 2, *Exégèse prosopologique et théologie*. Rome: Pont. Institutum Studiorum Orientalium, 1982, 1985.

Rordorf, Willy. "An Aspect of the Judeo-Christian Ethic: The Two Ways." In *The* Didache *in Modern Research*, edited by Jonathan A. Draper, 148–64. Leiden: Brill, 1996.

Rothschild, Clare K. *Hebrews as Pseudepigraphon: The History and Significance of the Pauline Attribution of Hebrews*. WUNT 235. Tübingen: Mohr Siebeck, 2009.

Rowley, Harold. "The Interpretation of the Song of Songs." In *The Servant of the Lord and Other Essays on the Old Testament*. London: Lutterworth, 1952.

Rubin, D. C., et al., "Things Learned Early in Adulthood are Remembered Best." *Memory and Cognition* 26 (1998): 3–19.

Ruysschaert, José. "Le manuscrit 'Romae descriptum' de l'édition érasmienne d'Irénée de Lyon." In *Scrinium Erasmianum* I, 269–76.

Sanday, W., and C. H. Turner, with A. Souter, eds. *Novum Testamentum Sancti Irenaei Episcopi Lugdunensis*. Oxford: Clarendon, 1923.

Scherer, Jean. *Entretien d'Origène avec Héraclide et les évêqes ses collues sur le père, le fils, et l'âme*. Cairo: Imprimerie de l'institut francais d'archéologie orientale, 1949.

Schmid, J. "Das textgeschichtliche Problem der Parabel von den zwei Söhnen. Mt 21.28-32." In *Vom Wort des Lebens: Festschrift für Max Meinertz zur Vollendung des 70. Lebensjahres 19 Dezember 1950*, edited by N. Adler, 68–84. Münster: Aschendorff, 1951.

Schmidt, C. "Irenaeus und seine Quelle in Haer. 1, 29." In *Philoktesia: Paul Kleinert zum 70. Geburtstag dargebracht*. Berlin: Trowitzsch, 1907, 315–36.

———, ed. *The Books of Jeu and the Untitled Text in the Bruce Codex*. Translated by V. MacDermot. Leiden: Brill, 1978.

Schmidt, Ulrich. "Citation Markers, Corrections and Some Preliminary Observations on Trends in the Textual Tradition of Both Testaments." Presented at the Society of Biblical Literature, November 23, 2009.

Schoedel, William R. "Enclosing, Not Enclosed: The Early Christian Doctrine of God." In *Early Christian Literature and the Classical Intellectual Tradition: In Honorem Robert M. Grant*, edited by William R. Schoedel and Robert L. Wilken, 75–86. Paris: Beauchesne, 1979.

———. "Philosophy and Rhetoric in the Adversus haereses of Irenaeus." *VC* 13.1 (1959): 22–32.

———. "'Topological' Theology and Some Monistic Tendencies in Gnosticism." In *Essays on the Nag Hammadi Texts in Honour of Alexander Böhlig*, edited by Martin Krause, 88–108. Nag Hammadi Studies 3. Leiden: Brill, 1972.

Schrenk, Gottlob, and Gottfried Quell. "πατήρ, πατρῷος, πατρία, ἀπάτωρ, πατρικός." *TWNT* 5 (1954), 946–1024 (English version in *TDNT* 5 [1967], 945–1022).

Scott, James M. *Geography in Early Judaism and Christianity: The Book of Jubilees.* Cambridge: Cambridge University Press, 2002.

Sesboüé, B. *Tout récapituler dans le Christ: Christologie et sotériologie d'Irénée de Lyon.* Jésus et Jésus-Christ 80. Paris: Desclée, 2000.

Siniscalco, P. "La parabola del figlio prodigo (Lc 15:11-22) in Ireneo." *Studi e materiali di storia delle religioni* 38 (1967): 536–53.

Skeat, T. C. "The Oldest Manuscript of the Four Gospels?" *NTS* 43 (1997): 1–34.

Slusser, Michael. "How Much Did Irenaeus Learn from Justin?" *Studia Patristica* 40 (2006): 515–20.

———. "The Exegetical Roots of Trinitarian Theology." *TS* 49 (1988): 461–76.

Smulders, P. "Some Riddles in the Apostles' Creed." *Bijdragen* 32 (1971): 350–66.

Snyder, Harlow Gregory. "'Above the Bath of Myrtinus': Justin Martyr's 'School' in the City of Rome." *HTR* 100.3 (2007): 335–62.

Spicer, Andrew. "Gallars, Nicolas des (c.1520–1581)." *ODNB* (electronic version).

Spicq, C. *L'Épitre aux Hébreux.* 2 vols. Paris: Gabalda, 1952.

Spoerl, Kelley McCarthy. "Two Early Nicenes: Eustathius of Antioch and Marcellus of Ancyra." In *In the Shadow of the Incarnation: Essays on Jesus Christ in the Early Church in Honor of Brian E. Daley, S.J.*, edited by Peter W. Martens, 121–48. Notre Dame: University of Notre Dame Press, 2008.

Staats, Reinharts. "Ogdoas als ein Symbol für die Auferstehung." *VC* 26 (1972): 29–52.

Stanley, Christopher D. *Paul and the Language of Scripture: Citation Technique in the Pauline Epistles and Contemporary Literature.* SNTSMS 74. Cambridge: Cambridge University Press, 1992.

Steenberg, M. C. *Irenaeus on Creation: The Cosmic-Christ and the Saga of Creation.* Supplements to Vigiliae Christianae 91. Leiden: Brill, 2008.

———. *Of God and Man: Theology as Anthropology from Irenaeus to Athanasius.* London: T&T Clark, 2009.

———. "Scripture, *Graphe*, and the Status of Hermas in Irenaeus." *St. Vladimir's Theological Quarterly* 53.1 (2009): 29–66.

———. "The Role of Mary as Co-Recapitulator in Saint Irenaeus of Lyons." *VC* 58 (2004): 117–37.

Stewart, Peter. *Statues in Roman Society: Representation and Response.* Oxford: Oxford University Press, 2003.

Stewart-Sykes, Alistair. *Hippolytus, On the Apostolic Tradition, an English Translation with Introduction and Commentary.* Crestwood: St. Vladimir's Seminary Press, 2001.

———. "The Baptismal Creed in *Traditio apostolica*: Original or Expanded?" *QL* 90 (2009): 199–213.

———. "The Christological Form of the Earliest Syntaxis: The Evidence of Pliny." *Studia liturgica* 41 (2011): 1–8.

———. "The Pseudo-Hippolytean Homily on the Theophany (CPG 1917): A Neglected Witness to Early Syrian Baptismal Rituals." *Studia Liturgica* 39 (2009): 23–39.

Styger, P. "L'origine del cimitero di S. Callisto sull' Appia." *Rendiconti Pontificia Accademia di Archeologia* 4 (1925–26): 91–153.

Tabbernee, William. *Fake Prophecy and Polluted Sacraments: Ecclesiastical and Imperial Reactions to Montanism.* Leiden: Brill, 2007.

———. "To Pardon or Not to Pardon? North African Montanism and the Forgiveness of Sins." *Studia Patristica* 35 (2001): 375–86.

Telfer, W. *The Office of a Bishop.* London: Darton, Longman and Todd, 1962.

Testini, P. *Le catacombe e gli antichi cimiteri cristiani in Roma.* Bologna: Cappelli, 1966.

Theissen, Gerd. *Untersuchungen zum Hebräerbrief.* SNT 2. Gütersloh: Mohn, 1969.

Theodoret of Cyrrhus. *Explanatio in Canticum Canticorum.* In PG 81: 27–214.

Thomann, Günther. "Grabe, John Ernest (1666–1711)." *ODNB* (electronic version).

———. "John Ernest Grabe (1666–1711): Lutheran Syncretist and Anglican Patristic Scholar." *JEH* 43 (1992): 414–27.

Thomas, Garth. "La condition sociale de l'église de Lyon en 177." In *Les Martyrs de Lyon (177): Colloque international du Centre national de la recherche scientifique, Lyon, 20–23 septembre 1977*, 93–106.

Thomassen, E. *The Spiritual Seed: The Church of the "Valentinians."* NHMS 60. Leiden: Brill, 2006.

Till, W. C. *Die gnostischen Schriften des koptischen Papyrus Berolinensis 8502.* TU 60. Berlin: Akademie, 1955.

Torisu, Yoshifumi. *Gott und Welt: Eine Untersuchung zur Gotteslehre des Irenäus von Lyon.* Studia Instituti Missiologici Societatis Verbi Divini Sankt Augustin 52. Nettetal: Steyler, 1991.

Tortorelli, K. M. "Some Notes on the Interpretation of Saint Irenaeus in the Works of Hans Urs von Balthasar." *Studia Patristica* XXIII (1989): 284–87.

Trevett, C. *Montanism: Gender, Authority, and the New Prophecy.* Cambridge: Cambridge University Press, 1996.

Turner, E. G. *Greek Papyri. An Introduction.* Oxford: Oxford University Press, 1968, 1980.

———. *The Typology of the Early Codex.* Philadelphia: University of Pennsylvania Press, 1977.

Uebel, Fritz. "Der Jenaer Irenäuspapyrus: Ergebnisse einer Rekonstruktion und Neuausgabe des Textes." *Eirene* 3 (1964): 51–109.

Van der Straeten, J. "Saint-Irénée fut-il martyre?" In *Les Martyrs de Lyon (177): Colloque international du Centre national de la recherche scientifique, Lyon, 20–23 septembre 1977*, 145–52.

Vansina, J. *Oral Tradition as History.* Madison: University of Wisconsin Press, 1985.

Van Unnik, W.C. *Newly Discovered Gnostic Writings: A Preliminary Survey of the Nag Hammadi Find.* London: SCM, 1960.

Verheyden, J. "The Shepherd of Hermas and the Writings That Later Formed the New Testament." In *The Reception of the New Testament in the Apostolic Fathers*, edited by A. Gregory and C. Tuckett, 293–329. Oxford: Oxford University Press, 2007.

Vielhauer, P., and G. Strecker. "Jewish-Christian Gospels." In *New Testament Apocrypha*, vol. 1: *Gospels and Related Writings*, edited by W. Schneemelcher, translated by R. McL. Wilson, rev. ed., 134–78. Cambridge: James Clarke, 1991.

Vokes, F. E. "Penitential Discipline in Montanism." *Studia Patristica* XIV (1976): 62–76.

Von Campenhausen, H. "Das Bekenntnis Eusebs von Caesarea." In von Campenhausen, *Urchristliches und Altkirchliches: Vorträge und Aufsätze*, 278–99. Tübingen: Mohr-Siebeck, 1979.

Von Harnack, Adolf. *Chronologie der altchristlichen Litteratur bis Eusebius I.* Leipzig: Hinrichs, 1897.

———. "Der Presbyter-Prediger des Irenaus, IV, 27,1–32,1: Bruchstücke und Nachklange der ältesten exegetisch-polemischen Homilien." In *Philotesia zu Paul Kleinert zum LXX-Geburtstage dargebracht*, 1–38. Berlin: Trowitzsch, 1907.

———. "Zur Abhandlung des Hrn. Holl: 'zur Auslegung des 2. Artikels des sog. apostolischen Glaubensbekenntnisses.'" In *Kleine Schriften zur alten Kirche: Berliner Akademieschriften 1908–1930*, 562–66. Repr. Leipzig: Zentralantiquariat der Deutschen Demokratischen Republik, 1980.

Von Soden, H. *Hand Commentar zum Neuen Testament*, vol. 3.2, *Hebraerbrief, Briefe des Petrus, Jakobus, Judas.* Tübingen: Mohr, 1899.

Waldstein, M. "The Primal Triad in the *Apocryphon of John.*" In *The Nag Hammadi Library after Fifty Years: Proceedings of the 1995 Society of Biblical Literature Commemoration*, edited by J. D. Turner and A. McGuire, 154–87. Leiden: Brill, 1997.

Westcott, B. F. *The Epistle to the Hebrews.* Grand Rapids: Eerdmans, 1984.

Westcott, B. F., and F. J. A. Hort, eds. *The New Testament in the Original Greek.* 2 vols. Cambridge and London: Macmillan, 1882.

Westra, L. H. *The Apostles Creed: Origin, History, and Some Early Commentaries.* Turnhout: Brepols, 2002.

Whittaker, John. "The Value of Indirect Tradition in the Establishment of Greek Philosophical Texts or the Art of Misquotation." In *Editing Greek and Latin Texts: Papers Given at the Twenty-Third Annual Conference on Editorial Problems, University of Toronto 6–7 November 1987,* edited by John N. Grant, 63–95. New York: AMS, 1989.

Widdicombe, Peter. "Justin Martyr and the Fatherhood of God." *Laval Théologique et Philosophique* 54 (1998): 109–26.

———. *The Fatherhood of God from Origen to Athanasius.* Rev. ed. Oxford: Clarendon, 2000.

Wiedemann, Thomas. *Adults and Children in the Roman Empire.* New Haven and London: Yale University Press, 1989.

Williams, Margaret. "The Jews of Early Byzantine Venusia: The Family of Faustinus I, the Father." *JJS* 50 (1999): 38–52.

Williams, Michael Allen. *Rethinking 'Gnosticism': An Argument for Dismantling a Dubious Category.* Princeton: Princeton University Press, 1996.

Williams, Rowan. *Arius, Heresy and Tradition.* Rev. ed. London: SCM, 2001.

Wisse, Frederik. "The Apocryphon of John (II,*1*, III,*1*, IV,*1*, and BG 8502, *2*)." In *The Nag Hammadi Library in English,* rev. ed., James M. Robinson, 104–23. Leiden: Brill, 1996.

Woolf, Greg. *Becoming Roman: The Origins of Provincial Civilization in Gaul.* Cambridge: Cambridge University Press, 1998.

Wright, W. *Apocryphal Acts of the Apostles.* London: Williams and Norgate, 1871; repr. Piscataway: Gorgias, 2005.

Zahn, Theodor. *Geschichte des neutestamentlichen Kanons.* 2 vols. Leipzig and Erlangen/Leipzig: A. Deichert, 1888–1992.

———. *Marcellus von Ancyra: Ein Beitrag zur Geschichte der Theologie.* Gotha: Friedrich Andreas Perthes, 1867.

Ziegler, H. *Irenäus der Bischof von Lyon.* Berlin: Georg Reimer, 1871.

Zirkle, Conway. "Animals Impregnated by the Wind." *Isis* 25, no. 1 (1936): 95–130.

Index

Passages of Irenaeus Specially Discussed

Index of Names and Subjects